ZULU
Isandlwana and Rorke's Drift
22nd–23rd January 1879

ZULU

**Isandlwana and Rorke's Drift
22nd–23rd January 1879**

Ian Knight

Colour plates by
**Michael Chappell
and
Angus McBride**

WINDROW & GREENE
LONDON

Dedication

For Carolyn, for her love and support

This edition first published in Great Britain
1992 by Windrow & Greene Ltd.
19A Floral Street
London WC2E 9DS

Second impression 1993

Third impression 1994

© 1992 Ian Knight
Colour plates © 1992 Michael Chappell &
Angus McBride

This book is typeset by
York House Typographic Ltd, Hanwell,
London and printed and bound by
World Print Ltd, Hong Kong

Designed by Victor Shreeve

A CIP catalogue record for this book
is available from the British Library

ISBN 1-872004-23-7

CONTENTS

CHAPTER ONE

Africans and Colonials

On the evening of 20th January 1879 the officers of the 3rd Regiment, Natal Native Contingent were relaxing in their mess tent over "a jolly little dinner". The Staff Officer, Lieutenant Henry Charles Harford, was chatting to Lieutenant Charles D'Aguilar Pope of Her Majesty's 24th Regiment of Foot; both of them were amateur artists (the skills required of Victorian officers for topographical sketching were often extended into a fashionable hobby), and they were comparing their work. They had had a tiring day's march with a British military column which had crossed from the Colony of Natal into the independent African kingdom of Zululand just over a week before. That same day their column of some 3,500 troops — Regular, Colonial and African — had advanced over difficult country, on a road unworthy of the name, to establish a large tented camp beneath a distinctive rocky outcrop known as Isandlwana. Their convivial evening was interrupted, however, when the commanding officer of the 3rd NNC, Commandant Rupert Lonsdale, returned from a conference with Lieutenant-General Lord Chelmsford to announce that the regiment was to parade before dawn the next morning; they had been given orders to reconnoitre the hilly country south of the camp.

"Poor Charlie Pope" was very disappointed that he was "not able to join our party the next morning . . . how eagerly he looked forward (like others) to the first real fight with the enemy". So far the Native Contingent had seen action only in one small skirmish; both their officers and the General's staff were anxious to see how they behaved in battle, and these new orders were suggestive of impending action. Two companies from each of the 3rd NNC's two battalions were to be left in camp for picquet duties, and the disappointment of their officers was no less intense than Pope's. Some managed to find colleagues willing to exchange places with them, and were able to go after all. Assistant Surgeon Buee started out with them the next morning, but his horse went lame, and to his disgust he was forced to return to the camp. The men were ordered to take a day's rations with them, and most of the officers took nothing but a few biscuits, expecting to be back before nightfall. It was a decision they would regret.

Harford described the carefree way the regiment moved off:

To anyone who watched our departure as dawn broke we must have afforded some considerable amusement going off as we did like a swarm of bees in a sort of "Devil take the hindermost" fashion. The Natives, who had been cooking and eating most of the night, still had pots full of smoking hot porridge which they had brought on parade with them, determined to leave nothing in the shape of food behind, and as it would never have done to take any notice of this irregularity we let them travel at their own pace and get well ahead so as to snatch time to finish their meal. A real cheery lot they all were — full of buoyant spirits and chaff, excellent fellows to work with . . .

Yet, for all this air of excitement, a sense of foreboding seems to have plagued many who marched out that morning. George Hamilton-Browne, the Commandant of the 1st Battalion, 3rd NNC later recalled a light-hearted conversation he had had with his friend Lieutenant-Colonel Henry Pulleine of the 24th Regiment. "A lot of you [levy] leaders will be knocked over today", said Pulleine. "If that is so," joked Hamilton-Browne, "when I return to camp I shall not find one of you alive". Harford sensed it, too, and saw portents in the beautiful South African dawn itself:

As the sun rose that morning there was a very wonderful sky scene. Overhanging Isandhlwana and the camps was a long, tortuous, more-or-less low-lying dark cloud, based on the horizon, much in the same form as a trail of smoke from the funnel of a steamer, and ending immediately above Isandhlwana hill, which as the sun got higher was first tinged almost blood red, then passing into ashy-brown with broad golden edges, assumed a marvellous variety of tints with the rise of the sun. And there it hung for the best part of the morning, frowning, as it were, over the fated Camp. I have never forgotten it.

Henry Harford was a young man who was keenly aware of his surroundings, and perhaps the possibility of imminent combat had sharpened his sensibilities. Yet Isandlwana does have a particular atmosphere about it which has fascinated European travellers for more than a century. The outcrop itself is a rocky spur of sandstone which rises abruptly some 300 feet from the surrounding plain, nestling in a basin of rolling, grassy hills. It dominates the almost treeless landscape and draws the eye for miles about, "towering grim and dark in the summer haze like a huge lion". Its moods shift with the weather; in brilliant sunshine it sits still and brooding, its pock-marked crags suggestive of some ancient mystery. On summer evenings the intense heat of the day can give way to sudden thunderstorms; the threatening sky seethes purple and mauve, and sudden winds come whipping through the grass ahead of heavy spears of rain — then the hulking mass of Isandlwana glowers leaden and sinister between heaven and earth. All in all, nature could hardly have contrived to produce a more appropriate backdrop for any darkly memorable human event.

Whatever his response to the bloody dawn sky, Henry Harford was delighted to be on active service in a part of the world that he knew better than many officers of the column. At 27 years of age he was a career soldier with eight years'

Lieutenant Henry Harford, in the undress uniform of the 99th Regiment, probably photographed at the end of the Anglo-Zulu War. As Staff Officer of the 3rd NNC he held the local rank of Captain. (Local History Museum, Durban)

service already behind him. He had joined the Army as an Ensign in 1870, and by 1877 had been appointed Adjutant of the 99th (Duke of Edinburgh's) Regiment, with the rank of Lieutenant. The Regiment had been stationed at Chatham, Kent, in 1878 when news first reached the home garrisons of an impending crisis in Zululand, and Harford had immediately volunteered for a special service post.

A constant round of small wars across the globe was the price Britain paid for her Empire, and on the whole the military profession greeted each new outbreak with enthusiasm. It meant an exotic break from the dull routine of garrison duty, where the main enemy was drunkenness in the ranks, and held out the prospect of adventure and promotion. Military laurels might be won in the form of brevet ranks — immediate promotions which took precedence over regimental rank — or even the coveted Victoria Cross; and were celebrated by a public at home who liked to romanticise the "thin red line of heroes", so long as the redcoats were not quartered in their own back yard. Even a military disaster could have its consolations for the individual: nothing accelerated promotion quite like it. Whenever the illustrated papers brought news of some bloody fiasco in a faraway place with an unpronounceable name, they heralded the advance of many a hitherto stagnant military career.

Coincidentally, Harford had grown up in South Africa. Ex-Army officers who had settled abroad to make their fortune were something of a sub-class in Colonial society, and Harford's father had been one of them. A retired Captain of the 12th Lancers, he had bought a farm at Pinetown, outside Durban in Natal, in 1864. At that time Natal, on the eastern seaboard, had been an official British Colony for just 19 years, and it held a great deal of promise for those with a hardy and optimistic temperament: which is to say that it was almost completely undeveloped. Britain had taken it largely to stop the Boers from getting it, thereby encapsulating much of the Imperial experience in South Africa. Even by that stage it had seen more than its fair share of bloodshed.

Britain had first come to the tip of the continent when she acquired the Cape of Good Hope in 1806, as part of the political fall-out of the Revolutionary Wars in Europe. Her sole interest lay in the fact that the Cape sat strategically astride the long sea-haul to India, which was the basis of much of her Imperial wealth. Nevertheless, with the Cape Britain had inherited the legacy of the previous colonial power, Holland, which had been in possession for more than two hundred years previously. The descendants of the original Dutch settlers, especially those living out on the wild borders of the colony far from the centre of authority in Cape Town, had developed into a hardy and self-reliant breed resentful of outside interference. Known as Boers, or Afrikaners, they lived a pastoral lifestyle, and their restless search for new

grazing land had led them into endemic conflict with the robust African societies which inhabited the eastern frontier. Nor were they much impressed by the British; many of them responded to the new administration by decamping for the interior, hoping to find new lands to call their own. Their progress was marked by a series of violent clashes with the African groups who lay across their path, and Britain found herself dragged reluctantly in their wake, cast in the role of Imperial policeman.

Until the 1820s Natal — so-called because the Portuguese explorer Vasco da Gama had logged its existence for the outside world on Christmas Day 1497 — lay beyond the sphere of interest of any white group. It was cut off from colonial penetration from the south by the border chiefdoms, and to the west and east by geography; it is framed inland by the barrier of the Drakensberg Mountains, while the crashing surf of the Indian Ocean limits the approaches from the sea. It was populated by a patchwork of African clans — a clan being a loose kinship group tracing descent from a common ancestor — who spoke broadly the same language, and shared a common culture based on polygamy and, significantly, cattle, which were the resource governing all social relations. These societies seem to have been comparatively static until the beginning of the 19th century, when they were propelled into conflict by an obscure combination of economic and ecological factors. From this crisis the Zulu kingdom emerged as the dominant regional power.

Strictly speaking, the Zulu heartland lay to the north of the Thukela River, the boundary of Natal proper; but during the reign (c.1816–1828) of King Shaka kaSenzangakhona, a dynamic and innovative military leader, Zulu influence was extended almost as far south as the Cape frontier. Many Natal clans acknowledged King Shaka's authority; others resisted him by clinging tenaciously to natural strongholds, and the remainder temporarily abandoned their homelands and placed themselves beyond his reach. It was tales of the fabulous wealth supposedly accrued by Shaka that drew the first white adventurers, a mixed group under the leadership of a British ex-naval officer, to his court. The wealth proved largely imaginary, although Natal was rich in elephants, and the whites made a good living from the ivory trade. They were sufficiently useful to Shaka to persuade him to grant them extensive rights in Natal; and during the reign of Shaka's successor, King Dingane kaSenzangakhona, the Zulus withdrew north of the Thukela and Mzinyathi Rivers and recognised them as an official boundary with Natal.

When they realised that the presence of the whites was recognised by the Zulu kings, and that Natal therefore offered a safe haven, the country began to fill up again with those clans who had fled before Shaka. Indeed, Natal became a refuge for many dissident elements within the Zulu kingdom itself, and

An officer (left), NCOs and soldiers of the Natal Native Contingent: a good impression of the motley appearance of the NNC, who were issued only with blankets and red headcloths — though most of the men here have odd items of cast-off European clothing — and mostly carried their own weapons.
(Local History Museum, Durban)

each political crisis there sent a new wave of refugees across the Thukela. The two countries remained politically and economically entwined, therefore, since the whites remained dependent on Zulu goodwill for their existence, while the blacks had inextricable ties of history.

The activities of the British traders received no official backing from their government, however; and in 1837 the vanguard of the Boer Trek movement crossed over the Drakensberg from the interior, lured by the promise of seemingly limitless grazing land. To the Boers the land seemed ripe for the taking, but their attempts to open negotiations with King Dingane were brutally rebuffed, and a vicious war broke out in which the Zulus were spectacularly defeated. The Boers then established their own republic in Natal; but their attempts to open contacts with rival European empires via the one practical harbour, Port Natal (later Durban), and their plan to dump the African population considered surplus to their labour requirements on the Cape's doorstep, rung alarm bells in the British Colonial Office. In 1842 a small British force was marched up from the Cape to seize the port. A sharp fight broke out in which the British were ultimately victorious, and the Boers retreated back over the mountains.

By the time Henry Harford's father arrived in the 1860s the British had established a colonial administration, but the countryside was scarcely changed from the wild days of half a century before. It was spectacularly beautiful: Natal drops in a series of terraces from the cool inland heights to the sub-tropical coastal belt, and the rain-laden winds blowing off the ocean have given birth to majestic river-systems which have cut deep valleys through the rolling blue hills. Most of the profitable game — elephant and buffalo — had been shot out in all but the most inaccessible parts of the country by the 1860s, but a wide variety of lesser wildlife still abounded. The commercial plantations of sugar and imported varieties of timber which chequer the landscape today were still a few years in the future, and ancient forests of indigenous wood (with exotic names like sneezewood, stinkwood, milkwood and ironwood) still crested the ridge-tops. The hot valleys were carpeted with thorn bush, and the hills between them with a wide range of sweet and sour grasses which matured at different times throughout the year. This, coupled with a relative absence of the tsetse fly, made Natal good cattle country. Cattle farming came to play an important part in both settler society and the African community. In order to satisfy the settlers' clamour for land the British had divided it up, allocating a disproportionate acreage to the whites and settling the blacks in reserves known as locations. Lacking the power to do otherwise, the British allowed the blacks to retain their traditional forms of administration, but kept a wary eye on them through a system of magistrates.

The white population was unevenly scattered and greatly outnumbered. There were only two towns of any note: the port at Durban, and Pietermaritzburg, the Boer capital 50 miles inland, which the British had adopted. The other settlements were mere hamlets consisting of a handful of houses and trading stores. A few were connected by unevenly maintained roads, while traders' wagon-tracks had to serve for the rest. In the more remote areas the settlers, while conscious of their vulnerability, learned to live tough and self-sufficient lives.

It was an environment better suited to the vigour of youth than to old age. Pinetown, so near to the metropolitan centre, offered little in the way of frontier challenges, and Colonial society was subject to all the petty distinctions and snobberies of its British model. Yet Henry Harford was typical of the younger generation of Colonials with whom he shared an adventurous boyhood, learning to ride and shoot, and to appreciate the rugged delights of camping out in Natal's unspoilt countryside. Harford had absorbed the Zulu language from his youth, and took a keen interest in everything

about him. He developed a passion for naturalism, and the Local History Museum in Durban still has many of the specimens he collected.

As we have seen, Henry Harford was with his regiment at Chatham when news spread of an impending war with the Zulus. Determined to exploit the advantages promised by his background in the race to secure a special service post, he wasted no time in applying. His senior officers were content to free him from his regimental duties, but he was obliged to resign the Adjutancy in favour of his friend (and fellow amateur naturalist) Lieutenant Arthur Davison. After a frustrating day spent trying to secure an interview with the Adjutant-General at the War Office in London — where "officers of all grades, from Generals to subalterns, belonging to all arms of the Service", ranged the corridors bent on similar quests — Harford was at last successful, and gained his appointment.

He had just two days to make his preparations, and in the time-honoured tradition of young officers about to depart on overseas service he scoured the best gentlemen's outfitters in London in search of the myriad necessities thought to make life on campaign bearable. At Dean's in the Strand he bought a pair of fine leather boots, which had been custom-made for a gentleman embarking on a shooting tour of Algeria but who had not yet claimed them. (Those boots were to have an interesting history.) Finally, in November 1878, he embarked on the steamer *Edinburgh Castle* bound for South Africa. Ironically, it was not long after his departure that the 99th Regiment received their own orders to sail for Africa; they were to be one of only two infantry battalions sent out from home to take part in the first phase of the Anglo-Zulu War. (Lieutenant Davison may later have regretted standing in for Harford: he would die of disease at Eshowe on 27th March 1879.)

Harford found a number of other special service officers on board the steamer. His cabin-mate was 20-year-old Horace Smith-Dorrien, a Lieutenant in the 95th (Derbyshire) Regiment. Smith-Dorrien had been one of three officers from his regiment whose services had been requested by name by the General commanding troops in South Africa, Lord Chelmsford. Chelmsford was a former commanding officer of the 95th, and the Colonel of the Regiment, and was obviously keen to see his old regiment represented in Zululand. Smith-Dorrien's superior had refused permission for him to go, however; so Smith-Dorrien had written to the War Office behind his back, accepting the post, and his CO received orders to release him that same day. Smith-Dorrien congratulated himself on the success of this "unwarrantable piece of cheek" (although, as we shall see, his superior's disapproval probably cost him the chance of a VC).

Also on board was Lieutenant William Francis Dundonald Cochrane, who had joined the 32nd (Cornwall) Light Infantry as an Ensign at the age of 19 in 1866, and had served for a spell in South Africa; Harford had met him before. Cochrane proved "simply the life and soul of the ship, always ready to sit down at the piano and sing a good song, or get up concerts, theatricals, and other amusements" on the long voyage out. The paths of all three men were to cross again beneath the slopes of Isandlwana.

The *Edinburgh Castle* did not stop on the voyage out until she reached Cape Town. Steaming up the eastern coast, she anchored briefly off Port Elizabeth to drop off some passengers; whilst "hanging about outside the harbour, another steamer from England passed, conveying a number of Staff College officers to Natal for special services. We at once dubbed them *aasvogels* [vultures], as we were afraid that, on reaching Natal before us, they would be selected for the best appointments". Harford need not have worried; when the *Edinburgh Castle* docked at Durban on 2nd December the port

Lieutenant Charles D'Aguilar Pope,
Harford's friend who commanded
G Company, 2/24th Regiment at
Isandlwana; he appears to be wearing
some individual variation of the British
officer's blue patrol jacket.
(Killie Campbell Africana Library)

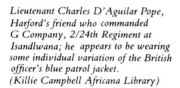

Captain Theophilus "Offy" Shepstone of the Natal Carbineers,
sketched by Lieutenant Fairlie, NNC. The Shepstone family were
very influential in the Colony; Offy's father, Sir Theophilus, was
the Administrator of the Transvaal, his brother George was
Durnford's Political Assistant, and another brother, Henrique, was
Natal's Secretary for Native Affairs. (Courtesy of the Director,
National Army Museum, London)

was alive with rumours of impending war, and there were plenty of appointments to go round. Pausing only to hand over a collection of insects he had made on the outward voyage to the embryonic Natal Museum, Harford reported to Chelmsford's headquarters. He was given a position ideally suited to his talents — Staff Officer of the 3rd Regiment, Natal Native Contingent. He was delighted: it "was a stroke of luck such as I had not counted on; no doubt my being able to speak Zulu had helped me into it".

* * *

The Natal Native Contingent was formed as an auxiliary force to help offset the shortage of Regular troops. There were over 300,000 blacks living in Natal, many of them with a strong history of antagonism towards the Zulu kingdom. Lord Chelmsford had been determined to realise something of their military potential, but in doing so he had cast light on the ambivalence of Natal's civil administration towards both its black neighbour and the Imperial power. Natal had grown up under the threat of the Zulu menace; on several occasions in the past the colony had been scared out of its wits by rumours of Zulu raids. The Zulu army was rumoured to be 40,000 strong, and the implications of this fact were much discussed by the kingdom's neighbours. Furthermore, the attitude of the incumbent Zulu king, Cetshwayo kaMpande, was said to be hostile, and a number of minor border incidents were held up in evidence. One in particular was to have a bearing on subsequent events.

In July 1878 the sons of a Zulu chieftain named Sihayo kaXongo, who lived across the Mzinyathi River border not far from Isandlwana, had crossed over in pursuit of two women who had fled to sanctuary in Natal following accusations of witchcraft and adultery. The women were abducted, taken back to Zululand, and put to death. Settler society was shocked by the brutality of the crime and by the infringement of its territorial integrity, which seemed to fit in with a broader

pattern of border wrangling. The Zulus had been involved in a boundary dispute with their north-western neighbours, the Boer republic of the Transvaal, for over 30 years, and when Britain had annexed the Transvaal in 1877 the problem had been dumped squarely in her lap.

The festering political crisis had not been orchestrated by Natal, but was in fact the result of a shift to a new forward policy by the Colonial Office in London. In 1867 diamonds had been discovered at Kimberley, north of the Cape, and at last southern Africa offered the promise of a return on the decades of British investment. In order to put the exploitation of the region on a sound footing a new economic infrastructure would have to be constructed. This policy was, however, at odds with the political realities of the region, in which British colonies, introverted Boer republics, and independent native states were locked in mutually antagonistic proximity. The solution devised by the Secretary of State for the Colonies, Lord Carnarvon, was Confederation: the bringing together of all these groups under British rule.

The first to succumb was the backward and bankrupt Transvaal. A hasty and highly unrepresentative canvass of public opinion gave Britain a pretext to march in apparently by popular demand, and in April 1877 the Union Flag was raised at Pretoria. Shortly afterwards a new British High Commissioner for Southern Africa, Sir Henry Bartle Frere, arrived in Cape Town with specific instructions to push the Confederation scheme through as quickly as possible. He soon became convinced that the quickest way to do so was to wage a short, successful war against the Zulus, who were by far the strongest independent black group in the region who were not yet drawn into the mainstream of colonial economic development. By defeating them Frere hoped to send clear signals to both black and white across South Africa: to the blacks, that resistance to the new order was hopeless, and to the whites, that British rule was ushering in an age of security and prosperity. He was particularly concerned to browbeat disgruntled republican elements in the Transvaal with an effective demonstration of British military might.

In the event, Frere's plans did not progress entirely smoothly. The head of the Natal administration, Sir Henry Bulwer, was opposed to a war with the Zulus, fearing that it could have dangerous long-term effects on Natal's economic development and on her relationship with the black population. He also suspected that such a war might prove a good deal bloodier than the Imperial party allowed. Bulwer moved to head off a confrontation over the disputed border by suggesting an independent commission to look into the question. Frere agreed, in the hope that a decision in favour of the Boers would provide him with a *casus belli*; but in fact the commission was scrupulously fair, and when it produced its findings in June 1878 it came down largely in favour of the Zulus. Frere delayed the release of the findings whilst he considered his next move. His position was further complicated by the fact that the home government, preoccupied with crises elsewhere in the world, was reluctant to embark on a Zulu war, and urged him to treat with the Zulus in "a spirit of forbearance". In the meantime Frere asked the senior British commander, Sir Frederic Thesiger, to prepare a military appraisal of the situation.

* * *

Deprived of any significant reinforcements from Great Britain, Thesiger hoped to arm some of Natal's blacks. Elaborate plans were drawn up for several British-style regiments to be raised, each supplied with old uniforms from outdated stocks, and trained in the use of firearms. Bulwer, however, was opposed to the idea, and in this he spoke for an influential sector of Colonial society, who were afraid to arm their own blacks in case this posed a threat to internal security. In the end the initial plans proved too costly, and a compromise was reached. Three regiments of black infantry were raised; No. 1 was to consist of three battalions, the others of two. Each battalion was broken down into ten companies, each with a complement of white leaders — one Captain, two Lieutenants and six NCOs — and one black Sergeant-Major, ten black NCOs, and 90 privates. Five squadrons of Native Horse were also to be raised.

The task of finding suitable recruits was given to Natal's Resident Magistrates, who in turn demanded them of the clan chiefs in their wards. The men were ordered to assemble at places behind the projected starting points of the various invading columns, and throughout December 1878 the regiments began to take shape. The 3rd Regiment mustered at Sandspruit, a few miles from the Msinga border magistracy, in preparation for an advance to the Helpmekaar heights, where Lord Chelmsford's Centre Column (No. 3) was being collected.

The 3rd Regiment, Natal Native Contingent consisted of men from a number of clans, but the largest groups were from Chief Pakhade's Mchunu and Chief Mganu's Thembu, both of which lived in locations in Weenan County to the west. The British made some attempt to keep men from the same clans together; the Thembu comprised four companies in the 1st Battalion, and the Mchunu six in the 2nd. Three companies in the 1st Battalion reflected the serious divisions which occasionally rent the Zulu royal house: they were formed from men of the isiQoza faction, who were followers of the Princes Mkhungo kaMpande and Sikhota kaMpande — half-brothers of King Cetshwayo who had fled to Natal during a bitter succession crisis in the 1850s and 1860s. According to Charles Norris-Newman, a journalist working for the London *Standard* and several local papers, who rode out to see something of the build-up: "Umkungu, the eldest, was not there himself, being too corpulent to march far, but his son was present in his place. The other brother, Isokota, accompanied his men into camp, and was on the Staff of the Commandant. Isokota is a fine looking man, for a Zulu, stands over six feet high, well made, and has a pleasant, though indolent, countenance".

The early hopes that the NNC could be properly armed and uniformed had come to nought, and the men were issued with no more than a blanket, and a red rag to twist around their heads to distinguish them from the Zulus. A few resourceful Commandants managed to find supplies of outdated uniforms, while some warriors had already dressed themselves in European cast-offs, but most simply wore their traditional dress. One in every ten — supposedly the best shots, but usually the NCOs — was issued with a breech-loading firearm and a bandolier with ten rounds of ammunition, while the rest carried their own shields and spears.

Providing officers for the NNC had also proved problematic. Most of the Commandants were chosen from Colonials with military experience. For the 3rd Regiment Chelmsford had picked men whom he knew well from the earlier campaign on the eastern Cape frontier. In overall command was Commandant Rupert LaTrobe Lonsdale. Then 29 years of age, Lonsdale had served as a Lieutenant in the 74th Highlanders from 1868 to 1874, but had apparently resigned following criticism that he had married on insufficient means. He had come to South Africa to nurse a sick brother, and had been appointed Magistrate for Keiskammahoek in the eastern Cape. His handling of Mfengu levies in the Xhosa campaign there (the so-called "Ninth Kaffir War", in the blunt terms of the 1870s) had drawn enthusiastic praise even from Imperial officers, who generally considered themselves professionally and socially superior to Colonial officers. Colonel Evelyn Wood, VC, of the 90th (Perthshire) Light Infantry — himself an authentic hero of the Crimea and the Indian Mutiny — had pronounced him "Brave as a lion, agile as a deer, and inflexible

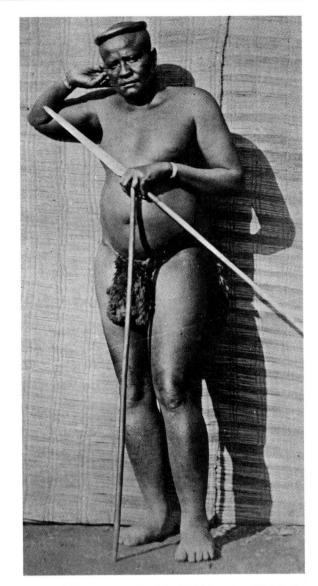

For most African groups in Natal the British invasion of Zululand afforded an opportunity to pursue their own conflicts with the Zulu kingdom. This is Sikhota kaMpande, a prince of the royal house who had opposed King Cetshwayo's succession. His followers, the isiQoza, made up part of the 3rd NNC. (Courtesy of the Director, National Army Museum, London)

as iron . . . the best leader of Natives I have seen". Curiously, given his subsequent adventures, no photograph of Lonsdale seems to have survived, although a written description by Chelmsford's Military Secretary suggests something of his appearance and character; he was physically short but his "face was redeemed from boyishness by the square jowl that tells of the determination which will make his name an unforgotten one as long as the tales of this war are told".

Lonsdale's battalion commanders were, for the 2nd, Commandant A. W. Cooper, another ex-Imperial officer who had served in the 95th Regiment; and Commandant George Hamilton-Browne. Hamilton-Browne was in his early thirties, an Irish adventurer who had knocked about the world; he had seen action with volunteer troops in the New Zealand Wars, where he had picked up the nickname "Maori" Browne. According to Robert Baden-Powell, who met him years later in what was then Rhodesia, Hamilton-Browne liked to be photographed in a belligerent pose, pointing a rifle at a cowering African: a sufficiently eloquent comment upon his attitude towards the men amongst whom he served. Thoroughly at home among the white roughneck element in his battalion, many of whom could command respect only with their fists, Hamilton-Browne brutalised and despised his black troops, to whom he regularly referred as "niggers", "curs" and "scum". Small wonder that he inspired little confidence among them in return.

The white NCOs were, indeed, a problem for the NNC. As the outbreak of war became more and more likely most Natal settlers who could ride and shoot joined the more prestigious mounted corps, and there were not enough left to fill the places in the NNC. Chelmsford was forced to fall back on men who had served on the Cape Frontier, and at his request Lonsdale had recruited many of his NCOs from among the recently disbanded irregular units around King William's Town. Few of these men spoke Zulu or had any understanding of conditions in Natal. They were given a hat with a red band, a jacket, trousers, boots, a blanket, a haversack, a gun and a bandolier — and their Commandants were left to make of them what they could. Despite the fact that Chelmsford's Headquarters issued a booklet with advice on *The General Management of Natives*, which urged officers to refrain from using abusive language and to look upon their men as upon "an intelligent child", the NNC's potential was largely squandered before it took to the field.

Nevetheless, the journalist Norris-Newman decided to attach himself to them: "I shared the Commandant's [tent], who, with his officers, was most anxious that I should remain with them throughout. Being pleased with what I had already seen, and naturally thinking that, if there was to be any fighting, the native contingents should naturally be in the van, I promised that I would go in with them". That was not quite how Henry Harford remembered it: the journalist had "quietly plumped himself down on us, and without a by-your-leave had attached himself to the Contingent. This was a quite un-looked for surprise, more especially as none of us had ever seen or heard of him before. Nevertheless, we made him very welcome, and he turned out to be an excellent and garrulous companion in our Mess. Lonsdale at once named him 'Noggs', and by this name he was subsequently known throughout the 3rd Column".

By the end of 1878 war seemed inevitable. Frere had decided his course. He gambled that, provided he could undertake a short and successful campaign before his superiors had time to interfere, he would be applauded afterwards on the success of the results. On 11th December his representatives had met with King Cetshwayo's envoys at the Lower Drift (a drift is the local term for a ford) on the Thukela River, to announce the findings of the boundary commission. Tagged onto the end of the award was what amounted to an ultimatum: the Zulus were given just 30 days to disband their military system, or take the consequences. It was a proposal devised solely to be refused.

As the days allowed for compliance with the ultimatum ticked by, the 3rd NNC left Sandspruit and marched up the road to Helpmekaar. They were in good spirits, but not everyone was impressed. As they marched in they passed a picquet of the Natal Carbineers, among them one Trooper Fred Symons. Symons was a conscientious member of his unit, but he was a sceptic when it came to military pretension, and he had his doubts about the NNC:

One day Ted Greene and I were standing and watching a regiment of the Native Contingent gweering and capering and singing and shouting as they came along the road when I passed the remark that these men had better have been left behind. Why? says Ted Greene; "Because they will not fight and will get in the way of our troops" said I. "Rot! Bloated rot!" said Ted. "They are a splendid body of men!" Alright, said I, we'll see. I bet they'll bolt at the first sign of the enemy, if I know the Natal kaffir. "Rot!" says Ted. If noise and capering makes a good soldier then Ted ought to be right in his estimate . . .

The Natal Carbineers were one of the oldest of Natal's Volunteer units, having been formed in 1858. The movement to provide a limited defence force from amongst the Colony's

white settler community dated back to the 1850s, when it became clear that the Imperial power had no intention of maintaining a large garrison in Natal. As such, they constituted Natal's only official defence force. Like the Rifle Volunteer movement in Britain, the men met to train once or twice a year, providing their own uniforms and horses but receiving government-issue weapons and equipment. Because of the nature of the country mounted units were more popular than infantry, and the men were drawn from much the same class as Henry Harford: the sons of the settler gentry and middle classes, literate men who could ride and shoot. They considered themselves a cut above the Regular military — despite the fact that the Army recognised their ranks as inferior to its own — and they were not constrained by the Articles of War when on active service. For any infringement of discipline the worst that could happen to them was to be stripped of rank and fined.

Officially, the Volunteer units were not required to serve outside the Colony; but during October 1878 they had been canvassed to see if they were prepared to cross into Zululand, and most had been willing. Nevertheless, Sir Henry Bulwer had been no more willing to call them out than he had been to sanction the NNC, and it was not until 26th November that the order was given for them to report on 3rd December. Most were taken by surprise, and suffered as a result; Symons was obliged to abandon the harvest of the year's mealie crop on his farm. He commented sourly that "the two thousand bags of mealies I expected to reap will be left to the pleasure of the [local Africans] . . ."

Lord Chelmsford reviewed the Carbineers before they marched to the front, promising each of them a farm in Zululand once the war was over: a promise which he had no right to make, and was to prove unable to keep. The regiment, just 60 strong, was commanded by Theophilus "Offy" Shepstone junior, the son of Natal's former Secretary of State for Native Affairs. Shepstone senior was a staunch supporter of Frere's policy towards the Zulus, and something of his attitude must have rubbed off on his son. Trooper Symons did not agree, and a remembered exchange between them points up the ambivalence of settler society towards the war. While many in Natal were afraid of the menace posed by the Zulu army, they had to live and work amongst the African population, and the war posed a threat to the region's political and economic stability:

One day . . . we halted on an eminence covered with soft green grass and as I lay there resting on the sward our Captain came up and said to me "Well, Symons! Wouldn't you like to see this slope covered with dead Zulus?". I replied "No. Sir, I wouldn't!" "Why not?" said he. "Because we have no quarrel with the Zulus and I consider this war an unjust one." He turned and walked away without a word.

The Carbineers were appointed to the Centre Column, together with the Natal Mounted Police and two smaller units drawn from the northern Natal border, the Buffalo Border Guard and Newcastle Mounted Rifles. The 150-strong Natal Mounted Police were a full-time regular body whose ranks included many ex-servicemen; they were less well-integrated into Colonial society than the Volunteers, and they were perhaps much closer in spirit to the Regular Army.

The Volunteers were disappointed to find that Chelmsford had placed them under the command of an Imperial officer, Brevet Major John Cecil Russell of the 12th Lancers. Russell was a special service officer who had been brought out from Great Britain to add a touch of professionalism to locally-formed Mounted Infantry troops. Quite why the Volunteers disliked him is unclear; undoubtedly, since they were responsible to the Natal civil authority rather than to the military, they expected to be under a Colonial officer, and they clearly felt slighted. Russell, it seems, was also very much the Regular officer, and the Volunteers may well have resented his high-handed attitude. Captain Offy Shepstone orchestrated their discontent:

Captain Shepstone spoke, and said, as nearly as I can remember, — "Men, you know under what conditions you signed your names and agreed to go into Zululand. One of those conditions was that Major Dartnell should have the command; by this order Major Dartnell is superceded in the command, and Captain Russell raised to the rank of brevet major, is placed in command over you. Now is your time to speak upon the subject; once you enter under the command of Captain Russell no murmuring or complaints of any kind must be heard or made. I ask you now, therefore — Do you accept Captain Russell as your commander or no?" The men, one and all, shouted most determinedly, "No!" Captain Shepstone then asked, "Are you willing to march tomorrow morning into Zululand, under the command of Major Dartnell?" One and all again shouted "Yes, to-night if you like!" "No, now at once" was shouted by some . . .

John G. Dartnell, of whom the Volunteers thought so highly, was another ex-serviceman who had settled in Natal. He had served with the 86th (Royal County Down) Regiment during the Indian Mutiny, and had been recommended for the Victoria Cross. He had retired in 1869 and bought a farm at Mvoti in Natal; but his wife had found the life too lonely, and Dartnell had secured an appointment to raise and train the Natal Mounted Police. He was a strict disciplinarian, but his strong personality had won him great respect throughout the Colony, and he was widely regarded as "an old, valued, tried and experienced officer in Natal . . . His estimable qualities as a man and a soldier [had] endeared him to the whole volunteer force".

Chelmsford was willing to compromise; his force was short of cavalry and he had no desire to alienate the Volunteers. Russell remained in his post, but Dartnell was co-opted onto Chelmsford's staff. Indeed, when Chelmsford planned his reconnaissance from Isandlwana on 21st January he appointed Dartnell its overall commander — which brings us back to that dawn, when young Henry Harford woke under the loom of the great rock after the "convivial little dinner" cut short by Commandant Lonsdale's orders; and marched out with his NNC unit, leaving Charlie Pope and his other friends in camp, disappointed at missing the excitement.

* * *

From Isandlwana, Chelmsford intended to advance along an old traders' track. About ten miles away this road skirted to the north of a range of hills which began to the west with a high rampart known as Malakatha Mountain, and continued eastwards in an undulating plateau called Hlazakazi. On the northern face the slope of Hlazakazi was easily ascended, but to the south, away from the camp, the whole range fell away steeply towards the valley of the Mzinyathi (Buffalo) River, which marked the Natal/Zulu border. At the far eastern end Hlazakazi dropped away almost sheer into a deep gorge cut by the Mangeni River. Chelmsford had already scouted Hlazakazi himself, and was concerned that the broken country might shelter a Zulu force lurking on his flank. He therefore decided that the NNC and the Volunteers should sweep through the range on the morning of the 21st. The NNC were directed to march due south from Isandlwana, and to sweep round the edge of Malakatha, beating through the valley beyond. The Volunteers were to take the northern route, patrolling the top of Hlazakazi, and the two forces were to affect a junction at the far end. Dartnell was to command the Volunteers, accompanied by two of Chelmsford's ADCs, Major Matthew Gosset and Captain E.H. Buller.

The Volunteers were paraded early on the morning of the 21st, and Dartnell asked for volunteers to join the patrol since a number of men had to be left in the camp for picquet duties. The patrol were ordered to take no more than a day's rations as they were expected back in the camp by noon. The Carbineers each snatched a handful of biscuits and a tin of preserved salmon.

Dartnell's party consisted of nearly 120 men in all: about 46 Mounted Police under Inspector Mansell, 27 Carbineers under Offy Shepstone, 20 Newcastle Mounted Rifles and 16 Buffalo Border Guard. Trooper Symons was with the Carbineers; so were his brother Jack, and his friend Ted Greene. The party rode out, following the track for several miles as it slanted towards Hlazakazi; then the Carbineers and Police separated, the Police continuing along the track while the Carbineers turned off to the right and up onto the summit of Hlazakazi. They rode across the top for only a short distance before a spectacular sight met their eyes: at the foot of Hlazakazi the Mangeni stream, flowing down through a basin on their left, suddenly plunged over a dizzying precipice and into a deep

Sub-Inspector Phillips and a detachment of the Natal Mounted Police who furnished Shepstone's escort during the annexation of the Transvaal, 1877. Of this formidable-looking group of frontier constabulary Trooper C.N. Sparks (fifth from left, back row) survived Isandlwana; Trooper J. Pleydell (fourth from right, back row) did not. The NMP wore a black corduroy uniform and were armed with Swinburne-Henry carbines in Zululand. (Natal Archives Depot)

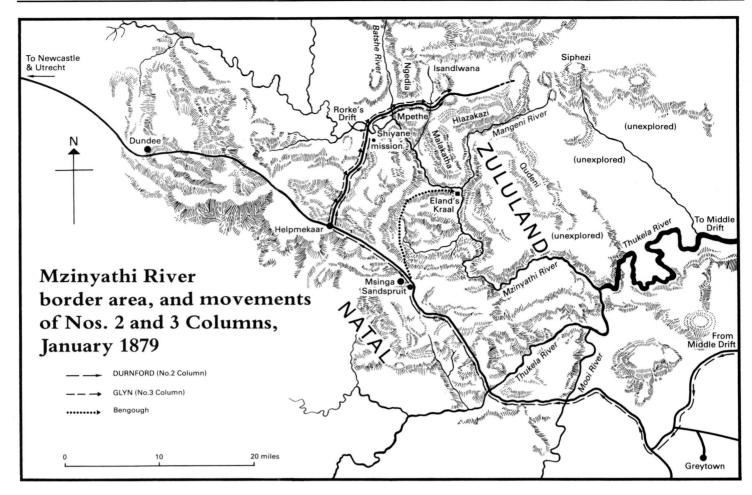

**Mzinyathi River
border area, and movements
of Nos. 2 and 3 Columns,
January 1879**

———→ DURNFORD (No.2 Column)

– – –→ GLYN (No.3 Column)

••••••••→ Bengough

gorge. To the right the gorge continued narrow for a mile or two, the floor choked with boulders and bush, until it opened out to reveal a view of range upon range of steep hills, extending for miles along the Zulu border. The Carbineers descended to the head of the waterfall and off-saddled, pausing to break out their rations and admire the extraordinary view. Suddenly, from the direction the Police had taken, there was a single gun-shot.

Trooper Symons was struck by the contrast with the extra-ordinary stillness of the day: "The day was warm and bright and not another sound broke the stillness, not even the distant lowing of cattle; or the chirp of a bird." The Carbineers were curious about the meaning of the shot, but do not seem to have been unduly concerned. They saddled up again, and moved slowly round the far edge of the gorge. There was no sign of the Police; nor, far below in the Mzinyathi valley, was there any sign of Lonsdale's NNC, who should by now have been coming round to meet them.

The 3rd Regiment NNC had marched more or less south from the camp until they struck the valley of the Ndaweni stream just below the deserted homestead of the chief Gamdana kaXongo. Both Lieutenant Harford and the journalist Norris-Newman, preoccupied as they must have been, were struck by the beauty of the view, which extended for miles along the southern edge of Malakatha: "We arrived at a beautiful spot where a stream that ran through the valley above us dropped over a precipice in a most picturesque waterfall.. the valley . . . was a dense mass of mimosa bush with precipitous krantzes and kloofs on either side, and Zulu kraals and mealie fields dotted about below." Here the regiment divided: the 1st Battalion, under Lonsdale, picked its way up the steep wall of Malakatha opposite, while the 2nd Battalion moved to its right, sweeping round the foot of the mountain in extended order.

The view over the "great Thorn Valley of the Malakata" has

hardly changed in more than a century. The green slopes are still dotted with dark bush, and Zulu homesteads are scattered here and there, though the dome-shaped thatched huts have long since given way to square structures of wattle and daub or corrugated iron. In the stifling mid-day heat the landscape seems lifeless and the air heavy and quiet; sound carries for miles on such days, but there is no noise from the distant huts, just a constant background whirr and hum of insects, and the occasional piercing, rhythmic cry of a bird. On a summer's day in January the temperatures regularly rise above 100 degrees Fahrenheit; for those not accustomed to such heat it creates a desperate need to drink. European skin turns to the colour of a lobster in one afternoon; the tops of your ears go red and peel, and sweat collects under the browband of your hat, dribbling down now and then to collect in drops on your eyelids. As you walk about your boots knock against boulders, and spiky aloes snatch at your clothes.

Most of the whites in Lonsdale's command were accustomed to the heat, but by midday it was taking its toll. "In going round", observed Norris-Newman, "we had some very difficult ground to get over, which seemed to try the powers of our non-coms — who were not mounted — very considerably. In fact, it is not to be disputed for one moment that white men cannot keep up with [Africans] in a day's march over stony and hilly country". The whites on foot were, admitted Harford, "very nearly dead beat". About noon a halt was made, and the men rested and partook of a "frugal meal". Not long afterwards Lonsdale's battalion, who had found the going easier on the summit, descended "an easy slope on the hills", and the two battalions were reunited.

The morning's work had not produced any dramatic results. The 1st Battalion had rounded up a large herd of unguarded cattle on the summit of Hlazakazi, but the 2nd Battalion had seen nothing. The Zulu homesteads appeared to be deserted apart from a few women and children. According to Hamilton-Browne, he had questioned some of these about the whereabouts of the fighting men:

> To a girl, I returned some goats which one of my men had taken from her and, through Duncombe, questioned her as to the movements of all the men. She replied, "That they had been ordered to join the King's big army." We again asked "where that was." She pointed with her chin over to the N.E., at the same time saying, "They would attack in two days' time." . . . In our next drive I captured two young men and questioned them. They had no goats to be given back to them, but there are more ways than one of extracting information. They were led apart and well questioned. War is war and you can't play at savage war with kid gloves on. The information amounted to this. They had both left the big army and come over to see their mother. We inquired, "Where is the big army?" They pointed in the same direction as the girl had done. "When was the attack to take place?" They did not know, but the moon would be right in two days' time.

It is difficult to know what to make of this incident. Hamilton-Browne's memoires reveal a distinct case of wisdom after the event, and it is curious that no-one else mentions it. Harford goes so far as to state flatly that "no Zulus were seen by anyone". Then again, with the regiment widely scattered over such difficult country, there would be no reason for a very minor incident to become common knowledge. Certainly, if it happened as Hamilton-Browne suggests, the implications were ominous.

At last the NNC rounded the southern spurs of Hlazakazi, and came in sight of the Carbineer vedettes on the edge of the gorge, who saw their white shields catching the sunlight far below. According to Symons, "upon perceiving us, Captain Lonsdale brought up the NNC" — a simple phrase which must conceal a good deal of sweat on the part of the men concerned, as there is no easy way up out of the narrow part of the Mangeni gorge near the waterfall. When they reached the crest the men were allowed a few minutes rest, and Hamilton-Browne suggested that a message be sent back to Isandlwana to report. Since the regiment was encumbered with a large herd of cattle it was decided to send back Captain O.Murray with two companies as escort. They had not been gone long when a messenger arrived from Dartnell, requesting the NNC to join him.

The Police, meanwhile, had returned to join the Carbineers above the waterfall. They had an interesting story to tell. After the force had divided they followed the track a little further, to a point where it crossed a "nek" (the local term for a saddleback ridge between two hills, which will be used throughout this book for the sake of consistency) and descended towards the Mangeni. To their left was a further circle of hills, arching in a horseshoe around the Mangeni stream. Just above the nek is a distinctive conical hill known as Mdutshana. Here they had seen "a body of Zulus on a hill to the left of the road to the number of seven or eight hundred; one of their scouts told us that upon another hill he saw several thousands of them." The news caused a buzz of excitement among the men, but the officers did not seem unduly concerned. The troopers were ordered to off-saddle by the Mangeni stream, presumably to await the arrival of the NNC, while Dartnell went off to see what had become of the Zulus: "strange proceedings I thought", commented Symons. The men settled down to brew tea, Symons noting glumly that "The Police were better provided for than the Carbs, they were wise enough to bring their camp kettles upon the packs". In the event few of them had time to enjoy their brew, as a rider came in from Dartnell almost immediately with orders to "saddle up and follow the Major". "Tired and disappointed for we cared more for a rest and some tea than for all the Zulu armies just then, we stood to our horses and mounting rode at a smart pace over very rough and stony ground", back up onto the eastern end of Hlazakazi, and down the same route they had ridden up in the morning. The NNC joined them on the heights, but seemed reluctant to descend towards the track.

According to Symons, the Volunteers and Police then descended and crossed the track. They had not gone far, and the NNC could still see them, which means that they must have been facing the hills immediately north of Mdutshane; these are known respectively as Magogo and, above it, Silutshana. It is difficult to be certain, but they were apparently drawn up facing a depression on the slope of Magogo. None of the Zulus previously seen by the Police were now in sight; but as they

The stern rampart of Malakatha mountain, looking eastwards along the southern face of the Hlazakazi range from a point south of the site of Gamdana's homestead. On 21st January the 1/3rd NNC ascended the mountain and swept across the summit, while the 2/3rd moved down into "the great Thorn Valley of the Malakata" (sic) to the right, the two battalions reuniting in the Mangeni valley at the far eastern end of the range. (Author's photograph)

Major John G.Dartnell, the highly-regarded commander of the Natal Mounted Police, who led the reconnaissance towards the Mangeni on 21st January 1879. (Natal Museum)

moved cautiously forward a young trooper in the Police named Parsons thought it wise to load his revolver. Unfortunately he accidentally let off a round, and his horse shied and threw him, much to the amusement of his colleagues. Dartnell ordered him back to the camp at once — a punishment which, as it turned out, would prove particularly harsh. At the foot of Magogo, in the middle of the range, they halted, and a small party under Inspector Mansell of the Police and Lieutenant Royston of the Carbineers was sent forward to look for the enemy. Symons described what happened next:

> We anxiously watched the small party disappear over the brow of the hill and when we saw them riding down the rocky hill side at a much more rapid pace than when they went up we knew something was after them and our surmise was correct for, from one end of the ridge to the other, as if by magic, rose a long line of black warriors advancing at the double in short intervals of skirmishing order. It was a magnificent spectacle and no British regiments could excel in keeping their distances in skirmishing at the double. They uttered no sound and on reaching the brow of the hill their centre halted while the flanks came on thus forming the noted "horns" of the Zulu impis.
>
> We all thought we were to be attacked but a shout came from the hill top answered by one from the right horn. The impi then halted, another shout, and the Zulus slowly retired till only three or four [were] visible on the ridge.

The opinion amongst the Volunteers was that the Zulus were trying to draw them up the slope after them, presumably with the intention of ambushing them in the broken ground beyond. Dartnell waited for the NNC to come and support him; but they showed no signs of moving down from Hlazakazi, so the Volunteers turned about and wearily retraced their steps, "leading our tired horses to the summit where as the sun sank behind the furthest range we met the NNC who were standing watching the Zulu tactics. I don't believe they ever intended joining us in the valley so near the foe", commented Symons sourly.

Watching from the vantage point of the heights, Harford estimated that the Zulu force was about a thousand strong, while Norris-Newman thought it was double that. At any rate it was a significant force, and it was impossible to say how many more warriors might be lying in the hills beyond. According to his original orders, Dartnell should have been back at Isandlwana hours before, but the discovery of a hostile force so near the camp and so late in the afternoon presented him with a dilemma. It would be difficult to attack it under cover of darkness; but if he disengaged it would be impossible to trace the Zulus' movements overnight, and the fruits of the

day's labours would be wasted. He decided to send the two ADCs, Buller and Gosset, back to Chelmsford to ask for fresh instructions, and in the meantime to bivouac on Hlazakazi heights.

The men made themselves as comfortable as they could. A small stream flowed across the summit, and nearby Symons and his comrades found some wild spinach. Beyond the stream was a deserted Zulu homestead, and the NNC gleefully pulled apart the thatched huts and stockades for firewood. The farmer/soldier Symons primly disapproved of their destructiveness — not because it made Zulu civilians homeless, but because "one [Zulu] hut means the destruction of about five hundred saplings and I know what it was to get the young trees planted out at Claridge" — but the Carbineers found it difficult to gather enough firewood elsewhere, and their meagre meal took an age to cook. When it was done, one mouthful proved enough for most of them, but "though hankering after the fleshpots of Egypt as much as any of them" Symons was determined not to waste in a time of want.

As it grew dark Dartnell placed his troops for the night. They were arranged in a hollow square; the NNC, two companies deep, formed three sides, and the Volunteers the fourth. "We were on the side furthest from the enemy whether by accident or design I cannot say, but design I believe", remembered Symons. The horses were tied inside the square, where the NNC built several large bonfires to keep their spirits up. They were already showing signs of nervousness, and Harford, placing a line of picquets out on the slopes facing towards the Zulu position, noted uneasily that his men were reluctant to form a line, preferring to huddle together for mutual support.

Nor were the white officers and NCOs of the NNC happy. Hamilton-Browne had been against staying out overnight from the beginning, and complained bitterly: "Here we were at least eleven miles from camp, no food, no spare ammunition, well knowing that a huge army of Zulus must be in our close vicinity". "Colonial officers are given to speaking their minds", he commented; "Even Captain Duncombe came to me and asked if everyone had gone mad. 'What in God's name are we to do here?' ". At least two officers, Lieutenants Avery and Holcroft, "went off without leave, evidently to ride back to camp, but were never seen or heard of again".

Not long after dark a party of 20 Mounted Infantry under Lieutenant Walsh rode in, bringing some comfort from the General. Gosset and Buller had reached Chelmsford safely,

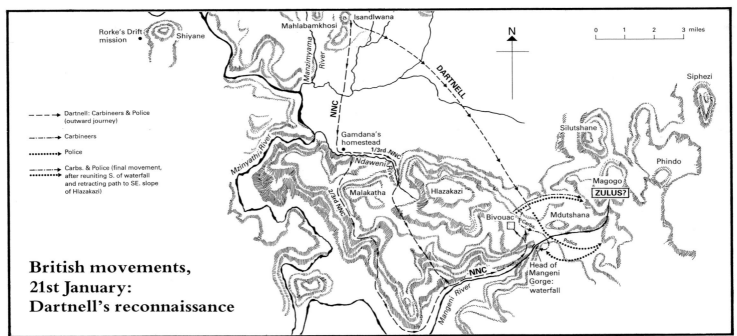

British movements, 21st January: Dartnell's reconnaissance

(Map legend:)
- – – – → Dartnell: Carbineers & Police (outward journey)
- –·–·– → Carbineers
- ·········· → Police
- –··–··– → Carbs. & Police (final movement, after reuniting S. of waterfall and retracting path to SE. slope of Hlazakazi)

and he had sent out Walsh with orders for Dartnell to attack the Zulus "when he saw fit". Walsh had with him "four pack horses with some few blankets, tea, sugar, biscuits and tinned meat. These were distributed amongst us, so far as it would go, and did a little to make us more comfortable." The Carbineers' blankets were among those sent out, "but", commented Symons, "someone else got [mine]." Walsh also brought news that another patrol had run into a small party of Zulus earlier in the day, near Siphezi mountain a few miles to the north-east, and shots had been exchanged. Walsh's men had seen small parties of warriors on their ride out from Isandlwana, and one of them told Lieutenant John Maxwell of the 2/3rd NNC that they had been fired on. This last information can hardly have been encouraging, especially as a disconcerting number of Zulu campfires could now be seen flickering across the valley on Magogo.

Fred Symons had been on "first relief camp guard" with Troopers Stirton and Macfarlane when the Mounted Infantry party arrived. They were relieved shortly afterwards, and tried to snatch some sleep, Symons sharing Macfarlane's blanket:

> When the 2nd relief went on duty the hum was gradually subsiding, and at length all was still the horses even being too tired to move about. I don't know how long we three of the 1st relief had been lying down, as I had no watch; it was very cold as I lay between sleep and waking when a shot was fired away in front, i.e. in the direction of the Zulu army. I was all there in two winks you may be sure! Then followed two more shots in quick succession . . .

The Carbineers scrambled up and rushed towards their posts when suddenly, "with a roar like the Howick Falls in flood, striking their shields with their sticks and firing their guns", they were overwhelmed by a wave of figures rushing up out of the darkness. Hamilton-Browne had fallen into a deep sleep, and had not heard the shots:

> I had loosened my revolver belt for a minute, meaning to buckle it on again, but went to sleep without having done so. I do not know how long I slept when I felt myself rushed over and trampled on. I tried to get to my feet, but was knocked down again. I then tried to find my revolver but was unable to do so. I never let go of my horse's bridle which I was holding in my hand, and at last staggered to my feet.
> The square was broken, natives rushing all ways mixed up with plunging horses, while the night was horrible with yells, shouts and imprecations. "My God", I thought, "why am I not assegaid?" as half-mad natives rushed by me jostling with their shields.

Norris-Newman struggled up, knocking one man down with his rifle, then went to find his horse, returning "with revolver in hand, prepared for anything". Trooper Symons heard the Sergeant-Major of the Police call out in ringing tones several times "Halt! Who goes there?" — "I liked that man's voice, it inspired confidence and courage". For a few frantic seconds, chaos reigned supreme, and then the penny dropped: the running men were not Zulus, but panic-stricken members of the NNC. In a fury, their officers snatched up weapons and began to cudgel them back into place. Dartnell sent a few men from the Police out onto the perimeter to look for the enemy, and some of the NNC, mistaking them for Zulus, promptly opened fire on them, fortunately without result. The Police Sergeant paced about calling out reassuringly "Don't fire! Don't fire!" in an attempt to restore order. Even so, several men of the NNC were severely wounded before the panic subsided. Someone handed Harford his pony — "for which I was more than thankful" — and he set off after his fleeing charges, worried that they might disappear into the night altogether:

> Luckily, however, I found them almost at the foot of the hill, squatting in various-sized clumps, and addressing them in anything but Parliamentary language, hounded them back to the bivouac. In the darkness of the night it was impossible to say whether everyone had been rounded up, but there was no time for further search as I had to get to the outpost line as quickly as I could.

Lieutenant Henry A. Walsh, 1/13th Light Infantry, photographed in 1887 as a Brevet Major; he served with the Mounted Infantry in 1879. It was he who brought food to Dartnell's bivouac on the night of 21st January, and carried Dartnell's second message back to Chelmsford. (Somerset Light Infantry Museum, Taunton)

Harford set out to find what had sparked the scare. Away from the bivouac the outpost lines were deserted, and strange shapes loomed up out of the darkness; " 'Zulus!' I said to myself, and rather a shiver went down my back. Everything was dead silence" — and the dark masses proved to be nothing more than huge boulders. At last Harford came across a group of men under Lieutenant Thompson still in place, and asked them what had happened:

> He solved the problem by telling me that an NCO of one of his sections, who should have been patrolling in company with a Native, had sat down and fallen asleep, then suddenly waking up and seeing, as he thought, a Zulu coming towards him, fired at him.

The NNC had taken this as the alarm, and panicked. It was some time before order could be fully restored; and the rest of the night passed fitfully, the officers pacing about calling out to their men to reassure them. Norris-Newman decided he had had enough of the Contingent for the night, and slept instead amongst the Volunteers. There was at least one more false alarm before morning.

It was probably after the first alarm that Dartnell sent a further message to Lord Chelmsford. Curiously, he left no report; but the number of campfires glowing on the Magogo heights opposite, and the jitteryness of his own command, cannot have made him confident that he could hold his position unaided. He asked for two or three infantry companies to be sent out to support him. Walsh was to be the messenger again, returning to Isandlwana with only three of his Mounted Infantry escort. Harford was impressed:

> Walsh's was a very perilous journey with a fifteen-mile ride in the dark over stiff country, hills, valleys, bush, kranzes, dongas, etc, all quite unknown to him. An occasional [Zulu] path, perhaps, leading to goodness knows where, and with every chance of being attacked by a lurking body of Zulus. However, he managed to reach Isandlwana safely . . .

While many on the hill must have doubted that they would see another morning, the sun rose on Wednesday 22nd January at about 4.30 a.m. to reveal a heavy mist hanging over the Magogo heights and Hlazakazi, obscuring the Zulu position of the night before. Across the plain to their left, out towards Isandlwana, Dartnell's men could clearly see the red coats of British infantry moving in their direction. At their head were Lord Chelmsford and his staff.

CHAPTER TWO

The Second Baron

At a quick glance, the photographs taken of Lieutenant-General Lord Chelmsford during the Zulu War do not give a very ready insight into his personality. Although dressed in the dark blue undress uniform that he wore throughout the campaign, there is little informal about them; they are pictures of Victorian propriety, of a man confident of his achievements and station in life. Equally, there is little that is overtly arrogant: he sits tall, straight-backed, darkly bearded, looking rather grave, yet not severe; there is a suggestion of humanity — a twinkle, even — about the eyes. They are portraits of a man who knew himself to be a gentleman, whose inner thoughts are therefore properly hidden, but who understood the importance of courtesy and good manners when dealing with others. So perhaps they reveal quite a lot, after all.

Frederic Augustus Thesiger, the 2nd Baron Chelmsford, was very much a part of the Victorian establishment; part, indeed, of an old military order which even then was giving way under pressure from a younger, brasher generation. Thesiger was born in 1827, the son of a highly successful barrister who, in 1858, was appointed Lord High Chancellor and enobled with the title Lord Chelmsford of Chelmsford, Essex. The younger Thesiger entered the Army in December 1844; his father had hoped to secure him a commission in the Grenadier Guards but, despite an appeal to the Duke of Wellington, he had to be content with the Rifle Brigade. Nevertheless, within a year he was able to purchase an exchange into the regiment of his choice. After various spells of peacetime soldiering overseas he first saw action in the Crimea, serving as an ADC to Lieutenant-General Markham in the trenches before Sebastopol, and finishing the war on the Headquarters Staff. In the Indian Mutiny he served as a Lieutenant-Colonel in the 95th Regiment in the campaign in Central India. A decade later he was on Sir Robert Napier's staff during the Abyssinian expedition, a foray which was widely applauded as much for its well-planned success in overcoming the difficult terrain as for its defeat of the Abyssinians. Thesiger emerged from the campaign as a CB, and advanced steadily in rank and influence; but he did not hold an independent command on active service until 1878, when he was sent to South Africa to bring to a close an uprising amongst the Xhosa on the Eastern Cape Frontier. It is important to understand something of his experiences there, and the lessons he learned, if one is to make sense of subsequent events in Zululand.

The Ninth Cape Frontier (or "Kaffir") War, the "War of Ngcayecibi", was the last in a series of bitter struggles between the indigenous African groups on the frontier and the more dynamically expansive settler communities spreading out from the west. Both parties had pastoral economies which were dependent on access to good grazing land, and the needs of one were all too often satisfied at the expense of the other. After more than a century of conflict the Xhosa were cramped and impoverished, and their political institutions and economic independence were in tatters. The revolt of 1877 — sparked off, significantly, by a clash between the Xhosa and the Mfengu, an African group enjoying the benefits of Colonial patronage — was to prove a last, hopeless gesture of defiance. Yet, for all that the Colonial forces possessed a vast technological superiority, warfare against the Xhosa had never been easy.

Xhosa society was politically fragmented, with no strong central authority, and it therefore boasted no large army. Instead the Xhosa fought in warrior bands under their immediate chiefs, waging guerrilla warfare from secure bases in their rugged bush-covered mountain homeland. They were completely at home in an environment which seemed utterly inhospitable to their enemy; with no commissariat to hold them back, they moved swiftly through the bush along trails that were invisible to the white man's eye, striking at isolated patrols, and harrying columns on the march. The frontier wars tended to follow an inevitable pattern: an initial Xhosa offensive, which foundered because they were unable to capture Colonial outposts, followed by withdrawal to their strongholds, and the long and gruelling reduction of each warrior band in turn. From the very beginning the British had found little in this mode of warfare that appealed to them; Brigadier-General Vandeleur, who was among the first to confront them early in the 19th century, commented that frontier warfare was "an unequal contest with savages in the midst of impenetrable thickets" which would add "little lustre to British arms". He was right; the Cape Frontier had proved

Lieutenant-General Sir Frederic Thesiger, 2nd Baron Chelmsford, in 1879.

Thesiger and his staff photographed on the Cape Frontier in 1878; left to right: Major J.N.Crealock, Captain W.C.F.Molyneux, Colonel H.Evelyn Wood, VC, Thesiger, Lieutenant-Colonel Redvers Buller, Brevet Major Matthew Gosset. (Author's collection)

something of a graveyard for glittering military reputations.

By the time Thesiger arrived on the Frontier in February 1878, however, he found that the back of Xhosa resistance had already been broken. In two uncharacteristic actions the Xhosa had abandoned their guerrilla tactics for the sort of mass attacks in the open which they had favoured in pre-Colonial days. This was a grave mistake in the age of the breech-loading rifle, and their columns had been shot to pieces. Those who survived and remained in the field had retreated once more to their inaccessible mountain strongholds, and Thesiger was faced with little more than a frustrating mopping-up operation. The troops under his command were a motley collection of British Regulars, Colonial volunteers and black levies, the latter mostly recruited from the Mfengu. Thesiger's strategy was to ring the rebel strongholds with troops, and try to drive through the bush, forcing the Xhosa to break cover: in an open fight they could easily be destroyed. The Xhosa were aware of this, naturally enough, and sought to avoid all contact except on their own terms. It made for a very frustrating war.

Thesiger threw himself into it energetically, riding great distances across rugged country each day accompanied only by his staff. He supervised the placing of troops himself, and painstakingly explained to them their places in his overall scheme of things. Nevertheless, it was difficult work; small parties of troops struggled through impossible terrain pursuing objectives which often remained imprecise simply because there was little reliable intelligence available. All too often Chelmsford felt let down by the indiscipline of Colonial troops and levies. Sometimes they were too enthusiastic, and could be lured away from important posts to chase easy quarry. Occasionally they stuck too rigidly to orders when the subtler judgement of a professional soldier might have secured better results; often, they simply refused to close in for the kill unless the odds were alarmingly in their favour. "Alas! it *was* trying," wrote Thesiger's Military Secretary after one unsuccessful operation. "Just as [the Xhosa] seemed to be at last in our grasp, just when after 3 days' doubt we should be able to understand what they were doing and orders could be given that could hold our scattered forces, up to now seperated by miles of forest, and by a new impulse secure a success too long deferred against the Caffres who were under our eyes now emerging from the Bush and following up our troops: and yet we were helpless. Of course, they did not know that the General was so near or that instead of retiring west he wanted [his troops] to advance east . . ."

Chelmsford was certainly not a snob; almost everyone he met was struck by his "most kind manner — a manner that endeared him to us all". He was prepared to deal with everyone regardless of their class and origins; but his background and professionalism gave him an innate confidence in his own judgement, and his experiences on the frontier confirmed his faith in himself at the expense of his trust in Colonials. And in the image of a will-o'-the-wisp enemy, lurking in impossible country, unwilling to risk a major confrontation but lingering dangerously on the flanks and rear, Thesiger found a view of the African warrior that confirmed his preconceptions. That image profoundly affected his outlook in the early part of the Zulu campaign, and with tragic consequences.

One more aspect of Thesiger's time on the Frontier should be noted before we move on. A former veteran of the frontier, Sir John Michel, had urged him "Do not hamper yourself with staff, they are useless, as Colonels of Regts. do all the work, with an efficient D.Assisstant, or Brigade Major . . . Staff officers of rank, without [African] experience, are not valuable; active, young, intelligent DAGs more useful . . . In the war of '46-'47, 7 Staff officers were sent out of rank: 5 of the 7 were useless". Thesiger certainly seems to have taken this advice to heart, as he scarcely burdened himself with any staff at all. He arrived in South Africa with just his Assistant Military Secretary — a misnomer, since there was no other military secretary — Major John North Crealock, and a couple of ADCs. Nor does he appear to have given any great thought to the appointment: "I had never thought of [Crealock] as my military secretary until he wrote and asked me to take him". Certainly, Thesiger was to be accused of an inability to delegate, of taking too much work upon himself, and not trusting sufficiently in the ability of his juniors — a pattern of behaviour not inconsistent with his Frontier War experiences. Crealock himself complained that "The general's headquarters staff is and has been all along (as I have so often said) miserably weak", and bemoaned the amount of work that fell to him as a result.

Yet Crealock himself was no insignificant player in the Zulu drama. Born in Devon in 1837, he had entered the 95th Regiment as an Ensign in 1854, and saw action in the closing stages of the Indian Mutiny. He was a graduate of the Staff College at Camberley — a progressive institution established in 1854 as part of the move towards greater professionalism in the Army — and had held a number of staff posts before his appointment to Thesiger. Nevertheless, he does not appear to have been particularly good at his job; his orders and despatches in the Zulu War reveal a certain carelessness, and, though he was generally loyal to Thesiger, he had a rare talent for making enemies elsewhere. Major C.F.Clery, another Staff College graduate who worked alongside him in Zululand, found Crealock "swaggering, feeble, self-sufficient, superficial and flippant". General Sir Garnet Wolseley despised him as neither a soldier nor a gentleman. To some extent these comments reveal the petty jealousies which plagued not only the Zulu campaign, but also the British Army in general: Clery and Crealock were later to cross swords over the responsibility for Isandlwana, while Clery resented the way "Crealock is indisposed to allow anyone of any ability to get near the general". Sir Garnet Wolseley, meanwhile, was an arch-snob who resented the fact that the Zulu War was prosecuted by members of the old order while he himself was excluded from the campaign until there were no more laurels to be won — he had nothing good to say about any of Thesiger's officers. Nevertheless, there is a good deal of truth in Clery's comments; Crealock had a facetious and sarcastic manner which most of his colleagues found off-putting and which made him difficult to work with; Sir Henry Bulwer summed him up as "a sort of military wasp". (Crealock's elder brother, H.H.Crealock, was a general, and would command a column in the final months of the war.)

* * *

It took four months to flush out and destroy the Xhosa, and then Thesiger moved on to Natal. By that time Frere was already committed to a tough Zulu policy, and rumours of an impending war were rife amongst the military. Frere asked Thesiger to investigate how such a war might be conducted.

Frere's political objectives gave Thesiger little room for strategic manoeuvre. Frere wanted the campaign brought to a successful conclusion as quickly as possible, before either the Home Government could object, or the reservations of Natal's civil administration could be confirmed. Frere and Thesiger in fact became firm political allies in their determination to circumvent the objections of Bulwer, whom Crealock dismissed as possessed of "essentially a small mind". Thesiger was therefore obliged to plan for an offensive campaign, with the view of bringing the Zulu army to a decisive confrontation

as soon as possible. In this he was hampered both by the terrain and by the inadequacies of his own forces.

The Natal/Zulu border ran for over 200 miles, marked in the north-east by the line of the Mzinyathi River down towards its junction with the Thukela, then following the latter to the sea. Both rivers flowed through very broken and difficult countryside; near Middle Drift the Thukela flowed at the foot of a spectacular escarpment. In the summer months, when the rivers rose with the seasonal rains, there were scarcely a handful of points where a British army could cross; in the winter, the dry season, a Zulu army could counterattack along any one of dozens of unguarded fords. Natal itself boasted little in the way of defensive arrangements; the civil authority had made tentative efforts to establish defensive laagers for its civilian population at the most vulnerable points on the border, but there was nothing resembling a border garrison, and no provision had been made for Natal's black population whatsoever. There were no more than a few frontier villages to serve as supply depots from which to launch the invasion; and across the border there were no roads, only a few traders' tracks. Few colonists had more than the haziest idea of the geography of Zululand, although there was general agreement that King Cetshwayo's principal homestead of Ulundi was a viable military objective.

Thesiger's plans reflect the extent to which he had been affected by his experiences on the Cape Frontier. Although he knew that the Zulu fought in a very different way to the Xhosa, he could not quite free his mind from the idea that they would avoid his army, and would have to be forced into a corner and made to fight. He was worried, too, that they might slip past him and strike into Natal behind him. To reduce the likelihood of this he planned to cross into Zululand with no less than five distinct columns, advancing from widely separated points along the border. This would risk dilution of his greatest asset — the massed firepower of his Imperial infantry battalions — but it would leave little room for a Zulu counter-thrust, and five converging columns would be sure to catch the Zulu army in the open at some point. Thesiger's critics were later to suggest that it would have been wiser to have concentrated his forces into one strong thrust; but by then they had the distinct advantage of hindsight.

In the event, this initial plan faltered for two practical reasons. Firstly, the British infantry would inevitably be the backbone of his columns, and Thesiger did not have enough of

Life on campaign on the Cape Frontier, in two sketches by Lieutenant W.W.Lloyd, 1/ 24th:"Our best drinking water" (left), and "A pair of Old Colony bush fighters" — the latter a fine impression of the extent to which field conditions had affected the appearance of the 1/24th. (Author's collection)

Chelmsford's Assistant Military Secretary, Brevet Lieutenant- Colonel (by 1879) John North Crealock; this 1868 portrait suggests something of the famously sarcastic manner of this "military wasp". (Ministry of Defence)

Major Cornelius Francis Clery, Colonel Glyn's Principal Staff Officer, photographed in 1870. Clery was a former Professor of Tactics at Sandhurst, whose judgement of his brother officers was less than charitable. (Ministry of Defence)

them to go round. There were just five Imperial battalions in South Africa, scattered between the Cape Frontier and the Transvaal, with a further battalion split between the Cape and Mauritius. When Thesiger requested reinforcements from Britain, he was sent only two more battalions and a tart reminder that Frere was expected to deal with the Zulus in a "spirit of forbearance".

The second problem was that it would prove impossible logistically to sustain even this number of men in the field with the transport and supply facilities available. Despite a series of committees which had sat since the well-publicised fiasco of the Crimean War, there was still no efficient transport and supply system available to the British Army. The Transport and Commissariat Department, which was in its infancy, was expected to produce a supply infrastructure to meet each emergency as it arose and, most importantly, to keep the cost to the Exchequer at a minimum. On the Cape Frontier this had caused so many problems that it had contributed to a rift between the civil administration and Thesiger's predecessor Cunynghame, and had provoked a stinging rebuke from the Home Government about the cost. In the months immediately preceding the Zulu War Thesiger's Commissary General, Edward Strickland, had just 19 officers and 29 men — several of whom had not yet returned to duty after sickness or injury on the Frontier — with whom to organise the supply and transport of Thesiger's entire army. Strickland faced up to his responsibilities manfully, but Crealock reflected a widespread belief when he commented that "the commissariat and transport department has utterly broken down as such".

The physical problem was enormous. Each British unit had to carry with it everything it needed to feed and equip itself: tents, provisions, baggage, equipment, and ammunition. In practice this meant that each infantry company required at least two wagons to sustain it, or 16 to a full battalion of eight companies, plus one for the battalion headquarters. Beyond a few Army General Service wagons — which proved unsuitable because, having been constructed with European roads in mind, their wheelbase was too narrow — there were no wagons available beyond what Strickland's officers could buy or hire from civilian sources. For the most-part these were large, heavy, robust ox-wagons, which could carry loads of 4000lbs. with easy, but needed 16 oxen to drag them — more, over difficult roads or through bad drifts. Working the oxen was an art in itself; it was safe to yolk them for no more than

four hours at a stretch, and they required long periods of rest and grazing if they were not to succumb to a frightening array of illnesses, and die like flies. Strickland respectfully drew Thesiger's attention to the fact that the Zulu War was promising to be a grander affair than the one on the Frontier, and that he could not possibly cope without help. Since trained Commissariat officers were not available, Thesiger cabled London with a request for special services officers to take on transport duties.

Smith-Dorrien, when he reported to the Headquarters in Pietermaritzburg, found himself assigned to such a task. For a young man it was not a life without appeal. The teams of oxen were managed on the road by black *"voorloopers"*, who walked alongside, controlling them with long whips, while the wagon driver sat on the box urging them on:

> It was a great experience for a boy. I found myself alone controlling the convoys, along a great stretch of road, supplying equipment, purchasing oxen, and generally keeping things going. The skilful handling of the teams of sixteen oxen made a great impression on me. The driver who wielded the whip was usually an Afrikander; the oxen were named and, when the pull became very heavy, were urged forward by name and pistol-like cracks of the whip. Such names as "Dootchmann", "Germann," and "Englischmann" were bestowed on them, and when a wretched animal possessed the last it seemed to me there was more emphasis in shouting it out, and more venom in the lash when applying it.

Needless to say, Smith-Dorrien had absolutely no experience of this work before he arrived in South Africa, nor was there time to give him any training; in this he was absolutely typical of most of the transport officers brought out from Britain. Most of them were hard-working and strove to be efficient; a few succumbed to the temptation to profit from their position, and most were simply acutely vulnerable to unscrupulous civilian contractors. Knowing nothing about wagons and less about oxen, they bought at extravagant rates, sold at a loss, and were often swindled.

To complicate matters still further, South Africa had suffered several years of drought prior to 1879. This had caused considerable hardship in the black locations — and across the river in Zululand — where crops had withered and cattle had died. The Colonial economy, too, had suffered; wayside pasture had dried up to such a degree that draught oxen could no longer survive along many of the main trading routes. As Thesiger tried to assemble his forces he found himself hamstrung by a system which had simply ground to a halt.

Determinedly, Thesiger issued a General Order in November 1878 in which he specified how he expected his transport to operate. Each of his invading columns would include one Transport Officer, assisted by a (civilian) head conductor, and by a sub-conductor for every ten wagons. Wagons were to be moved in sections of ten or columns of 20; each column was to carry sufficient supplies for 15 days, and should be ready to move ten miles in a day. Nevertheless, it was obvious that the number of invading columns would have to be reduced.

Thesiger decided to retain three offensive columns, but to keep the remaining two in a largely defensive role. The offensive columns would be No.1 (Right Flank), under the command of Colonel C.K.Pearson of the Buffs (3rd Regiment), based at the Lower Drift near the Thukela mouth; No.3 (Centre) Column, under Colonel Richard Glyn of the 24th Regiment, crossing at Rorke's Drift on the Mzinyathi; and No.4 (Left Flank) Column, commanded by Colonel H.E.Wood, VC (90th Light Infantry), based at Utrecht on the Transvaal border. No.2 Column, commanded by Colonel Anthony Durnford, RE, was placed on the Kranskop escarpment above the Middle Drift on the Thukela; while No.5, under Colonel H.Rowlands, VC, of the 34th (Cumberland) Regiment, was situated in the far north at Derby in the Transvaal, where it could also keep an eye on the disgruntled republican Boers.

The starting point for the Centre Column had been chosen largely because Rorke's Drift was one of the oldest and best-established routes into Zululand. It was also on one of the most unsettled parts of the border. It lay not far south of the disputed territory — indeed, the boundary commission had convened at Rorke's Drift in March 1878 — and across the river in Zululand lived the powerful border chieftain Sihayo kaXongo, whose sons had been responsible for the infringement of Natal's border in July. White settlement in the area was sparse: a scattering of farmers, trading posts and mission stations, with a small village at Dundee 20 miles north-west of Rorke's Drift. The nearest towns were Newcastle, further to the north, and Ladysmith to the west.

Thesiger planned to supply the Centre Column via the main road from Pietermaritzburg, the so-called border road; this passed north through Greytown, with Zululand on its right, then plunged into the steep thorn valley of Msinga, emerging again onto a high, table-topped ridge, a spur of the Drakensberg called the Biggarsberg. The Voortrekkers who had first blazed the route had united to make a cutting through the slope of the Biggarsberg, and when a small settlement was established there it was named Helpmekaar — "help one another" — in honour of the occasion. From Helpmekaar a hunters' and traders' track wound eastwards down into the Mzinyathi valley, to the crossing where the trader Jim Rorke had once lived, giving his name to Rorke's Drift. Thesiger decided to establish the main supply base for the Centre Column at Helpmekaar. This had less to do with the settlement itself (which in 1879 consisted of just two buildings, with a chapel built by a local farmer a mile or so away), than with the area's excellent strategic location, and with its supposedly bracing atmosphere. From the edge of the escarpment there are stunning panoramic views for miles over the Mzinyathi valley, stretching to Zululand. A line of cliffs which marked the site of Sihayo's homestead were clearly visible, and a few miles away Isandlwana nestles like a grey smudge below the horizon. Because of its height Helpmekaar catches any breeze that blows, and even in summer the temperature at

night is cool. As a result it was widely regarded as being healthy, and free of horse-sickness.

In the middle of December 1878 the Centre Column began to assemble at Helpmekaar. The first to arrive were four companies of the 1st Battalion, 24th Regiment, who pitched their tents on a stretch of open land to the left of the road. Then came members of the Natal Volunteer corps, who camped by unit further down the road; the 3rd NNC; and, at the end of December, the 2/24th. Convoys of wagons plied the road back and forth to Greytown, and a huge stockpile of stores began to accumulate. Commissary-General Strickland had managed persuade the War Office to send out several large wooden sheds with galvanised iron roofs, and three of these were erected at Helpmekaar to protect the more perishable provisions. Five large "wildebeest" huts — a local term for an improvised hunting camp — were put up nearby to shelter sacks of mealies (maize, the ubiquitous local grain crop) and forage. It was particularly necessary to protect the stores, since no sooner had the build-up begun than the three-year drought broke, and the rains began to fall.

At first the rain offered a welcome break from the stifling summer heat, but as each new day dawned and brought with it only overcast skies and fresh downpours the appeal soon wore off, and serious problems emerged. Crealock, who had served in India and knew something of the monsoon, thought the summer rains in Natal at the end of 1878 comparable: "I *never* got such a ducking as my waterproof could not be got at until I was drenched. This is the second 36 hours continuous rain in a week". In a very short time the camps became a sea of mud, and road transport came almost to a standstill once more. Streams and rivers that had been dry for years past filled and became impassable within hours, and the constant traffic of heavily-laden wagons and their oxen churned the roads to a quagmire. Norris-Newman describes a night spent with the NNC at Helpmekaar not long after their arrival:

The British Regular infantry on campaign in Zululand, 1879.
Although this photograph in fact shows the 91st Highlanders it gives
a good impression of any Imperial battalion in the field. Note the
greatcoats worn horseshoe-fashion. (Courtesy of the Director,
National Army Museum, London)

. . . just as the cook was preparing the savoury viands down came such a storm of wind, followed immediately by heavy rain, as not only put out fires, but even to blow over some tents, and quickly flood us all out. The Commandant and myself bore it patiently for some time, but when things began to float about and small streams flow through our tent, we thought the time for action had commenced; so divesting ourselves of some of our clothing, we put on our waterproofs, made a rush to the nearest tent for spades, came back and commenced to dig a good-sized trench outside the tent, so as to direct the water into some other channel. In this we succeeded after everything was wet through, and then, as our misery was at its height, we made a journey through the camp to see how others had fared. The result proved that there were many worse off than we were . . .

With Christmas coming on, "Noggs" Norris-Newman, never one to suffer discomfort without good reason, abandoned the camp and went down to Pietermaritzburg. Others were not so lucky; the Natal Mounted Police ordered a wagon-load of luxuries, including plum puddings, up from Pietermaritzburg, but the wagon was swept away as it crossed Keate's Drift on the Mooi River and Quarter-Master Sergeant Hobson was almost drowned. Most of the stores were later salvaged, but they did not reach Helpmekaar — apparently none the worse for their adventures — until 8th January. By the time Norris-Newman returned in the last week of January, marching up with companies of the 24th, the Column was almost complete, and the Union Flag which marked Thesiger's Headquarters fluttered in the middle of a sea of tents.

Thesiger, indeed, was no longer Thesiger: on 5th October 1878 his father had died, and when he heard the news the following month Thesiger adopted the title Lord Chelmsford. Since he expected the Centre Column to bear the brunt of the fighting, he had decided to join it in person. It was a decision which was to rob the nominal commander, Colonel Glyn, of any real authority.

The arival of Chelmsford's army had had a devastating impact on the local community. The army was desperately in need of stores, horses, oxen, wagons, drivers and interpreters,

and many settlers either profited by their proximity or temporarily entered their employment. For the civil officials the coming of war heralded a new responsibility, since they were required to organise a local defence. The government had reluctantly authorised the erection of a number of protective laagers for the (white) civilian population, and many farmers had built their own on their own land. By the beginning of January many settlers had abandoned outlying farms and moved to the safety of the laagers. Five miles from Helpmekaar was Fort Pine, an impressive stone structure built as a garrison for the Volunteers; this remained under the authority of the civil power, and provided a secure place of refuge.

Amongst those who threw themselves energetically into the military life was the magistrate of Msinga, Henry Francis Fynn junior. Fynn had been particularly well qualified for his job, since his father was the most famous of the white adventurers who had first come to King Shaka's court. Fynn spoke Afrikaans and fluent Zulu, which was just as well, since the population of his ward was overwhelmingly black. Fynn's post was a neat stone magistracy below the Biggarsberg where he had been living for four years with his wife and three young daughters. His interpreter, Jackson, lived in a wattle-and-daub hut nearby, but otherwise his closest neighbours were the Brickhill brothers who lived at Knox's store a mile away. The nearest church was the Gordon Memorial Mission four miles to the east. Since the total white population of Msinga numbered only 232, the colonial goverment had suggested that Fynn abandon his post in the event of an emergency. He stoutly refused to do so, and asked that the post be fortified instead; in December its defences were improved by the addition of loopholed iron shutters.

Fynn's ward bordered the Mzinyathi to the north-east, opposite the difficult country facing the Mangeni gorge. Fynn was in charge of a number of black Border Police, and he used these to scout out the situation across the river. In the weeks after the delivery of the ultimatum his agents tested the

Chelmsford was dependent on locally hired civilian transport to keep his army in the field; these are typical Colonial ox-wagons, photographed in June 1879. ("SB" Bourquin)

The Buffalo Border Guard in the field, c.1879; Quartermaster-Sergeant Dugald Macphail stands at right, with beard. For a small frontier troop the BBG wore an impressive black, braided uniform, with an ornate buffalo-head forage cap badge; the men at the front have helmets. (Killie Campbell Africana Library)

reaction of the important border chiefs, and found that while most of them were clearly prevaricating, Sihayo's brother, Gamdana kaXongo, was contemplating defecting to the British. When Chelmsford rode through Msinga on his way to Helpmekaar, Fynn took the opportunity to meet him and acquaint him with his intelligence. He obviously found the presence of the army and the imminence of hostilities stimulating, and he filled his despatches with improbable plans for border defence. More significantly, in the first week of January, he was able to tell Chelmsford that the fighting men who had previously been gathering at the homesteads across the river had left to report to the king — a sure sign that hostilities were imminent.

For both the black and the white population, the immediate threat of war made it inescapable that they should take to the field to protect themselves. Outside the ambit of the NNC, Chelmsford had ordered magistrates to raise black border guards and border levies from amongst the local clans. The border guards were stationed in groups of 100 above the most vulnerable drifts on the border, and rotated every few weeks, so as to provide a reliable warning of any Zulu invasion. The border levies were only to be called out in time of emergency.

Two white units were recruited from the Mzinyathi border, both of which camped with the Carbineers and Police at Helpmekaar. The senior of the two, the Buffalo Border

Guard, mustered just 23 men, most of them from Dundee and its outskirts. They had been raised in 1873 during the dismal "rebellion" of Chief Langalibalele's Hlubi people in the Drakensberg foothills. The influential Smith family was well represented: Captain Tom Smith was in command, seconded by Lieutenant William Craighead Smith. The Quartermaster was a 38-year-old Scot from Inverary, Dugald Macphail. Trooper Fred Symons remembered one of the Smiths with some disdain from their days together at Helpmekaar:

> On the Zulu side was a long line of rocks (small kranz) and here men were placed [on picquet duty at night] singly at intervals of about fifty yards or more. It was bad enough to find your way about in the dark on this line, but much worse when an officer of the Buffalo Border Guard named S. was on duty. It might have been timidity on his part as be it what it might he was a perfect nuisance to the men on night guard. Relieved from guard we would just have settled down for a much needed sleep when clank, clank, clank, along would come the "Man with the Knife" as we called him, on his visiting rounds. Of course he was not afraid to visit the line of sentries by himself, not at all! He only wanted to take the old guard along to shew him the way in case such a valuable officer got lost! . . . He . . . would leave one man with each sentry we came to and then pick them up on his return so that he was never alone. I am pleased to say he disappeared from the scene shortly after and never troubled us any more — sent to buy horses or something of this kind.

The Newcastle Mounted Rifles had been formed as recently as 1875, and, with 30 members, were not much stronger. They

Lieutenant Horace Smith-Dorrien, 95th Regiment; a special service officer attached to Glyn's No.3 Column for transport duties, this future General, photographed c.1887, was one of only five Imperial officers to escape Isandlwana. (Ministry of Defence)

The windswept Biggarsberg heights at Helpmekaar. The Centre Column's original supply depot consisted of three large zinc-roofed sheds; they can be seen in the right background, surrounded by an earthwork hastily raised in the aftermath of Isandlwana. ("SB" Bourquin)

had been raised from among the population of Newcastle, and their commander was Captain Robert Bradstreet — possessor of a truly impressive set of whiskers, and apparently the darling of local society. His second-in-command was Lieutenant Charles Jones, whose younger brother Samuel was a trooper in the ranks. (A third brother, Ruben, was too young to fight but obtained work as a wagon-driver.) The Lieutenant, worried that his brother's adventurous temperament might lead him into trouble, tried hard to keep him away from the scene of any potential danger. Firstly he secured him a commissariat post on Colonel Wood's column, which was assembling at Utrecht 200 miles further north. Sam Jones would have none of this, however, and promptly reported to Wood, begging to be allowed to rejoin his unit. Evelyn Wood admired his desire to serve with his own comrades and granted permission: by the time Jones returned to Newcastle, however, the unit had departed for the front, and he found that his brother had anticipated his move, and

> in order to put a further spoke in my wheel . . . had sold my horse, saddle and bridle. Horses were scarce and I was in an awful rage. The expense did not worry me, but the thing was to find someone with a horse to sell. In this unhappy frame of mind I took a walk up the street when I was hailed by an old friend, who was riding along on horse-back. Looking at me he asked what the trouble was. My pent up feelings then found expression in a torrent of words while I poured out the whole story to him. In the end he agreed to sell his mount, saddle and bridle to me . . . . A couple of hours later I set off after my troop. I rode the whole night through and caught them up at Helpmekaar over sixty miles away. I reported myself and had a few words with my brother over the sale of my horse in my absence, but things panned out all right . . .

Frere's ultimatum had given King Cetshwayo 30 days to respond fully to his demands; 10th January 1879 was the last date allowed for compliance, and, as no response had been forthcoming, the Column began to descend from Helpmekaar to Rorke's Drift on New Year's Day. A party of Natal Native Pioneers led the way; they established a camp 400 yards from the drift, and began work preparing the road for the heavy traffic to come. The next day the 3rd NNC and Volunteers were pushed forward to Knostrope, a farm on the eastern ledge of the escarpment offering a wonderful view over the valley. (Knostrope was owned by Trooper William Adams senior of the Buffalo Border Guard, who was Jim Rorke's brother-in-law.) On the 5th the infantry companies marched

out. Rorke's store, two stone buildings roofed with thatch, had recently been taken over by the Swedish Evangelical Mission, and the Reverend Otto Witt was in occupation with his wife and three daughters. The military soon requisitioned one building as a store to house the wagon-loads of supplies trundling down from Helpmekaar, while the medical department took over the other as a makeshift hospital. By the 9th the entire column was camped on the Natal bank overlooking the drift. It consisted of the two battalions of the 24th Regiment (less several companies left on garrison duty); N/5 Battery, Royal Artillery; the 3rd NNC; No.1 Squadron, Imperial Mounted Infantry; and the Natal Carbineers, Buffalo Border Guard, Newcastle Mounted Rifles and Natal Mounted Police: a total of 4,709 men, 302 wagons and carts, 1,507 oxen and 116 horses.

After weeks of heavy rain it was impossible to move such a large concentration across the Mzinyathi without help. At Rorke's Drift the river flows between two even banks, with flats on either side; but after the summer rains it is a wide torrent of dark tea-coloured water. At low water it is possible to cross via a rocky island in mid-stream, but when the river is

The Jones brothers photographed in the 1890s; in 1879 Charles (centre) was a Lieutenant in the Newcastle Mounted Rifles, Sam (left) was a Trooper in the same unit, and Ruben (right) was a young transport driver. (Talana Museum, Dundee)

Captain Robert Bradstreet of the Newcastle Mounted Rifles; he was the senior officer of mounted Volunteers left in the camp at Isandlwana on 22nd January. (Author's collection)

raided Natal in July, Sihayo kaXongo, whose territory lay directly across the river, was widely held to be an aggressive and defiant commander who was sure to contest the crossing. As the date for the impending invasion grew near all heads in the British camp craned towards the river, hoping to see signs of the Zulu response. On the 8th there was a flurry of excitement when a sentry reported a group of horsemen riding down to the drift on the other side; but they turned out to be a party of officers, including Captain Barton and Baron von Stietencron, from the Frontier Light Horse — one of the irregular units attached to Wood's Left Flank Column. They had ridden down from the north, through Zulu territory, to bring the news that Wood had crossed the Ncome (Blood) River into Zululand two days before — five days before the ultimatum expired. During their journey of over 30 miles they had encountered no hostility from Zulus they met on the way; nevertheless, it was considered unwise to let them return that same evening, so they stayed with the column until the morning.

On the 9th Chelmsford announced his intention to review the NNC the following morning, with one unfortunate consequence. The men were scattered about on various duties, and Lonsdale and his Staff Officer, Henry Harford, were riding out to gather them in when

> *Lonsdale's pony shied at something and threw him off. I saw him fall. He appeared to have struck his head and then, rolling over on his back, lay quite still with one of his arms projecting in the air at right angles to his body. I got off at once and ran to his assisstance, only to find that he was unconcious, and rigidly stiff.*

up the water surges over the rocks in a foaming torrent. Nevertheless, there is a wide, sandy-bottomed stretch below the island where a determined traveller can cross under most circumstances. It was clearly quite impossible to cross with the wagons, however, and in early January an improvised pontoon bridge was brought up in sections and assembled at the site by the Native Pioneers, assisted by a party of Royal Engineers. Another large pontoon was built out of barrels and planking, and hawsers were stretched across the river ready for the crossing.

Chelmsford had no Head of Intelligence on his staff, believing that such a post was unnecessary, and was dependent on the reports of the black Border Police, and on rumour, for his information concerning Zulu intentions. Since his sons had

No.3 (Centre) Column crossing the Mzinyathi valley, Harness' N/5 Battery RA in the foreground. This sketch published in the Illustrated London News *shows dramatic scenery strongly resembling a point on the road between Helpmekaar, above the escarpment, and Rorke's Drift, although the direction of march has been reversed for some reason — the Column was in fact descending the heights. (Author's collection)*

The Anglo-Zulu War begins: the dawn crossing of the Mzinyathi at Rorke's Drift on 11th January captured in a quick sketch by J.N.Crealock. Soldiers of the 24th cross on the pont, foreground; the barrel-raft and a small boat can be seen beyond. (Sherwood Foresters' Museum)

Lonsdale was not seriously injured, but he had suffered a bad concussion, and was taken back to the hospital tent at Help-mekaar to recover: he did not rejoin his regiment until the 20th, by which time it was camped at Isandlwana. Chelmsford's inspection went ahead; he professed himself much pleased with the regiment, and offered them what Norris-Newman considered "good advice — saying that no prisoners, women and children were to be injured in any way".

The next morning, Saturday, 11th January 1879, the Anglo-Zulu War began.

The night was fine until four in the morning when, as so often happens at that time of year, a dense fog came down. Reveille had sounded at 2 a.m., and the men shivered in a drizzling rain as they waited to cross the river. The job of covering the crossing had fallen to the artillery and the 2/24th; the infantry battalion lined a low ridge which overlooked the ponts, while the six 7-pdrs. of N/5 Battery unlimbered on a rise a few hundred yards down stream which commanded the drift. The 1/3rd NNC and the Volunteers were to cross by the drift while the men of the 1/24th began to file onto the ponts. Harford was ordered to take the 2/3rd NNC to a point upstream which had been spotted as a potential crossing; he plunged his horse into the water. It kept its feet despite the strong current, with the water reaching up to the saddle flaps; the far bank was steep and slippery, but it was possible to get across. Harford clearly found the whole experience exhilarating:

Then followed a truly unforgettable scene, first of the Natives crossing over and then of the impressive ceremony when the Regiment had formed up again on the other side and were addressed by old Ingabangi, the witch-doctor. In order to scare away any crocodiles that might be lurking in the vicinity, the leading Company formed a double chain right across the River, leaving a pathway between for the remainder to pass through. The men forming the chain clasped hands, and the moment they entered the water they started to hum a kind of war-chant, which was taken up by every Company as they passed over. The sound that this produced was like a gigantic swarm of bees buzzing about us, and sufficient to scare the crocodiles or anything else. Altogether, it was both a curious and grand sight.

All being safely over, the men were formed up into quarter-column on

the hillside, and one or two Officers on their ponies were sent out in different directions to try and find out in the dense fog where any of the other troops were, and what was going on. While this was in progress, old Ingabangi asked permission to address the men. Never shall I forget his extraordinary elocutionary power, and the splendid oration he delivered. The old fellow got to the head of the Column, and then started off at a trot, going backwards and forwards at this pace for nearly half an hour. He would have gone on much longer, had we not received orders to move. Without stopping for breath, he recounted the history of the Zulu nation, which was frequently applauded by a loud "Gee!" and rattling of assegais on shields from the whole Contingent. It was a wonderfully impressive scene, and one which will always remain fresh in my memory. The drift at which we crossed was subsequently known as Harford's Drift, but I don't suppose it's ever been used since.

Norris-Newman crossed with Captain Krohn's company of the 1/3rd NNC, and (ever the journalist) prided himself on being "actually the first man in Zululand after the war was declared". The water was flowing at a rate of over six knots, and in some places the men were up to their necks. Hamilton-Browne commented sourly that he lost several men in the crossing, but did not know how many as he had never bothered to take a roll; however, no-one else mentions the incident, and there were no casualty returns submitted.

The men waiting on the Natal bank had a tense time of it. The mist was so thick that they could see nothing across the river except for a few shapes moving dimly about. There was a very real concern that the Zulus would attack; yet, as the minutes dragged by, the party in Zululand became more and more secure. The mounted men dumped their kit in the pontoons, then rode down to cross at the lower drift. As each company of the 1/24th crossed over they formed up on the far slope.

Then, almost suddenly, the mist began to lift, and the sun shone through bright and hot. The NNC shook themselves out, and pushed forward up the gentle slope on the Zulu bank to a rise. Four companies of the 1st Battalion formed up in skirmishing order on the right, with their flank anchored on a bend in the river, and their remaining companies behind them in reserve. Several companies of the 1/24th extended in similar order on their left; then came the 2/24th and 2/3rd NNC. The whole line stretched for almost three miles.

The men began to relax at their posts, letting the sun warm their chilled limbs, while the long and exhausting process began of ferrying the supply wagons across. The only Zulu in sight was a solitary herdsman, and a patrol set off enthusiastically to capture his cattle. The Anglo-Zulu War had begun on a cheerful note.

The heat of the day has a detrimental effect on the alertness of a typical four-man picquet of the 24th at Rorke's Drift; Shiyane hill rises in the background. (Author's collection)

CHAPTER THREE

The Red Soldier

The backbone of the Centre Column was inevitably its Imperial contingent: the two battalions of the 24th Regiment, N/5 Battery RA, and No.1 Squadron of the Imperial Mounted Infantry.

For a few days at the beginning of January 1879, when the 2nd Battalion of the 24th joined the four companies and headquarters of the 1st Battalion already encamped on the sodden heights at Helpmekaar, the two battalions were re-united. This was an unusual event for any regiment on active service, and it was all the more so for the 24th since, temporarily at least, the two battalions were commanded by brothers. By even happier chance the reunion had occurred within days of the anniversary of the 24th's most famous battle-honour. On 13th January 1849 the 24th had been part of an Anglo-Indian brigade which assaulted an enemy position at Chillianwallah during the Sikh Wars. The 24th had charged an enemy battery head-on through thick jungle, carrying the assault "at the point of the bayonet, without firing a shot". They had suffered terrible casualties as a result: both the brigade commander and the regiment's commanding officer were killed, along with 11 officers and over 200 men, and many more had been wounded. The Colour party, the focus for regimental pride, had been devastated, and the Queen's Colour lost; according to one story a Private had torn it from the Colour pole and wrapped it round his body in an effort to save it, but he was later killed and the Colour, unnoticed, was buried with him.

The officers of the 1st Battalion had made themselves as comfortable at Helpmekaar as the weather allowed, and had improvised a mess out of wooden biscuit boxes and crates of supplies roofed over with a tarpaulin. They had been carefully hoarding the last of their wine, and invited their brother officers from the 2nd Battalion over to join them for dinner. Two of the hosts, Captain William Degacher and Lieutenant Francis Porteous, offered a toast to the memory of Chillianwallah — "that we may not get into such a mess and have better luck this time". The toast was "laughingly drunk" by all concerned.

* * *

The British Army in the 1870s was in a state of flux. The much-publicised shambles of the Crimean War had proved that reform was long overdue, and the campaign was spearheaded by Edward Cardwell, appointed Secretary of State for War by Disraeli in 1868. The Army of the early Victorian era had reflected the desperate divisions in British society itself; it was run as a gentlemen's club by officers who disdained efficiency and professionalism, and had little regard for the ranks, whom they regarded — often quite rightly — as the dregs of society. Cardwell was determined to reduce the Army's dependence on patronage, to increase the emphasis on training, and to attract a larger number of better quality recruits into the ranks. His objectives were bitterly opposed by a powerful conservative element within the Army led by the Commander-in-Chief himself, the Duke of Cambridge; and the subsequent wrangles dogged the Army through two decades, until the old school at last died away and a younger generation of zealous reformers, epitomised by Sir Garnet Wolseley ("Britain's Only General"), took control.

By the late 1870s Cardwell's reforms were beginning to bite, and the consequences of many were to emerge during the Zulu War. One of Cardwell's first acts was to abolish the system whereby officers purchased their commissions: a system which had filled the senior ranks of fashionable regiments with social butterflies who had neither the experience not the training necessary to do their job, while leaving less popular regiments to be commanded by the younger sons of minor gentry. Officers who had purchased their commissions under the old system were allowed to retain them, but newcomers were required to prove their suitability by means of an entrance exam. Of course, the "right background" and the necessity of a large private income ensured that the officer class remained a social elite throughout the Victorian period; but the old stigma attached to Engineer and Artillery officers — who were trained in their technical specialities and therefore among the most professional in the Army, but who were thought to be "not quite gentlemen" — began to die away.

It is interesting to see exactly who did make up the officer class in the 1870s. Of the 19 officers of both battalions of the 24th who fought at Isandlwana, six were the sons of clergy, and four were following their fathers' military profession. No less than seven had passed through the Royal Military Academy at Sandhurst; while two had university degrees, including the Adjutant, Lieutenant Teignmouth Melvill, who was a Cambridge graduate. Geographically, they came from homes as scattered as Toronto, France and Northumberland, but four of them had Irish connections, reflecting the close links between the Anglo-Irish "ascendancy" and the officer class. Lieutenant Nevill Coghill was the son of Sir Jocelyn Coghill, Bt., of Drumcondra, County Dublin; his letters reveal him to be a bright, ambitious young man who shared the class-consciousness of his age, preoccupied with social pursuits which included a good deal of riding and hunting, and with the inadequacy of his Army pay to support the necessary expenses of his lifestyle. There is nothing to suggest that he was anything other than a typical subaltern of the period.

Lieutenant-Colonel Henry J. Degacher, who commanded the 2/24th throughout the Isandlwana campaign. (Royal Archives)

The High Commissioner, Sir Henry Bartle Frere (seated centre) with officers of the 1/24th, and others, photographed in 1878 at King William's Town on the Cape Frontier. (Standing, left to right:) Captain W.T.Much, Captain T.Rainforth, Paymaster F.F.White, Captain Hiller (Staff), Captain H.H.Parr (Staff), QM J.Pullen, Lieutenant F.B.Porteous, Major H.B.Pulleine, Lieutenant G.F.J.Hodson, Lieutenant-Colonel F.W.Walker (Staff), Mr.Sivewright, Lieutenant C.J.Atkinson, Captain G.V.Wardell. (Seated, left to right:) Lieutenant J.P.Daly, Hon.C.P.Brownlee, Frere, Lieutenant-General Sir A.Cunynghame, Colonel R.T.Glyn, Hon.J.X.Merriman. (Front:) Lieutenant N.J.A.Coghill (Staff), Hon.W.Littleton. (Africana Museum, Johannesburg)

Captain (Acting Major) William Degacher of the 1/24th in dress uniform. He would be killed at Isandlwana. (Royal Archives)

One of Cardwell's most controversial reforms was the introduction of the short-service system. Previously a man enlisting in the ranks was required to sign up for a minimum of 12 years' service with the Colours, but under the short-service system the minimum period was reduced to six years, with a further six on the Reserve. Cardwell hoped to make the ranks more attractive to a better class of recruit, and it is true to say that by the 1870s the Army was gradually losing its role as society's dustbin. Literacy and general educational standards were improving, as the prolific letter-writing from the Zulu War demonstrates; while the abolition of the more brutalising aspects of the Army regime, including flogging as a punishment in peacetime, meant that the life of the ordinary soldier was no longer as unrelentingly grim as it once had been. Nevertheless, Jack Frost and unemployment were still the best recruiting-sergeants, and drunkenness in the ranks was still a serious problem. Partly because of this, the British public as a whole remained decidedly ambivalent towards its "thin red line of heroes", whom it preferred to be holding the frontiers of Empire on the other side of the world rather than carousing in the local canteen. The opponents of the short-service system regretted the passing of the grizzled old sweats who were supposed to excercise a steadying influence in the ranks. They argued that short service meant too great a proportion of inexperienced young soldiers; and to some extent the frequent night-time panics in the ranks of battalions sent out for the closing stages of the Zulu War would prove them right.

From 1871 infantry regiments were associated with a particular district within the United Kingdom, where they were required to establish a barracks and from whence they were to draw most of their recruits. Many regiments already had established local connections: the 3rd Regiment, the Buffs, for example, were the East Kents, and the 13th Light Infantry, Prince Albert's Own, were the 1st Somersetshires. Not all of these connections were honoured under the new system; the 24th also bore the title 2nd Warwickshires, reflecting 200 years of associations with that county, but in 1873 their depot was established at Brecon in South Wales. From that date on they began to recruit extensively amongst the English counties on

*B Company, 1/24th, photographed at Port St.John's in 1879.
Lieutenants W.E.D.Spring and the Hon.N.de R.B.Roche recline in
the foreground; the figure in civilian dress at left may be Captain
H.Harrison. This company remained in southern Natal throughout
the Anglo-Zulu War, but the photograph gives a good impression of
the mature soldiers who made up the Battalion.
(Royal Regiment of Wales Museum, Brecon)*

the Welsh borders, many of which had large Welsh populations.

The effects of these changes could be seen in the different composition of the two battalions of the 24th. The battalion, rather than the regiment, was the standard fighting unit: a self-contained community of over 800 men, composed of eight lettered companies each with a theoretical strength of a hundred men. Few companies were ever up to full strength on overseas service, however; there were always a number of men on detached duties or on the sick list, and it was the practice to replace natural wastage — men whose period of enlistment had expired — by periodic drafts from home. It was not unknown for a battalion in the field to number as few as 400 men. The 1/24th had been overseas since 1867, before Cardwell's ministry, first in Malta and then in Gibraltar; most of its men had enlisted under the old long-service system. When the Battalion sailed to South Africa in 1875 it was made up to strength by a draft of 300 men from the depot in Wales, and it therefore gradually took on a Welsh character which it had not previously enjoyed. Two further drafts, totalling 230 men, joined the Battalion before August 1877; but the remainder, just less than half, were long-service men, and the Cape press commented favourably on the high proportion of long service and good conduct stripes in evidence on the men's right cuffs when the Battalion landed. The 2nd Battalion, by contrast, sailed to South Africa in 1878 direct from the depot at Brecon, and observers were struck by the apparent youth of the short-service men in the ranks.

Many of the NCOs, the backbone of any infantry unit, had an impressive history of service behind them. Two of the 1st Battalion Colour-Sergeants who fought in Zululand, Joseph George Ballard and Frederick Wolfe, had achieved that rank as early as 1874, while Ballard had enlisted in 1864 at the age of seventeen. Most of the Sergeants were in their late twenties or early thirties, men in "what may be regarded as the prime of life and experience". Sergeant Thomas Cooper may be taken

as a typical example; he was born in 1850, lying about his age in order to enlist in 1866 at the age of sixteen. He re-enlisted at the end of his first term of service in 1873 as a Corporal, and was promoted Sergeant in August 1874. He was aged 29 at the time of the Zulu War.

Before their time in South Africa the 1/24th had not seen active service since the Indian Mutiny, but by 1879 they had already earned themselves Frere's approval as a "seasoned Battalion under an excellent, steady, sensible Commander, Colonel Glyn, and with very good young officers". They had not been long at the Cape when it was necessary to despatch an expeditionary force to quell an incipient republican rising in the diamond fields at Kimberley. Three companies of the 1/24th — C, D and F — made up the bulk of the expedition, and although the prospective revolt collapsed as soon as it was known that the troops had been called out the 24th proved themselves more than capable of withstanding the rigours of campaigning in the worst the South African landscape had to offer. They had to march over 350 miles from Cape Town to Kimberley, much of it through the dry, arid wastes of the Karoo. They covered it at a rate of 20 or even 30 miles a day, spurred on by the infrequency of fresh water supplies. By day it was bakingly hot, and the air was heavy with dust; at night the temperature dropped below freezing. General Cunynghame, who joined the expedition on its final phase, was impressed: "Those who were on picquet duty were sorely tried; but there were no complaints, and every man looked more healthy daily".

It was in the fighting on the Cape Frontier that the Battalion was really tested, however. When the rising broke out the 1/24th was stationed at Cape Town, and, since the recent annexation of the Transvaal was tying down most of the other Imperial troops in South Africa, the Battalion was best placed to meet the emergency. Despite the opposition of the civil administration, who insisted that it was merely a local police matter, the 1/24th were deployed in small detachments at a series of posts along the Kei River. When the situation deteriorated Colonel Glyn led a sweep through the Transkei in pursuit of King Sahrili's Gcaleka Xhosa. Cunynghame had to stretch his resources thin to cover the necessary ground, and the Battalion was frequently broken down into small detachments of half-companies or less, or mixed up completely. It was a situation which encouraged self-reliance, since the men could not always serve under their own company officers and

No.1313 Thomas Cooper, 1/24th — a distant relative of the author. He is photographed as a Private, c.1873, and as a bearded Sergeant, c.1879; the Battalion grew their beards during the Cape Frontier campaign the previous year, which suggests that the second picture was taken shortly before the outbreak of the Anglo-Zulu War. Cooper served with Captain Mostyn's F Company, and was killed at Isandlwana. (Author's collection)

detachments were often commanded in action by nothing more than a Lieutenant. The Battalion band was pressed into service to man two 7-pdr. guns for which there were no crews, and their response drew eulogies from Cunynghame: "The rapidity with which they learned this exercise was amazing. After ten days' instruction, they were able to load and come into action in *fifteen seconds*; but there was no duty whatever which the 24th Regiment could not be found equal to."

Much of the fighting took the form of debilitating skirmishing in thick bush, but the 1/24th did take part in two stand-up fights, which are significant because they shaped the attitude of the unit's officers — no less than that of Lord Chelmsford himself — towards African warfare. On 13th January 1878 Colonel Glyn commanded a force including nearly 200 men of the 24th which defeated the Xhosa at Nyamaga. Glyn had marched out from a fortified camp at Kwa Centane to intercept a large Xhosa force which was gathering to attack an isolated outpost. The Xhosa were drawn up along the crest of a ridge when Glyn's column arrived; he immediately drew up his men in a long line at the foot of the hill, with the guns in the

centre, and Mounted Police on either flank. A second line was placed some distance behind the first to act as support. When the guns opened fire the Xhosa retired behind the crest, and Glyn immediately ordered his men to advance. By the time they reached the top of the hill the Xhosa had regrouped on a ridge opposite them. For a while they stood their ground and a stiff fire-fight broke out, but as Glyn committed his reserves the fire grew too hot for the Xhosa, who broke off and fell back, chased by the Mfengu auxiliaries.

On 7th February a combined force of Ngqika and Gcaleka Xhosa attacked the base at Centane itself. The post was built on one end of a bare spur which sloped away on three sides. It had been protected by a simple square earthwork, a trench with the soil piled up inside to form a rampart; and was

Corporal Henry Richardson and Pioneers of the 1/24th on the Cape Frontier, 1877/78; Richardson was killed during the flight from Isandlwana. Note the appearance of these old soldiers, and the four LS & GC stripes worn by the man on the right. (Africana Museum, Johannesburg)

Captain F.Glennie and men of the reconstituted G Company,
2/24th, photographed at the end of the Anglo-Zulu War. Although
the 2nd Battalion had a higher proportion of short-service men, this
photograph suggests that there were still a number of "old sweats" in
its ranks. Glennie is wearing the officer's undress scarlet frock; and
the men appear to have drab canvas helmet covers. (Gavin
Edgerley-Harris)

guarded by F and G Companies of the 1/24th, about 80
Colonial police, two guns, a rocket battery, and over 500
Mfengu levies, all under the command of Captain Russell
Upcher of the 1/24th. The Xhosa build-up had been obvious
for several days preceeding the attack, and Upcher had
ordered the 24th to dig rifle pits on the forward slope of the
spur, while the guns were placed in the earthwork; a wagon-
laager was built to corral the transport oxen.

It was pouring with rain on the morning of the 7th when
picquets reported the approach of a Xhosa force estimated at
between 5,000 and 6,000 men. The mounted men and G
Company were sent out to draw them on, falling back as the
pace of the Xhosa advance quickened. The 24th retreated to
the cover of the shelter trenches and opened a heavy fire on the
Xhosa, whose attack stalled several hundred yards away. A
dense mist moving up the valley allowed some of them to
creep forward to within 200 yards of the camp, but the steady
fire of the 24th, supported by the artillery, drove them back.
When their attack wavered the mounted men and the Mfengu
were sent out in pursuit. The attack appeared to be over, and
the men had been allowed to stand down for breakfast when
another body of the enemy was discovered approaching from
the north-west. A company of the 24th was sent out to
disperse them, but was almost cut off when the Xhosa made a
determined attempt to get between them and the camp.
Upcher fed more men into the fighting, however, and the
Xhosa attack collapsed, caught in turn in a devastating crossfire. By 10.30 they had been driven from the field; their losses
were recorded as 200 dead, but were widely held to be higher.
Upcher had lost three Mfengu killed and three Police
wounded. He was particularly pleased with his men's performance: "The 24th skirmished with great steadiness and
rapidity, making the best use of cover whilst advancing under
fire, to which fact I attribute the small loss on our side".

General Cunynghame added another relevant observation.
Concerning Nyamaga, he noted: "At no time had the power

of the Martini-Henry rifle been more conspicuously shown;
indeed, it was perhaps the first occasion when it had been fairly
used by soldiers of the British army." Since the Martini-Henry
had no small role to play in the events of January 1879, it is
worth pausing to consider its merits.

The 1/24th had been issued with the rifle in 1873, replacing
the breech-loading percussion Snider. The Martini-Henry was
a single-shot breech-loader with a "falling block" action,
activated by a lever behind the trigger: pull the lever down and
the breech falls opens, allowing a cartridge case to be pushed
into the exposed end of the chamber. After firing the same
action ejects the spent case. The cartridges themselves were the
.450 inch rolled brass Boxer variety, firing a heavy, hard-lead,
unjacketed slug.

The rifle was sighted up to 1,700 yards, but at longer ranges
it must have been difficult to hit anything; at that range it is
necessary to fire over raised backsights, and it is not possible
for the rifleman to nestle his cheek alongside the stock —
instead you have to move your head back and crane your neck
at an awkward angle to get a glimpse of the foresight. When
firing in a standing position it soons becomes difficult to keep
your left arm steady, and the foresight begins to wobble. At
shorter ranges the rifle is much easier to use; at 400 yards the
backsight can be folded down, and at last the marksman can
settle in closer and draw a bead down the barrel. Even at that
range a cross-wind can have a marked effect on the fall of the
shot, and the velocity seems slow; there is time to look up to
see the thick spurt of dust which marks the bullet-strike.
Firing with the bayonet fixed is even more difficult, since it
obscures part of the foresight, and the rifle seems to be being
pulled away from you. At ranges of 200 yards or less, however, it becomes extremely effective, especially when firing
from a steady kneeling or prone position, and even relatively
inexperienced riflemen could expect as many as eight out of
ten hits on a stationary target.

The rifle fires with a sharp crack that feels like a clap round
the ears, and produces a thin cough of white smoke which
blows away quickly on a breezy day but lingers in still air. The
recoil produces a steady thump on the shoulder — not as sharp
as the kick of modern, high-velocity military firearms, but
after ten rounds it becomes difficult not to flinch in anticipation. After 40 or 50 rounds the firer can expect some significant
bruising. After ten rounds, too, the barrel becomes too hot to

The Mark II Martini-Henry rifle, the British infantry arm in the war of 1879. (Courtesy of the Director, National Army Museum, London)

The Martini action: the lever behind the trigger guard is depressed to allow access to the chamber. (Author's collection)

Boxer pattern .45 in. calibre rounds, with rolled brass cartridges and paper-wrapped lead bullets; and some expended cartridges reputedly found after Isandlwana. Note the seam just above the cartridge base; the rolled brass body often tore free at this point during extraction from a hot, fouled chamber.

touch, and the spent cases spill out covered in a thick greasy deposit. The cartridges are pulled out by extractor hooks on either side engaging with the cartridge rim. This was a system prone to damage; either the extractors themselves became broken, or they tore the rim and base section off the rather flimsy rolled-brass cartridges, softened by the heat of the breech.

When the lead slug hit a human target the effects could be devastating. Because of its velocity it often clipped through muscle and flesh cleanly, but if it encountered any obstruction it splintered bone unmercifully, and the resultant injuries often caused death through shock. The British Army considered that the Martini's effective battle range was between 300 and 450 yards, although firing was often opened at 800 yards. On one occasion Crealock noticed a company of the 2/24th cutting off a Xhosa retreat and "at a distance of 1300 yards were making good practice". There is no reason to suppose that either Battalion was anything other than proficient in its use by the beginning of 1879.

It is also interesting to note that at neither Nyamaga nor Centane did the 24th take up an all-round defensive position and stand shoulder to shoulder in tight formation. Both battles were essentially fluid and fast-moving: in one Glyn had dispersed the Xhosa by attacking in an open line, while in the other infantry skirmishers had been used to draw the enemy on, then drive them from the field. On neither occasion were the 24th in serious danger of being overrun by the Xhosa attacks and, while some attempts were made to threaten their flanks, they were never effectively surrounded. Nevill Coghill, who underwent his baptism of fire at Nyamaga, regarded it as a significant victory, and noted the coincidence that it had occurred exactly on the twenty-ninth anniversary of Chillianwallah.

Centane marked a turning point in the Ninth Frontier War. It broke the back of resistance amongst the Transkei Gcaleka Xhosa, and heralded a return to the traditional guerrilla warfare amongst the Ngqika Xhosa, whose territory lay east of the Kei within the Colonial border. The fighting there fell to the lot of the 2/24th, who had arrived in South Africa in March 1878 along with General Thesiger. Although Thesiger begged his staff to take great pains not to offend his predecessor Cunynghame he was, despite being the younger man, a more conventional general. He did not approve of Cunynghame's habit of splitting infantry companies down into small irregular detachments, and he insisted that Glyn collect the Battalion together. The 1/24th remained on garrison duty across the Kei, however, and it was the 2/24th who played a prominent role in Thesiger's campaign against the Ngqika. He deployed them in groups of two or three companies in a ring around the Amathole Mountains, the Ngqika stronghold; here the 2/24th learned the art of South African warfare, struggling through thickets of dense thorn bush, scrambling down rocky precipices or toiling up steep hills. It was a baptism of fire no less effective than Centane, though it boasted no set-piece battles; and it confirmed the prevailing opinion that black South Africans could not be made to stand and fight.

By the time the war ended and the battalions were despatched to Natal the youngsters of the 2/24th looked no less like veterans than their comrades in the 1st Battalion. They were lean and bronzed, used to the rough life in the field, and most now sported the beards which Army regulations permitted on active service. Even Coghill had grown one: he sent his sister a photograph of himself, and commented proudly "it is now a very presentable Van Dyke", but added "I shall be very glad indeed when I take it off". The rigours of campaigning had taken their toll on the men's uniforms; the clean white

The 24th on the march from King William's Town to Natal at the end of the Ninth Cape Frontier War. Note the cased Colours in the centre, and the officer (left) wearing a forage cap. The artist, Charles Fripp, who had a good eye for detail, curiously shows several men with spears apparently thrust down the barrels of their rifles — presumably these were trophies. (Author's collection)

foreign service helmet mounted with the 1869–78 pattern shako plate had been stripped of its glittering badge and dulled down with a khaki dye improvised from tea, coffee or boiled mimosa bark; and many men had sewn a length of cow-hide around the stock of their rifles to save their fingers from getting burnt in action. The thorns of the Amatholes had ripped out the seat of many a pair of trousers and the rocky ground had scuffed elbows and knees; the men had cut squares from their blankets or any other available material to make patches. Few of them had any illusions but that further fighting was in the offing; Coghill spoke for them all when he wrote as early as February 1878: "one thing is clear that Cetewayo wants a beating and sooner or later he must get it."

* * *

The Regiment moved up to Natal in stages. The 2nd Battalion went first, embarking at East London in July 1878, "leaving", as the regimental records state wryly, "the women and children and heavy baggage behind". With a complement of 21 officers, 39 sergeants and 707 other ranks it was close to full strength. It disembarked at Durban and marched up to Pietermaritzburg, where it arrived on 6th August, and remained at Fort Napier for three months. On 30th October F, G and H Companies under Major Wilsone Black marched up to an abandoned earthwork near the border named Fort Buckingham. The remainder of the Battalion joined them there shortly afterwards, and the Regiment was reunited at Greytown.

The 1st Battalion sent two companies — C and D, under Captains Younghusband and Upcher respectively — to Natal in September 1878. B Company, under Captain Harrison, was left at Fort Buckingham, at the mouth of the St.John's River in southern Natal, and was destined to remain there throughout the Zulu War, guarding against a possible rising by the ama-Mpondo. The Headquarters and A, F, G and H Companies

arrived in Natal on 19th November, the remaining company, E, joining them later from East London. As the Battalion marched to the front it collected C Company from Fort Napier, and detached F Company. At Greytown, where it overtook the 2nd Battalion, it detached G Company, so that by the time it reached Helpmekaar it consisted of just the Headquarters and A, H, C and E Companies. F Company finally caught up with it on 21st January at Isandlwana, by which time D and G Companies were at Helpmekaar.

The later stages of this march were accomplished in alternate baking sunshine and torrential rain. The Natal Carbineers were with the 1st Battalion when they marched out of Pietermaritzburg; the Battalion band, now reassembled, had been restored to its proper duties. Trooper Fred Symons noticed that the music was interrupted twice, however; perhaps he was overly superstitious, but it struck him as faintly sinister. The band were in the middle of a tune called *Nancy Lee*, and:

> *when they had gone far enough they wheeled to the side and continued playing till Fletcher's horse became restive at the sound of the drums and rearing up fell with him almost on top of the big drum. Thus our music came to an untimely end, a bad omen . . .*
>
> *. . . The 24th came marching in [to Helpmekaar] in due time and another ominous incident occurred, a huge bull frog, red and green, hopped up and stopped the band again, and the whole battalion swerved aside so as to avoid his bullfrogship who sat placidly blinking at the men.*

Curiously enough, the red jackets of the 24th had green regimental facings.

However, most of the rank and file had more to preoccupy them than Trooper Fletcher's skittish horse or the eccentric behaviour of a bullfrog. For the 1st Battalion companies at Helpmekaar the advent of Christmas brought no change in the daily duties, and a Christmas lunch just as dour as the one consigned to the Volunteers. It made Private Owen Ellis homesick:

I was on sentry duty on Christmas morning — from one til three o'clock, and as I was parading backwards and forwards, I thought what a row there was at Carnarvon that night. There was not a sound to be heard around where I stood; the night was as dark as pitch and heavy rains descended from three till five o'clock in the morning. We afterwards enjoyed pleasant sunshine all day long; indeed, no-one would have believed that it had been raining. Well, I had Christmas Day all to myself; but there was no difference in the supply of food — we only got what we got on ordinary days. Being many miles from any town or village, we did not expect anything else . . .

Even this was comparative comfort, for the men of the 2nd Battalion spent Christmas Day on the road. Corporal H. Brown complained bitterly to his wife:

At three o'clock the same day we left Mooi River, marching twelve more miles, that was altogether twenty-three miles that day; to make it worse we had to go through a wood seventeen miles long. At eight o'clock that night we got to the Thukela River, and it was that dark we could not see one another, and raining in torrents, and we had to sleep on the ground wet through without anything to put under or over us. That was the joyous Christmas I spent in South Africa in the year 1878, one that none of us will forget while we live.

Four days later Corporal Brown marched into Helpmekaar, and was delighted to find that the band of their sister battalion had turned out:

[We were] played into camp by the band of the 1/24th Regiment who were there before us. They had a nice bit of dinner ready for us, and did all our work for us when we got in; it was very good of them for doing it for we were all tired.

Clearly the two battalions were happy to be working together. Curiously, the 2nd Battalion was commanded by Lieutenant-Colonel Henry Degacher, whose younger brother, Captain (acting Major) William Degacher, was serving in the 1st Battalion. The 1st Battalion had left its Lieutenant-Colonel, Henry Pulleine, on temporary administrative duties at Pietermaritzburg, so that when Colonel Glyn gave up his regimental duties to take over command of the Column the command of the Battalion devolved onto the senior Field Officer — who happened to be William Degacher. The two battalions were therefore briefly commanded by brothers.

Throughout the first week of January the remaining Imperial contingents joined the column. Lord Chelmsford had inherited the chronic shortage of cavalry which had plagued the British Army in South Africa in the wars of the 1870s. Neither he nor Cunynghame had been able to call upon the services of any regiment of Regular cavalry, and both had had to make do with local Volunteer units. As a step towards rectifying this imbalance attempts had been made as early as 1875 to raise a unit of Mounted Infantry. Thirty-six men who could ride had been selected from the 1/24th and given horses, and had served throughout the abortive Kimberley rising, but had been disbanded and returned to their normal duties at the end of the expedition. In April 1877, however, No. 1 Squadron, Imperial Mounted Infantry had been formed at Pietermaritzburg from men of the 1st Battalion stationed at the Cape and on the Frontier, commanded by Lieutenant Fred Carrington and Lieutenant Edward Browne. It was subsequently joined by a small party from the 1/13th Regiment under Lieutenant Walsh, and a similar party from the Buffs under Lieutenant Nathaniel Newnham-Davis; total strength was about 120 men. The Squadron's first duty was to escort Sir Theophilus Shepstone, the newly-appointed Administrator of the Transvaal, to Pretoria. They were then distributed in small detachments to garrison the territory, or to act as roving troubleshooters. A section under Carrington and Walsh accompanied Shepstone to a meeting with King Cetshwayo's representatives on 19th October — a meeting that was so stormy that Shepstone declared his intention of sending the MI into Zululand to express his displeasure. Carrington, who thought the idea meant ''certain death'', was relieved when the Administrator changed his mind.

Carrington later left the Squadron to raise an irregular unit — Carrington's Horse, later the Frontier Light Horse — for the war on the Frontier. Newnham-Davis' section, meanwhile, had been blooded in a brief campaign in Griqualand West, north of the Orange River; one man was killed, and in the action on the Gobatse Heights Private John Power of the 1/24th earned himself a recommendation for the Distinguished Conduct Medal. In September 1878 Brevet Major (later Lieutenant-Colonel) J.C. Russell had taken command of the Squadron, and had led part of it in the unsuccessful Sekhukhune expedition. By the time the various units were ordered to re-unite on the Zulu border and to join the Centre Column, No. 1 Squadron, IMI, had already seen a good deal of South Africa and had been tested in the field. Indeed, the men's appearance — they retained their jackets from their parent regiments, but were issued with buff cord riding breeches — had deteriorated to the extent that they were nicknamed the ''Bashibazooks''. They were armed with the Swinburne-Henry carbine, and carried 70 rounds in a leather bandolier over the left shoulder.

Amongst the last to arrive were the six guns of Brevet Lieutenant-Colonel Arthur Harness' battery of the Royal Artillery. Harness was a member of the old school but, like many Gunners, he was proud of his professionalism. He had joined the Army in 1853 at the age of 25, and after more than 20 years of peacetime soldiering he was promoted Major and given command of N Battery, 5th Brigade, in August 1877. Five months later it embarked for service on the Cape Frontier. Harness, who was regarded as a thorough, steady soldier and an ''excellent judge of men'', approved of Lord Chelmsford, whom he considered a gentleman, but disapproved of the irregular way troops had been used on the Cape Frontier. He had a particular disdain for Colonial volunteers, born of both professional distaste and an awareness of his own social position: ''We expect Buller with the Frontier Light Horse (a band of about two-hundred villainous-looking Colonist volunteers) to join us'', he wrote from the Frontier, adding that ''they are undisciplined and preserve little system in camp, so that the river water wherever we camp, which is very precious, will hardly be kept free of their touch anywhere. The 90th are bad enough, but the volunteers will be far worse . . . '' Nor was he much impressed by the pretensions of settler society, writing from Greytown of the locals: ''A very curious lot they look, of the commonest class, with a mixture of Dutch blood in them; not a single nice looking person among them, and I dare say there were forty or fifty white women among them . . . ''

The fastidious Harness took his duties very seriously. His Battery consisted of six 7-pounder Rifled Muzzle-Loading guns, which had originally been designed to fit light mountain carriages. These carriages were too unstable for South African conditions, and instead they had been mounted on ''Kaffrarian'' carriages — slightly modified versions of the carriage for the heavier 9-pounder gun. The guns themselves had a maximum range of 3,100 yards, but their effectiveness was a matter of some controversy; it was argued that at longer ranges the velocity of the projectile had decreased to the extent that the shell-burst was largely ineffective.

Nonetheless, Harness and his friend and second-in-command Major Stuart Smith struggled to keep N/5 up to a high level of efficiency. The men were regularly drilled, and Smith scoured South Africa in search of suitable horses, which were in short supply. In the age of horse-drawn transport an absence of good horses could have a crippling effect, and it was one of Harness' major grievances against South Africa that English horses did not thrive on the local grasses, whilst local horses were seldom up to the rigorous duties of a good gun-team. With so little artillery to go round Harness reluctantly had to admit the necessity of splitting his battery, which was scattered around the Frontier in one- or two-gun detachments.

By the time the campaign ended in 1878 N/5 was perfectly used to South African conditions and had seen a good deal of action, much of it in co-operation with "our old friends of the 2nd Battalion, 24th Regiment", as Harness called them. For the impending campaign against the Zulus Harness had been delighted to find that his Battery was to be reunited. Unlike the 24th, it marched overland to Natal as part of Colonel Evelyn Wood's Column. When Wood moved up to the Transvaal border, however, N/5 stayed in Pietermaritzburg, switching over to Colonel Glyn's command. It arrived at Helpmekaar, six guns, 130 officers and men, 73 horses and 36 mules strong.

The Commander of No.3 Column, Colonel Glyn, was in his late forties in 1879, and had nearly 30 years' service behind him. He had served in the Crimea, and then with the 24th in the Indian Mutiny. He had purchased his Lieutenant-Colonecy in 1867 and had commanded the 1st Battalion ever since. In photographs, taken both at the time and in old age, he has an appearance aptly described by one historian as "bristling", but this was belied by his temperament. Frere's opinion of Glyn as steady and sensible has already been noted, whilst Nevill Coghill, who shared Glyn's passion for hunting, thought him "as good a little man as ever breathed". Coghill, who had spent much of the Frontier War as General Cunynghame's ADC and who had feared that his General's recall might have spelt the end of his own staff appointment, had been considered as Adjutant of the 1st Battalion when Melvill secured a place at the Staff College. In the event, however, Chelmsford decided that Melvill was too good an officer to lose on the eve of a new campaign, and Coghill had been appointed Glyn's orderly officer instead.

The senior Staff Officer for No.3 Column, Major Francis Clery, described Glyn as "a guileless, unsuspicious man, very upright and scrupulously truthful, yet of a slow, not to say lethargic temperament". Clery, however, was not entirely happy with his own appointment; a dashing Irishman, with a touch of vanity about his appearance, and a pronounced tendency to disparage the efforts of others, Clery was a Staff College graduate and a former Professor of Tactics at Sand-hurst. He had arrived in South Africa in the hope of securing a plum staff job, and had been attached to Colonel Wood's column. He was an old friend of Wood, whose energetic style suited his own, and he was looking forward to serving with him until, at the last moment, he was transferred to Glyn's column and ordered down to Helpmekaar. The acerbic Crealock was dismissive of Glyn — "do not expect anything [of him]. He is a purely regimental officer with no ideas beyond it." If that view reflected Chelmsford's opinion, one wonders why he had appointed him to the command.

In fact, when Lord Chelmsford brought his Headquarters to Helpmekaar on 4th January, he effectively displaced Glyn and his staff. With Chelmsford taking all the important military decisions — his Frontier War experience having exaggerated his natural tendency not to trust anything to his subordinates — it was inevitable that Glyn was reduced to little more than a figurehead.

Clery commented bitterly that "Colonel Glyn and his staff were *allowed* to work the details — posting the guards, etc, and all the interesting work of that kind". This impotence seems to have had an adverse effect on Glyn, who became withdrawn and uninterested: he "was scarcely ever seen or heard of — the more so as he got anything but encouragement to interest himself in what was going on". This was surprisingly tactless behaviour on Chelmsford's part, and no doubt exacerbated by a damaging clash of personalities between Clery and Crealock, two egotists who clearly detested one another. As well as his Military Secretary, Chelmsford was accompanied by three ADCs: Brevet-Major E.H.Buller, Lieutenant-Colonel Gosset, and, as a courtesy to the Navy, who had landed a contingent to join Chelmsford's forces, Lieutenant Berkeley Milne, RN. Chelmsford had still not appointed a Chief-of-Staff; and indeed, there was a dangerous ambiguity at the heart of the structure of command of No.3 Column.

* * *

The Column first went into action on 12th January, the morning after it had crossed the Mzinyathi. The track from Rorke's Drift meandered to the right, crossing the valley of the Batshe stream a mile or two above the point where it joins the Mzinyathi, then disappearing through the hills to the east. The western side of the valley was marked by a long, low, stony ridge (the southern tip of which, incidentally, is still known as *Masotsheni*, "the place of the soldiers", reflecting its proximity to Chelmsford's camp). On the eastern side, however, the valley was bordered by a steep hill known as Ngedla, which was scarred by a line of cliffs which extended for almost

Brevet Colonel Richard T.Glyn, CB, Commanding Officer of the 1st Battalion, 24th Regiment and also of No.3 Column, though Chelmsford's presence effectively deprived him of a role. (Royal Archives)

The site of the skirmish at Sihayo's stronghold on 12th January? A view along the cliffs on the western face of Ngedla mountain; this shallow horseshoe gorge matches descriptions of the fight. Note the tangle of brush and boulders at the foot of the cliff, where the skirmishing took place. (Author's collection)

the whole length of the side facing the Batshe. At the north end of the valley, about four miles above the track, Chief Sihayo had built his homestead, kwaSokhexe, on a rise nestling at the foot of the cliff. There was no sign of a significant Zulu force in the Batshe valley; although small parties of men were seen moving amongst the hills on the eastern edge, the homesteads and mealie fields scattered across the fertile valley floor were quiet and deserted. Yet Chelmsford could hardly afford to ignore any potential threat along his line of communication; furthermore, since the actions of Sihayo's sons had been one of the ostensible causes of the war, it was only right in British eyes that he should be punished.

At dawn on the morning of the 12th a force set out to attack Sihayo's homestead, commanded by Glyn but, typically, accompanied by the General and his staff. It consisted of the four companies of the 1/24th, both battalions of the 3rd NNC, and the Volunteers and Mounted Infantry under the command of Lieutenant-Colonel Russell. The force marched four miles, descending into the valley and following the track until it reached the point where it crossed the stream; here it halted whilst Glyn and Chelmsford planned the attack. Across the valley small parties of warriors could be seen moving about amongst the boulders at the foot of the cliff, and the sound of a war-chant, mixed with the lowing of cattle, carried through the still morning air. Captain Henry Hallam-Parr, one of Bartle Frere's ADCs who had secured permission to join the Column, recognised some of the shouts as taunts — "Why are you waiting there?", the Zulus were asking, "Are you looking to build kraals? Why don't you come on up?"

Neither Sihayo kaXongo nor his senior son, Mehlokazulu, were present with the Zulu force, which consisted of a number of Sihayo's retainers led by his son Mkhumbikazulu. Most of the fighting men had gone to Ulundi to answer the king's summons; this party had been left to keep an eye on the chief's property. They had taken up a secure position in one of the horseshoe gorges which scallop the line of the cliffs. The exact location cannot be identified today, and unless some battlefield relics are discovered by chance it probably never will be. Like most battlefield accounts, the eyewitness descriptions left by the British are vague, and often confined to features which played a significant part in the individual's experience; and, although the area is thickly settled today, any folk memories amongst the local Zulus have been overwhelmed by the more dramatic events at Isandlwana.

Glyn's plan was to attack the gorge on three sides. The cavalry were to move round to the southern edge of the heights, where they sloped down to a nek and could easily be climbed, while the NNC were to advance straight into the mouth of the gorge, with the 1/24th attempting to scale the spur at the point of the gorge on their left. Hamilton-Browne's 1st Battalion, 3rd NNC was to lead the assault, supported by Cooper with the 2nd; since Lonsdale was still recovering in the hospital tent Major Wilsone Black, a peppery and resourceful Scot from the 2/24th, had been placed in overall command. Henry Harford, who started out with the supports, noted that Hamilton-Browne's battalion advanced enthusiastically enough until it got within range of the boulders and caves where the Zulus were hidden. As they drew near a voice cried out in English, "By whose orders do you come to the land of the Zulus?" Norris-Newman heard it, but thought there was no reply; Hamilton-Browne claimed that his interpreter, Lieutenant Duncombe, shouted back "By the orders of the Great White Queen!" In any case, it was enough to open the ball, and the first shot fired by the Zulus struck an NNC man close to Harford, breaking his thigh.

As they pushed into the mouth of the gorge Hamilton-Browne told off his flanking companies to try to work up amongst the boulders on either side. Despite the inspiring personal leadership of his NCOs, who tried to encourage their

men to the attack by beating them with clubbed rifles, the advance bogged down at the foot of the cliffs under a galling fire from Zulus hidden in the rocks above. Major Black saw the problem, and brought some of the 24th up in support; Hamilton-Browne suggested that the sight of the glittering bayonets of the 24th behind them was all that put new heart into his men. This was characteristically ungenerous: Black's leadership had something to do with it. He had drawn his sword and strode to the front, calmly and clearly urging his men on in ringing tones. Trooper Symons was told by a friend in the Contingent that Black was waving his hat when a bullet clipped it out of his hand; he calmly bent down, picked it up, and carried on cheering his men. At one point a boulder dislodged by the Zulus struck the rocks nearby and bounced up, catching him from the rear, but Black's curses only added to his warlike demeanour.

Meanwhile, Henry Harford had advanced part of the 2nd Battalion to support Hamilton-Browne. It was his first time under fire, and he had expressed his nervousness to Hamilton-Browne the night before, afraid that his nerve might fail him.

The brave and resourceful Major Wilsone Black, apparently photographed in somewhat unorthodox campaign kit in 1879. Black commanded the 3rd NNC while Lonsdale was sick, and was in the forefront of the fight at Sihayo's stronghold. (Local History Museum, Durban)

The crag of Isandlwana, in an aerial view looking roughly south-east. (Peter Engblom/Arthur Konigskramer)

The distinctive outline of Isandlwana mountain, looking back westwards towards Natal; the Helpmekaar plateau is on the distant skyline, and Shiyane hill in the right middleground. The camp was arranged on the flats at the foot of the mountain; note how the ground falls away where the huts are today, towards the dongas. (Ian Castle photograph)

As he came up to Hamilton-Browne, Harford suddenly dropped to the ground:

> *"Good God, Harford," I said, "You are hit!". "No, sir," he replied, "not hit but I have caught such a beauty." And there the lunatic, in his first action, and under heavy fire, his qualms and nervousness all forgotten, had captured some infernal microbe or other, and was blowing its wings out, as unconscious of the bullets striking the rocks all around him as if he had been in his garden at home . . .*

Hamilton-Browne reminded Harford of his priorities, and sent him off to the flanking company on the right to try to move them forward; they were pinned down by Zulu snipers firing from a deep cave in the cliff face opposite them. This cave had been attracting the attention of a company of the 24th on the far side, and several dead Zulus had fallen out and were suspended grotesquely below it, tangled up in creepers and bush. Harford, nothing daunted, ordered one of the NCOs to follow him, and:

> *Clambering at once over a big piece of rock, I got rather a rude shock on finding a Zulu sitting in a squatting position behind another rock, almost at my elbow. His head showed above the rock, and his wide-open eyes glared at me; but I soon discovered that he was dead.*
>
> *Scarcely had I left this apparition behind than a live Zulu . . . suddenly jumped up from his hiding place and, putting the muzzle of his rifle within a couple of feet of my face, pulled the trigger. But the cap snapped, whereupon he dropped his rifle and made off over the rocks for the cave, as hard as he could go. Providence had again come to my aid, and away I went after him, emptying my revolver after him as we scrambled up. Of my six shots only one hit him, but not mortally. I stopped for a second to reload, but finding the wretched thing stuck I threw it down into the valley below, at the same time turning round and shouting to the NCO, who I thought was following me, to let me have his revolver. But he remained behind, where I had left him at the start, and all he did was to call out, as loud as he could, "Captain Harford is killed!" However, I soon put this right by shouting down, "No, he is not, he is very much alive!"*

Harford followed his man to the mouth of the cave, calling out to him to surrender, and assuring him that he would not be ill-treated. The man squatted down in submission. Harford asked him if there were any others in the cave; the Zulu answered no, and with some misgivings Harford edged forward and peered into the gloom. A wounded man was lying with his feet towards the entrance; he was unable to rise, but he was clutching a spear by his side. Harford told him to drop it, and asked him how many more men were inside. The Zulu denied that there were any, but as Harford became accustomed to the gloom he could see several likely looking fissures and crannies. He kept repeating over and over that he knew there were men in the cave, and that the Zulus were lying; then three men cautiously emerged from the darkness, and squatted down in submission. Harford triumphantly led his prisoners out of the cave and down through the rocks to the valley, where Chelmsford and the staff were watching. Clery called over to him: "Well, Harford, I congratulate you on your capture, the General and I have been watching your gallantry for some time."

By that time the Zulu stand had collapsed. The 1/24th had worked their way up to the top of the cliff via a steep fissure in the rock, and had cut off several Zulus fleeing up from the cliffs below, scattering them across the summit. Once on the top the infantry pushed on along the cliff, reaching a point which overlooked Sihayo's homestead itself. The 2nd Battalion had left the camp after the first party, and had swung up through the Batshe valley, driving through the mealie fields and long grass. When they reached Sihayo's homestead they formed up in skirmishing order and advanced cautiously up the slope, only to find it deserted, and that their colleagues had

been watching them from above and enjoying a good laugh at their expense. Although the homestead itself was deserted they were sure that they detected signs that the big central cattle pen — the foundations of which can still be seen to this day — had been loopholed and prepared for defence.

The mounted division, meanwhile, had also had its share of adventures. There was no sign of the Zulus at the southern end of the ridge, and the cavalry turned to their left to move up the slope, the Volunteers moving slightly to the right so that they were out of sight of the Mounted Police on the left. Some mounted Zulus were seen moving on the crest of the heights, but they disappeared behind a rocky outcrop. Russell ordered the Carbineers to send forward some men to draw fire, and Sergeant Methley took Trooper Symons and two others further to the right, which provoked a sudden volley from the rocks ahead — Symons remembered the "V-o-o-rrr" sound made by an irregular missile whirring overhead. The Police seem to have born the brunt of the volley, for they dismounted and hurried forward in skirmishing order, driving the Zulus before them. Symons recalled that "we opened fire, too, along the whole line — a frightful waste of ammunition".

The Volunteers did not halt, but pushed up the slope, presumably still out of sight of the skirmishing on their left. They could see no Zulus in front of them, just the horses they had left when they took up the position in the rocks. A few of the Carbineers rode on to round them up, when suddenly a large body of warriors appeared and bore down towards them. Symons shouted a warning to the Carbineers off to the left but by now they were too far away to hear, and the isolated detachment dismounted and prepared to make a stand. Their carbines had a nine-inch knife with a bayonet attachment; they fixed these, and presented arms. Sergeant-Major Dan Scott called out a challenge, *"Ulipi?"*, but the warriors showed no signs of slowing. "Ulipi? twice. Ulipi? thrice", remembered Symons, "and by this time the natives were about forty yards from us and I had one spotted fairly in the wind and was pressing the trigger when up went their hands and a shout of 'Nombulwan' ". The warriors turned out to be men of the Native Contingent, who had pulled off their distinguishing red headbands to save themselves from attack by the Zulus.

The action had been completely successful from a British point of view. It had lasted perhaps half an hour, and after the Zulus had abandoned their positions in the rocks and caves they had fled across the summit, to be cut off by the various

British parties pursuing them. About 30 Zulus had been killed in all, among them Sihayo's son Mkhumbikazulu. Despite the ever-gracious Hamilton-Browne's conviction that his men had accounted for about 30 of their own comrades with their wild firing, the British losses were confined to Lieutenant Purvis, Corporal Mayer, and 15 unnamed soldiers of the NNC wounded, and three NNC rankers killed. The Volunteers had not suffered a scratch; now they roamed the surface of the heights, rounding up cattle, and examining a deserted homestead. They found a number of obsolete firearms, and a new wagon, reputedly one of Sihayo's. The whole force then descended, and moved back to the camp at Rorke's Drift. They had captured a number of Zulu civilians, including members of Sihayo's household; and over 400 head of cattle, 30 horses, and a large number of goats and sheep. The Volunteers, who had been promised a share of the prize money, were delighted at the profits in store. (Alas, they were to be disappointed; most of the loot was sold off cheap to meat contractors, who later sold it back to the Army at inflated prices.) As the column marched back they were drenched by a sudden thunderstorm.

Nevertheless, everyone was highly delighted with the results of the Centre Column's first action. The troops had acquitted themselves well, and Chelmsford was particularly pleased with the conduct of the Native Contingent, who "behaved very well, and not a native touched a woman or child or killed a wounded man". If the Zulus had fought well, this was only cause for further self-congratulation. Chelmsford had been told that "Sihayo's men have always been looked upon as the bravest in the country, and certainly those who were killed today fought with great courage". Crealock thought that "our fight . . . showed the pluck of these Zulus. Of course, they had every advantage being in a most difficult position. If we are not attacked tonight it is thought we shall not meet a Zulu army for some time. On hearing of our having attacked his people, it is thought [Cetshwayo] will have taken instant action". Fred Symons, sceptical as ever, merely commented that the fight at Sihayo's homestead was "a big fuss over a small matter."

If Crealock seriously expected an immediate Zulu counter-attack he was to be disappointed. In fact, a sense of anti-climax seems to have prevailed amongst the Centre Column over the next few days. "I see no chance of our advance for seven days", Chelmsford wrote to Wood on the 13th; "Road near camp over a swamp must be drained and supplies must be stored at Rorke's Drift; at present there are scarcely any there. The rain latterly all over Natal has been incessant and the roads are reported impassable". "The rains and storms are simply the devil", agreed Crealock; "it would save us an amount of trouble if the Zulus would come down and attack us, fail, and sue for peace". To call the projected line of advance a track, let alone a road, was somewhat optimistic, since it was little more than a line of overgrown wagon-ruts which marked the passage of an occasional trader. At places in the Batshe valley it disappeared completely into patches of rocky ground or under a boggy morass.

On 14th January Chelmsford sent forward four companies of the 2/24th under Major W.M.Dunbar, and several companies of Hamilton-Browne's 1/3rd NNC, to repair the road and make a temporary storage camp just beyond the point where it crossed the stream. The work was all too necessary, but Hamilton-Browne did not find it congenial:

> The Colonial officers turned sulky. They had come out to fight not to make roads. None of the natives had ever used a pick or a spade before, and it took me all my time get them turned to. Certainly it is not a pleasant job to make roads in Zululand in the summer-time, the sun is hot, flies bad, and men sulky. The Colonial officers were not at their best, and men who would willingly stand up to their middles all day long in the drift of a river plugging oxen over, grumbled and swore. It required no small amount of tact to get them started, but when they saw me off shirt and turn to, they could not hang back and once we started we soon made things hum and the road grew apace.

Major Dunbar was not happy either. Physically a big man, he had the most distinguished war record of any officer in the 24th, having taken part in the final attack on the Redan in the Crimea, and in the Indian Mutiny. He was clearly not a man who was easily daunted, but the camp on the Batshe lay too close for his liking to the cliffs where the action on the 12th had taken place, and was surrounded by thorn bush, with no field of fire. The camp was completely exposed, especially by night, and Dunbar was forced to mount strong guards every night simply to ensure advance warning in case of attack. When, on the 16th, Lord Chelmsford and his staff visited the camp, Dunbar made his reservations known; but Crealock dismissed them in pointlessly offensive terms, snapping that "If Major Dunbar was afraid to stay there, we could send someone who was not." Deeply insulted, Dunbar walked off in a rage, resigning his commission on the spot. Chelmsford tried to smooth matters over as best he could and persuaded him to retract for the time being; but the story must have circulated amongst the officers of the 24th, and can hardly have improved the strained relations between Chelmsford and Glyn.

Behind Crealock's impatient dismissal of an experienced officer's professional opinion lay the supreme self-confidence of Lord Chelmsford and his staff. Neither the supply depot at Rorke's Drift, nor the camps on either side of the Mzinyathi crossing, nor the camp in the Batshe had been in any way fortified. Before the campaign had started, in November 1878, Chelmsford had issued a booklet entitled *Regulations for Field Forces in South Africa, 1878*. This had laid down exactly how he expected his commanders to operate their forces, including such details as the time of "lights out", the daily ration, and so on. The Orders relating to camps specified:

> (17) By day the camp should be guarded against surprise by vedettes thrown out at some distance on all surrounding points of observation. Horses and oxen when out grazing should have mounted guards. The former will be knee-haltered.
> (18) By night horses should be picketed and oxen placed in a wagon-laager.
> (19) The camp should be partially entrenched on all sides.

The last order seems surprisingly casual, but in fact it had not been common practice to entrench temporary camps on the Cape Frontier. True, fortified posts had been established at strategic points around the Xhosa strongholds; but these were intended as long-term bases to support offensive operations. Russell Upcher had fortified the camp at Centane, but only when he expected it to be attacked. There was no clear view in January 1879 of the necessity of entrenching camps; it was not until February that a revised edition of the *Field Force Regulations* insisted that camps should be fortified by earthworks, or at the least protected by entanglements of bush cobbled with broken glass, and that columns on the march should laager their wagons "when halting, though but for a few hours". But by February circumstances were very different.

In fact Chelmsford had no fear of a Zulu attack in the middle of January. He was in constant touch with Evelyn Wood's Left Flank Column, which was gaily raiding the homesteads of local Zulus to the north, and thereby seemed to secure Chelmsford's left flank. On the 15th Russell was sent out to patrol with his mounted Volunteers as far as Siphezi mountain, about 20 miles to the east. He returned to report that the country seemed empty of Zulus, but it was his description of the track which most concerned Chelmsford: it did not "sound promising. Country seamed with deep nullahs [the Indian term for water-courses, dry or otherwise — in South Africa they were called *dongas*] some nearly 100 yards broad, stoney hills and no wood". Chelmsford therefore resolved that "Our first move must therefore be to the Isandlwana Hill where there is wood and water . . . I shall hope to move [there] in 4 days".

On the 15th, Chelmsford rode with his staff to reconnoitre Isandlwana himself. Since the place features significantly in the story of the Centre Column it is worth pausing to describe it in detail. Emerging from the Batshe valley, the track crested the nek at the southern foot of Ngedla, then dropped into a wide, undulating valley, bordered to the north by a range of hills stretching away eastwards from Ngedla. Here it crossed a shallow stream, the Manzimyama or "black water". Beyond the stream the track rose steeply again towards another nek, passing between Isandlwana mountain on the left and a hill known to the Zulus as Mahlabamkhosi on the right. Isandlwana itself, lying on a north-south axis, is an isolated spur of the hills beyond, and at the southern tip, where its cliff face is at its sheerest, it rises 300 feet above the plain. To the west the mountain drops away in a steep slope at its base, but to the east the slope is gentler, striking flat ground which runs almost level for 300 or 400 yards before dipping towards two dongas, the Mpofane and Nyogane, which run down from the slopes to the north. In that direction the view beyond Isandlwana is open for miles, extending to the bulk of Siphezi 19 miles away; but the hills to the north, known locally as the Nyoni, cut off the view in that direction; while to the south-west the great wall of the Malakatha obscures the course of the Mzinyathi River.

The name Isandlwana confused the British, and it appears variously in contemporary reports as Isanlahana, Insanalwana and Isandula. The name itself, which some say was bestowed by Chief Sihayo but which was probably much older, means literally "something like a small hut", from the noun *ndlu*, meaning hut, and the diminutive *wana*. This was a term by which the Zulus, obsessed as ever with cattle, knew the second stomach of a cow, apparently because they were struck by the similarity of purpose of that organ and a small grain storage hut. Contemporary speculation often translated it as "the little hand", Isandlana. Until 1948 it was usually spelt Isandhlwana, but the scientific analysis of the Zulu language, officially accepted in that year, rendered the combination *dhl* gramatically inaccurate.

In any event, little hand or cow's innards, Isandlwana offered a reasonable supply of wood and water, and from a defensive point of view it was no more or less vulnerable than any other camp ground in the vicinity. Provided the heights were properly patrolled and the broken ground to the rear adequately secured, there was no reason why it should not make a perfectly adequate camp site.

On his return from his reconnaissance Chelmsford visited a homestead to the south of Isandlwana, at the foot of the Malakatha. This was the home of Gamdana kaXongo, Sihayo's brother. Gamdana was reputed to be wavering in his support for King Cetshwayo, and Chelmsford was surprised to find "a large number of men, women, children and cattle all ready to move somewhere. The chief said they were coming in to surrender, which may possibly have been the truth." Chelmsford ordered them to hand over their weapons, which they did — "20 guns (none of a high class) and about 50 assegais" — and told Gamdana that if he did not annoy the British troops he would be left in peace. He was rather indignant to find that Gamdana was already in contact with the magistrate of Msinga, Henry Francis Fynn, with whom he was negotiating to surrender. "Feeling very strongly that grave complications may arise if a Natal magistrate is in correspondence with a chief whom I may possibly find it necessary to attack", wrote Chelmsford, "I have sent a summons to Mr [Fynn] to join me here at once . . . ". Fynn was delighted; he had hoped for a chance to join the invading force, but Sir Henry Bulwer had been reluctant to allow him to leave his post. Fynn left his wife, children and magistracy in the capable hands of his dashing colleague William Beaumont, the resident magistrate of Newcastle, and arrived at Chelmsford's Headquarters on the 19th.

On the same day, Chelmsford received the first information that King Cetshwayo had launched his army towards the Centre Column two days beforehand. Ulundi lay 50 miles to the east; the mobility of the Zulu army was legendary, and if the information proved correct Chelmsford could expect to be attacked at any time after about the 20th. But Chelmsford was still not convinced that the Zulus would try a direct attack. Colonel Wood's column could take care of his left flank; however, Chelmsford was still concerned about his right, and the difficult country which stretched south down the banks of the Mzinyathi to the nearest British outpost above the Middle Drift on the Thukela, 40 miles away. On the Zulu side of the border the country was extremely hilly and broken, running into the wooded heights of Qudeni mountain. On the Cape Frontier the Xhosa had regularly used such country to good effect as a base for raiding, and an increase in Zulu activity in the region suggested that their strategy might be similar.

On the 19th, Hamilton-Browne's outposts noted large numbers of cattle in the broken country away towards the river. It was a tempting prize, but Hamilton-Browne, who had "matriculated in ambush work in New Zealand", refused to be drawn. He sent a small patrol down into the valley, whereupon a force of about 1,500 Zulus showed themselves and fell back before it. Hamilton-Browne recalled his men and passed on the information to Headquarters, where Fynn, who had just arrived, suggested that these men might be the followers of Chief Matshana kaMondisa who lived near Qudeni. Matshana's reputation amongst the British was ambivalent; he had lived for a while in Natal territory, but fled after a fracas with Colonial forces, reverting to his allegiance to the Zulu royal house. Because of his experience of the Colonial regime he was regarded as a possible defector to the British cause, while at the same time being considered something of an untrustworthy customer. In fact his experience of the Colonial system had made Matshana determined never to live under it again if at all possible.

Another chief named Matshana kaSitshakuza, who ruled a section of the Mchunu, also lived in the vicinity; the British found it difficult to distinguish between them, and Chelmsford spoke of them collectively as "the two Matyanas".

On 20th January 1879 the Centre Column moved from Rorke's Drift, picking up Dunbar's detachment along the way, and established a new camp at Isandlwana. It was not an easy journey; in the valley of the Manzimyama the road broke down once more, and the NNC had to be employed dragging boulders out of the track and piling stones in the stream. After this halt the Column set off on the final stretch in great form, as Trooper Symons described:

> The Mounted Infantry under Col. Russell formed the advanced guard followed by their wagons. Natal Police supported, Carbineers bringing up the rear. Then came the 1st 24th Regiment, with band playing merrily, succeeded by the long dark lines of Native Allies, the 2/24th Regiment forming the rear-guard. No. [5] Battery R.A., was also with the Column.

Curiously enough, during a tune called *Don't you love me, Mollie darling?*, the band broke off playing suddenly — for the third time on its march to the front, as Symons noted.

Chelmsford and his staff had ridden on ahead. According to Fynn, no decision had been made as to the exact location of the camp, and "I pointed out the open flat two miles farther as good camping ground. Some said it was too sandy, they not

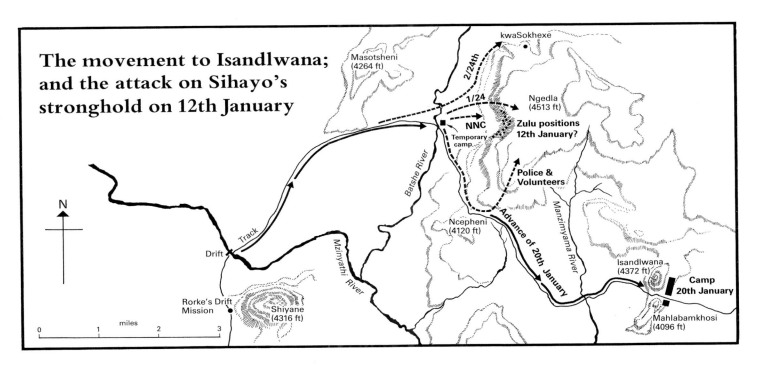

The movement to Isandlwana; and the attack on Sihayo's stronghold on 12th January

Isandlwana, photographed late in 1879, looking roughly north-west from the camp area. (Killie Campbell Africana Library)

knowing otherwise, when it was observed that [Major Clery], Col. Glyn's Chief of Staff, had already begun marking off the encampment on the southwards of Sanhlwana slope; and there the matter rested". Since Glyn had had little opportunity to order anything beyond the routine life of the camp, this seems quite likely; Hamilton-Browne confirms that it was Clery who told him where to pitch the tents of the 1/3rd NNC. It seems that the exact choice of the site happened almost by accident.

The camp was in fact spread out on the eastward side of Isandlwana, on the sloping ground immediately at the foot of the mountain. The tents were pitched in blocks according to units, with their wagons parked behind: the 1/24th on the right of the wagon-track, then the Carbineers, Mounted Infantry and Police, Royal Artillery, 2/24th, 1/3rd NNC and 2/3rd NNC. The Headquarters Staff were located on the slope of the mountain above the Royal Artillery camp, whilst Glyn and the Column Staff camped a little to the south, above the nek. Some of the officers of the 1/24th noticed that the mountain bore a striking resemblance to the shape of the sphinx motif on their collar badges, and immediately christened it the "Little Sphynx": not all of them thought it was a good omen. Not all of the wagons could be brought in that day, and they were left under guard at the Manzinyama, where a camp was pitched beside a deserted homestead which would have made a good defensive post. "Here a company of the 1st battalion 24th, under Captain Mostyn and Lieutenants Daly and Anstey, came up on their way to their battalion. They were in high spirits; had had a long march that day and dreadful roads up country; but, 'Thank goodness, here we are at last' Captain Mostyn said. As the drift was blocked, they pitched their camp with the rearguard for the night, and marched into Isandlwana camp with it next morning."

While the Column attended to the wearisome chores of hauling the lumbering wagons into place and unloading, Chelmsford rode out at about 9 a.m. to scout round. Running eastwards from the Malakatha, the Hlazakazi heights hid the dangerous country bordering the river from the camp; and accompanied by Dartnell, Gosset, Crealock, Milne, Fynn, Glynn and his orderly officer Coghill, and the Adjutant of the 1/24th, Melvill, Chelmsford rode up along the top of the heights until he reached the eastern edge, where it falls in a sheer drop into the valley of the Mangeni. The party off-saddled on the top of a precipice, and searched the valley below through their binoculars. The view was astonishing: row upon row of hills piled one upon another, disappearing off to the blue horizon. Crealock had time to paint a water-colour of the scene; down below them the cattle on the valley floor looked like ants. There were no warriors in sight, but the general opinion was that they were there somewhere.

The party descended to the head of the Mangeni, looking for a possible camp site, then rode back across the plain towards Isandlwana. They were just passing a deserted homestead when someone spotted a chicken, and Melvill, Coghill and Milne set off after it. Coghill, however, fell, and badly dislocated his knee; although he was a fit and active young man his letters home from South Africa reveal a propensity for strains, sprains and rheumatism — perhaps his body was weaker than he gave it credit for, or perhaps he was simply accident-prone. He was in such pain that when they reached the camp Coghill went to lie down in the tent which he shared with Melvill.

It was that night that Chelmsford called Major Dartnell of the Natal Mounted Police and the commanders of the 3rd NNC to his tent, and ordered them to be ready to march out before dawn to thoroughly scout the Malakatha and Hlazakazi, as described at the beginning of Chapter One .

At Isandlwana, no attempt had been made to fortify the

camp or form a wagon-laager. The wagon-laager, a defensive circle in which the wagons were run end to end and lashed together, had been the standard Boer defence in African warfare, perfected in the 1836 campaign against the Ndebele in the Transvaal, and at Blood River, against the Zulus, in December 1838. More than one Afrikaner pioneer had warned Chelmsford against neglecting to laager the camp; Paul Kruger, the republican leader from the Transvaal (who was himself destined to give the British a run for their money 20 years later) was among them, and so were Gert de Jager and James Gregory, both of whom had been at Blood River. On the whole, the British were not impressed. Chelmsford had not neglected to assess the fighting capability of his enemies — his officers had all been issued with a pamphlet describing the organisation and methods of the Zulu army in detail — but knowing was not quite the same as believing. Laagers had not been necessary on the Cape Frontier, and it seemed highly unlikely that the Zulus would stand up to the disciplined fire of the Imperial redcoats any better than the Xhosa had done. When Colonel Glyn suggested to Chelmsford that the camp at Isandlwana be laagered he received a curt reply which can only have reminded him of the superfluity of his position as Column commander: "It is not worth while, it will take too much time, and besides the wagons are most of them going back at once to Rorke's Drift for supplies".

There were admittedly practical difficulties in laagering the camp. According to the *Field Force Regulations*, every Column was to have an appointed Laager Master, an experienced man whose duty was to oversee the difficult task of organising the laager safely and quickly. Although Glyn had approached several likely individuals, none had been persuaded to join the Column. And the wagons were, indeed, needed to go back to Rorke's Drift to collect the mountain of stores that had been ferried down there from Helpmekaar. Furthermore, Chelmsford did not anticipate staying long at Isandlwana; as soon as the Malakatha had been pronounced safe he intended to advance to the Mangeni gorge. The *Field Force Regulations* were, however, quite specific in that all camps should be "partially entrenched on all sides". No attempt was made to do so, because on 20th January the men were too tired after their march, and on the 21st half the force was out of camp whilst the other half was unloading the wagons and repairing the road. Nor was the ground suitable; it is extremely hard and rocky, and to have dug a shelter trench around such an extended camp was a practical impossibility.

And yet . . . there were other means available to fortify the

position had Chelmsford so desired. Later in the war it became common for columns to build small piled-stone bastions on some commanding position near a camp; these served as a rallying point and a redoubt on which to anchor the defence. Nor did they post-date the Isandlwana campaign: on the same day as Chelmsford was establishing himself at Isandlwana, Evelyn Wood was operating from Fort Thinta, a base he had established on the White Mflozi headwaters, which was protected by a chain of these small rock sangars. There were plenty of rocks at Isandlwana; the truth is simply that Chelmsford did not think defences necessary.

Not all of his officers agreed with him. The following day the veteran Major Dunbar, who was out on picquet duty, expressed reservations to an unnamed staff officer about the broken ground at the rear of the mountain. "Well sir", replied the staff officer, "if you are nervous we will put a picquet of the pioneers there". Dunbar's reaction to this new slur is not recorded. Later, Lieutenant Melvill said to the same staff officer: "I know what you are thinking by your face, sir; you are abusing the camp and you are quite right! These Zulus will charge home, and with our small numbers we ought to be in laager, or, at any rate, be prepared to stand shoulder to shoulder".

As described at length in Chapter One, Dartnell's force departed at dawn on the 21st. Lieutenant Jones of the NMR made one last attempt to keep his brother Sam out of danger; Sam's horse had gone lame and he had bound its leg with a piece of red rag, and on seeing this Charles ordered him to remain behind. Sam simply went to Captain Bradstreet and exchanged his horse for another; he was allowed to go on the patrol.

After breakfast, at about 9 a.m., Chelmsford, Glyn and their staffs again rode out to see Chief Gamdana. Gamdana's homestead was situated south of Isandlwana, on a rise just above the Ndaweni stream, facing the Malakatha. When they arrived it was deserted; Gamdana and his followers had apparently fled into the Mzinyathi valley. Chelmsford's party off-saddled and Crealock made another sketch, looking back towards Isandlwana. The NNC had passed down the Ndaweni only about four hours before but, try as they might, the staff could see no sign of them. The landscape seemed to have simply swallowed them up.

Chelmsford returned to camp, and was about to ride out again, this time up onto the hills to the north of Isandlwana, when Gamdana came hurrying in after him. He had been in hiding, he explained, because Cetshwayo had sent an "*impi* to eat him up, for giving up his arms to the English; he had expected the *impi* that morning (21st) but it had not arrived". If this information struck Chelmsford as significant none of his staff recorded the fact. The conversation with Gamdana then developed into a wrangle about the number of guns he was to

Crealock's sketch of Isandlwana, drawn from above Gamdana's homestead (left) to the south-east of it during Chelmsford's patrol of 21st January. Malakatha mountain is on the right. (Sherwood Foresters' Museum)

surrender, and ended with Gamdana being sent away. Chelmsford did not allow the interview to interfere with his plans. He was riding up towards the Nyoni ridge when the two ADCs, Major Gosset and Captain Buller, found him on their return from Dartnell's reconnaissance on the Hlazakazi, bearing the first report of a significant presence above the Mangeni.

* * *

It will be remembered that we left Dartnell's force of mounted Volunteers and jittery NNC at the end of Chapter One, bivouacked on the heights of Mlazakazi during a disturbed night, very conscious of the presence of at least a thousand Zulu warriors camped opposite them on Magogo hill. Unwilling to attack an enemy of unknown but certainly far superior strength late in the day; and equally unwilling to return to Isandlwana, abandoning his reconnaissance and leaving the Zulus to move off at will, under cover of darkness and relatively close to the camp; Major Dartnell had sent Gosset and Buller back to report to Chelmsford while the Volunteers and NNC mantained their position.

Since Gosset and Buller had been with Dartnell during the encounter, and since both must have known something of the General's intentions, it seems highly unlikely that they had not concurred with Dartnell's decision to stay put. Equally they were able to give the General a first-hand account of what had occurred; and since his response was unhurried he cannot have been alarmed. He sent Lieutenant Walsh out to Dartnell with his Mounted Infantry, pack horses, and orders that Dartell was to attack the Zulus "when he saw fit". Chelmsford was obviously in a relaxed frame of mind at the prospect of Dartnell spending the night away from the camp; and this is significant, since he later claimed that Dartnell's actions were unauthorised, and compromised his own intentions.

After the meeting with Gosset and Buller, Chelmsford rode up onto the lip of the Nyoni ridge, and looked out across the undulating surface of the plateau from a high point where two vedettes had been posted earlier in the day. The vedettes said that they had seen a small party of mounted Zulus several times during the day, and had reported the fact; Milne spotted them now, about 14 miles away. They disappeared behind a low rise. "From this point", observed Milne, "the ground was very nearly level; there were slight rises, however, every now and again, which would prevent our seeing any men who did not wish it." When Chelmsford returned to camp he expressed his intention to scout the hills again the following day.

That evening tatoo was sounded at about 8 p.m., and all lights in the camp were extinguished. It was apparently the custom of the bands to play tatoo in turn; it is not recorded which one played that night, but it is tempting to imagine that it was that of the 1st Battalion. Before playing *God Save the Queen*, it struck up with *Home Sweet Home*. In the Natal Mounted Police camp Trooper Hayes, one of those left behind on camp duties, found this unsettling; he disturbed his tent-mate Trooper Dorehill by warning that disaster was imminent, and by crying out several times in the night that the Zulus were coming. Hayes died two months later of fever; perhaps it was already working in his veins.

Dartnell's second message from the Mangeni, carried through the night by the fearless Walsh after the false alarm had raised doubts about the reconnaissance party's unaided prospects in any serious encounter, reached Isandlwana long after everyone but the night picquets had turned in. Clery left the best account of what happened next, and, since it had a crucial bearing on subsequent events, it is best to let him tell the story in his own words:

> *About 1.30 that night a message written in pencil was brought to my tent from the commander of the force bivouacking out, to say that the enemy had shown in increased force and that it would not be prudent to attack them in the morning without some white troops. I took this at once to Colonel Glyn, who simply said I must take it to the general. The general's tent was close by, so I roused him up. Lying on my face and hands close by his camp-bed I can still remember how I read from that crumpled piece of notebook paper written across in pencil, word after word what I had previously had such difficulty in deciphering in my own tent.*
>
> *The general did not hesitate much. He said, "Order the 2nd Battalion 24th Regiment, four guns, and all the mounted troops to get ready and start at daybreak." He also added "Order up Colonel Durnford with the troops he has to reinforce the camp" (Colonel Durnford was then here, Rorke's Drift, 12 miles off). This was overheard by Crealock in the next tent, so he joined in (very properly I think), "Is Major Clery to issue orders to Colonel Durnford?" — for Durnford's was an independent command hitherto. So the general said, "No, let you do it." I might add that Crealock was acting as [Deputy Adjutant General] in the field . . . As I did not want to give any warning to the enemy or disturb the camp I went direct to each of the commanders and gave the general's orders. This took some time and the general was soon dressed and impatient to be starting. The troops turned out well. The general had given no orders about the camp, except that Colonel Durnford was to move up there; but in trying to gather my wits together after giving out the different orders for the march personally myself, as to what further should be cared for before marching off, it occurred to me that some instructions should be left to the officer in command of the camp. It was too late to refer to Colonel Glyn, who of course would only have referred me to the general, so I ventured on the responsibility of issuing them myself. So I wrote to poor Colonel Pulleine who commanded the 1st Battalion 24th Regiment, officially as follows: "You will be in command of the camp in the absence of Colonel Glyn. Draw in your line of defence while the force with the general is out of camp. Draw in your infantry outpost line in conformity. Keep your cavalry vedettes still well to the front. Act strictly on the defensive. Keep a wagon loaded with ammunition ready to start at once, should the general's force be in need of it. Colonel Durnford has been ordered up from Rorke's Drift to reinforce the camp".*

Just before he left the camp Clery walked over in person to Pulleine's tent to make sure that he had received the message and understood it. Clery stressed that Pulleine was simply to hold the camp; although, of course, "nobody from the general downwards had the least suspicion that there was a chance of the camp being attacked".

By this stage, it seems, Chelmsford's mind was already set on the idea that any Zulu threat would develop from the direction of Qudeni, via the Mangeni valley. Dartnell's encounter seemed to have confirmed this; Chelmsford's orders suggest that he was expecting to march into action — a battalion of infantry, four guns and most of the mounted men was clearly an offensive force, and the instruction to Pulleine to keep a reserve supply of ammunition ready to be sent out suggests an expectation of a heavy engagement. He also took with him two ambulances and a medical detachment led by Civil Surgeon Thrupp — a clear indication that he expected to take casualties. He seems to have overlooked the camp completely; later, when Clery remined him that he (Clery) had left orders that Pulleine should "act strictly on the defensive", Chelmsford said "I cannot tell you what a relief it is to me to hear this."

The General rode out of the camp first, accompanied by his staff and a number of officers who went along for the ride, and an escort of the Mounted Infantry. Captain Hallam Parr remembered the disappointment of those who had to remain behind:

> *On looking back to that Wednesday morning, how every little detail seems to stand out in relief! The hurried and careless farewell to Nevill Coghill, who shared my tent, and whose name will not be forgotten while the Zulu War is remembered; my servant, who was to leave for Natal that very morning, saying when he brought my horse, "I shall be here, sir, when you come back; the wagons are not going to start to-day, now that this force is going out"; the half-laughing condolences to the 1-24th as they watched the troops move out of camp; the men not for duty turning out for the routine work of the camp; the position of the tents and of the wagons — many trifles fixed in the mind serve to make stronger the contrast between the departure and return to that ill-fated camp.*

CHAPTER FOUR

A Day in the Hills

Chelmsford and his escort crossed the valley towards the Mangeni without encountering any Zulus. By the time they had reached the eastern end of Hlazakazi, where Dartnell and the NNC descended to meet them, the artillery and most of the infantry had lagged behind. The plain was seamed with dongas, and the guns found the going particularly difficult, the men having to haul the carriages across obstacles with drag-ropes.

It was about 6.30 a.m. when Chelmsford met up with Dartnell; in the cold grey light of dawn the hills were just taking shape around them, and dense mist still hung on the tops of Hlazakazi, Magogo and Silutshana. For most of the men in Dartnell's party the sight of the General was a great relief after the alarms of the night before, but Hamilton-Browne was still uneasy:

> Colonel Glyn rode over to me and drawing me aside said "In God's name, Maori, what are you doing here?" I answered him with a question, "In God's name, sir, what are you doing here?" He shook his head and replied "I am not in command." And fine old soldier as he was, I could see he was much disturbed.

As the sun came up, the mist lifted to reveal no sign of the Zulus who had camped on Magogo the night before, and Chelmsford and his staff did not trouble overmuch to conceal their disappointment and frustration. The force was drawn up to the north of the track, with Hlazakazi on the right and Mdutshane a little way off to the right front, facing towards Magogo. Although the guns had not yet caught up Chelmsford was eager to press on and try to locate the missing Zulus. The Police and Volunteers were ordered to proceed to the right, following the track across the Mangeni, then sweeping north through the hills beyond. The NNC were directed up the slope of Magogo to the front, whilst Chelmsford and the Mounted Infantry rode further to the left, heading towards a valley which separated Magogo and Silutshana. A message was sent back to the infantry and guns ordering them to follow the General's route.

The Police and Volunteers crested the nek between Mdutshane and Hlazakazi, and had not gone far beyond the Mangeni when they spotted a group of warriors on the hills ahead. Trooper Fred Symons described the exhilarating chase that followed:

> It must have been about eight o'clock when a body of Zulus shewed itself on our right. The Major [Dartnell?] mounted his steed and before we were ready started off shouting "Come on boys" and we followed at a gallop, best horses first. The Zulus (about eighty) drew in line on a low ridge shields to the front as though meditating resistance but changed their minds and made for a high hill one side of which was precipitous and the other a grassy slope but steep. We echeloned to the left to prevent them from reaching the rocky heights but only managed to turn them onto the grassy side.

Symons and his brother dismounted and opened fire on a party who were making for some caves in the hillside. They fired in turns, each taking his range from the other's shot, until Jack hit a man who tumbled over down a rocky cliff. Captain Shepstone rode up to upbraid the brothers for dismounting, and ordered them to join the others, who were firing at the same groups a little way off. One Zulu in particular attracted their attention; he was walking casually along the slope, oblivious to the bullets striking around him. When he came to a solitary boulder he crouched down behind it and tried to fire back, but

each time his gun missed fire; Symons could hear the percussion caps snapping in the clear morning air. After a few minutes the Zulu stood up and walked quietly over the brow of the hill, "amidst a shower of dust sent up by the bullets" of the Carbineers.

Most of the Zulus had disappeared over the crest of the hill or into caves amidst boulders on the slopes, but Shepstone gave chase to a man mounted on a black horse, whom he claimed to recognise as the untrustworthy chief Matshana kaMondisa. The man managed to slip off his horse and disappear into a crevice in the nick of time, but his horse, at least, was captured. Another Zulu tried to bolt past the Carbineers, making a break for the Mangeni valley behind them; Trooper Hayhow set off in pursuit, but the Zulu gave him a run for his money, and it was a mile or two before he was ridden down and brought back a prisoner. Those Volunteers who had pursued the Zulus as far as the caves found it dangerous work; Trooper Harry Pennefather was peering over a jumble of rocks when he heard a Zulu loading his gun — Pennefather just spotted his man in time and managed to shoot him first.

This running action had taken place in a curve to the Volunteer's left, the Zulus fleeing north to the foot of a hill called Phindo, which lay eastwards of Magogo and Silutshana. A rocky valley separated the two ranges; and on Magogo the NNC, who had had a hard climb before sweeping across the top of the ridge without, as Norris-Newman put it, "finding

Lieutenant-Colonel (local rank) John C. Russell, 12th Lancers. Russell commanded No. 1 Squadron, Imperial Mounted Infantry, and was in effect Chelmsford's commander of No. 3 Column mounted troops throughout the Isandlwana campaign. (9th/12th Lancers)

The mouth of the Mangeni gorge, with the conical hill Mdutshane above it. Chelmsford intended to establish his new camp on the flat ground to the centre and right of the picture. (Author's photograph)

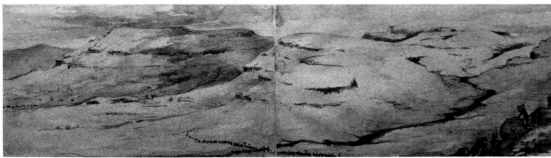

Crealock's sketch of troops deploying at the Mangeni, 22nd January, drawn from the Hlazakazi heights looking north towards Magogo (centre) and Silutshana (left). The line of the 3rd NNC is seen in the foreground, about to sweep across Magogo. Dartnell's skirmish of the previous night probably occurred somewhere along the valley to the right. (Sherwood Foresters' Museum)

ebony", could see the skirmishing taking place on the slopes opposite. Lieutenant John Maxwell, on the extreme right of the NNC skirmish line,

> heard firing in that direction, and saw about a mile off some natives, I should say about 400 or 500, coming over a kopje. They were running in all directions followed by the Carbineers, who appeared to be in skirmishing order. The enemy made for a kranz — or in other words a precipice in which there were some caves. I passed the word down the line of skirmishers that the enemy was on my right and waited for orders. Commandant Lonsdale came up and asked me to intercept them in their rush for the caves. We endeavoured to do so but the enemy got to earth with a few exceptions.

Nevertheless, the Contingent crossed the valley and tried to winkle the Zulus out. Both Lonsdale and Hamilton-Browne disappeared in pursuit of solitary mounted Zulus, and Henry Harford found himself in temporary command of the regiment. He allotted the various companies their positions, and sent them forward into the rocks:

> Being day instead of night, our men shewed nothing of the fear they had exhibited at the bivouac, and under the leadership of the officers did uncommonly well, tackling several very nasty situations. At one spot alone thirteen men were shot down one after another, and others were quite game to make further attempts had I not gone up myself and put a stop to an impossible undertaking. Nothing but some high explosive like dynamite could have affected an entrance to the cave, which was evidently cut well into the hillside, and the only way to get into it was by a hole underneath a massive overhanging rock, above a rather deep donga. A widish crack through the rock enabled those inside to fire straight down the donga, and made it certain death to attempt to cross it, and above again an extension of the crack provided another place to fire through, making any attempt to get at anyone inside the cave from there impossible, so I ordered the men to leave it alone and get on.

A short while later he spotted a sniper behind another rock taking aim at him. Harford fired first, and the man disappeared into the shadows behind with Harford in hot pursuit. He found his man lying wounded in a cave, with a dead man beside him; Harford dragged the wounded man out and sent him on to the doctor. Norris-Newman, who had been watching the incident from a distance (he was "a smart fellow, but wary", according to Maxwell) thought Harford had a charmed life; "May he keep it long! was our wish at this time".

Maxwell, meanwhile, had been trying to induce the Zulus in the first cave to surrender. At last one warrior ventured out and explained that there were six more men inside who were afraid to come out. Maxwell told him to return and tell them that they would be well treated if they came out. The Zulu disappeared inside — and remained there. A member of the NNC poked his head round the opening, and was promptly shot dead. This stalemate persisted until the recall was sounded.

The Volunteers had been called off when the NNC had come up. Fred Symons was guarding a prisoner and watching the NNC at work when he, Ted Greene and some others decided to repair to a nearby stream for a drink. One of the men spotted a shield lying abandoned by the side of the stream and, looking round, they noticed that the water below a rock was muddy:

> So we knew a man must be concealed beneath. We shouted to him to come out, but he refused to come out until I told him the Natal Natives were approaching from whom he would receive no quarter. This news had a magical effect upon him and an immediate resurrection took place.

Asked if there were any more men hiding nearby, the prisoner pointed down stream, and was just calling on them to surrender when a man from the NNC rushed up and struck him a heavy blow in the back. Trooper Symons indignantly

> *gave him a thump in the ribs with my carbine and told him if he touched my prisoner again I should put a bullet in him. He didn't appear to understand my behaviour and stood assegai poised about to stab the prisoner but he soon saw I was in earnest and moved off. I think Ted Greene's opinion of this splendid body of men is on the back track . . .*

Three more Zulus crawled out of hiding, two of them middle-aged married men, and one a young warrior wearing a fur coat. One of the older men carried an Enfield carbine and a table knife; the other had been shot through the leg. The young man refused to give up his weapons and laughed at the idea "at first". The Carbineers questioned them closely, but the Zulus could give no useful information — they knew nothing of the presence of a Zulu army, they said; they had merely heard that English soldiers were in the vicinity, and had turned out to see if it was true. The Police and Volunteers had taken a total of nine prisoners, who were handed over to some mounted men in the Contingent. Symons was shocked later to hear that the NNC killed them all: "The wounded one was seen being shot by a mounted officer with a revolver". It is not clear exactly when this incident took place, but it was presumably after the news of events at Isandlwana reached the unit. If so, it was the first of several such summary reprisals.

While this skirmishing had been going on, Chelmsford and his escort had moved up the valley between Silutshana and Magogo, climbing a steep rise to a nek at the top end. From this point they could see Phindo to their right front, and the splutter of shots from its base alerted them to the action taking place there. Directly in front of them was the valley across which the NNC had advanced, and it opened out to the left in a wide plain. In the distance on the left front was the imposing bult of Siphezi mountain itself. There were "large clusters" of the enemy on the hills to the front, but they soon disappeared into folds in the ground.

It was at about this time that a messenger arrived from Isandlwana, and delivered an enigmatic note. It read: "Staff Officer — Report just come in that the Zulus are advancing in Force from left front of Camp. 8.5 am. H.B.Pulleine, Lieut-Col." Hallam-Parr took the note, scribbled the time of receipt on it — 9.30 a.m. — and handed it to Clery. Clery, of course, should have reported to Glyn, but he had clearly tired of the pretence of following protocol, and took it straight to Chelmsford:

He returned it to me without a word. I said "What is to be done on this report?" He said "There is nothing to be done on that".

Clery did not press the point, and excused himself later with the comment: "the fact is that, whether from overwork or other causes, the general has got rather irritable since we knew him and particularly touchy about suggestions being made to him." It is not strictly true that Chelmsford did nothing; he sent his naval ADC, Lieutenant Milne, and Captain W.Penn Symons of the 24th up a hill on the left to look at the camp through their glasses. Reported Milne:

> *On reaching the summit I could see the camp; all the cattle had been driven in close around the tents, I could see nothing of the enemy on the left. The main body of the enemy who had been on our front all morning, were now assembled at the foot of the [Siphezi] hill, watching the movements of the Mounted Infantry, who were scouring the plain some short distance off, but on their approach they all retreated to the table-land on top of the [Siphezi] mountain.*
>
> *I also saw small clusters of the enemy on every hill top around us, observing our movements. Distinct firing was heard at small intervals in the direction of the Mounted Police.*

Exactly how much could Milne have seen from his position? Isandlwana is clearly visible 12 miles away across the plain from Mangeni, and at a quick glance it seems improbable that anyone with a good glass could have missed signs of a battle taking place at its foot. Yet the mountain itself is below the skyline, and the distant hills of Natal beyond camouflage its outline, while any mist or heat-haze would obscure objects at its foot. The white blur of the tents would probably have been clear enough; for the rest, Milne would have had to interpret a few dark smudges according to whatever circumstances he thought most likely. Since no member of the staff expected anything unusual to be taking place at the camp, Milne assumed that the dark patches near the tents were cattle. He was later forced to admit that he may have been wrong in that judgement.

Back on the nek, Chelmsford was still concerned about the Zulu forces to his front. Despite his own troops making contact over a wide area he still had no very clear idea about the Zulu strength or intentions, other than that they seemed to be falling back, away from the immediate hills and towards the bastion of Siphezi. Whilst Milne and Symons were clambering up the hillside Chelmsford had despatched the Mounted Infantry into the valley below.

Russell and his men rode down into the valley, turning to their left towards the point where it opened out into a plain to

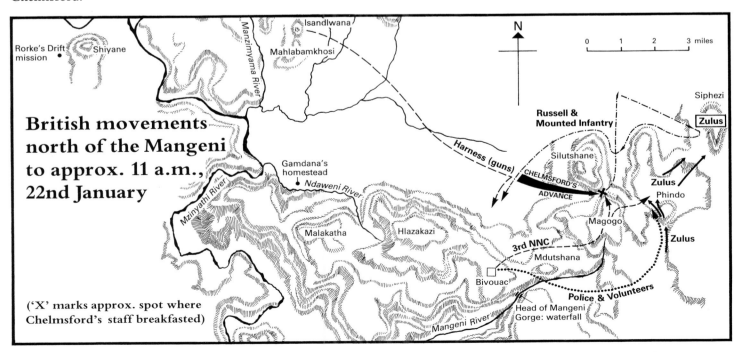

British movements north of the Mangeni to approx. 11 a.m., 22nd January

('X' marks approx. spot where Chelmsford's staff breakfasted)

Lieutenant F.J. Durrant Scott of the Natal Carbineers (right), who commanded the mounted vedettes at the camp on the morning of Isandlwana, and died with Durnford. The other two men are believed to be his brothers, Sergeant-Major Dan Scott (left) and Trumpeter C.Scott, both of whom were out with Chelmsford that day. Durrant Scott is wearing the Carbineer officers' braided dark blue patrol jacket with white collar and cuffs. (Local History Museum, Durban)

the north. There were small parties of warriors on the plain, and Russell immediately gave chase, but the Zulus scattered and moved off at such a rapid rate that Russell called a halt, turned about, and moved off towards Siphezi:

> This hill was covered with the enemy in very large numbers and we saw the spoor in the valley where their masses had come down from the hills where they had been in front of the General that morning. This valley is about four miles long and terminated in a high neck from which there is a rapid slope to a very broken country in which we could not recognise any tracks or landmarks.
>
> Instead of entering an unknown bit of country, therefore, and allowing my retreat to be cut off — I retired down the [Siphezi] valley again, and decided to try and rejoin the General. A good many of the natives came down from the hill and commenced firing at us, but a long way off.

When Russell reached the foot of Silutshana once more he off-saddled for an hour. While his men were resting there, a lone European from the NNC rode up and asked if they knew of Chelmsford's whereabouts. He explained that he had been sent to tell him that the camp was under attack. Russell does not seem to have been unduly concerned by this message; if he asked who sent it and for more details, his report does not mention the fact. Probably, as the man was not a fellow Regular, he did not take it seriously. He pointed the man towards the nek where he had last seen Chelmsford, but later admitted that he thought the man had been too frightened to go alone and had given up on his quest. He may well have done.

Nevertheless, since Russell had received no further instructions from Chelmsford, it was not at all clear what was expected of him; so he ordered his men to move "quietly along the outside of the hills", round the northern edge of Silutshana, while he rode off in person to try to find the General. In this he had no luck, and when he rejoined his squadron the officers told him that they had heard the sound of distant cannon fire. Shortly after this another man rode up with effectively the same message. By now rather concerned, Russell sent off Lieutenants Walsh and Davey, each with a small escort, in an attempt to find Chelmsford "and give him the information which we had received".

Where was Chelmsford? After watching something of the

skirmishing at Phindo from the nek between Silutshana and Magogo, he had retired into the valley to breakfast. Two companies of the 2/24th who had caught up with him (A and C) were sent over the hills to support the NNC; they arrived too late to take part, much to their disgust. Two more companies, D and E, were still struggling up the valley. The remaining two companies, F and H, were with Harness' guns and the wagons, which were still struggling across the plain. By this time Chelmsford seems to have recognised that the big battle he had anticipated was not about to take place, and he began to make more mundane plans for the Column's next advance. Hamilton-Browne's 1/3rd NNC was recalled from the skirmishing, and moved back up onto Magogo. Hamilton-Browne, as ever, was disgusted with the whole proceedings:

> Getting my men together and advising Lonsdale of my orders, I requested him to take over my skirmish, and on his relieving me with the 2nd battalion I moved down a valley and found the general and staff quietly at breakfast.
>
> Never shall I forget the sight of that peaceful picnic. Here were the staff quietly breakfasting and the whole command scattered over the country! Over there the guns unlimbered, over the hills parties of Mounted Infantry and volunteers looting the scattered kraals for grain for their horses, a company of the 24th in one place, and another far away . . .
>
> As soon as I halted my men, the General rose and kindly greeting me asked if I had had any breakfast. I replied, "No, nor had any of my men had any." I might have added "and no dinner or supper the night before." Of course he understood, that as commandant, I could not eat in the presence of my fasting men . . .
>
> Colonel Crealock came to me and said "Commandant Browne, I want you to return at once to camp and assist Colonel Pulleine to strike the camp and come on here." I nearly fell off my horse. Could these men know of the close proximity of the enemy? Were we all mad or what? However, I was only a poor Devil of a Colonial Commandant and as a simple irregular not supposed to criticise full-blown staff officers, so I saluted and said, "If I come across the enemy?" 'Oh,' he said, "just brush them aside and go on," and went on with his breakfast.

According to Clery (but it must be remembered that he detested the man), it was at about this time that he heard Crealock mutter, in response to the rumours of a Zulu presence at the camp, "How very amusing! Actually attacking our camp! Most amusing!". . . .

And so Hamilton-Browne set off at the head of his command, down the valley which opened into the plain and towards Isandlwana. It was a long, hard march across broken ground, and the white officers and NCOs were beginning to suffer from their sleepless night and lack of food; perhaps the African soldiers were suffering too, but no-one noticed their discomfort — although somehow over the whole command

Sketches by Horace Smith-Dorrien of a soldier of the NNC; and "Warriors on the war-path", a lively impression which captures the appearance of Zulus in the field — no ceremonial regalia, and a mixture of firearms and traditional weapons. (Imperial War Museum)

Lieutenant Archibald Berkely Milne, RN, of HMS Active, *Chelmsford's ADC, who observed the camp at Isandlwana through a telescope from the hills above the Mangeni without detecting any signs of trouble. (Royal Archives)*

What could Milne see? This photograph was taken to the left of his position, on the nek between Hlazakazi and Mdutshane, where a number of officers looked back towards the camp. It was taken with a 200mm telephoto lens to simulate the effect of a telescope; although the outline of Isandlwana is dimly visible below the horizon it is impossible to discern any detail of what lies at its base. (Author's photograph)

"there seemed to hover a black cloud." It certainly was not due to the weather; despite everything, several men noticed the weather on 22nd January. The stifling heat stuck in the mind of one as much as 60 years later, while Hallam-Parr had noted that "the morning became very hot, the sky perfectly clear, and only the faintest breath of wind." Henry Fynn, writing years later, thought the day dull and overcast; but Trooper Symons noted that there was an uncanny stillness in the air, "an oppressive gloom" that pervaded the whole atmosphere. Later he learned that it was due to a partial eclipse of the sun.

Having despatched Hamilton-Browne, Chelmsford sent Captain Alan Gardner, an officer of the 14th Hussars who had been appointed to general staff duties on the Column, with orders to Pulleine to pack up the tents and move the entire camp towards the Mangeni. A number of officers elected to ride back to Isandlwana with Gardner; Adjutant Henry Dyer of the 2/24th, and 2nd Lieutenant Thomas Griffith, "a young officer thoughtful beyond his years" who had been doing duty as commissariat officer, offered to go back to supervise the loading of the 2/24th camp. Since the men had hurried out at 2 a.m. that morning with only their haversacks, water-bottles and ammunition pouches, "all their small belongings, of such comfort to a soldier campaigning, were necessarily scattered about the tents". Griffith seems to have been affected by the melancholia which touched the more sensitive spirits that morning; according to an enigmatic comment in the Historical Records, "he took a gloomy view of things". Gardner's party, which set off at about 10.30 a.m., was completed by Lieutenant MacDowel of the Engineers and Lieutenant Andrews of the Native Pioneers. (At some point Major Stuart Smith of the artillery also joined Gardner's party, possibly joining them as they passed Harness' force on their way.) Chelmsford then rode over the crest of Magogo and down towards the Mangeni stream, looking for the best place to pitch the new camp.

Hamilton-Browne was just emerging from the hills when

> . . . myself and Adjutant-Lieutenant Campbell, who were riding some distance in front, flushed two Zulus. They bolted and we rode them down. Campbell shot his one, but I captured mine, and on Duncombe coming up we questioned him.
>
> He was only a boy and frightened out of his life so that when asked where he came from, he pointed to the line of hills on the left flank of the camp saying "he had come from the King's big army." "What are you doing here?" we asked, to which he replied "that he and his mate had been sent by their induna to see if any white men were among the hills" we had just left, "but as they were sitting resting under the shade of a rock, they did not see the white men and were caught." "What was the size of the army?" He answered "There are twelve full regiments."

This was a disturbing piece of news, if true. Hamilton-Browne claimed in his memoires that it confirmed his existing fears of the danger to the camp, but this is surely the wisdom

of hindsight. As he admitted himself, "I rode forward and used my glasses, but everything so far was peaceful." Not only did an attack on the camp seem intrinsically improbable; most of Chelmsford's scattered detachment must have thought it highly unlikely that any significant enemy force could have slipped round behind them without any sign of it being apparent just 12 miles away. Nevertheless, Hamilton-Browne sent Lieutenant Pohl with a message to Chelmsford to report this information; it may have been Pohl who encountered Russell at the eastern foot of Silutshana. Hamilton-Browne, meanwhile, continued his march, and a short while later he encountered two men loaded with food. They had been sent out by Assistant-Surgeon Buee — whose horse had gone lame the day before — with food for the officers, and also carried a light-hearted message from two officers of the 1/24th whom Hamilton-Browne had befriended. Lieutenants Edgar Anstey and Patrick Daly had apparently gone to Hamilton-Browne's tent the night before, and found that his servant had prepared him dinner. With no-one to eat it they had helped themselves, and now sent out a couple of bottles of whisky in exchange. The arrival of these supplies cheered Hamilton-Browne, and can hardly have reinforced any misgivings about the safety of the camp. He distributed the food and drink amongst his NCOs, and prided himself on taking nothing himself (although presumably his black soldiers received nothing either).

In truth, there is something uncanny about the way small groups of men had crossed and re-crossed the plain between Isandlwana and the Mangeni hills without so much as a hint of danger. When the blow fell, however, it fell suddenly, and Hamilton-Browne at least grasped the situation immediately:

> At about 11 o'clock I was on ahead and looking through my glasses when I saw a puff of smoke rise from the hills on the left of the camp. It was followed by another. They seemed to come from a huge black shadow that lay on the hills. Presently another puff, and in a moment I knew they were bursting shells. Not a cloud was in the sky, and I knew that the shadow resting on the hills must be the Zulu army moving down to attack the camp.
>
> At once I despatched a second message: "11 a.m. — The Zulu army is attacking the left of the camp. The guns have opened up on them. The ground here is still suitable for guns and mounted men. Will push on so as to act as support to them."

This message, carried by a Sergeant Turner, was presumably the second one received by Russell, which prompted him to send Walsh and Davey looking for the General. Lord Chelmsford claimed that neither of these messages reached him; if true, then the fault lay with his own restlessness, and in his failure to make his whereabouts known to the men under his command.

Remarkably, under the circumstances, Hamilton-Browne's

The scourge of the 3rd NNC: Commandant George "Maori" Hamilton-Browne of the 1st Battalion, photographed c.1879. (Author's collection)

Lieutenant Edgar Oliphant Anstey of Mostyn's F Company, 1/24th, who sent Hamilton-Browne a gift of food and whisky from the camp on the 22nd, lulling his suspicions about an attack at Isandlwana during Chelmsford's absence. (Royal Archives)

NNC battalion kept up their march towards Isandlwana, their commander scouting ahead and examining the camp though his field glasses. By about 12 noon — at least an hour and a half after they had left Magogo and encountered the Zulu scouts — they were close enough to make out some of the details of the

fighting. Hamilton-Browne could see the guns positioned away from the front of the camp, and supported by two companies of the 24th. They were firing at large enemy masses descending from the Nyoni heights. Some of these bodies were advancing rapidly across the NNC's front, apparently oblivious to their presence but cutting them off from the camp. Hamilton-Browne, whose temper must by now have been on a decidedly short fuse, sent a third message to Chelmsford:

> The camp is being attacked on the left and in front, and as yet is holding its own. Ground still good for the rapid advance of guns and horses. Am moving forward as fast as I can.

This message did not reach Chelmsford either. Hamilton-Browne shifted his own advance to the left, hoping to cut round behind the Zulu forces in front of him, and enter the camp from the south. At about 1.30 p.m., however, he saw one of the guns alter its position and shell the Zulus massed on the plain. Shortly after this the guns ceased firing, and heavy fighting seemed to be going on "in the camp". In his memoires his account is graphic:

> Good God! What a sight it was. By the road that runs between the hill and kopje, came a huge mob of maddened cattle, followed by a huge swarm of Zulus. These poured into the undefended camp, and at the same time the left horn of the enemy and the chest of the army rushed in. Nothing could stand against this combined attack. All formation was broken in a minute, and the camp became a seething pandemonium of men and cattle struggling in dense clouds of dust and smoke.

The sight seems to have shocked Hamilton-Browne's command, all the more so because some of the Zulus to their front seemed to have spotted them and to be preparing to attack. Conscious that even those few of his men with rifles had only 15 rounds each, Hamilton-Browne faced them about and retreated to a ridge by the side of the road to his left rear. From here he despatched Captain Develin with a message which could hardly have been more explicit: "For God's sake come back, the camp is surrounded, and things, I fear, are going badly."

Back towards the Mangeni, Colonel Harness of the Royal Artillery had been continuing with the difficult advance of his party towards Chelmsford's breakfast spot when he received orders to abandon that approach, to move south to an easier track, and to make instead for the head of the Mangeni gorge, where the new camp was to be pitched. (Major Stuart Smith, Harness' second-in-command, rode back to Isandlwana to prepare the remainder of the battery.) The first part of this instruction was carried out easily enough, but it was not at all clear to Harness where the Mangeni gorge was. His men halted on a slight rise while Major Wilsone Black, who was with him, rode off to find Chelmsford and determine his exact intentions. With Harness were F and H Companies of the 2/24th under Captains Church and Harvey respectively, and about 50 Native Pioneers. Black had hardly departed when Harness' party heard the reports of guns from the direction of Isandlwana; Church judged them to be about eight miles away:

> We did not know what to make of this, and were puzzled how to act, when about one o'clock a body of about 1000 natives suddenly appeared on the plain below and between us and the camp. Our Native Sappers pronounced them to be Zulus; and as it was advisable to ascertain for certain, I suggested to Colonel Harness that, if he would let me have one of his artillery horses, I would go and find out. He at once gave me a horse and sent a mounted sergeant RA with me. I galloped towards them, and when I was getting near, a European rode out to meet me, and said "The troops behind me are Commdt Browne's contingent and I am sent to give you this message — Come in every man for God's sake; the camp is surrounded and will be taken unless helped at once."

Church immediately rode back to Harness, where he found that Black had returned with Chelmsford's ADC Major Gossett. Gosset was not impressed: "It's all bosh", someone heard him say, "I do not hear big guns. You had better continue your march as ordered." He offered to bet a hundred pounds to a brass farthing that the camp was safe. Harness and Black were not convinced. Captain Develin was a credible messenger, and they pointed out that Chelmsford could not possibly know of any changed circumstances at Isandlwana from his position. Harness turned the guns, and, with the 24th companies, started to march back to Isandlwana. He sent a Lieutenant Parsons with Gosset to Chelmsford to explain his decision. They had gone not quite two miles when Gosset returned with an order from Chelmsford repeating that they should return to the campsite at the Mangeni.

If it is hard to believe Chelmsford's apparent complacency, Clery provides something of an explanation:

Curious reports arrived during the day, first of the camp being attacked, next of the camp being taken; but these were generally treated lightly, for it was presumed the general had any correct information that arrived . . . even I who thought we had been acting imprudently, could not still realise that any such calamity hung over us as the loss of our camp.

Clery's casual references to the "curious reports" is interesting, since Chelmsford denied having received any from Hamilton-Browne, and it is difficult to know to which others Clery might have been referring; but in any case it is clear that neither Chelmsford nor his staff felt the camp could be in any danger. In the Cape Frontier War large bodies of Xhosa had gathered near camps without posing a serious threat; that morning the Zulus seemed to have been behaving in the same way at the Mangeni.

Chelmsford himself had ridden down to the stream to meet the Volunteers and Police under Dartnell who had been recalled from Phindo hill. A number of officers had waited on the nek above, from where the camp was visible; and, according to Norris-Newman, they had seen bodies of warriors in the distance. Some of the men captured in the skirmishing were being questioned when they heard the distant thud of shells bursting against the Nyoni. "Do you hear that?" said one of the Zulus, "There is fighting going on at the camp". A messenger was sent down to Chelmsford, who immediately rode up to the nek, and "every field glass was levelled at the camp. The sun was shining brightly on the white tents, which were plainly visible, but all seemed quiet. No signs of firing, or of an engagement could be seen." Men were moving about at Isandlwana, but they were assumed to be the camp garrison. Reassured, Chelmsford returned to mark out the new camp

site. At about this time Gosset and Parsons came up, and Chelmsford issued the order for Harness to continue his march. "The time was now about 1.45 p.m. and not the faintest idea of disaster occurred to us."

Out on the plain, Hamilton-Browne was stunned to find that his messages provoked no response. At one point he saw the Mounted Infantry, who had drawn ahead of Harness, halt across the plain to his right, and he sent a message by Captain Hayes suggesting that Russell support his advance. Russell acknowledged the message, but his men stayed put; shortly afterwards they mounted up and rode back towards the Mangeni. Russell reached Harness just as he was turning the guns again. Russell had received another message, apparently from Pulleine, indicating that he had a battle on his hands and could not move the camp immediately. Russell and Gosset rode back together to find Chelmsford.

At last, Chelmsford had decided to ride back to Isandlwana himself to find out what was going on. He had finished marking out the new campsite, and intended to leave Glyn and his men at the head of the Mangeni. The Volunteers and Mounted Infantry would provide his escort.

After they had been pulled back from Phindo, Trooper Symons noted that the Carbineers had off-saddled by the Mangeni stream, "and those who had tea made it and shared it with those who had none". The men had eaten nothing since they had left camp the day before apart from the biscuit and tinned fish they had brought with them: "I thought I should never care to taste the fish again. Tinned fish on an empty stomach is not good." Sometime after noon Symons heard the "low boom" of a cannon a long way off; it was about the time of the eclipse, and "I had a presentiment that something was going to happen either to us or those at the tents, and I chaffed inwardly as I walked to and fro listening to the booming of the guns at Isandlwana and wondered why on earth we were not ordered back to assist the garrison." Yet no order to return came for some time. By the time the Carbineers had gathered their horses and saddled-up, Chelmsford was already on his way back to Isandlwana.

There still seems to have been little urgency about Chelmsford's return ride. Along the way he met Russell, who found that he already knew of the attack on the camp, and was ordered to join him as an escort. Together they passed Harness and Black with the guns and the two companies of the 24th,

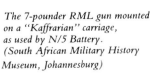

Lieutenant-Colonel Arthur Harness, the commander of N Battery, 5th Brigade, Royal Artillery. (Royal Archives)

The 7-pounder RML gun mounted on a "Kaffrarian" carriage, as used by N/5 Battery. (South African Military History Museum, Johannesburg)

Brevet Major Stuart Smith, RA, Harness' friend and second-in-command, who returned in time to command the N/5 detachment at Isandlwana. Wounded during the action, he managed to reach the Mzinyathi valley only to be killed on the final descent to the river. (Royal Archives)

who were now marching back to the Mangeni. No further orders were given to them, however; Black was so astonished that when he arrived he sought out Degacher of the 2/24th: "Colonel, have you heard the news? They say the camp is attacked and hard pressed; we were on our way back to help them, but they have brought us back here!"

At last Chelmsford came up to Hamilton-Browne's NNC battalion. Hamilton-Browne describes the encounter:

The long afternoon passed slowly away, and towards evening I saw a small body of horsemen riding towards us. On using my glasses I discovered it was the General and his staff and I at once mounted and rode towards them.

He looked very surprised when he saw me and said, "What are you doing here, Commandant Browne? You ought to have been in camp hours ago." I replied "The camp has been taken, sir."

He flashed out at once "How dare you tell me such a falsehood? Get your men into line at once and advance." I did so and led my 700 miserables supported by the staff against the victorious Zulu army.

We moved on about two and a half miles until we had opened out a good view of the camp, when he called me to him and said, in a kindly manner, "On your honour, Commandant Browne, is the camp taken?" I answered, "The camp was taken at about 1.30 in the afternoon, and the Zulus are now burning some of the tents."

He said, "That may be Quartermaster's fatigue burning the debris of the camp." I replied, "Q.M.'s fatigue do not burn tents, sir," and offered him my glasses. He refused them, but said "Halt your men at once," and leaving me, rode back to the staff and dispatched an officer to bring up the remainder of the Column.

A few minutes later Hamilton-Browne had an encounter which destroyed the last of the General's hopes. A white man on foot leading a pony came up to the NNC from the direction of Isandlwana, and to their astonishment it turned out to be their CO, Rupert Lonsdale. He had become separated from them earlier in the day when chasing a mounted Zulu on the slopes of Phindo, and had decided to ride back to Isandlwana to prepare for the movement of the camp. According to Norris-Newman, who was with the staff, he had ridden to within 300 yards before he had realised anything was wrong. Perhaps it was closer; in some versions he was amongst the tents before a Zulu emerged from one with a bloody stabbing spear, and he realised that the red coats wandering about were all on the backs of Zulus. Perhaps the story just grew with the telling; in any case, it was extraordinary enough. He only just had time to turn his pony, Dot, away from home, and to ride away with bullets whistling past his ears. A few Zulus chased him, but soon gave up; no doubt they were exhausted, and the delights of the camp were more tempting than the prospect of killing one more solitary white man.

It was now about 3 p.m., and it was quickly clear that the Zulus were in possession of the camp at Isandlwana. The fate of the garrison remained to be seen.

Captain Alan C.Gardner, 14th Hussars, attached to Glyn's staff for general duties. One of the five Imperial officers to survive Isandlwana, he later rode on to warn Wood's Column of the disaster; he was consequently considered (briefly) for a recommendation for the Victoria Cross but, according to Francis Clery, was the subject of unflattering doggerel: "I very much fear/That the Zulus are near/So hang it, I'm off to Dundee" . . . (F.W.D.Jackson Collection)

CHAPTER FIVE

Pulleine and Durnford

It is clear that when Chelmsford marched out of the camp at Isandlwana at 2 a.m. on the morning of 22nd January he felt that it was secure. Not only were there sufficient troops on hand to defend it; he clearly did not expect it to be attacked — in fact, he hardly gave the matter a thought.

The camp was left under the command of Lieutenant-Colonel Henry Burmester Pulleine of the 1/24th. Pulleine was 40 years old at the time of the Zulu War. He had passed through Sandhurst; first commissioned into the 30th Regiment in 1855, he had joined the 24th three years later, purchasing his majority in 1871. For all his 20 years with the Regiment he remains something of a shadowy figure — which is a shame, since his actions on that day were crucial, and it would be valuable to have some insight into his thought processes. In the best-known photograph he looks rather like a typical Victorian self-made man; he beams robustly off to one side, sporting a pair of mutton-chop whiskers, with an air of self-satisfaction. It comes as something of a surprise to see in a group photograph that he was actually below average height, and that he is wearing his forage cap at a jaunty angle. His personality does not seem to have provoked much comment, but was evidently amiable enough. He had a clear talent for administration, and had spent most of his time in South Africa on detached duties.

He had been partly responsible, with Lieutenant Fred Carrington of his Battalion, for raising a tough irregular cavalry unit, the Frontier Light Horse; and had also raised an infantry unit known as Pulleine's Rangers. These had been recruited from the dross of settler society, and had proved almost as much trouble as they were worth; Hamilton-Browne, who served with them for a while, nicknamed them with heavy sarcasm "Pulleine's Lambs". These duties had kept him away from the front during the entire period of his Battalion's active service on the Cape Frontier. When the 1/24th arrived in Natal Pulleine had been appointed commander of the garrison at Fort Napier in Pietermaritzburg, but he petitioned Chelmsford to be allowed to rejoin his unit. He finally rejoined it in Zululand on 17th January, assuming command from Captain Degacher. Despite, therefore, having had a good deal of military experience, and being well known to the men under his command, Pulleine had never yet commanded a force in action. Perhaps it was because of this that, after his death, Mrs. Glyn — who presumably knew him well enough within the regimental family — cast aspersions on his personal bravery, suggesting that he would be found "hiding behind a wagon wheel or a large stone." No more serious imputation could be made against the reputation of any Victorian officer; but there is nothing in Pulleine's known conduct on the 22nd to support it.

The core of Pulleine's command was the 1st Battalion of his own Regiment. Three companies had still not rejoined it — B Company was in southern Natal, while D and G had only recently reached Helpmekaar — but with Mostyn's F Company now in, the headquarters and remaining five companies totalled 16 officers and 400 men. Apart from Pulleine, the officers were William Degacher (acting Major); Lieutenant and Adjutant Melvill; Captain Mostyn and Lieutenants Anstey and Daly (all F Co.); Captain Cavaye and 2nd Lieutenant Dyson (E Co.); Captain Wardell and Lieutenant Atkinson (H Co.); Captain Younghusband and Lieutenant Hodson (C Co.); Lieutenant Porteous (A Co.); Paymaster (Honorary Major) White, and Quartermaster Pullen. Nevill Coghill, Glyn's Orderly Officer, was also in the camp, not having recovered from his knee injury on the 20th. In addition, G Company of the 2nd Battalion, under Lieutenants Pope and Godwin-Austen, had been out on picquet duty on the night of the 21st and were still in camp the next morning. A significant number of unattached men from the 2/24th were also in camp, making a total of 173 including G Company, and presumably came under Pope's command.

In addition to the infantry, Pulleine had a detachment of two 7-pdrs. from Harness' N/5 Battery under the command of Lieutenant Curling. There were some 70 gunners in the camp, of whom about 50 were not attached to the guns. Thirty men of No. 1 Squadron, Imperial Mounted Infantry had been left in the camp, together with just over 100 Police and Volunteers, under the command of Captain Robert Bradstreet of the Newcastle Mounted Rifles.

The orders conveyed by Clery to Pulleine had been quite specific: he was to remain on the defensive, throw his cavalry vedettes well out, but keep his infantry outposts close at hand. Clearly nothing further was expected of him, and Pulleine no doubt shared the general opinion that whatever Zulus might have been in the vicinity, the General was dealing with them, and that an attack on the camp was most unlikely. No doubt he expected to be ordered to advance the camp at some point in the near future.

Pulleine must have been aware of Chelmsford's instructions to column commanders issued on 23rd December 1878. These instructions are of particular interest for a number of reasons, not the least of which is that they have only recently become available to historians. The only copy which has apparently

Lieutenant-Colonel Henry B. Pulleine, 1/24th Regiment. (Author's collection)

53

survived was one found on Colonel Durnford's body, and for more than a century its contents remained resolutely illegible. Since the commanders of the surviving columns had also presumably been issued with the same instructions, one cannot help but wonder whether they were discreetly lost in the aftermath of subsequent events.

Amongst other things these instructions contained tactical advice on how to deal with a Zulu attack. The column commander was to draw up his guns in line, with Regular infantry companies on either side. The companies on the flanks would be set back slightly to provide some protection for the flanks, while behind them on either side the NNC would be placed in echelon. Behind the Native Contingent, on the right and left rear, were to be placed the mounted men, with an infantry reserve behind the centre. The whole formation was entirely in keeping with Chelmsford's experience on the Cape Frontier; it recognised that the encircling tactics favoured by African enemies posed a threat to the flanks, while at the same time seeking to concentrate his firepower in one direction. There is no mention of a tight defensive formation, of standing shoulder to shoulder in a square, or of entrenchments.

It has been suggested that this formation ignored the lessons of Centane, but this is based on a misunderstanding of the tactics followed on that occasion. Certainly, Upcher had protected his camp with a square earthwork, and sheltered his guns in it, and Chelmsford's *Field Force Regulations* insisted that camps should be "partially entrenched" — but it had been the 24th, lying down in rifle pits, or sweeping through the bush in skirmishing order, who had broken the Xhosa at Centane. There had been no "defensive square" in the sense that one understands the formation as used in the later battles of the Zulu War. At Nyamaga Glyn had won using almost exactly this formation. Interestingly enough, a comment Chelmsford made to Hamilton-Browne on the 19th falls into place in the light of this document: "In case he was attacked, I was to move down and attack the right flank of the enemy. I suggested that as I lay in their road, they would eat me up long before they reached him. He thought not . . ."

Before dawn the camp was up and about its business. Mounted vedettes were despatched to take up position on the surrounding heights, and the infantry outposts were relieved. A party was sent out under Lieutenant Anstey to work on the

A remarkable record of some of the defenders of Isandlwana: H Company, 1/24th, photographed on the Cape Frontier. The officers sitting at front are (left to right) Lieutenants Charles W. Cavaye and Charles J. Atkinson, and Captain George V. Wardell. The Colour-Sergeant (third from left, front row) is probably Frederick Wolfe, whose body was found with others on the rocky rise at the right of the firing line. H Company were wiped out. (F.W.D. Jackson Collection)

Three officers of the 24th photographed on the eve of the Anglo-Zulu War: Lieutenants Cavaye (left) and Porteous (centre), with Captain William Degacher. Porteous wears the officers' scarlet frock, the other two dark blue patrol jackets. All three would die at Isandlwana. ("SB" Bourquin)

road somewhere to the east. If Chelmsford had ever communicated his intention to scout the Nyoni ridge to anyone, it had been forgotten in the excitement of the previous night. The infantry were stretched in a curve around the front of the

serving under him again. Durnford himself was obviously looking forward to the coming fray; it was a chance to see some proper action, and to prove the worth of his black troops. Durnford trained his men as vigorously as he thought practical, and refused to allow his officers and NCOs to abuse or insult them. Given their limitations, by the time the ultimatum expired the 1st NNC had been moulded into a surprisingly efficient light infantry force.

Chelmsford had not entirely settled on a role for Durnford's column. His first plan, outlined at the end of December, suggested that Durnford should cross into Zululand once Colonel Pearson's Right Flank Column to the south had reached its first objective, the Eshowe mission station, and should clear the country between the Middle Drift and Eshowe. He changed his mind almost immediately, ordering Pearson to clear the country to the west of him instead; and directing Durnford to move down to cross at the Lower Thukela and support Pearson's advance. When he reached Helpmekaar on 4th January, the plans were changed again; Durnford was now to move two of his best battalions to Sandspruit, since the Msinga district had been unprotected since the 3rd NNC had moved to Helpmekaar. The remainder of the column was to support Glyn's advance if necessary, and four days later Chelmsford added that Durnford might cross the Drift into Zululand if the situation allowed, providing he did not remain there. Chelmsford can hardly be blamed for changing his mind — flexibility in the face of a changing situation was a necessity in African warfare, and confused and contradictory reports were coming out of Zululand every day. Nevertheless, Durnford must have felt frustrated that his mission was not more clearly defined, though consoled that he could expect to be given a more active role at any time.

On 13th January, the day after Glyn's Centre Column went into action at Sihayo's stronghold, Durnford received information that a Zulu force was preparing to raid into Natal across the Middle Drift. The information seems to have emanated from Bishop Schreuder, a missionary who had fled Zululand but whose spies were still at work across the border. Durnford, who had not yet detached his men to Sandspruit, prepared to advance his column to the drift to head the raiders off. He sent a note to Chelmsford to inform him of his intentions; but before he had time to move he received a curt reply:

Unless you carry out the instructions I give you, it will be my unpleasant duty to remove you from your command and to substitute another officer for the command of No.2 Column. When a column is acting SEPARATELY in an enemy's country I am quite ready to give its commander every latitude and would certainly expect him to disobey any orders he might receive from me, if information which he obtained showed that it would be injurious to the interests of the column under his command. Your neglecting to obey the instructions in the present instance is no excuse. You have simply received information in a letter from Bishop Shroeder, which may or may not be true, and which you have no means of verifying. If movements ordered are to be delayed because report hints at a chance of an invasion of Natal, it will be impossible for me to carry out my plan of campaign. I trust you will understand this plain speaking and will not give me any further occasion to write in a style which is distasteful to me.

This is a surprisingly tart response from a man renowned for his dislike of offending people, especially in the light of his order to Durnford of 8th January, and their previous good relationship. Perhaps it reflects that "certain tetchiness" which Clery noted; it certainly only makes sense in the light of Chelmsford's experience of disobedient subordinates in the Cape Frontier War. Durnford, keyed up for action, read the message with "disgust".

The next day Durnford was ordered to leave the major part of two battalions of the 1st NNC — the 1st and 3rd — at Kranskop, and to move up to Rorke's Drift with three companies of the 1st, the whole of Bengough's 2nd Battalion, the Native Horse, and the Rocket Battery. The three companies of the 1st Battalion were Chief Zikhali's Ngwane, under the command of Captains Nourse, Stafford and Hay; since Hay was required to stay behind for other duties, his company was divided up between the other two. After a hard march, part of it at night, they reached Sandspruit at 3 a.m. on the morning of the 18th. The next day Major Spalding, the DAA&QMG, brought a fresh order from Chelmsford which outlined something of his current thinking:

No.3 Column leaves tomorrow [for] Isandlwana hill and from there as soon as possible to a spot about ten miles nearer to the Qudeni forest. From that point I intend to operate against the two Matyanas if they fail to surrender . . . I have sent you an order to cross the [Mzinyathi] river at Rorke's Drift tommorrow with the force you have . . . I shall want you to cooperate against the Matyanas but will send you fresh instructions on this subject.

This message was particularly significant because it undoubtedly shaped Durnford's understanding of the role he reasonably believed Chelmsford expected him to play: he was to continue as a separate command, in support of any offensive action undertaken by the General.

Edendale Horse veterans of the 1879 Anglo-Zulu War and 1906 Natal Rebellion, photographed c.1910. Edendale, outside Pietermaritzburg, was a Christian community, and many of its members were landowners; they volunteered to support the Colonial authorities despite moral reservations. All those standing served in the Zulu War: Jabez Molife (fourth from left) and Simeon Kambule (right of him, in light suit) distinguished themselves at Isandlwana. Kambule was the Troop Sergeant-Major; his father had died fighting with Durnford at Bushman's Pass. (Killie Campbell Africana Library)

On 20th January Durnford's column crossed Rorke's Drift and established a camp on the Zulu bank. Bengough's battalion stayed behind, as it had been ordered to strike eastwards from Sandspruit, crossing the Mzinyathi downstream of Rorke's Drift at Eland's Kraal, which — significantly — lay opposite the mouth of the Mangeni gorge. Durnford's force had therefore been denuded of infantry, apart from the two companies (D and E) of Zikhali's Ngwane, who totalled about 240 men including nine whites. What remained were the five troops of the Natal Native Horse under the overall command of Captain Barton. Of these, three were also composed of Zikhali's Ngwane: No.1 Troop, under Lieutenant C.Raw, was about 52 strong; No.2 Troop, under Lieutenant J.A.Roberts, had about 55 men; and No.3 Troop, under Lieutenant W.Vause was 50 strong. The Hlongwe BaSotho troop, Hlubi's men, was about 50 strong and commanded by Lieutenant A.F.Henderson, whilst the Edendale Troop, commanded by Lieutenant H.D.Davies, was 52 strong. All of these men were dressed in European clothing, and the Edendale men, being Christians, prided themselves on their smart appearance. They were armed with Swinburne-Henry carbines. Finally, there was the Royal Artillery Rocket Battery commanded by Brevet Major F.B.Russell. Durnford's "Political Officer" — in effect his Staff Officer — was Captain George Shepstone, a son of Sir Theophilus and brother of "Offy" of the Carbineers: George had known Durnford since King Cetshwayo's coronation, and had been one of the few Volunteers to stick by him after the Bushman's Pass debacle. Durnford had been pleased with the appointment, but Shepstone's father had had his misgivings:

> *It is strange but true that when I heard he had been appointed to serve with Colonel Durnford, I felt as if I had heard his death warrant. I had no confidence in Durnford's prudence or capacity to suit himself to the circumstances in which he might be placed.*

Lieutenant Charles Raw was also a veteran of Bushman's Pass. Attached to the Column as Transport Officer was Lieutenant William Cochrane of the 32nd Regiment, whom Henry Harford had met again on the voyage out, and who had so entranced his fellow passengers with his skill at the keyboard.

On the 21st Durnford wrote a letter home to his mother, which reveals both his state of mind and his understanding of his orders:

> *We arrived here and camped on the Zulu shores about dusk. The mission station is in sight on the Natal side, where also is a company of the 24th regt. and the hospital, with, I am happy to say, but few patients in it. I have sent on to ask for instructions from the general, who is about ten miles off, forming a camp at or near the Isandhlwana mountain (see my map of Zululand). My movements are to operate against the two Matshanas, and, if they won't submit, make them. I have as a guide a man who, having lived nine years in this part of the country, ought to know it. This wet weather we have had is most depressing in every way, but today has been very hot, and quite a pleasant change for me, and, indeed, for all of us, black and white. The general has gone on with the 1st and 2nd battalions of the 24th, etc., and we follow on. I have no news, am stupid, and dull, and "down", so adieu for the day.*
> *P.S. I am "down" because I am left behind, but we shall see.*

* * *

Shortly after dawn on the 22nd, a messenger from Isandlwana arrived at the river bank opposite Rorke's Drift. It was young Horace Smith-Dorrien:

> *I rode back, about 10 miles, arriving just before dawn on the morning of the 22nd, and delivered my dispatch. It ought to have been a very jumpy ride, for I was entirely alone and the country was wild and new to me, and the road little better than a track; but the pride at being selected to carry an important dispatch and the valour of ignorance (for I only realised next day that the country was infested with hostile Zulus) carried me along without a thought of danger.*

Durnford had already ridden out that morning with Cochrane, Davis and an escort of four men to search the Biggarsberg farms for wagons to increase his transport park; Smith-

Brevet Major Francis Broadfoot Russell, RA, who commanded the Rocket Battery with Durnford's No.2 Column. (Royal Archives)

Dorrien handed the note to Shepstone, who read it, and ordered Lieutenant Henderson to take it to the Colonel. Shepstone immediately gave orders to break up the camp, while Smith-Dorrien crossed the river and rode up to Rorke's Drift. As Transport Officer, it was part of his duty to supervise the making of reims, tough leather ropes, and he organised a party to build a gallows about 15 feet high to stretch the hides. He was just passing the time of day with Lieutenant "Gonny" Bromhead of the 2/24th when they both heard the sound of distant firing. It was now about 8 a.m.; Smith-Dorrien cadged 11 rounds for his revolver from Bromhead, then set off back to the camp. Henderson, meanwhile, had caught up with Durnford. Cochrane, who was also present, remembered Durnford's comment when he read his instructions: "Just what I thought. We are to proceed at once to Isandlwana camp. There is an impi about eight miles from the camp which the General moves out to attack at daybreak."

The note itself, scribbled by Crealock at 2 a.m. that morning, gave no precise instructions as to what Durnford was to do on arrival at Isandlwana; it reflected Chelmsford's carelessness about the camp, and his opinion that if a battle was to be fought, it would be fought at the Mangeni:

> *You are to march to this camp with all the force you have with you of No.2 Column. Major Bengough's battalion is to move to Rorke's Drift as ordered yesterday. 2/24th, Artillery and mounted men with the General and Colonel Glyn move off at once to attack a Zulu force about ten miles distant. J.N.C.*
> *If Bengough's Battalion has crossed the river at Eland's Kraal it is to move up here. (Nangwane Valley)*

Quartermaster-Sergeant J.C.Bullock of the Natal Carbineers, killed at Isandlwana. (Local History Museum, Durban)

At the camp at Rorke's Drift Durnford found his men ready to move, and they marched out towards Isandlwana at about 7.30 a.m. The Natal Native Horse led — the Hlongwe troop, then the Edendale men, then Zikhali's Horse with Raw's Troop first, then Roberts, and finally Vause. The Rocket Battery came next, followed by the infantry, and the column's wagons. It took about two and a half hours to reach Isandlwana; by that time, the mounted men had drawn well ahead. About half a mile short of Isandlwana, Durnford met Lieutenant John Chard, RE, who had arrived at Rorke's Drift on the 19th and had ridden up to the camp for orders. Chard's handful of Sappers from No.5 Company, Royal Engineers had been stationed at Rorke's Drift, working on the ponts, but had accompanied Durnford's force. On hearing of the Zulu presence on the hills Chard had ridden back to Rorke's Drift, worrying that the Zulus might be preparing to slip round behind the camp and attack the crossings. He told Durnford his news, and Durnford sent a messenger back to hurry Russell's Rocket Battery along, and to detach one of the NNC infantry companies to guard the wagons. The message must have reached Russell at the Batshe, for he ordered Captain Nourse's D Company to press on, while Stafford's E Company marched with the wagons. Nourse's men reached Isandlwana not long after the mounted men, with the Rocket Battery lagging behind.

Once at the camp, Durnford ordered his men to dismount "somewhere in the centre of the camp just beyond the Ambulance wagons", but not to off-saddle. Hlubi's men took the bits from their horses' mouths and fed them. Durnford himself went off to report to Pulleine.

It was at this meeting that the inconsistencies in Chelmsford's intentions became apparent. Durnford was the senior officer; although his Brevet Colonelcy was probably not yet known in Africa, he had been a Lieutenant-Colonel for four years longer than Pulleine. Pulleine brought Durnford up to date with the situation in the camp, and told him of the General's orders to "defend the camp". According to his Transport Officer, William Cochrane, Durnford took command of the camp, but he clearly had no intention of remaining in it for long. According to Cochrane, the conversation was along the following lines:

Colonel Pulleine said, "I'm sorry you have come, as you are senior to me and will of course take command." Colonel Durnford replied "I'm not going to interfere with you. I'm not going to remain in camp."

Perhaps Durnford had expected to find fresh orders from Chelmsford awaiting him; but there had been no word from the General, not even in response to Pulleine's message earlier in the day warning him of the Zulu presence on the hills. By now the gunfire in the distance had been noticed by almost everyone. The messages from the picquets on the hills were confusing, however: "The enemy are in force behind the hills"; "the enemy are in three columns", "the columns are separating, one moving to the left rear and one towards the general"; "the enemy are retiring in every direction".

The prospect of a Zulu column slipping round behind Isandlwana was worrying, as Durnford's wagons were still about four miles from the camp. He returned to his men — Davies thought it was now about 10.15 a.m. — and ordered Vause's No.3 Troop of Zikhali's Horse to ride back out and bring in the wagons. Nourse's infantry company, which had only just arrived, was also sent back after them. While he had been away, Quartermaster-Sergeant Bullock of the Carbineers had come over with several of his men and told Davies of the Zulu presence out towards Itusi. Durnford then ordered his men to move further to the left of the camp, to a position in front of the NNC tents. Here one of the NNC picquets came in and reported that Barry's men on the spur had seen about 600 Zulus to their front. Clearly these Zulu movements, whatever they meant, could not be allowed to continue indefinitely, and Durnford decided to send out two troops of Zikhali's men to sweep them off the heights. Raw's No.1 Troop and Roberts' No.2 Troop were selected, and George Shepstone, the Zikhali *induna* Nyanda, and Captain Barton were to go with them. (This Captain Barton is an enigmatic figure; he has often been confused with Captain Geoffrey Barton of the 7th Fusiliers, who was the Staff Officer of the 1st Regiment NNC, but who had remained at Kranskop; although several witnesses remember Barton setting off with Shepstone, his movements after that are obscure.) Durnford told Nyanda that No.1 Troop should drive across the heights, while No.2 Troop should search through the valley beyond. The two troops were to support each other if necessary, and Raw was to take with him Barry's infantry company if he felt he needed it.

Durnford then went off and took a hurried lunch with Pulleine and the officers of the 1/24th, standing up while he ate. The immediate danger seemed to have passed, and at Durnford's suggestion the men of the 24th — who had been lined up in columns in front of the camp all the while — were ordered to stand down. They were not to take off their equipment, however, and were to eat their lunches as quickly as possible. While they were eating, Lieutenant Higginson came in from Barry's NNC outpost to report. He went to Pulleine, but Pulleine referred him to Durnford. Durnford listened to what he had to say, asked if any lookouts had been placed on the top of Isandlwana, and when told that they had not, ordered Higginson to despatch some. This was a good idea in theory; it is perfectly possible to scale the mountain at the northern end, where the sheer rock wall drops to only about 15 feet in height, an easy scramble for an active man; but in practice it served little use, since the peak of Isandlwana is about the same height as the Nyoni range and commands no great view across the surface.

Over lunch, Durnford announced that he intended to take his men out across the plain. He was concerned that the Zulu column earlier seen retiring in the General's direction might have been trying to circle round to cut him off from the camp; Durnford proposed to march out after it and intercept it. He wanted to take two companies of the 24th with him; quite what for remains a mystery since two Imperial infantry companies would only have slowed him down on the march. Nevertheless, perhaps Durnford thought the threat of redcoats might force the Zulus away; or perhaps he felt he needed their firepower. In any case, although Durnford put his case in a "persuasive" rather than a "peremptory" fashion, Pulleine was uneasy. His orders had been to "defend the camp": he had not been specifically ordered to hand over command to Durnford, nor had Chelmsford given him any fresh instructions which might have caused him to alter his original position. At last, however, Pulleine said, "Oh, very well; of course if you order them I'll give you them." Pulleine then went over to discuss this with his officers, but the 24th were clearly unhappy; and shortly afterwards Lieutenant Melvill walked over to Durnford and said, "Colonel, I really do not think Col. Pulleine would be doing right to send any men out of camp when his orders are to 'defend the camp'." Durnford replied, "Very well, it does not much matter; we will not take them".

Nevertheless, at about this time a company of the 1/24th — E Company under Lieutenant Charles Cavaye — was sent up onto the ridge by the spur. It is not certain who gave the order, but since the movement was clearly intended to support the sweep across the heights, it was presumably at Durnford's instigation. Quite what purpose this served is also obscure, although once Barry's men set off after Raw there was no picquet on that side of the camp.

Durnford then went back to his men to prepare them to march out and to check on the progress of the Rocket Battery. They still had not come in; and after a while, impatient for news, Durnford went back to Pulleine's tent. There had been no news from the men on top of the mountain, and Durnford told Higginson to send a man up to find out what was

happening. He returned with the news that the Zulus were retiring. "Ah! Is that so; well then, we will follow them up." Durnford asked if Higginson could be spared — Pulleine said he could — and Durnford told him to ride after the party now on the heights, and tell them to work to their right, eastwards along the ridge, since he himself was going to work along the foot of the hills.

Durnford returned to his men and told them to mount up. He told the officers that the enemy were retiring, and that he intended to follow them up: "If they are going towards the General we must stop them at all hazards". By this time Russell's Rocket Battery had been in camp for about 15 minutes, and Durnford ordered them to follow him, with Nourse's NNC company to support them. It was now about 11.15 a.m., and all this activity had taken place in less than an hour since Durnford had arrived at Isandlwana.

Up on the ridge Raw's Troop, accompanied by Shepstone and Nyanda, found "the enemy in small clumps, retiring before us for some time, drawing us four or five miles from the camp". Some of the Zulus had cattle with them, and may well have been foraging parties. North of the Nyoni escarpment the land was comparatively level, an undulating plateau broken by patches of rocky outcrop. The horsemen were cantering after the Zulus, Roberts' Troop only about half a mile to the left of Raw's, when suddenly the warriors disappeared into a fold in the ground in front of them. In the cool words of an official report, Nyanda described the chilling sight which greeted them next:

We saw a handful (not many) of Zulus who kept running from us. All of a sudden, just as Mr. Shepstone joined me on the crest of a ridge, the army of Zulus sprung up 15,000 men . . . Mr. Shepstone said to me you must retreat fighting and draw them towards the camp . . .

"They turned and fell upon us", commented Raw laconically, "the whole army shewing itself from behind the hill in front where they had evidently been waiting."

When Lieutenant Raw of Durnford's Natal Native Horse looked down from this ridge shortly before noon on 22nd January 1879, some 20,000 Zulus of the main impi *were bivouacked at the bottom: the Ngwebeni valley, from the rocky slope of the Mabaso heights, looking eastwards. Siphezi mountain, where the Zulu army had camped the previous night, and where the Mounted Infantry skirmished on the 22nd, is on the right skyline. (Author's photograph)*

Lieutenant Wyatt Vause, who commanded No.3 Troop of Zikhali's Ngwane Horse at Isandlwana, and who survived the battle. (Local History Museum, Durban)

CHAPTER SIX

Cetshwayo's Kingdom

When Crealock hoped, in the aftermath of the attack on Sihayo's kwaSokhexe homestead on 12th January, that King Cetshwayo would thereby be provoked into an attack on the Centre Column, he was being prophetic; the news soon reached the king at Ulundi, and brought an end to months of prevarication stretching back to July 1878.

The possibility of a conflict with the British had become apparent following their reaction to the border incident in that month involving the sons of Sihayo kaXongo. The king and his advisors were somewhat bewildered by the evident change of mood, since the Zulu royal house had a history of good relations with the British dating back to the time when King Shaka had first allowed them to establish a client chiefdom at Port Natal. Nevertheless, it was apparent that since their annexation of the Transvaal the British were intent on some sort of confrontation and, while Cetshwayo was only too aware of the potentially disastrous consequences of a war with the whites, his own internal political considerations allowed him little room for manoeuvre.

He was a vigorous ruler, jealous of both his personal position and the prestige of the monarchy; for much of his reign he had been concerned to halt the decentralisation of political power within his kingdom which had begun 40 years earlier during the reign of his father King Mpande. On the border question, Cetshwayo was adamant that the Boer claim was unjust; spurred on by powerful economic considerations — in a time of drought the lush grazing lands around the upper Ncome River assumed a particular importance — he was unable to give way on his basic claim. He was, however, prepared to accept the findings of the Boundary Commission as impartial; but while he no doubt greeted their award with some satisfaction, this was negated by the demands contained in Frere's ultimatum.

The ultimatum precipitated a crisis within the kingdom. Cetshwayo was happy to make some reparation for the deeds of Sihayo's sons, but only within limits. Sihayo was a personal friend of the king, and had been a loyal supporter since the civil war of 1856. In 1874 Cetshwayo had confirmed Sihayo's position as head of the Qungebe people, whose territory, facing Natal across the Mzinyathi River border, was strategically important. Sihayo's son Mehlokazulu was also something of a royal favourite; he was one of a group of youths who were required periodically to attend upon the king in person, and he was a commander within the iNgobamakhosi ibutho (an age-group society, and in time of war a regiment). The iNgobamakhosi was the king's favourite, and one of the youngest and most vociferous of his regiments; the king could not afford to alienate it, and the iNgobamakhosi were outraged that he might sacrifice one of their own to placate the whites. Despite the opposition of some of the more influential members of his inner council, who thought Sihayo's sons a small price to pay for peace, Cetshwayo could not give them up.

The second demand which all agreed was unacceptable was the disbandment of the amabutho system (amabutho is the plural form of ibutho). To the British the amabutho were simply a standing army who were a menace to their neighbours, but in fact their role within Zulu society was much more complex. The Zulu kingdom was essentially a conglomerate, made up of the clans who had either allied themselves to King Shaka or been conquered by him. Most of these clans survived intact, and had hereditary chiefs of their own. The chiefs were required to acknowledge the superiority of the king; but their interests were often opposed to those of the monarch, and many had used the political crises of the previous reign to buy themselves a considerable degree of political and economic independence. These chiefs, together with the male members of the royal house — whose blood conferred on them an enormous degree of respect — constituted the izikhulu, the "great ones" of the nation, who sat on the ibandla, the king's council. The king could not make any important state decisions without their consent, and such was their power that the king could not often overrule the ibandla when it was united against his policies.

The amabutho system, however, worked against this gradual dispersal of power to the chiefs, since it concentrated the nation's most important resource — its manpower — directly in the hands of the king. Scattered around the country were royal homesteads known as amakhanda, or "heads" (singular ikhanda), which served as regional bases for the administration of royal authority; the British called them "military kraals". Physically, these were ordinary family homesteads (umuzi; plural imizi) writ large: a collection of dome-shaped huts built round a central cattle-pen, and surrounded by a stout stockade. Amakhanda were, of course, much larger than ordinary homesteads; the smallest of them contained two or three hundred huts, while Ulundi (or oNdini), the king's principal residence, comprised 1,500 huts. The amakhanda were, most importantly, the headquarters of the amabutho.

When a Zulu man reached the age of 18 or 19 he was required to report to his local ikhanda to offer service to the king. Here he would spend his time tending the king's cattle, looking after his huts, and undergoing an elementary military training. When there were sufficient young men gathered across the kingdom, the king called them together and formed them into an age-set society or ibutho. They were then directed to go and build their own ikhanda at a specified spot, where they were required to serve the king until such time as he allowed them to marry. Marriage — signified by the assumption of the isicoco, a head ring of fibre woven into the hair and plastered with glossy black beeswax — marked the transition from youth to full adulthood, and the point at which men transferred their immediate allegiance from the king back to their own clan chiefs and families. The king often refused permission for an ibutho to marry until the men were nearly 40, thus maximising the time they were available to him as a resource.

The amabutho performed a number of crucial services within the kingdom: they were, of course, the basic tactical blocks which constituted the national army, but they were also the kingdom's police force; they tended the king's cattle, kept his homesteads in good repair and tended his fields, and took part in mass ceremonial hunts and important national gatherings. Because the amabutho were assembled from men of the same age from across the country, regardless of clan origins, they effectively took power out of the hands of local chiefs and vested it in the monarch. Furthermore, the army was run by a

continued on page 65

63

COLOUR PLATES A-D by Michael Chappell

Plate A1: Brevet Colonel Anthony Durnford

This figure is based on photographs, and on his own description of his field service dress. He wears the Royal Engineers officer's dark blue patrol jacket; riding breeches and boots; and a wide-brimmed hat with the red puggaree which was the distinction of the Native Contingent and some irregular units. In 1879 holstered revolvers were normally worn on a shoulder strap; Durnford wore a cartridge pouch and a knife on his waist belt. Rank badges – here still the crown of Lieutenant-Colonel — were worn on the jacket collar.

Plate A2: Trooper, Natal Carbineers

The Carbineers wore a foreign service helmet with white metal fittings and crowned "NC" badge; and a dark blue uniform with white facings and shoulder cords. They were armed with a revolver, holstered on a shoulder strap, and a Swinburne-Henry carbine; ammunition was carried in a brown leather back pouch on a broad shoulder belt, and a haversack (and presumably a water bottle) were also slung from the shoulders.

Plate B1: Colour-Sergeant, 1st Battalion, 24th Regiment

The foreign service helmet was locally dyed various light khaki shades; the brass regimental plate was ordered removed (although some have been found at Isandlwana). He wears the Other Ranks' scarlet serge five-button frock, with green regimental facings as collar patches and outer cuff panels, and white piping to the collar, shoulder straps and cuffs. Line Infantry NCOs wore their badges of rank only on the right sleeve of the frock; opinions differ as to whether the Colour-Sergeant's badge illustrated here was worn on the frock, or only on the seven-button tunic, but contemporary photographs suggest that it was sometimes seen on the former. The same ambiguity surrounds the use in the field of the crimson sash worn over the right shoulder by Sergeants. The frock, and the "Oxford mixture" trousers, show evidence of the Battalion's hard campaigning in South Africa. The rifle is the .45 inch Mark II Martini-Henry, with 33 inch barrel, and weighing 8lb.10 ½ ounces; it has here an improvised cowhide hand guard laced round the forestock. Unlike junior ranks, Sergeants were issued with the 22 ¾-inch "Bayonet, Sword, Pattern 1856 Enfield, Converted", of so-called "yataghan" shape. The plain crimson ribbon is that of the Long Service and Good Conduct Medal.

Plate B2: Private, 2nd Battalion, 24th Regiment

He wears the same order of dress as the Colour-Sergeant. Photographs show some men of the 2nd Battalion wearing khaki cloth helmet covers in 1879, although this was not general practice. The two white chevrons above the right cuff are Long Service and Good Conduct badges, denoting between five and twelve years' service. Hidden here by the belt and the bunching of the frock at the back are two lengths of white piping passing vertically from buttons in the small of the back to the bottom edge of the jacket. More visible are the scarlet seam welt of the Oxford mixture trousers, and the laced black marching gaiters. Like the Colour-Sergeant, he wears the 1871 Valise Pattern "Light Marching Order": waist belt with regimental clasp; two ammunition pouches with the black "ball bag" hanging below the right one; on the left hip the frog for the 1876 Pattern 22-inch socket bayonet; and slung over right and left shoulders respectively, the haversack and the Oliver pattern water bottle.

Plate C1: Drummer, 24th Regiment

This was the official term, although the company Drummer in fact carried a bugle in the field; note the worsted drum badge on his right upper sleeve. The standard five-note infantry bugle is carried by a simple cord; more ornate plaited cords were used when in full dress. The Drummer stayed in close attendance on his officer, passing tactical orders by blowing "sounds" — the term "calls" was associated only with cavalry trumpeters. Photographs show that a fife case was carried on the right of the waist belt. The Drummer's only weapon was the ornate 1857 Pattern drummer's sword.

Plate C2: Captain, 24th Regiment

This figure is based upon photographs of Captain Reginald Younghusband, commanding C Company, 1/24th. He wears the foreign service helmet, and the officer's scarlet serge undress frock which — with the blue patrol jacket — was the most popular field uniform. It bears the distinctions of his rank on the cuffs and, in this case, the collar; subalterns of the 24th seem to have worn only the Regiment's sphinx collar badge, or no insignia at all, on the undress frock, and field officers the badges of rank; but Captains seem to have worn rank badges or not at personal choice. The trousers resembled the men's, and were worn in the field to individual taste with various types of boots and gaiters. Photographs and memoires confirm that the 1846 Pattern infantry officer's sword was carried in action by numbers of officers in 1879; the steel scabbard is slung from a waist belt worn beneath the jacket. The Adams Mark II .45 inch service revolver illustrated was regulation, but many officers' revolvers were of various other models, privately purchased — as were field glasses.

Plate D1: Quartermaster-Sergeant, 24th Regiment

His rank is indicated by the four-chevron badge above the right cuff of the frock; like B1, he wears the ribbon of the LS&GC Medal. He has a holstered Adams Mark II revolver, and, hooked up on his left hip, the Staff Sergeant's sword — a brass-hilted pattern similar to the officers' sword. The undress headgear for all ranks was the plain dark blue Glengarry, with black tape and ribbons and a dark blue tuft, worn with a brass badge at front left by Other Ranks and NCOs. He holds ten-round ammunition packets from the opened 600-round Mark V ammunition box at his feet.

Plate D2: Second Corporal, Royal Artillery

Photographs indicate that this plain dark blue frock was the uniform most commonly worn by the Royal Artillery in Zululand. His rank badge is worn on the upper sleeves and two LS&GC badges on the lower right sleeve, in the red-trimmed yellow of the RA; an appointment badge identifying this man as a Shoeing Smith, in yellow, on the upper right sleeve; and the Artillery's bursting shell badge, above the Battery letter N, above the Brigade number 5, in brass on his shoulder straps. He is armed with a service revolver and an 1853 Pattern cavalry sword; only two carbines were provided per gun, carried on the limber. He holds a rammer staff.

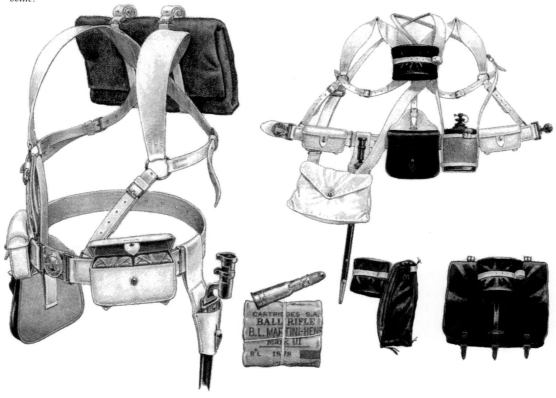

The 1871 Pattern Valise Equipment, as worn by the 24th. (Left) The basic belt, braces, pouches and frog; to these was attached the valise (bottom right). Water bottle and haversack were slung over the shoulders to form marching order. (Top right) The period equivalent of "battle order". The equipment could be worn in several configurations other than marching order; some troops in 1879 wore only belt and pouches, others belt, braces and pouches. A blanket or greatcoat was worn strapped to the rear of the braces; the greatcoat cape was carried under the flap of the valise. (Detail) Martini-Henry round, and ammunition packet. (Michael Chappell)

Plate A

A1: Brevet Colonel A.W. Durnford, RE

A2: Trooper, Natal Carbineers

Plate B

B1: Colour-Sergeant, 1/24th Regt.

B2: Private, 2/24th Regt.

Plate C

C1: Drummer, 24th Regt.

C2: Captain, 24th Regt.

Plate D

D1: Quartermaster-Sergeant, 24th Regt.

D2: Second Corporal, Royal Artillery

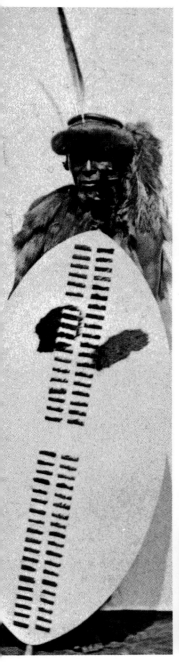

class of state officials called *izinduna* (singular *induna*), who were appointed by the king; although often men of hereditary rank, they were not necessarily so, and were therefore a further means of strengthening royal authority.

The *amabutho* system had been perfected by King Shaka, working on existing structures, but by the late 1870s there had been a number of significant changes. Because of the relative decentralisation of power it was no longer possible to enforce the most rigid aspects of the system. Some men felt able to marry without waiting for the king's consent, whilst others did not bother to join the *amabutho* at all — although they suffered the scorn of the majority who did. Those who were enrolled no longer spent much of their time living in the *amakhanda*; they lived in their fathers' homesteads, and only reported for duty when the king called up their *ibutho* for a specific purpose. The only occasion when all the *amabutho* were mustered was at the annual *umKhosi* ceremony, the harvest festival which ushered in the first fruits every January, and served as an affirmation of the unity and continuity of the nation.

Indeed, in 1879 there are suggestions that some of the more

Three excellent studies of warriors in the characteristic dress of the Zulu army in 1879. (Left) The typical ceremonial regalia of a senior regiment: headring, otterskin headband, crane feather, and white shield. (Right) The costume of the younger amabutho: *a stiff headdress of white cowhide with tails attached to the tips, called* amapovela; *a dense bunch of sakabuli feathers, and a predominantly black shield. Both of these men carry the full-size* isihlangu *shield. (Centre) A warrior in war-dress, an abbreviated form of ceremonial regalia; in fact, most of the regiments would not even have retained this much headdress in the field in 1879. Note the smaller* umbhumbhulosu *shield. (Royal Archives)*

important *izikhulu*, living a long way from the centre of royal authority at Ulundi, no longer allowed their young men to join the king's assemblies but had formed *amabutho* of their own. Nevertheless, even those whose interests were most directly opposed to those of the king feared the consequences of the break-up of the nation, and it was clear to all that this would be the consequence of the overthrow of the *amabutho* system. Compliance with Frere's ultimatum was therefore quite impossible — as, indeed, he had anticipated.

The king and his councillors adopted no firm policy towards the threat of war in the month between the delivery of the ultimatum and its expiry. Cetshwayo sent various placatory messages to the British, while at the same time calling up the *amabutho* when the obvious military preparations across the river sent shock-waves of alarm through the kingdom. It seems that the king did not decide on a military strategy until after British troops had crossed the border and attacked Sihayo's followers on 12th January.

Whilst Lord Chelmsford's intelligence system was able to tell him virtually nothing about the country through which he was travelling, or of the intentions of the enemy, King Cetshwayo not unnaturally knew almost everything about the British. They were operating in his territory, and news of their strength and movements was brought to him not only by military patrols, but by those civilians who had lingered in the vicinity of the invading armies. He was therefore able to plan his campaign accordingly. He was determined to wage a defensive war; the terrible cost of fighting Europeans had been only too apparent since the days of Blood River in 1838, and the king believed that his only real hope was to launch a quick and decisive attack which would cause the British to fall back. If he contained his action within his own borders he hoped to be able to portray himself as a victim of unwarranted aggression, a stance which might weaken the resolve of the British to renew the campaign. The king was well aware that Lord Chelmsford had accompanied the Centre Column, and news of its action on the 12th January confirmed his impression that it was the strongest and most dangerous of the invading columns.

The king had called up the *amabutho* in the middle of January, leaving small groups drawn from the border communities to watch the British progress. This was, in any case, the time of the *umKhosi* ceremony; but this year the *amabutho* were ordered to gather without their full ceremonial regalia and in readiness for war. The *umKhosi* ceremony was not held that year; instead, the army underwent a modified version of the ritual specifically designed to prepare the *amabutho* for combat. This was an immensely important ceremony which lasted over several days; it was designed to cleanse the nation on the eve of war, to bind the army together, and to ensure the assistance of the spirit world in the coming fight. The army gathered in the several *amakhanda* scattered over the rolling

countryside surrounding Ulundi on the Mahlabatini plain. The ceremony was organised by the nation's greatest war-doctors who, in 1879, included an unknown Sotho doctor.

On the second day of the ceremony the doctors selected a wild black bull from amongst the king's herds, and treated it with medicine thought to have magical properties. One of the younger *amabutho* were ordered to kill the bull with their bare hands; after it was dead the doctors cut the flesh into strips, roasted it and sprinkled it with more medicines. The entire army was then drawn up in a huge circle, and the doctors tossed the strips of meat into the crowd. Each warrior was supposed to catch a piece, bite off a mouthful, then throw it back into the air. The warriors were not supposed to swallow the flesh; but the provisioning arrangements for such ceremonies were usually inadequate, and in the excitement many of the hungry warriors did swallow the meat. Then the doctors prepared more medicine and set fire to it, wafting the smoke over the warriors and spattering them with the ashes. Once this part of the ceremony was complete the army filed down to the banks of the eNtukwini stream, which flows into the White Mfolozi near Ulundi, and, in groups of three or four, were called up by the doctors to vomit into a deep, narrow hole especially dug for the occasion. The vomiting was intended to cast out any lasting evil influences from the individuals, and the vomit was regarded as extremely powerful. A sample was taken to the king and added to the *inkhata*, a grass coil bound in python skin which embodied the unity of the nation; the remainder was carefully buried to prevent any of it reaching the hands of the enemy.

The Sotho doctor paid particular attention to the firearms carried by the warriors. King Shaka had been the first of the Zulu kings to appreciate the value of firearms; although the evidence was carefully concealed by them, it seems that his British clients at Port Natal had supplied him with a limited number of muskets. This clandestine trade had grown during King Dingane's reign, but by the 1840s King Mpande was openly demanding firearms as the price of a concession to hunt and trade in the Zulu country. In the 1860s, during the political uncertainty following the civil war of 1856, Cetshwayo's white friend and advisor, the trader and hunter John Dunn, had imported large numbers of guns to bolster Cetshwayo's cause. Although the practice was officially frowned upon in

A sketch by Charles Fripp, the "special artist" for The Graphic, *who later painted the famous "Last Stand of the 24th at Isandlwana". His sketch of warriors in the field gives an excellent impression, full of accurate detail, of the type of costume and mixture of weapons actually carried into battle in 1879; the smaller* umbhumbhulosu *shields are well conveyed. (Author's collection)*

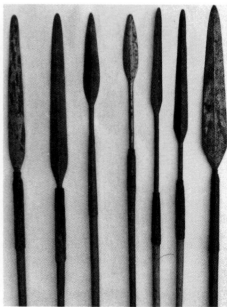

A selection of Zulu spears, most of which date from the 1879 war. Note the broad-bladed stabbing spear (right), and the narrower variants (left); those in the middle are throwing spears. (Author's collection)

Natal firearms were sold illicitly across the borders, while many thousands were imported through Portuguese Delagoa in the north. At one point in the 1870s it was estimated that as many as 10,000 guns a year were shipped into Africa by this route, the majority for the Zulu trade; although the British put diplomatic pressure on the Portuguese to close off this source in 1878, there were undoubtedly thousands already inside the country.

With the rapid advance of firearm technology in Europe, where armies had only recently adopted single-shot breech-loading rifles taking metal cartridges after decades of using muzzle-loaders with percussion cap locks, models soon became obselete; and it was common practice to dump them on unsophisticated markets around the world. Many of the guns in Zululand were old Brown Bess flintlock (or converted percussion action) smoothbore muskets, bearing the Tower mark on the lock; but in the 1870s the much more accurate Enfield percussion rifle (which had proved deadly in the American Civil War, and which had been until recently standard British military issue) could be bought for as little as the cost of a sheep.

Most of the guns were of British or European manufacture, but there were some American and more exotic types. One report in August 1878 suggested that there were as many as 20,000 stands of firearms in Zululand, of which 500 were modern, good quality British breech-loading weapons, a further 2,500 were recent percussion models, 5,000 were older percussion weapons, and the rest were old muskets. A correspondent from the *Natal Witness* examined those taken at the battle of Nyezane on 22nd January, and provides a revealing insight into the variety and quality of guns available to the Zulus at the beginning of the war:

> I saw two Natal guns only, viz. Nos N 5867 and N 9604. Who imported these? . . . There were all sorts of guns. From Potsdam, from Danzig, Mutzig, and Tulle, from "Manchester, N.H., United States" etc. The majority, however, were Tower muskets. The foreign weapons are very ancient indeed; some of them being manufactured in 1835. As far as I could make out by the inscriptions, the continental weapons were condemned army ones. The sights were the most extraordinary contrivances.

Not only were these guns old, but many were in poor condition, and the Zulus had no means of keeping them in good repair. Indeed, they often did not see the need, and the barrels and locks of many were deeply etched with rust. There were no spare parts available, and only the most rudimentary supplies of powder and ammunition. Where proper musket balls were not available they were improvised from stones or likely pieces of metal. The king had Sotho advisers who were able to make powder for him, and maintained a supply of several hundred pounds in a store a few miles from Ulundi, but it was not of the best quality. Nor did many Zulus fully understand their weapons; although there were numbers in the country who had worked with the professional hunting parties that scoured Zululand in the 1850s and '60s, and were competent marksmen, the majority had no training and little experience, and believed rumours which suggested that the higher the sights were set, the further a gun would shoot. In November 1878 the king, who was acutely aware that firepower would prove a deciding factor in the war, had ordered some of his men to practise their marksmanship. When the uVe *ibutho*, the youngest in the army, reported to the muster,

> Cetshwayo came out by the inner gate at 9 a.m. He said, "Is this the whole impi, then? Lift up your guns." We did so. "So there are no guns?" Each man with a beast from his place must bring it up next day and buy guns from Dunn.

In the doctoring ceremony, the Sotho doctor burned his medicines on pot-sherds and the warriors were required to file past, with their guns pointed downwards, so that the smoke wafted up into the barrels. This was intended to make the bullets flow fast and accurately.

Vumandaba kaNtati photographed as a member of the Zulu delegation who received Frere's ultimatum at the Lower Drift on 11th December 1878. An influential councillor, he commanded the uKhandempemvu regiment, which he led at Isandlwana. ("SB" Bourquin)

Prince Ndabuko kaMpande, a younger brother of King Cetshwayo, probably photographed c.1874. He accompanied the army to Isandlwana, and urged the warriors to cross the Mzinyathi in pursuit of the fugitives. ("SB" Bourquin)

Chief Zibhebhu kaMapitha (centre), head of the Mandlakazi Zulu lineage; an important izikhulu *despite his youth, he commanded the* uDloko *regiment. ("SB" Bourquin)*

Once the ceremonies were complete, and the warriors had undergone a short period of exclusion from society, the king called up his favourite *amabutho* in pairs which were of roughly the same age group, and ordered them to challenge one another. Men from each *ibutho* would step out in front of the ranks and boast of the deeds they would commit in the coming fight, while their comrades cheered them on. They would challenge members of the opposite *ibutho*, offering extravagant bets that they could outdo them. A warrior named Mpashana kaSodondo of the uVe has left a detailed account of the ceremony:

> Before the Isandlwana battle the warriors harangued one another about their fighting prowess. The king called up the uKhandempemvu and iNgobamakhosi into the cattle enclosure, he being present, and directed them to challenge one another. A man from the iNgobamakhosi lot got up and shouted "I shall surpass you, son of So-and-So. If you stab a white man before mine has fallen, you may take the kraal of our people at such-and-such a place . . . you may take my sister so-and-so". Having said this he will start leaping about (giyaing) with his small dancing shield and a stick (for assegais are not carried on such occasions in the presence of the king, for it is feared that the troops may stab one another with them). The other who has been addressed may now get up and say "Well, if you can do better than I do, you will take our kraal . . . and my sister". He will then giya. Whilst the giyaing goes on, he is praised by those of his regiment and, if the man happens to be known to the king and is trusted . . . by the king, the king will hold out his arm towards him, pointing the first, or first two fingers at him, and shaking them and the hand approvingly. Many others will do the same in their turn, each again giyaing, and so it goes on until sunset.

A day or two later the uNokhenke and uMbonambi were called to go through the same ceremony.

How large was the Zulu king's army? According to an account carefully compiled to F.B.Fynney, a Natal border agent, at Chelmsford's request, there were over 40,000 men enrolled in *amabutho*, although many of these were too old to fight; the king had ordered a number to remain in their home districts to watch the British, while a few had no doubt refused to muster. In the event the king had perhaps 30,000 men directly available to him. After carefully weighing up the

British movements, he decided to use those men living in the north-west and south-east of the country to harass the approach of Wood's and Pearson's Columns. A detachment of the main army was sent down to the coast to reinforce those opposing Pearson, while two regiments of middle-aged men were kept as a reserve at Ulundi. The king was concerned that the British might try another foray, either from the coast, or through Swaziland in the north; these two regiments might not have provided much protection against a determined attack, but they were all he could spare. The remainder, the main Zulu army, between 20,000 and 25,000 strong and composed of the youngest and fittest men in the country, was sent to attack Lord Chelmsford's Centre Column.

The army moved off on the afternoon of 17th January. As Professor John Laband has pointed out in his masterly analysis of the Zulu army in 1879, it remains difficult to be precise about the composition of the force despite the considerable evidence collected by the British at the time. The Zulus did not necessarily compute an army's strength in terms of complete *amabutho*, but rather in terms of their component companies, which varied from as few as 50 men apiece to as many as two hundred. Many men who lived in the parts of the country threatened by the British stayed to fight with their local forces; elements from some *amabutho* were split between the different fronts. Neverthless, it is possible to say that the uThulwana, iNdluyengwe, iNdlondlo, uDloko, uDududu, iSangqu, iMbube, uNokhenke, uKhandempemvu (also known as the uMcijo), uMbonambi, iNgobamakhosi and uVe *amabutho* were there in strength, together with some companies of the uMxhapho.

The commanders were Chiefs Ntshingwayo kaMahole of the Khoza and Mavumengwana kaNdlela of the Ntuli. Ntshingwayo was nearly 70 years old, an extremely powerful man within the kingdom who sat in the inner circle of the king's council and was commander of the kwaGqikazi *ikhanda*. Mavumengwana was a younger man, the commander of the uThulwana *ibutho* — in which King Cetshwayo himself had served — and the son of Ndlela kaSompisi, who had been King Dingane's chief *induna*. A number of other notables were present with the force, including Zibhebhu kaMapitha, the head of the Mandlakazi, a section of the Zulu clan which traced its descent from King Shaka's uncle; Zibhebhu was the king's cousin. He was an independent and aggressive man who had fostered close links with white traders, and who was an excellent rider and a good shot; he commanded the uDloko. The Princes Ndabuka kaMpande and Dabulamanzi kaMpande represented the Zulu royal house, while Vumandaba kaNtati — one of the king's representatives who had received Frere's ultimatum — commanded the uKhandempemvu. Sihayo may have accompanied the force; his son Mehlokazulu was certainly with his regiment.

Despite the emphasis on firearms, the majority of this great army, which marched out across the Mahlabatini plain late in the afternoon with the uNokhenke in the van, were armed in the traditional Zulu way, and were wedded to a concept of fighting which had hardly changed since Shaka's day. Their principal weapon remained the stabbing spear, a long-bladed, short-hafted weapon designed for wielding underarm at close quarters. The *iklwa*, the prototype weapon introduced by King Shaka, had a fearsome blade some 18 inches long and an inch and a half wide at the base, mounted on a 30-inch haft. By 1879 such impressive weapons were losing their popularity in favour of a number of narrower, shorter-bladed variants, but the stabbing spear remained an extremely effective weapon under the right circumstances. It was wielded in practised harmony with the movements of the big leather shield (see below), recalling the classic combat technique of the ancient Roman legionary with his shortsword.

Most men also carried one or two lighter throwing spears, *izijula*, with smaller blades. Zulu males had been accustomed to throwing weapons in their daily lives from childhood, when a favourite game involved throwing sticks at a target rolled down a hillside; throwing spears were also used extensively for hunting. In flight the weapon could achieve considerable velocity, and it must have been able to transfix a human target easily; on the whole, however, the British were unimpressed. Evelyn Wood, who enlivened his men's routine with the occasional sports day, once organised a spear-throwing competition; he was disappointed to find that it was won by a Koi man from the Cape, who reached a distance of 70 yards,

"while no Zulu threw an assegai farther than 50 yards." British medical staff found that providing no vital organs were damaged, spear-thrusts left clean wounds which could be healed easily. Some men would also have carried knobkerries — *iwisa*, a stout stick with a round, polished club end — and a few may have had axes of Pedi or Swazi design, with "winged" blades set on a tang into a wooden haft.

Each warrior carried the characteristic oval cow-hide war shield of the Zulu. These shields were the property of the state rather than the individual, and were kept in special stores in the *amakhanda* to be issued only when an *ibutho* mustered for duty. In King Shaka's time each *ibutho* was required to tend a herd of cattle, carefully selected according to the colour of their hides, and from these hides in due course it made its shields. The original Shakan shield, the *isihlangu*, was as much as five feet tall by 30 inches wide, and was designed to shelter a warrior from chin to ankles. By 1879 most *isihlangu* shields were perhaps six inches smaller all round; and a smaller type of shield was, in any case, more popular. This was the *umbhumbulosu*, which had been introduced by King Cetshwayo amongst his followers in the civil war of 1856, and was about 40 inches long by 20 inches wide. Both shields do seem to have been carried, even within the same regiment, but the *isihlangu* was probably confined to older, more conservative men.

The practice of differentiating between the *amabutho* by shield colours was also dying away; in Shaka's time regimental shields had very specific, and often quite subtle colour variations, and in general, even in 1879, senior *amabutho* carried white shields while younger regiments carried black and spotted shields. It is a frustrating business trying to determine some of these colours; surviving examples are often poorly documented, whilst contemporary evidence is contradictory and clearly fragmentary. In some cases it is possible to suggest that particular colours were associated with a particular *ibutho*; on other occasions, some regiments seem to have carried shields of no uniform colour whatsoever. It may be that the

Chief Ntshingwayo kaMahole of the Khoza, probably the most senior Zulu general, who fought with the main army throughout the war of 1879. The younger man standing behind him with a knobkerry, not identified in the original caption, bears a strong resemblance to Mehlokazulu kaSihayo. (Royal Commonwealth Society)

Sicwelecwele kaMhlekehleke of the Ngadini, the senior commander of the iNgobamakhosi ibutho; he fought at Isandlwana. ("SB" Bourquin)

Mehlokazulu kaSihayo Ngobese, photographed with Border Police guards after his arrest at the end of the war. His violation of Natal's border in June 1878 had been one of the pretexts for the British ultimatum; he was an officer in the iNgobamakhosi, and fought at Isandlwana, Khambula and Ulundi. ("SB" Bourquin)

epidemic of bovine pleuro-pneumonia which decimated the royal herds following Cetshwayo's great coronation cattle review in 1874 had made it impossible to maintain the old colour-matching system.

It is possible to be a little more definite with regard to the costume worn by the *amabutho* in the Isandlwana campaign. The lavish ceremonial uniforms worn on festive occasions were expensive and fragile, and the king ordered his men to report to the muster without them. Most men probably wore little more than the everyday loin-covering, the *umutsha*, with a square of soft hide, the *ibeshu*, over the buttocks. Some probably retained cow-tail ornaments around their arms and legs; and many would have worn pouches of animal or snake-skin filled with medicine, and small blocks of wood burnt at the edges, tied to a thong around the neck as charms to ward off evil. Some perhaps wore stuffed headbands of otter or leopard-skin around their foreheads; and many would have carried snuff-spoons in their hair or earlobes, and snuff containers made from horns or gourds hanging round their necks. Commanders may well have worn specific items to identify themselves, such as the tall tail feathers of the blue crane, or bunches of waxy scarlet and green lourie feathers, both of which were marks of rank. On the whole, the older men probably retained more regalia than their younger counterparts, who made up the bulk of the army.

If the army followed its usual practice, it would have been followed on the first day or two by boys between the ages of about 14 and 18; these *udibi*, together with some female members of the warriors' families, carried the men's food supplies and mats. After that the warriors would have to fend for themselves. An army usually moved in a single column until it approached the enemy, when it would divide in two. A body of selected scouts then screened the advance; these men were chosen for their courage and stamina, and often moved in quite large groups so as to confuse the enemy into thinking that they were part of the main army. A few individuals would be sent out ahead of this vanguard to spy out the enemy's movements.

When committed to battle, the whole force would draw up in a circle, *mkhumbi*, to observe the last rituals and to hear the commanders' instructions. Then they would move out to the attack, taking up an encircling formation dating from Shaka's time, the *impondo zankomo* or "beast's horns". The regiments

of younger, fitter men formed two wings or "horns", *izim-pondo*, which rushed out to surround the enemy on either flank. A stronger body, *isifuba*, often formed of more senior men, launched a head-on frontal assault. A reserve, the *umuva* or "loins", was kept at hand to plug any gaps. Senior commanders did not often lead their men in battle, but observed from some convenient eminence, communicating orders by runners and signals.

An unknown warrior of the uNokhenke, who subsequently deserted to the British, confirmed that the Zulus did not significantly depart from their normal order of march in 1879:

> We accordingly left Nodwengu late in the afternoon, and marched in column to the west bank of the [White Mfolozi], about six miles distant, where we bivouacked for the night. Next day we marched to the [isiPhezi] military kraal, about nine miles off, where we slept; and on the 19th we ascended the table-land near the Isihlungu hills, a march of about equal duration with that of the previous day. On this day the army, which had hitherto been marching in a single column, divided in two, marching parallel to and within sight of each other, that on the left consisting of the [uNokhenke, uMcijo and Nodwengu] regiments, under the command of [Ntshingwayo], the other commanded by [Mavumengwana]. There were a few mounted men belonging to the chief [Sihayo] who were used as scouts.

The army was almost certainly the largest ever fielded by the old Zulu kingdom. Five months later Captain William Molyneux, serving with the British forces then closing in on Ulundi, saw where it had passed: "The track was as plain as if lately made, the long grass trodden down in one direction into the mud, just as if a huge roller had been passed over it."

On the night of 20th January the army bivouacked on the northern slopes of Siphezi mountain; on the 21st it passed north of Chelmsford's patrols, moving in small detachments, and took up a position in the Ngwebeni valley, nestling under the steep, rocky slope of the Mabaso heights which separated it from the Nyoni escarpment. Once the march was underway the army was provisioned by foraging parties which scoured the countryside along the route; most Zulu civilians had fled to inaccessible parts of the country on the British approach, and the grain pits of their deserted homesteads provided a welcome source of food for the army.

With so many small parties inevitably moving along on the fringes of the army, it does seem extraordinary that such a large force managed to move to within five or six miles of the

British camp and escape detection. The countryside around Siphezi is generally open, and even given the Zulu capacity for concealment in the slightest dead ground it would seem unlikely that British patrols would not have stumbled on it had they been sent in that direction. Twice, indeed, the Zulus thought they had been discovered; on one occasion a patrol saw part of the army in the open, but apparently failed to realise its significance — which patrol this was remains obscure. On another occasion a mounted patrol was chased away by Chief Zibhebhu kaMapitha, who was in charge of the Zulu scouts — this was presumably Lieutenant Browne's patrol, which Walsh knew had been fired upon, as he told Norris-Newman so on the Hlazakazi heights later that night. What really saved the *impi*, however, was Dartnell's encounter on the afternoon of the 21st, which confirmed Chelmsford's opinion that the Mangeni valley was the main source of danger, and distracted him from his intention to scout the hills to the north of Isandlwana.

One question which continues to intrigue historians is whether or not the men encountered by Dartnell on the 21st were part of a grand plan to lure Chelmsford out from Isandlwana and split his force. While admitting that there is little enough evidence to prove the point either way, Professor Laband thinks it likely. A warrior named uGuku of the uKhandempemvu had this to say on the subject:

> It was intended that Matshana kaMondisa was to be chief in command, but having been a Natal [African], the other three were jealous of him, and did not like him to be put over them; they therefore devised a plan of getting him out of the way on the day of the battle. They accomplished this plan by getting him to go forward with Undwandwe to the [Phindo hill] to reconnoitre, and promised to follow. As soon as he had gone they took another road, north of Babanango, while Matshana and Ndwandwe went south of it, accompanied by six [companies].

As an ordinary warrior, there is no reason why uGuku would have been privy to the decisions of the Zulu high command, and the jealousies he cites as the cause for the spilt in the forces — not necessarily implausible in themselves — may have been an outsider's view of a more complex tactical decision. Yet there are problems with this interpretation; it is extremely unlikely that King Cetshwayo would have given a command as important as this to anyone outside his immediate trusted circle. Matshana may well have been brought in because of his local knowledge; perhaps he was scouting out a possible route, one of many, to approach the British. On the whole, however, it seems more likely that the movements were unco-ordinated. Certainly the Zulus showed no such subtlety in later battles during the war; the army simply advanced on the British positions, and attacked. Most of the Zulus captured by Chelmsford's force on the morning of the 22nd seem to have been local men — who, as Symons recalled, claimed to have "heard the British were in the area, and came to see." Of course, they may simply have been unaware of a wider strategy; most of them seemed to have been trying to fall back on Siphezi when intercepted, however, and Russell noted that Siphezi was a natural stronghold. They were not trying to join the main *impi*, or indeed trying to lure Chelmsford onto the army hidden in the Ngwebeni valley. If a broader strategy had been planned, most of the warriors in the main *impi* were unaware of it; they fought at Isandlwana without making any provision for the troops in their rear, and most were shocked to find later that a portion of the British force had escaped the attack.

Furthermore, there is some confusion about the Zulu intentions on the 22nd. The king had apparently ordered his commanders to make one last attempt to negotiate with the British before attacking them. While this seems naive in retrospect, consultations on the eve of battle were not unknown, and it is possible that the Zulu commanders were hanging back, at least until they had a clear idea of the British

intentions. In any case, it was widely known amongst the army that the night of the 22nd/23rd was the new moon; the moon was "dead", an inauspicious omen for the day of battle. The army was apparently preparing to spend the 22nd resting quietly — the warriors lit their usual campfires, but were told to put them out for fear of giving away their position. If Matshana's movements were a carefully planned decoy, his timing was incompetent.

An eclipse of the sun, the night of the new moon: it seems as if nature itself was conspiring to make 22nd January 1879 a memorable day.

The army camped with the uDududu *ibutho* on the extreme right, towards the west, followed in succession by the iMbube, iSangqu, uNokhenke, uKhandempemvu, uMbonambi, iNgobamakhosi, uVe, iNdluyengwe, uThulwana, uDloko, and, on the extreme left, the iNdlondlo *amabutho*. The dense masses of warriors were such an extraordinary sight that the Ngwebeni valley is still known to some local Zulus as Makheni — "the place of shields". In the morning the army heard the sound of distant firing, and the rumour spread among the uKhandempemvu regiment that the iNgobamakhosi were engaged. The uKhandempemvu and some elements of the uNokhenke clambered up the steep slope in front of them, and moved out, unsupported, across the heights to investigate. It was probably this move, which apparently continued until the regiment reached the Nyoni ridge and could see for themselves that no battle was taking place — that the firing was coming from the direction of the Mangeni — which caused the first alarm at Isandlwana. When the uKhandempemvu saw Durnford's men ride into camp they fell back to the gorge. They remained hidden for another hour, until George Shepstone, Charles Raw, Nyanda and their men put an end to all hopes of concealment until the 23rd.

That first extraordinary contact made as much impression on the silent warriors as it did upon Zikhali's Horse. Said the warrior of the uNokhenke:

> Just after we had sat down again, a small herd of cattle came past our line from our right, being driven down by some of our scouts, and just when they were opposite to the [uMcijo] regiment, a body of mounted men, on the hill to the west, were seen galloping, evidently trying to cut them off. When several hundred yards off, they perceived the [uMcijo], and, dismounting, fired one volley at them and then retired. The [uMcijo] at once jumped up and charged . . .

It was perhaps 11.45 on the morning of Wednesday 22nd January 1879, and the battle of Isandlwana had begun.

The original caption of this 1930s photograph desribed this man as a veteran of Isandlwana. Since he is wearing the prized iziqu, the necklace made of interlocking beads of willow wood granted by the king to regiments which distinguished themselves in a specific battle, this is undoubtedly correct. (Killie Campbell Africana Library)

CHAPTER SEVEN

Isandlwana

It is one of the clichés of the military historian's art that the material with which he must reconstruct the events he studies is essentially obscured by the fog of war. Few battles seem to their participants to proceed in the logical sequence of action and reaction which they present when re-told on the written page; and the perception of officers direct-ing events is very different from that of the men in the ranks. In action a man's attention is totally preoccupied by the confusing and often terrifying events immediately around him. He is often aware only of the men on either side of him, and of those facing him. He may have only the dimmest recollection of other troop movements nearby — he may not be aware even of whose side they were on — and he is unlikely to have anything but the haziest awareness of topographical features. After the event the mind inevitably rearranges the jumble of intense, perhaps traumatic impressions into a logical sequence which they did not necessarily follow in the white-hot chaos of the moment. Even the act of analysing and describing a battle years later, of weighing up the evidence and seeking explanations for the decisions taken and the reactions displayed, imparts a certain dignity and rationality which is often at odds with the events themselves.

All of this is particularly true of Isandlwana, where, to complicate matters still further, all the most valuable evidence is missing, and the earliest reconstructions are littered with ommissions and contradictions. None of the senior British officers who were taking major command decisions survived; one has to try to reconstruct something of their thinking from the accounts of men who were often only involved on the periphery, and who did not always understand what they were seeing. It is like trying to discern the picture in a jig-saw puzzle when only a few pieces from the outside edges survive. Above all, it should be remembered that the battle happened very quickly: from the time Raw's men discovered the *impi* in the Ngwebeni valley to the time the Zulus took the camp it probably lasted only about two and a half hours. The battle of Isandlwana was over and done in less time than it takes to read about it. It was, in short, a bloody shambles.

* * *

In that electric moment when Raw's men appeared over the lip of the Mabaso heights, the uKhandempemvu regiment below them knew instantly that there could be no more waiting on propitious omens. They rose up immediately and charged up the steep slope in front of them, and the *amabutho* on either side streamed out of the more open ends of the valley to support them. It was a completely spontaneous movement; if Ntshingwayo and Mavumengwana had already made plans to attack they had not communicated them to their men, nor had they time to observe the final doctoring ceremonies and address the men. In fact they rushed forward to try to restrain the regiments and impose some sense of order on them. They were unable to restrain any but the regiments on the far left, however (the uNdi *amabutho*), and even then some impetuous elements such as Qethuka kaManqondo, an *induna* of the uThulwana, broke away to join the rush. The father of young Muziwento was amongst the Zulu ranks, and his son con-veyed something of the confusion of those first few minutes: 'The Zulu generals forbad [an advance], seeking to help the white men. But the regimental officers simply mutinied. They

marched forward; they went into battle. They . . . were rolled along together towards Isandlwana."

Zikhali's Ngwane riders dismounted and fired a volley into the Zulu ranks, knocking over a few warriors but making no impression on their advance, before mounting up again and beginning to fall back before them. The Zulus returned their fire. Barry's infantry company (Pakhade's Mchunu of No.5 Company, 2/3rd NNC) were close in support of Raw; but they took one look at the masses surging out of the valley, and fled — their officers were left alone to fight alongside the Ngwane. The seriousness of the situation was immediately apparent to Shepstone, who ordered Nyanda to make a fight-ing retreat to draw the Zulus towards the camp. Then, accom-panied by a friend (a civilian conductor named Hamer), he rode back to Isandlwana to warn Pulleine.

He had just arrived in the camp when he met the interpreter Brickhill, and asked him if he knew Pulleine's whereabouts; Brickhill took him to the Column Headquarters, and just as they reached it they encountered Captain Alan Gardner. Gardner had brought Chelmsford's order to break up the camp and move it to the Mangeni; he had left the officers who had come in with him somewhere in the camp, and they had gone off to rejoin their units. Gardner delivered the General's message, but Shepstone broke in with, "I'm not an alarmist, sir, but the Zulu are in such black masses over there, such long black lines that you have to give us all the assistance you can. They are now fast driving our men this way." While they were speaking some of Zikhali's men came into sight on the high ground to the left of the camp, falling back and firing. It was a crucial moment of decision for Pulleine — in effect, it was his first taken under combat conditions. He seemed undecided; Brickhill, indeed, thought that he looked thor-oughly perplexed. Up to that moment the general opinion had been that there was no serious threat to the camp. Curling of the Royal Artillery commented later that he had seen equally large bodies of warriors on the Cape Frontier, and never dreamed the Zulus would attack; the prevailing opinion was that "the enemy had no intention of advancing during the daytime, but might possibly be expected to attack during the night. No idea had been formed regarding the probable strength of the enemy's force".

Seeing Pulleine hesitate, Gardner said: "Under the circum-stances I should advise you disobeying the General's order, for the present at any rate. The General knows nothing of this, he is only thinking of the cowardly way in which the Zulus are running before our troops over yonder." Pulleine and Gardner then walked out of Brickhill's hearing, so any comments Pulleine may then have made are lost to us; shortly after this, however, Pulleine sent the message to Chelmsford in reply, reporting that as heavy firing could be heard from the hills to the left, he could not move camp *at present*. This was a very reasonable response under the circumstances, but upon consi-deration Gardner felt that the note was not detailed enough, and sent another after it:

Heavy firing near left of camp. Shepstone has come in for reinforcements and reports the Basutos falling back the whole force turned out and firing about 1 mile to left flank. Alan Gardner, Captain.

This note did not reach Gosset until 3 p.m. that afternoon.

Having presumably received some assurance of support,

Shepstone and Hamer rode back to join their men. Brickhill, who had no rifle, went off to find one, and when he failed to do so he took himself to the slope just above the middle of the camp to watch the fight. Unfortunately no-one witnessed any subsequent discussions between Pulleine and his Adjutant or officers, so we have no idea what plans he was making at this stage.

The 24th were, however, ordered to stand-to once more, and they formed up in columns in front of the camp. Curling's detachment of two 7-pdr. guns had remained limbered since the first alarms of the morning, and were ready to go into action. Krohn's No.6 Company, 1/3rd NNC, was drawn up in front of the Native Contingent camp. If Captain O. Murray's two NNC companies (sent back by Hamilton-Browne the night before) were in the camp no-one mentioned them, but it is possible that they also fell in in front of the NNC tents.

Apart from the Ngwane horse there were two other companies posted out from the camp. J.F. Lonsdale's No.9 Company, 1/3rd NNC, was out on the low stony ridge which separated the Mpofane and Nyogane dongas, directly east of the camp and about a thousand yards from it. It is possible that they were on the forward slope of the ridge, where it drops down towards the Nyogane; certainly Brickhill, who was in a commanding position, commented that he could see little of what was happening out on the line because of the low-lying ground. Perhaps this partly explains the traditional confusion about the part played by the NNC at Isandlwana; this, and the fact that Regular soldiers had no great opinion of black levies and tended to ignore them.

Captain Cavaye's E Company, 1/24th was deployed to the north of the camp. A sloping spur ran north from below the tail of Isandlwana, ending in Mkwene hill, a high point on the western end of the Nyoni ridge. To the left the hills curled round behind Isandlwana, and Cavaye's men had disappeared out of sight towards the west of the spur. After a while an increase in the sound of firing indicated that they, too, were engaged.

At this stage nothing was visible from the camp beyond some of Zikhali's men falling back, and perhaps some of Barry's men in flight. It must have seemed that the attack was developing on a very specific front — from the north, above the spur — and Pulleine reacted accordingly. He sent another company of the 1/24th, Captain Mostyn's F Company, out to support Cavaye. Mostyn's men had only marched into Isandlwana the day before on their way up from Pietermaritzburg: they were in luck, it seemed — they had arrived in time to see the fun . . . At about the same time as Mostyn's men set off towards the spur, Curling's artillery detachment was sent out to a position on the left front, in front of the NNC camp. Just as they were setting off Major Smith, who had come in with Gardner, joined them and took over command. The guns trotted out about 400 yards, and unlimbered facing the hills to the north. At this stage they were unsupported, the rest of Pulleine's men still being in front of the camp. Shortly afterwards, however, one of the 24th companies was sent out to take up a position behind the guns.

Captain Edward Essex of the 75th (Stirlingshire) Regiment, a special service officer who had been appointed Glyn's Director of Transport, had retired to his tent after the alarms of the morning, and was busy writing letters when:

> About noon a sergeant came into my tent and told me that firing was to be heard behind the hill where the company of the 1st Battalion 24th had been sent. I had my glasses over my shoulder and thought I might as well take my revolver; but did not trouble to put on my sword, as I thought nothing of the matter and expected to be back in half an hour to complete my letters. I got on my horse and galloped up the hill, passing a company of the 24th on its way to the front . . .

Mostyn, who was on foot, asked Essex to take a message to Cavaye, telling him to look out for his right flank, as Mostyn

Captain Edward "Lucky" Essex, 75th Regiment, Glyn's Director of Transport, who fought with the 24th at Isandlwana and was one of the five Imperial officers to survive. (Ministry of Defence)

intended to take up a position on his left. This is an interesting remark, since it implies that such a disposition had been planned in advance. As he rode up the slope Essex could see the Ngwane falling back, but nothing of Cavaye's E Company or the Zulus until he crested the ridge. Below him, Cavaye's men could then be seen spread out to the left in extended order, with a detached section under Second-Lieutenant Dyson 500 yards further to the left. They were firing across a low valley at a long column of Zulus who were making their way across their front, from right to left, on the opposite slope about 800 yards away. The Zulus were in impressive formation: "their line was about 1,000 yards in extent, but arranged like a horn — that is, very thin and extended on their right, but gradually thickening towards ours. They did not advance, but moved steadily towards our left, each man running from rock to rock, for the ground here was covered with large boulders, with the evident intention of outflanking us." The Zulus were coming round from behind Mkwene hill, which blocked their reserve from the infantry's sight, but there seemed no end to the enemy masses: "they skirmished very beautifully, and I saw that very few, considering we now had about 3,000 opposed to us, were hit". As Mostyn's men came up they formed up in the gap between Cavaye and Dyson. Essex was well known to the men of the 24th, and he now assumed the duties of a company officer, cheering the men on, directing their fire, and encouraging them not to waste ammunition. The Zulus were returning their fire, but Essex noticed that most of their shots fell short or whistled over the men's heads. Essex was also aware that there were some black infantry on his right; he "did not notice the latter much; except that they blazed away at an absurd rate".

It is a shame that he did not pay more attention to these men, as it would be very useful to know who they were. It is possible that they were Barry's men, who may have rallied on the spot where they had been on picquet duty the night before; but Higginson's report suggests otherwise. Higginson had been ordered by Durnford to follow the Ngwane men up onto the plateau, and he had reached the heights, with Sergeant-Major Williams of Krohn's company, just in time to see the Ngwane fall back before the Zulu advance. Higginson left Williams with Barry and rode back to the camp, where he rejoined his company. Not long afterwards Williams came in,

*Captain James Faunce Lonsdale,
whose No.9 Company, 1/3rd NNC,
was on picquet duty east of the camp
on the morning of the 22nd.
(Author's collection)*

bringing both Barry and Lieutenant Vereker with him. Both men seem to have lost their horses, and Williams had let them take turn about on his. The implication of this, surely, is that Barry's men had fled completely by that stage, and that their officers no longer felt any obligation to remain on the ridge. So, if the NNC men to Essex's right were not No.5 Company, 2/3rd, the most likely alternative is that they were Captain Erskine's No.4 Company of the same battalion. The only other possibility is that they might have been the companies under Captain Murray which Hamilton-Browne had sent in from Hlazakazi the night before.

When the Ngwane had retreated to the foot of the escarpment they found that their remaining troop, No.3 under Lieutenant Wyatt Vause, had come out to reinforce them, together with about 50 men of Captain Stafford's E Company, 1/1st NNC. Stafford's early account suggests that he came into camp once the fighting had started; and a longer account written half a century later, while a little confused, suggests that he arrived in camp before Durnford left. He reported hearing Durnford's conversation with Pulleine about the command of the camp. Durnford ordered him to distribute ammunition to his men, and some time later he was sent out to the left — by whose order is not clear. Vause certainly arrived in the camp after the fighting had already started, and rode out to the left in the hope of finding Durnford. Instead he met Shepstone, who ordered him to dismount his troop and reinforce Roberts' and Raw's men, who were at the bottom of the slope firing at parties of Zulus who were beginning to move down the slope towards them.

At this point there must have been some danger of Mostyn and Cavaye's men being outflanked, since any Zulus descending the spur to their right could conceivably have cut them off from the camp; but Essex does not seem to have been aware of this, and it may be that the crest of the ridge cut off the view of both parties. Leaving their horses in a donga, the Ngwane men advanced back up the slope on foot in skirmishing order, driving the Zulus before them. In the ranks of the uKhandempemvu the warrior uGuku remembered this phase of the battle: "the engagement now became very hot between the Mangwane . . . and us, the Mangwane being supported by the infantry, who were some distance to their rear. We were now falling very fast. The Mangwane had put their horses in a donga, and were firing away at us on foot."

The advance of Stafford's NNC company up the slope must have taken place at about the time the Ngwane counterattacked, and indeed this may have been orchestrated by Shepstone, who was clearly directing operations among this section of Durnford's column. Stafford fell in to the west of the British line: "I was placed on the extreme left of the ridge. Essex was next to me, and next to him was Wyatt Vause." By this time Stafford — who, incidentally, is one of the few who

refers to Captain W.Barton being present with the mounted men at this stage — estimated the number of Zulus to their front at about 2,000. As his men came into action Stafford's *induna*, Ntini, came to him and asked him how to regulate the sights of his rifle. Stafford set the sights at 700 yards and fired a shot which fell short. He adjusted it to 800 yards, "and that bullet struck amongst them."

It is interesting to note that even at this stage the line resembled Chelmsford's preferred defensive formation: infantry in the centre, auxiliaries and mounted men on either flank. Having no very clear idea of the Zulu numbers, it is quite possible that the 24th were fighting Isandlwana as another Nyamaga. It is also possible that the other mounted force in the camp — the mixture of Volunteers and Mounted Infantry left in camp under Captain Robert Bradstreet of the Newcastle Mounted Rifles — moved up the escarpment at this time. Brickhill claimed to have seen them near the Native Horse and the guns, at the foot of the hills, but the time of this is uncertain, and Malindi, a soldier in J.F.Lonsdale's NNC company, saw them pass up the slope to his left about the time Mostyn ascended.

At this point, the full strength of the Zulu army was still not apparent. The men passing in front of Mostyn and Cavaye were the uNokhenke regiment who formed the right of the Zulu centre. On their immediate left were the uKhandempemvu; these two regiments had outstripped the rest of their army in pursuit of the Ngwane. It seems that so far only the advanced guard had reached the escarpment, since the Ngwane had no trouble in dispersing them. Once back on the heights again, however, Raw noticed that the Zulu numbers were steadily increasing, being fed by dense masses coming up behind. The attack appeared to be directed to the left of the Ngwane position, and Raw turned his men slightly to meet it. Until now no Zulus had appeared on the left of the uKhandempemvu, but at about this time parties began to appear on the Nyoni ridge.

It soon became clear, indeed, that the position on the hills was too exposed. The concentrated fire of the entire line did not seem to be slowing the Zulu advance at all; and both Raw, whose men were the first to be engaged, and Vause, whose

NE HILL

NYONI RIDGE

AMATUTSHANE
(CONICAL KOPPIE)

ITUSI

APPROXIMATE LINE OF INFANTRY

GUNS?

NGOYANE DONGA

MPOFANE DONGA

OLD ROAD — PROBABLY PASSED
ABOVE DURNFORD'S STAND

DURNFORD'S
STAND

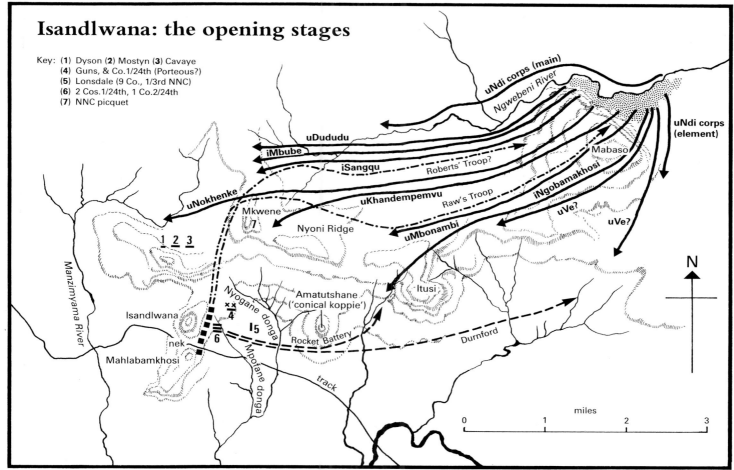

Isandlwana: the opening stages

Key: (1) Dyson (2) Mostyn (3) Cavaye
(4) Guns, & Co.1/24th (Porteous?)
(5) Lonsdale (9 Co., 1/3rd NNC)
(6) 2 Cos.1/24th, 1 Co.2/24th
(7) NNC picquet

men had not paused on their way through the camp to top up their supply, were running short of ammunition. Not long after Mostyn's men had come into action — Essex thought it was only five minutes, but it was probably more — Lieutenant Melvill rode up with an order from Pulleine. The Zulus were developing a fresh attack along the Nyoni ridge to the right, and the men on the spur were in danger of being cut off. They were to retreat to the bottom of the escarpment.

This retreat took place in some disorder, but the men recovered themselves well at the bottom of the slope. Essex became separated from the main body, and found himself descending a particularly steep slope on his own; by the time he reached the bottom Mostyn and Cavaye's companies were formed up again at the foot. Nyanda remembered that Zikhali's Horse "retreated to the bottom of the hill, mixed up with the company of the Red Coats that had supported us."

Roberts' troop apparently came down by a deserted homestead with the Zulus close behind them, and were accidentally struck by covering fire from the artillery. Stafford heard that Roberts himself had been killed; Vause wrote that he last saw Roberts shortly before the retreat, and this has often been taken to refer to a later stage in the battle, but in fact does not necessarily contradict Stafford. Bradstreet's men must also have fallen back about this time. A retreat in the face of the enemy is always dangerous to morale, and it proved too much for Stafford's NNC company; many of them simply threw down their shields and spears and fled. At the bottom of the hill Essex noted that Captain Reginald Younghusband's C Company, 1/24th had been drawn up in echelon a little way to the left rear of Mostyn and Cavaye, presumably to cover their retreat. The uKhandempemvu, encouraged by the sight of the men falling back before them, shouted the particular war-cry of their regiment, *"Izulu!"*, and pressed forward to seize the abandoned ridge. From there they began to descend the escarpment.

Major Stuart Smith's guns had opened fire at a range of 3,400 yards, firing shrapnel over the heads of the Ngwane at the Zulu masses appearing on the skyline. This was at the extreme limit of the 7-pdr.'s effective range, and it is unlikely that they did much damage. After they had been in action for some minutes, according to Curling, "the 1st Battalion of the 24th Regiment soon came up and extended in skirmishing order on both flanks and in line with us." Neither Curling nor anyone else identifies these companies, but Pulleine had only two companies of the 1/24th still available to him: Lieutenant Porteous' A Company and Captain Wardell's H Company. One of them (presumably Porteous') had been lying in support of the guns, and passed a little way to the left as Wardell's came up and deployed to the right. In the camp, Higginson had heard Pulleine order give the order "March all of the men out of the camp who can carry arms"; he was presumably making a fresh deployment to cover the retreat of the men on the ridge, and to meet the new Zulu threat which Melvill had described to Essex.

Lieutenant Charlie Pope's G Company of the 2/24th, perhaps enlarged by the number of unattached men of the 2nd Battalion in the camp, also seems to have marched out at about this time, moving further to the right and extending across the boulder-strewn ground at the head of the two dongas facing north. With J.F.Lonsdale's No.9 Company, 1/3rd NNC, still in position to their right rear, Pulleine had thus formed a new line at the foot of the hills. On the extreme left was Younghusband's C Company, 1/24th; then Mostyn and Cavaye; then, according to Raw, "a company of [Rupert] Lonsdale's footmen". Once again it is difficult to be sure who these men were, but Lieutenant Wally Erskine of Stafford's E Company, 1/1st NNC, who came into camp at the head of the wagon-guard at about this time, marched up to join them, and noted that they were Pakhade's men; most probably, therefore, they were Captain C.A. Erskine's No. 4 Company, 2/3rd NNC. Next to the NNC were the Ngwane, then, apparently, Porteous' Company, Smith's guns, Wardell, and Pope. Lonsdale's men were, in effect, in echelon behind Pope's right flank, and once again the line is similar to the formation prescribed by Chelmsford's standing orders.

* * *

Beyond Lonsdale's company to the east there was nothing but the open plain, and Durnford's men disappearing in the distance. Durnford had ridden out of the camp at the head of the Edendale and amaHlongwe BaSotho troops, and had ordered Captain Francis Russell's Rocket Battery to follow behind with an escort of Captain Cracroft Nourse's D Company, 1/1st NNC. Russell's rockets were loaded on pack-

mules; his command consisted of Bombardier Gough of the Royal Artillery and nine men seconded from the ever-adaptable 1/24th. The ground was difficult, however, seamed with dongas and strewn with boulders, and Durnford's men had inevitably drawn ahead. They were moving parallel to the Nyoni heights, and when they passed round the bulk of the Itusi shoulder they turned slightly north and disappeared from sight. Russell and his escort were left alone on the plain.

The Rocket Battery was a cumbersome apparatus, consisting of three metal troughs firing 9-pdr. Hales' rockets. The rockets themselves were infamously inaccurate; they were sighted by the elevation of the trough, which was supported by a tripod contraption which needed to be set on flat ground to work effectively. The rockets themselves had no stabilising mechanism beyond three crude flanges which deflected the jet and imparted a spinning motion in flight. If they struck any obstacle in the course of their trajectory they were liable to bounce off at totally unpredictable angles; they had even been known to fly back towards their own crew. They were fired by means of a friction tube inserted into one of the jet-vents. This was attached to a lanyard, and the man firing was supposed to lay the lanyard under his foot, then launch the rocket by giving it a sharp tug — an operation which cannot have markedly improved its already dubious accuracy. Even if the rocket did land on target there was no guarantee that it would explode, since it carried no detonating warhead. The rockets did, however, give off a truly fearsome screech in flight, vomiting out smoke and fat yellow sparks, and it was generally considered that they would have an immense psychological impact on "unsophisticated" enemies.

Russell's battery had not long passed Amatushane, the Conical Koppie, and were about a mile and a half from the camp, some two miles behind Durnford's men, when they met Troopers Barker and Hawkins of the Carbineers. After the Zulus had retreated from the heights earlier in the day Lieutenant Scott had pushed his vedettes out again to follow their movements. Barker and Hawkins had gone up onto the hills again, possibly as far as Mabaso and within sight of the Ngwebeni valley; Barker claimed that they had seen "a large army sitting down" on a hill about 600 yards in front of them. The Zulus began to advance slowly, and the vedettes fell back before them. They had ridden down the heights, and were heading back towards Lieutenant Scott's position when they met Russell. By now the sound of distant firing could be heard off to the left, and Russell asked them if he could get his battery up onto Itusi; Barker and Hawkins advised him to return to join Lieutenant Scott. Russell, however, decided to press on in any case; presumably, in the best military tradition, he was "advancing towards the sound of the guns", though some of his command thought they were heading either to join Zikhali's men or taking a short cut to Durnford.

Russell, who was mounted, had ridden on ahead, with his command straggling behind, when he must have caught sight of warriors appearing on the crest above him, and he turned and shouted "Action front!". The battery set up the troughs as quickly as possible, and had time to fire one rocket, which passed over the heads of the warriors who were streaming down a gully on their left. (In 1882 the traveller Bertram Mitford met one of these warriors; the man "was marked about the chest and shoulders as if he had been tatooed with Chinese white" as a result of being struck by the sparks). The rocket overshot its target, however; the Zulus, showing no obvious signs of terror, immediately fired a volley from some rocks about a hundred yards away, and Russell's command promptly fell apart. Two of the mules tumbled over a boulder in panic and were killed, and the rest bolted. Nourse's NNC company fired a few shots, and one of the battery crew,

The rocky rise or knoll between the dongas, where the right of the 24th firing line was secured during the battle. The boulders provided ample cover for men kneeling or lying down to fire; but the line was a long way out from the camp. (Author's photograph)

Private Johnson of the 24th, noticed that several of them were having trouble extracting the cartridges after firing. He offered to help them, but the men threw down their weapons and ran. Nourse himself had lost his horse in the confusion, and could do nothing to rally his men; "from that moment I saw no more of them with the exception of five who remained with me." Private Grant thought Russell himself was killed in the first volley, but Johnson said that he was only wounded; as Johnson tried to help him away another shot struck him and he was killed. The surviving members of the battery then made off after the Contingent men, heading back towards the camp.

It is difficult to say at what time the battery was overwhelmed; it was probably before the Ngwane men retired down the spur, at about the same time that Cavaye's company first came into action. The Zulus who overwhelmed the battery were apparently the advanced guard of the iNgobamakhosi; they had apparently taken the shortest route from Mabaso to the lip of the Nyoni, and had struck a notch to the west of Itusi where a donga has cut into the slope. Rushing down this, they encountered Russell just as he was coming up. They did not make a determined attempt to follow up their success, however, as they were clearly unsupported by the main body; Nourse and the five of his men who stayed with him were able to keep them at bay, although four out of those five were eventually killed. This fight was still going on when Durnford and his men rode back round the foot of Itusi.

Durnford's men had ridden out about four miles from the camp, following the curve of the heights to their left, which then blocked off the view of the camp. They had come within sight of another low ridge to the front when two Carbineers rode up, sent by Lieutenant Scott with a message. Harry Davies, the Lieutenant with the Edendale men, recalled:

> The message was to the effect that we had better return as the enemy were in fact surrounding us. Col.Durnford remarked "the enemy can't surround us and if they do we will cut our way through them." He asked me where the Rocket Battery was, I told him a very long way behind. He then told the two Carbineers to return and tell Lieut.Scott to support him with his picquet — the N.C. replied that Lieut.Scott would not leave his post on any account whatever, as he had strict instructions from Col.Pulleine not to leave his post on any pretext whatever. Col.Durnford replied "I am Col.Pulleine's senior, you will please tell Lieut. Scott to do as I tell him".

There is more than a tone of frustration, even anger, in Durnford's voice; faced with the prospect of action, his emotions, usually so carefully controlled, seem to have got the better of him. Jabez Molife, one of the Hlubi troop, heard him snap, "What are those scouts I sent out about?" While this conversation was taking place Durnford's scouts came in, and reported that the Zulus were in sight. The officers looked up: about 1,500 yards away the enemy were just coming over the ridge, "steadily advancing and firing at us." Durnford ordered

his men to extend, Davies' troop on the left, Henderson's on the right, and when the Zulus got to within 400 yards they opened fire. They then fired and retired alternately, slowing the Zulu advance.

When they came round onto the plain they rode past the debris of the rocket battery. Nourse and his handful of men were still making a stand, and Nourse told Davies that the rocket battery had been scattered, remarking that the mules had bolted. It is possible that Nourse had not seen Russell killed in the confusion, as Davies does not mention it, and Durnford remained uncertain about his fate. One of the mules was in view a little way off, and Davies sent a man to bring it in; "he had to go pretty close to the enemy to do so, as the mule was between us and the enemy". There were also a number of ammunition or rocket boxes lying about, presumably thrown from the mules or cast down by Nourse's men in their flight, and Davies ordered his men to pick them up. By this time the Zulus were so close, however, that they soon had to drop them. As they fell back towards the camp they met Private Johnson. Durnford was clearly indignant that he had left his post, but Johnson, who was alone and on foot, replied phlegmatically:

> He asked me where my battery was; I told him that the Battery was cut up and the Captain shot, when he said you had better go back and fetch him. I then pointed out to him that the enemy had nearly surrounded us.

Durnford's men retired steadily on the camp, still extended in a long line. Jabez Molife describes this running fight:

> After this we remounted and retreated 20 yards, always in a long thin line, then dismounted and fired, up again for another ten yards, dismounted and fired again, and so on ten yards at a time, firing always, slowly back towards the camp. We were not very many, but because of the way we were handled by our leader we were enough to stop the Zulus on that side for a long time.

Ten or twenty yards seems a very short distance to retreat each time; with the Zulus pressing so close behind, the inevitable delay in mounting and dismounting must have made such a procedure extremely hazardous. Durnford's force numbered only about a hundred men, and was spread thin — there was a very real chance of individuals being cut off. Perhaps the danger made the distance seem shorter to Molife than it really was.

By now the Zulu attack was beginning to develop fully. The regimental commanders had managed to instill some order into their men, and they had instinctively taken up the traditional "chest and horns" formation. The uNokhenke and uKhandempemvu were on the right of the chest, while the regiments on the right of the original bivouac — the uDududu, iMbube and iSangqu — had swung out beyond them to form the right horn. To the left of the uKhandempemvu the uMbonambi, with elements of the uMxhapho and those who had broken away from the reserve, pushed up towards the Nyoni ridge. The iNgobamakhosi and the uVe made up the left horn. Part of the left horn, probably elements of the iNgobamakhosi, had struck out southwards from the Ngwebeni valley, separated from the rest of their men, and it had been they who appeared in front of Durnford. Mavumeng-wana and Ntshingwayo had only been able to restrain the *amabutho* on the extreme left of the bivouac: the uThulwana, iNdluyengwe, uDloko and iNdlondlo. The rest advanced in a leisurely fashion, screened by skirmishers, their main body in open order, with supports following close behind. As they spilled over the lip of the heights, bunching here and there to make the best use of the ground, they must have been an awesome sight. According to an anonymous survivor, they "appeared almost to grow out of the earth. From rock and bush on the heights above started scores of men; some with rifles, others with shields and assegais."

As the main body of the iNgobamakhosi came over the crest, Mehlokazulu kaSihayo noticed that there were some small bodies of horsemen in front of them who had fallen back on Amatushane, the "Conical Koppie". These were Lieutenant Scott's Carbineer picquets, who now took up a position in one of the dongas nearby (from where Trooper Barker saw the rocket battery come to grief) and began to open fire. Flickers of light played along in front of them, either the muzzle-flash of their carbines or the sun glittering on their bayonets; and a warrior in the iNgobamakhosi called out *"Mbane, mbane wezulu, kuyagewazimula"* — "Lightning, lighting of heaven, see its glittering flash" — and the whole regiment took up the cry as an impromptu war-chant. Generally, however, the Zulus could be heard making no great war-cries, but rather a low murmuring sound.

* * *

Far away on the left, Essex thought the fresh Zulu advance ominous: "Affairs now looked rather serious as our little body appeared altogether insignificant compared with the enormous masses opposed to us. The 24th men, however, were as cheery as possible, making remarks to one another about their shooting, and the enemy opposed to them made little progress; but they were now within 500 yards of our line." Ahead of them the uNokhenke tried to push down the escarpment, but were caught for a few minutes against the skyline, and the fire from the infantry companies was so intense that they had to retire. Instead they extended more to their right, advancing out of sight behind the ridge. Further to Essex's right, however, where the uKhandempemvu were a little out of the line of fire, they had managed to push down to the bottom of the slope, and were massing in the hollows there. According to one of these warriors, uMhoti, some of the troops opposing them had not properly adjusted their sights:

The soldiers fired low, most of the bullets striking the ground in front of us and ricocheting over the foremost men. It appeared to me as though the soldiers were opening the breeches of their rifles with their feet in their haste to reload.

According to Essex, "The enemy's fire had hitherto been wild and ineffective; now, however, a few casualties began to occur in our lines." The band of the 1/24th doubled as stretcher bearers, and Private E.Wilson remembered that when the first alarms of the morning had taken place the stretcher-bearers had fallen in with the companies on their parade grounds. They stood down later when the situation seemed to improve, but were sent out again subsequently when the 24th were all committed to the line: "The stretcher-bearers were out with their companies for some ten minutes when we were ordered by Doctor Sheppard [sic] to go to the Hospital tents, as he said there would be too many wounded for us to attend to." This seems a curious order; presumably Shepherd felt that the men could be treated more effectively at the hospital tent with the bearers in attendance.

Surgeon Major Peter Shepherd was No.3 Column's senior medical officer, and the prospects for the patients under his care were good, since Shepherd had had a relatively dis-

tinguished career which suggests something of the advance in professionalism made by the medical establishment in the Army in the decades since the Crimean War. Born at Leochel-Cushnie, Aberdeenshire, in 1841, and completing his medical training in 1864, he entered the Army as an Assistant-Surgeon in that year. By 1876 he had reached the rank of Surgeon-Major and had seen two spells of overseas service, in India and at the Cape. He became an instructor to the St.John's Ambulance Association shortly after its formation in 1877, and impressed the Order with his "clearness, thoroughness and tact." He was an advocate of the principles of first aid, and in fact the notes he compiled as an aide memoire for service in Zululand were later to appear as the first pamphlet on first aid to be published by the St.John's Ambulance Association. They give some idea of the sort of treatment those first British casualties could expect:

A tourniquet can be made by placing a stone over a main artery, tying a handkerchief loosely over it and then twisting it tight with a stick.
Bleeding from arteries
Head:– Pad and bandage the wound.
Neck:– Place thumb in wound and press backwards against spine.
Armpit:– Press thumb into wound. Second person to press main artery behind middle of collar-bone . . .
Bleeding from veins
For all situations:– Elevate the part and apply pad and bandage.
Flesh wounds:– Wash, stop bleeding, fix parts in natural position without delay.
Gunshot wounds of Chest or Belly:– Place patient on wounded side with knees drawn up; give complete rest, no stimulants.
Bruised Wounds:– Wash, apply wet cloths: if about head, poultices.

Since the Zulu firing was erratic, and the British were poor targets, there were probably only a few men making their way back to the hospital tent at this stage. Pulleine's position must still have seemed comparatively secure, although the companies on the left were steadily shuffling back towards the tents. Out on the far right Pope's company seems to have fallen back, too. A warrior of the uMbonambi told Bertram Mitford in 1882 that when his regiment came down from the hills, "there were some parties of soldiers in red coats" close to Amatutshane, who "kept up a heavy fire upon us as we came over. My regiment was here and lost a lot of men," he recalled,

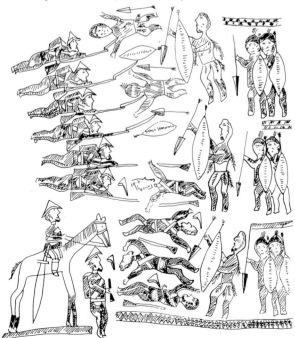

An extremely rare African representation of British soldiers and Zulus in battle. These images were engraved on cow horns, apparently in c.1880, and show considerable familiarity with British military detail; the artist may have been one of the black auxiliaries who took part in the war. (Natal Museum)

"they kept tumbling over one upon another". "Close to" is, of course, a highly subjective phrase, but it is possible that Pope's men had been sent out initially over a mile from the camp. This position was obviously too extended in the face of the mass attack which was now developing, and Pope's men probably fell back closer to Wardell, who had secured himself on a rocky rise on the crest of the ground between the two dongas. In any case, the line was still spread perilously thin.

The men were in extended order, and according to the instruction books of the period a company firing in skirmishing order could take up a single line, allowing 30 inches between each man. At Isandlwana it may well have been more: when Chelmsford reviewed the 2/24th at Pietermaritzburg before the war he ordered the spaces between the files to be doubled. (It was on this occasion that an anonymous staff officer commented, "Do you not think, General, that single rank extended would be sufficient for this scum?"). On that basis, taking an average company as 80 men field strength, it would take up just over 170 yards of frontage in a single row of men five feet apart — a very thin red line indeed. If the men were in a double rank the frontage would be reduced, but, given the distance they were covering, this can have only increased the gaps between the companies. Captain Penn Symons of the 24th believed that in the donga there were as much as ten paces between the files, but that on the left the men were closer together.

Beyond Pope's company, to the British right, the flank was wide open; there was nothing except the shattered remnants of the rocket battery, and Durnford's men retreating steadily across the plain. J.F.Lonsdale's NNC company was still in position on the ridge between the two water-courses. Pulleine had no reserve available to him, beyond Captain Krohn's NNC company still drawn up in front of the tents. A crowd of camp casuals — servants, cooks, grooms, the Artillery men not attached to Curling's section, and men with no other duties — had taken up a position in front of the camp, and were blazing away at the Zulus in the distance.

Despite Essex's reservations, the 24th seem to have been in good spirits. Although the flats on the left of the line offered very little in the way of cover, the rise between the dongas was strewn with boulders two or three feet high, and the men were crouching or even lying down behind them. According to the Field Excercise manual, "men in extended order will at all times assume such positions as may be most convenient and may render their fire most effective. The line may be ordered to lie down, or single soldiers may do so for the sake of cover; when firing in this position, both elbows must rest on the ground to support the body." (Firing the Martini-Henry from a prone position is more comfortable and more stable than firing kneeling or standing, though it must have been difficult to do so wearing the foreign service helmet; in such a position the shoulders push up the brim at the back, so that the peak falls over the eyes.) The 24th were holding their ground well, and Smith-Dorrien remembered them as "no boy recruits, but war-worn men, and fresh from the old colony where they had carried everything before them. Possessed of a splendid discipline and sure of success, they lay on their position making every round tell, so much so that when the Zulu Army was some 400 yards off, it wavered."

From their position at the foot of the escarpment, the warriors facing the 24th companies were indeed experiencing a terrible ordeal. According to uMhoti of the uKhandempemvu, "the soldiers who lay on the flat ground in front of the camp poured volley after volley into the *impi*; we crouched down and dared not advance." It is no coincidence that the attack slowed at 400 yards: not only was this the distance from the infantry companies to the hollows at the foot of the slope, it was also the Martini-Henry's most effective range. To get close the Zulus had to rise up and run, virtually naked, up the

continued on page **81**

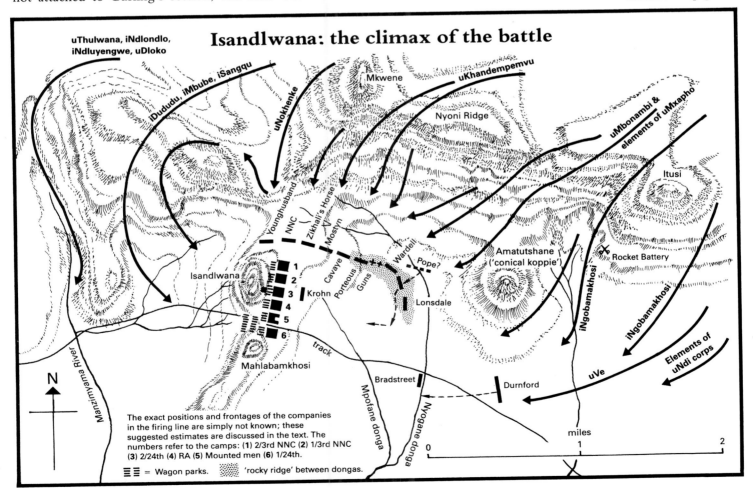

Isandlwana: the climax of the battle

The exact positions and frontages of the companies in the firing line are simply not known; these suggested estimates are discussed in the text. The numbers refer to the camps: (1) 2/3rd NNC (2) 1/3rd NNC (3) 2/24th (4) RA (5) Mounted men (6) 1/24th.

≡ ≡ = Wagon parks. ⠿ 'rocky ridge' between dongas.

COLOUR PLATES E-H   by Angus McBride

Plate E1: Senior Zulu induna

This man's appearance hearkens back to the days of King Shaka: he is wearing the full ceremonial costume of a Zulu general which, though probably limited to only a handful of the most senior commanders in 1879, would be characteristic of the conservatism of old age. The magnificent "kilt" is made of twisted civet and monkey fur; cow tail festoons are worn around the neck and limbs; he has a stuffed otter skin headband, and blue crane and red and green lourie feathers — both marks of seniority. He carries the full-size isihlangu shield, and an axe of the tanged pattern most common in Zululand.

Plate E2: Warrior, uThulwana ibutho

The uThulwana, who fought at Rorke's Drift, were a senior age-group regiment of married men in their mid-forties, who consequently wore the headring. This experienced warrior wears typical simple war costume; and carries the smaller umbhumbhulozu shield in the red-spotted white colour associated with this regiment. He carries an 1856 Enfield .577 inch percussion rifle, typical of the best firearms available to the Zulus, and a number of throwing-spears; powder, caps and shot are carried slung in a horn and pouches on trade and improvised belts. He has a snuff spoon thrust under his headring.

Plate F1: Induna, uDloko ibutho

Evidence concerning the costume of this regiment of warriors aged about forty is contradictory, but they apparently wore an otter skin headband and a single crane feather, both of which were typical components of married warriors' costume. This officer's rank is indicated by the bunch of red and green lourie feathers. His shield is the large isihlangu type; and he carries a polished hardwood knobkerry. The snakeskin pouch worn round the body on a cord is an amulet containing charms and medecines of ritualistic significance. The uDloko also fought at Rorke's Drift.

Plate F2: Warrior, uDududu ibutho

This regiment fought with the original "right horn" of the Zulu army at Isandlwana, swinging round the west of the mountain to move south and cut off the defenders falling back over the nek. In his mid-thirties, this warrior is wearing slightly abbreviated cow tail festoons on his chest, elbows and knees, and two bunches of sakabuli feathers thrust into his otter skin headband. He carries the smaller shield, with two throwing-spears and a stabbing-spear.

Plate G1: Warrior, uKhandempemvu ibutho

This regiment, also known as uMcijo, were in their early thirties; they made the first contact with the Natal Native Horse in the Ngwebeni valley on the morning of 22nd January, and played a leading part in the fighting against the firing line at Isandlwana. This warrior wears typical war-dress: a headband, loin-covering, and cow tail leg festoons. His charm necklace consists of small blocks of ritually-burnt wood, animals' teeth, and amulets. The regiment carried black or brown shields with white markings, although King Cetshwayo also granted them several other patterns: white, black with a white central patch, and shields which were dark on one side and white on the other. His firearm is an old European flintlock converted to percussion, perhaps dating from the 1840s.

Plate G2: Warrior, uMbonambi ibutho

Another warrior in his early thirties, wearing minimal war-dress: loin-covering and a single cow tail armlet. He is taking snuff, carried in a horn-tip bottle on a neck cord, with the type of spoon typically carried thrust into the hair or through the pierced earlobe. The colours of the uMbonambi's shields are uncertain, although there are references to them being speckled — as here — or spotted. Note the typical stabbing-spear. This regiment was recognised by King Cetshwayo as the first to "stab" the enemy at Isandlwana: the first to break through the British line and reach the camp.

Plate H1: Warrior, iNgobamakhosi ibutho

The iNgobamakhosi was Cetshwayo's favourite regiment; composed of fiery young men in their mid-twenties, it was heavily engaged against the British right flank at Isandlwana. This warrior has his hair worked up in a fashionably ornate three-horned style, but wears no costume beyond loin-covering, headband and fur wristlets; he has snuff spoons in his earlobes and snuff containers hung round his neck. The regiment seem to have carried shields of brown and black intermingled, with white spots. His weapon is an ancient Brown Bess, typical of the majority of poor quality Zulu firearms.

Plate H2: Warrior, uVe ibutho

The uVe, in their early twenties, were the youngest of the Zulu regiments at Isandlwana; closely associated with the iNgobamakhosi, they too fought in the "left horn". They appear to have worn no ceremonial regalia whatever. This man is armed solely with traditional weapons — throwing and stabbing spears.

Zulu ammunition belt taken from the body of a warrior killed at Ulundi. The belt and cap pouches appear to be of an obsolete Volunteer or military pattern; while the powder horn is so typical of those used by the Zulus that one wonders if these also were supplied in bulk by traders. (Local History Museum, Durban)

Plate E

E1: Senior Zulu *induna*

E2: Warrior, uThulwana *ibutho*

Plate F

F1: *induna* , uDloko *ibutho*

F2: Warrior, uDududu *ibutho*

Plate G

G1: Warrior, uKhandempemvu *ibutho*

G2: Warrior, uMbonambi *ibutho*

H1: Warrior, iNgobamakhosi *ibutho*

H2: Warrior, uVe *ibutho*

incline in the teeth of a terrible fire. Driver Elias Tucker of the Royal Artillery noted that the 24th's fire was "cutting roads through them", while Higginson, away in the camp, thought it "simply swept them away." Chief Zimema, a warrior of the uMxhapho, who was fighting under similar circumstances at Nyezane that same day, has left a graphic account of the effect of such fire: "Some of our men had their arms torn right off by the bullets of the [artillery]. The battle was so fierce that we had to wipe the blood and brains of the killed and wounded from our heads, faces, arms, legs and shields after the fighting." A warrior of the uNokhenke assessed the damage caused by British firepower at Isandlwana: "The [uMcijo] suffered very severely, both from artillery and musketry fire; the [uNokhenke] from musketry fire alone; while the [right horn] suffered least."

Major Stuart Smith's 7-pdrs. seem to have achieved mixed results. According to uMhoti, "as we descended the Nqutu the guns opened fire on us and we received each shot with a shout of '*Umoya*' (it is wind)". The Zulus noticed that each shot was preceeded by the gunners standing away from the gun, and they threw themselves down to let the "wind" rush past. Facing them, Wally Erskine could hear them shout "*Moya!*" and, defiantly, "*Qoka amatshe!*", "Catch stones!" — it was a boast of the uKhandempemvu that they would treat the bullets of the enemy as if they were just stones hurled at them in play. Brickhill noted that throughout the fight, "The Artillery threw about 25 shots from different parts of the field during the battle. Four of these were very effective, each tearing up what appeared to be about an acre of ground in the enemy's masses. One of the guns however always appeared to shoot high, whilst one shot burst half way, nearly over our foot Native Contingent." For the most part the guns fired on the *amabutho* facing them to the north, but at one point Smith took one gun off a little distance to the right to fire at the Zulu attack developing there, before returning to his original position.

Of course, the 24th could not sustain such a heavy rate of fire indefinitely. The men had apparently gone into action with 70 rounds each — 20 rounds in packets in each pouch either side of the waist-buckle, and a further 30 loose in the expense pouch or "ball bag" worn on the right hip in action. The expense pouch was not a particularly efficient item — it came undone easily, and the rounds fell out — but overall this would not have affected the rate at which a company used up its ammunition. Private John Williams, Colonel Glyn's groom, was amongst the unattached men who had taken up a position in front of the camp:

> I myself and Private Hough, the Colonel's cook, went to the left beyond the General's tents where we were joined by three of the General's servants, and began to fire from the left of No.5 Company, 1/24th Regiment [E:Cavaye's]. We fired 40 or 50 rounds each when the Native Contingent fell back on the Camp and one of their officers pointed out to me that the enemy were entering the right of the camp. We then went to the right, No.5 Company still holding their position, and fired away the remainder of our ammunition.

Williams' account is particularly interesting because it confirms that he, at least, had something like 70 rounds, and that he blazed away at a rapid rate. Nevertheless, there is no reason to suppose that the men in the ranks were expending ammunition so quickly. The expenditure per man in other Zulu War battles was often surprisingly low; Evelyn Wood noted that at Khambula the Imperial infantry "expended in four hours an average of 33 rounds a man". The fighting at Khambula was no less intense than at Isandlwana, although arguably individual companies were in action for longer periods of sustained firing at the latter. Even so, the 24th were "old steady shots", and we know from Essex's comments that their officers were exercising strict fire discipline.

Since the whole question of ammunition has become part of the popular mythology of Isandlwana, it is important to consider what arrangements the 24th had made to resupply their men in action. Unfortunately the Quartermasters of both battalions were killed in the battle, but it seems quite clear that

C.E.Fripp's famous painting of "The Last Stand of the 24th at Isandlwana" combines an accurate eye for detail with all the conventions of a Victorian battle painting. The central group, arranged around the stalwart Sergeant and heroic Drummer Boy, reflects the romanticised public view of "the thin red line". Fripp had covered the Zulu War as special artist for The Graphic, however, and knew something of its realities — as the fierce fighting in the background suggests. In fact, most of the stands took place closer to the mountain; and the presence of a Regimental Colour is fanciful. (Courtesy of the Director, National Army Museum, London)

they had fulfilled their duties properly. According to the *Field Force Regulations* a supply was "to be constantly in possession of regiments and detached companies in the field . . . at a rate of 270 rounds per man, viz 70 in possession of each soldier, with a reserve of 200 rounds". There were over 400,000 rounds in the camp, representing the regimental reserve of both the 1st and 2nd Battalions; Chelmsford had not taken the 2nd Battalion's reserve with him, but had ordered Pulleine to have it ready to be despatched if necessary.

The cartridges were carried in boxes containing 600 rounds, so the reserve for a battalion of some 800 men would take up about 60 boxes. The official transport wagons were designed to carry 30 ammunition boxes, but were not used in South Africa, where mule-drawn "scotch carts" were employed instead; such a cart could easily accommodate 30 boxes, although the load might have proved heavy for the mules. In any case, two or three carts would be sufficient for a battalion reserve supply.

It has been assumed by some writers that the ammunition wagons were amongst those on the nek on the morning of the 22nd, but this is almost certainly not so; these were empty supply wagons about to return to Rorke's Drift. The regimental equipment was parked immediately behind the tents of each unit in the camp. Nor should there have been any difficulty in identifying them; Chelmsford's *Field Force Regulations* had insisted that each wagon should bear a small identification flag — red for ammunition, blue for the commissariat, red and the colour of the facings for regimental transport, red and white for the staff, blue and red for the artillery.

The ammunition boxes themselves were stoutly made of teak or mahogany, and were secured by a copper band around each end. Access, however, was through a sliding wedge-shaped panel in the centre of the lid, which was held in place by one screw. This screw was supposed to be removed with a screwdriver issued to the Quartermasters, but in an emergency a sharp blow to the edge of the panel would break the screw-housing and free the panel. This basic design dated from the mid-1860s, before the introduction of the Martini-Henry; the Mark V pattern, intended for overseas service and lined with thin tin to protect the contents, had been authorised in 1876. The tin lining had a wire handle at the top which enabled it to be torn back. The cartridges themselves were packed in brown paper packages of ten rounds. It is difficult to see how Martini-Henry cartridges could have been issued from anything other than these boxes.

Shortly after Mostyn and Cavaye's companies had retreated to the bottom of the hill, Essex observed that they were

now getting short of ammunition, so I went to the camp to bring up a fresh supply. I got such men as were not engaged, bandsmen, cooks etc, to assist me, and sent them to the line under an officer, and I followed with more ammunition in a mule cart. In loading the latter I helped the Quartermaster of the 2nd Battalion 24th to place the boxes in the cart, and while doing so the poor fellow was shot dead. The enemy's fire was now increasing and I could hear the whiz of bullets all over the place.

The reference to "an officer" is intriguing — it may well have been Smith-Dorrien who, as a junior transport officer, would have been under Essex's command. Smith-Dorrien, in a letter written to his father two days later, recalled "I was out with the front companies of the 24th handing them spare ammunition." In his memoires, written nearly 40 years later, he expanded: "I, having no particular duty to perform in camp . . . had collected camp stragglers, such as artillerymen in charge of spare horses, officers' servants, sick etc., and had taken them to the ammunition boxes, where we broke them open as fast as we could, and kept sending the packets out to the firing line." Later, Smith-Dorrien had a famous conversation with Quartermaster Edward Bloomfield of the 2/24th, the same man mentioned by Essex:

Bloomfield, the Quartermaster of the 2/24th, said to me in regard to the

boxes I was then breaking open, "For heaven's sake, don't take that, man, for it belongs to our Battalion." And I replied "Hang it all, you don't want a requisition now, do you?"

This story has been much misunderstood, and upon it has been built the myth of the over-zealous Quartermaster, husbanding his precious supplies in strict adherence to the regulations at the expense of the men who desperately needed them. Yet Smith-Dorrien told this story not as an example of bungling and inflexibilty, but of "the coolness and discipline of the regiment." A different reading of the passage suggests that Smith-Dorrien's reply might even have been a light-hearted one. Writing so many years later, Smith-Dorrien suggests that this incident took place late in the battle, when the British position was deteriorating rapidly; yet if Essex, writing just four days later, is to be believed, Bloomfield was shot quite early in the fight. In fact, the conversation probably occurred when Essex first arrived at the 2/24th camp with Smith-Dorrien and the casuals in tow; after that, as Smith-Dorrien himself admits, he went out to the line, and he would not have seen Bloomfield killed. Furthermore, Bloomfield was probably showing a very proper concern for the supplies which Chelmsford had ordered to be kept ready for despatch to the 2nd Battalion; to have done otherwise would indeed have been failing in his duty. In any case, Bloomfield clearly overcame his reservations or found another supply, since Essex got his ammunition boxes. And since Smith-Dorrien described breaking them open "as fast as we could" and keeping "sending the packets out to the firing line", there seems no reason to believe that he had any difficulty in opening them — with or without a screwdriver.

It remains a moot point, too, whether the men in the firing line were running *out* of ammunition, or merely running *low*; Mostyn and Cavaye's men had been in action for longer than the rest of the line, and would no doubt have expended more rounds, but runners would presumably have been sent back in plenty of time to secure fresh supplies long before they had run out. The situation was perhaps more difficult for the men on the right, whose runners had to brave the gauntlet of Zulu fire which had passed over the heads of the line, and was striking the ground to the rear. Nevertheless, there are numerous references to runners coming in and going out again, so it was clearly not an impossible task. Although it is possible that many runners did make for the 1/24th camp, on the extreme right, furthest away from the line, it is equally clear from Essex's experience that supplies were to be had from elsewhere. Private Williams, it is true, thought that "the greater part never got there, as I saw horses and mules with ammunition on their backs galloping about the Camp a short time afterwards"; but the Regimental Records of the 24th suggest that confusion set in only after Bloomfield was killed, and perhaps much later. Both Williams and Vause thought that the fire from the 24th slackened, but if this is so it does not necessarily follow that it was because the men were out of ammunition — the Zulu accounts are unanimous that the 24th were still putting down a heavy fire when the line collapsed. There is, in short, no evidence to suggest that shortage of ammunition was responsible for any tactical decisions taken by the officers of the 24th.

The same cannot be said of the NNC and Ngwane. Stafford, who had stayed with the NNC despite the desertion of his men, went back to the camp with his *induna* Ntini and fetched a box of cartridges because "the ammunition by this time was running very short." Both Raw's and Vause's troops were running low, and it is unlikely that Barton's troop were any better off. If their fire slackened, it may have been this which Williams and Higginson noticed.

While the line was holding the Zulus to the north at bay, however, the steadily increasing numbers of warriors swinging down from the hills and south across the plain were posing a serious threat to the British right. Brickhill described the attack:

> They came on in lines, but very evenly distributed. Nowhere could you catch three men walking together and rarely two, so that in some places their front was three-quarters of a mile in advance of their rear.

Smith-Dorrien noted the peculiar sound they made as they advanced: "They were giving vent to no loud warcries, but to a low, musical murmuring noise, which gave the impression of a gigantic swarm of bees getting nearer and nearer."

To the right of the guns there were only Wardell and Pope to meet this attack, and Captain Lonsdale's NNC company. This company was now very exposed, but it kept its position well, though it soon ran out of ammunition. However, it had no difficulty in obtaining a fresh supply; Higginson, in the camp, noted that "a Sergeant of Captain Lonsdale's Company came in for ammunition, and then went out again." Malindi, who was with that company, recalled that "our ammunition failed once but we got fresh from the camp, and remained firing until the Zulus were within 100 yards".

Nevertheless, the right flank was still very open, and Captain Gardner spotted the danger. Rounding up "30 or 40" mounted men from somewhere out to the left, he asked Pulleine for permission to take them out to the right, and Pulleine agreed. These were the Volunteers and Mounted Infantry under Captain Bradstreet. Alan Gardner, the Hussar, thought that "had there been a regiment or even two squadrons of cavalry, the disaster . . . would not have occurred. The enemy's advance across our front which was requisite in order to turn our right, was in extremely loose order, the ground was an open plain and could easily have been cleared by a determined charge." But there was no cavalry regiment present: just Bradstreet's men, and Gardner took them out "and lined the spruit running across the front of our camp." Bradstreet had not been in position long when Durnford's men, still retiring across the plain, fell in beside them. Gardner then rode back to join Pulleine, leaving Bradstreet in charge.

The defence of the right flank has become part of the epic legend of Isandlwana, yet it is surprisingly difficult to piece together a correct sequence of events, or even the exact location. There were, of course, two dongas running across the plain between the camp and Amatushane, the Mpofane and the Nyogane. The Nyogane, the further of the two, is a good defensive position; it is about 40 feet wide, with a flat, shaley bottom, and the eastern edge is high enough to shelter a man crouching behind it. Certainly a stand took place here; a warrior of the uMbonambi told Mitford that a party of mounted men had made a stand in a donga "which intersects the field about a mile from the camp." Durnford seems to have left his command here, and ridden into the camp. Trooper Barker of the Carbineers recalled that after their initial skirmish with the Zulus Lieutenant Scott's vedettes — with or without that officer — had ridden back into camp looking for fresh ammunition. Barker found Quartermaster London in the Carbineers camp, opening ammuniton boxes; he had been struck by a stray bullet, but was not badly wounded, and the vedettes got their resupply. Shortly after this,

> As we left the camp Col. Durnford rode up to us, followed by some mounted natives, and shouted to us, "Carbineers hurry up and follow me". We followed him to a donga about a mile from camp, where we dismounted, Hawkins, myself and others giving our horses to one of Durnford's natives to hold, promising to tip him when the fight was over. However, he left our horses after a time and rejoined his troop. Colonel Durnford collected all the mounted men, police and Volunteers, some eighty in all, and here for about half an hour we kept the Zulus in check.

There seems to be no doubt from Barker's statement that he was referring to the Nyogane. Gardner, however, was quite certain that Bradstreet's men were in position before Durnford joined them. Had Gardner reinforced the Mpofane in anticipation of Durnford's further withdrawal? Certainly Lieutenant

Davies of the Edendale Troop was convinced that he met Bradstreet's men in a donga only about 300 yards from the camp, which can only have been the Mpofane. With Durnford's men firing and retiring alternately, it is quite possible that stands were made at both places. Then again, it is equally possible that in the confusion of the fight Davies misjudged the distance.

Why did Durnford return to the camp? Presumably to confer with Pulleine, though no evidence has survived of what passed between them. The ambiguities of the divided command, and of Durnford's parting remark to Pulleine earlier in the day — that he would expect to be supported if he got into difficulties — must now have been all too apparent to both of them, however. As the senior officer present Durnford should now have taken command of the whole battle, and remained at some place where he could properly exercise it. In fact it seems that he may have issued some orders, and then returned to his own men, leaving Pulleine to juggle two contradictory imperatives: to defend the camp, and to support Durnford. With Durnford so far out to the right Pulleine could only support him by stretching his line dangerously thin, and thereby compromising his defence of the camp. At about this time Pope's company left its original position and, passing behind Lonsdale's NNC, took up a new position in the low ground between the rocky ridge and the road. The manoeuvre was carried out smartly, as if the company were on parade, but before they had time to complete it Durnford's men fell back again, perhaps to the Mpofane. Lieutenant Davies recalled that when he made a stand 300 yards from the camp he had redcoats on his left, but that there was nothing to the right. Pope's company was now very exposed to attacks from the uMbonambi, whose men Davies could see rushing past to his left to attack them. Davies ordered the Edendale Troop to fire "one or two volleys on the flank of the enemy to our left" to try to disperse them.

Durnford was clearly exhilarated by the excitement of battle. Jabez Molife has left a vivid account of Durnford's stand. Giving no more clues than that they were at "a bad stony place and a little stream quite close to the camp", he says:

> Here we made a long stand, firing incessantly. The Colonel rode up and down our line continually, encouraging us all; he was very calm and cheerful, talking and even laughing with us. "Fire! my boys", "Well done, my boys," he cried. Some of us did not like his exposing himself so much to the enemy, and wanted him to keep behind us, but he laughed at us and said "All right! Nonsense!" Sometimes as he passed amongst us one of the men brought him his gun with the old cartridge sticking and he dismounted and taking the gun between his knees, because of having only one hand with strength in it, he pulled the cartridge out and gave back the gun.

Molife was clearly deeply impressed by Durnford's behaviour — "Now we say we shall always remember him by his voice and the way he gave us all some of his own spirit as he went up and down the line that day" — and claimed the Sotho would have gladly dragged Durnford away to save him, despite the protests he would have made. There can be no doubting Durnford's personal courage; at last he had found the chance to test himself in action which fate had previously denied him. Yet, as at Bushman's Pass, his judgement seems to have suffered in the heat of the moment; was it really his place to be in the thick of the fighting when he had left the responsibility of overall command to a subordinate? Certainly Lieutenant Alfred Henderson, commanding the amaHlongwe Sotho troop, was not impressed: "If I had known what sort of man Durnford was (when he got into action) I don't think I would have gone with him. He was close to me during most of the fight and he lost his head altogether, in fact I don't think he knew what to do."

Nevertheless, Durnford's men held the donga for perhaps 20 minutes or half an hour, and the cost to the Zulus was staggering. The uVe, the youngest *ibutho* with the army, was in the forefront of the Zulu attack on their left flank, and the terrible fire forced them to fall back until the larger iNgobamakhosi, coming up behind, reinforced them. Mehlokazulu was with the iNgobamakhosi:

We could not advance against their fire any longer. They had drawn their horses into this donga, and all we could see were the helmets. They fired so heavily we had to retire; we kept lying down and rising again. The Edendale men were in this donga, but we did not see the Basutos. The former were mixed up with the Carbineers.

As many as three times the Zulu left was forced to retire. The fire from Durnford's men was reinforced by that of Major Smith's gun, which moved to the right at this time; at least one of the devastating shots observed by Brickhill fell amongst the left horn. Brickhill thought that "a thousand Zulu dead must have lain between the Conical Hill and the gully. They lay just like pepper-corns upon the plain. The leading Zulus, finding they were being mown down so terribly, threw themselves flat on the ground to wait for the others to come up, when they jumped up and came on again." In fact, as Mehlokazulu explained, the iNgobamakhosi could make no headway against this fire, and "we retired towards the left wing." With nothing to protect his right, this movement threatened to

An example of the Mark V ammunition box, unlined, but showing the copper retaining bands, and the access covered by the sliding central panel (missing here). This was held closed by a single screw, and could be broken open in an emergency with a heavy blow or kick which sheered the screw housing. The white screwed washer seen here is a display fixture and not original to the box. (Royal Regiment of Wales Museum, Brecon)

H.T.Curling, photographed in later life. Lieutenant Curling commanded the two N/5 Battery guns at Isandlwana until Stuart Smith returned just as the battle began, and was another of the five Imperial officers to escape. (Royal Artillery Institution)

outflank Durnford and, abruptly, he ordered his men to withdraw.

In fairness, Durnford could not have held his position much longer, since his men were by now running low on ammunition. Davies claimed that he had only fired a couple of vollies into the uMbonambi on his left when "my men called out they were short of ammunition." Molife said, "at last our cartridges were nearly done. The Colonel had sent a messenger back to the camp for more, but none came. Then he sent Mr. Henderson and another." It seems odd that Durnford sent both Henderson and Davies, because when he left the command himself later the two black mounted troops had no white officers left. Davies and a small party who had accompanied him tried to find the regimental reserve supply, but could not; it had come into camp with Vause that morning, but no-one knew where the wagons had been left. Since Durnford's men had not pitched their tents, there was no obvious place to look for it; Vause may have left it on the nek, near the wagons waiting to go back to Rorke's Drift, or he may have taken it to the NNC camp. In any case, the best Davies could do was to find an open box with about 200 rounds in it in the Carbineers' tents. By the time he returned to the front, however, he "found everybody leaving it and the Zulus close on us."

Durnford's retreat must have horrified Pulleine, since it left the British right wide open. Both Essex and Gardner rode over to find out what had gone wrong; Gardner met Bradstreet and his men, who told him that it had been ordered by Durnford. Durnford himself then came up, and told Gardner that he had considered the position was too exposed to hold any longer. Essex met Durnford somewhere near the centre of the line — "He had, I think, already observed the state of affairs, and was looking very serious. He asked me if I could bring some men to keep the enemy in check in our rear." On the right the Zulus had got amongst the herd of cattle which had been grazing on the slopes of Mahlabamkhosi, and were driving them forward in an attempt to break up the line; far out across the plain, Hamilton-Browne had seen the same movement. Davies' men shot some of the Zulus as they came close. At this point, the British position suddenly collapsed.

* * *

Several things happened very quickly at about the same time. It is difficult now to work out their exact sequence, but in any case they were over in a matter of minutes. Lieutenant Higginson was still waiting with Captain Krohn and No.6 Company, 1/3rd NNC, in front of the tents. Higginson had noted with some concern the number of men coming in from the outlying companies searching for ammunition, and:

It was with great difficulty we kept the men in their places, for the bullets were dropping amongst us, and every one that came near made them all jump up, and try to run away.

A Carbineer rode by, looking for ammunition; he called out to Higginson "Col. Durnford is shot" — which seems unlikely at this stage — and Higginson saw that the Zulus had now swept round towards the right of the camp,

and as they got on the right flank they made a rush for the camp, and drove back the few men that opposed them, when my company saw them coming on, nothing could stop them, they all jumped up and ran and though I knocked a man down with my rifle, it was no use. I then saw the men of the 2nd Batt. N.N.C. running and looking for the 24th men, I saw that they were retreating also, but very slowly. All the mounted men were riding past as fast as they could . . .

In fact, the 2/3rd NNC men — whatever remained of Barry's company, with Erskine's men — who had been in the firing line at the north of the camp, had been slipping away throughout the fight as the companies gradually fell back. With the Zulus in danger of cutting them off, those who had so far held simply turned and fled.

According to Molife, Durnford had gone to Pulleine's tent,

and about this time someone seems to have given an order for the 24th to fall back and take up a close defensive position nearer to the tents. At the same time, "a simultaneous forward movement was now made by all the Zulus". In the ranks of the uKhandempemvu, uMhoti remembered, "then, at the sound of a bugle the firing ceased at a breath, and the whole British force rose from the ground and retired on the tents. Like a flame the whole Zulu force sprang to its feet and darted upon them . . . ."

The Zulu commanders, who had taken up a position on the Nyoni ridge near Mkwene hill, had been concerned for some time that the attack along the centre had stalled. Just below them on the slope the uKhandempemvu had ground to a halt in front of the steady fire of the 24th. One of the uKhandempemvu's *izinduna*, Ndlaka, was sent down to urge them on. He called out in a loud voice, "The little branch of leaves that beats out the fire did not order this!" (this was a well-known praise name for King Cetshwayo); and the uKhandempemvu rose up and charged forward with a great shout of *"Izulu!"*. As they did so Ndlaka himself fell dead, shot through the head, but the uKhandempemvu's example spurred the army on. Sikizane kaNomageje, an *induna* of the iNgobamakhosi, called out, "Why are you lying down? What was it you said to the uKhandempemvu? There are the uKhandempemvu going into the tents . . . Stop firing. Go in hand to hand!" The entire army seemed to rise up and rush forward, shouting out the war-cry *"Usuthu!"*. It was a terrible moment for Curling and his gunners:

> The enemy advancing still we began to fire case, but almost immediately the infantry were ordered to retire. Before we could get away the enemy were by the guns; and I saw one gunner stabbed as he was mounting on the axle-box. The gunners did not mount, but ran after the guns.

To the right, Malindi described the retreat of No.9 Company, 1/3rd NNC:

> We were then ordered to retire as we were also threatened on our rear by the advance left of the Zulus, and fall back on the camp, which we did, crossing the watercourse opposite the camp of the General. The company of soldiers [Wardell?] was with us and on nearing the tents knelt down and commenced firing at the enemy. Below them, some distance to the west, was another company or more of soldiers [Pope's men?], also kneeling down and firing.

Captain Lonsdale dismounted from his horse and gave it to Malindi, "telling me to take it to the ammunition wagons, and, turning back . . . he joined the red soldiers who were firing and I never saw him again." By this time his company were already streaming from the field. The isiQoza had lost their chance to wreak their revenge on Cetshwayo's regime; Muziwento heard that Sikhota himself was in the line until it collapsed, when he joined the stream of men making towards the safety of the nek.

On the right, the Carbineers and Bradstreet's men had dismounted by the road about a hundred yards in front of their tents. "After firing about a dozen shots" Barker noticed "or rather heard, a rush from behind, and on looking round I saw the soldiers who were left in camp literally surrounded by Zulus, who had evidently come in from the rear, and as soldiers and natives repassed us in confusion we retired back to our Carbineer lines." Essex says that he was talking to Durnford when "those natives who had not already stolen away rushed past us followed by thousands of Zulus, assegais in hand."

They had gone, too, from the middle of the line to the north, and Nyanda recalled the confusion as the Ngwane fell back: "the whole of the force, white and black, foot and horse mixed together and being assegaid." Wally Erskine was amongst the Mchunu facing the hills and could see no white officers with them, "no commander at all. They were acting entirely on their own account." They kept firing until the Zulus were about 300 yards away, and then fled. One of their

black *izinduna* called out to them *"mani buya"*, "return to the fight," but they did not listen, "that is, if they heard him."

Was there a general panic? The interpreter Brickhill thought so, claiming that "men were running everywhere but I could see no officer." Brickhill's tentmate was Quartermaster James Pullen of the 1/24th, and Brickhill saw him shouting to the running soldiers "Come on men — rally here — follow me — don't be running away like a parcel of old women — let's try to turn their flank." Pullen said calmly, "Mr. Brickhill, do go to Colonel Pulleine and ask him to send us help, as they are outflanking us here on the right." He went away towards the front of Hlabamkhosi, and Brickhill saw him no more.

Essex noticed that as the 24th fell back, "the men became unsteady. A few fixed bayonets, and I heard the officers calling on their men to keep together and be steady." They did so, which, under the circumstances, is an extraordinary tribute to their courage and discipline. The comment about bayonets is interesting; Stafford claimed that the last order he heard was one of the 24th officers shouting "Fix bayonets!" Mehlokazulu of the iNgobamakhosi later said that the soldiers had no time to fix bayonets; yet his own statement reveals the dread which the Zulus soon learned to feel for the bayonet.

As the Zulus surged forward, getting close enough to throw their spears, those who could understand them heard them shouting "It is beaten!" and "They are running!". Brickhill heard someone call out "The Usuthu has swallowed up!", while someone near Stafford shouted "You are fooling yourselves, tomorrow night we will sleep with your wives and sisters in Pietermaritzburg!" In the camp Trooper Sparks of the Mounted Police said to Trooper Pearce, "Things look black". "My oath, they do!", replied Pearce. Sparks heard the Zulus nearby yelling "Kill the pigs!", and urged Pearce to join him in a ride for their lives; but Pearce turned away to find a piece of equipment, and Sparks saw him no more.

After the war, the *amabutho* apparently argued amongst themselves as to who had the honour of being the first into the camp; it was eventually decided that it belonged to the uMbonambi, followed by the iNgobamakhosi and the uKhandempemvu. When Curling's guns reached the camp he found that the Zulus were already amongst the tents, and as his limbers rattled through it towards the nek most of the gunners were killed.

The three companies on the left tried to retire through the camp, pursued by the uKhandempemvu. The warrior uMhoti saw one company "standing four deep with their backs towards Sandhlwana". This was presumably Younghusband's C Company which, judging from the position of the subsequent graves, appears to have retired along the foot of Isandlwana, behind the tents, climbing an incline which runs from the northern edge up onto a shoulder of the mountain below the southern crag. Because they were a little further away from the Zulu breakthrough they managed to maintain some sort of order. Another party — presumably Mostyn and Cavaye's men — fell back in front of the tents, and bore the brunt of the uKhandempemvu's attack. "As we rushed on the soldiers retired on the camp, fighting all the way, and as they got into the camp we were intermingled with them." The fighting raged hand-to-hand, and these companies begun to suffer heavy casualties.

Wardell and Porteous seem to have managed to fall back from the rocky ridge in good order. Twenty men of Wardell's company, including Colour-Sergeant Wolfe, were cut off and killed among the rocks, just above a Zulu homestead; perhaps this section had been acting as a rear-guard, or perhaps they were simply overwhelmed by the speed of the attack. Two heaps of dead soldiers, amongst them the bodies of Wardell and Lieutenant Dyer, the Adjutant of the 2/24th, were later found in the area of the 1/24th camp, where they had tried to make a stand. Pope's company also fell back, and made a stand a little further down the slope above the road. The companies were presumably trying to draw together, but the Zulu pressure was too intense.

While the 24th were being driven in, Durnford made a stand on the right. As Shepstone's men fell back through the camp Nyanda had caught a glimpse of Durnford "near the middle of the camp". Shepstone must have seen him, too, for he was seen riding off towards the tents, and someone heard him say "I must go and see where my Chief is." On the right, Davies of the Edendale Troop with his small group of ammunition runners had tried to take up a position on the side of Hlabamkhosi to the right of the wagons, but it seemed too late to make any sort of determined rally. He had noticed that once the Zulus had got behind them all but a dozen or so of his men seemed to lose heart. He saw the guns moving through the Carbineers' camp, and not long afterwards he saw Durnford nearby, with his orderly next to him, with a drawn sword.

When the line had collapsed the men breaking away had fled over the nek, on the road towards Rorke's Drift. Davies saw them go, and the terrible sight which greeted them:

> I saw from here a great many wagon drivers, leaders, and many others leaving the camp they were making direct for the River. I saw from here the Zulus pouring down in great numbers at the back of the Isandhlwana hill thereby cutting off our retreat.

This was the Zulu "right horn", which had worked its way round the back of Isandlwana without the British noticing it. The uNokhenke, driven back over the ridge by the 24th's fire, had swung round to the right, and descended into the valley of the Manzimyama where, according to one of them, "The ground is high, full of dongas and stones, and the soldiers did not see us until we were right upon them." The original right horn, the uDududu, iMbube and iSangqu *amabutho*, had passed across the hills to the north of Isandlwana before descending into the Manzinyama valley further to the west. They had moved down the valley cautiously, cutting the road towards Rorke's Drift, then swinging up towards the nek.

George Shepstone must have tried to keep them at bay. Nothing was seen of him after he left to find Durnford in the camp, but his body was found on a steep rocky knoll at the south-western edge of Isandlwana. This spot is littered with boulders and falls away steeply to the dongas behind the mountain; and scattered amongst the aloes and bush which grow there today are some 30 graves, each containing between two and four bodies. This indicates a considerable stand; and, as the site itself is a commanding one, it must have slowed the Zulu advance. There is no record of this fight, and it is not known who these men were. Almost certainly, however, they were black troops, since the 24th and Volunteers were later meticulous in recording where the bodies of their own dead were found. The casualty returns of the NNC suggest that Pakhade's men suffered the most at Isandlwana, which means that these men might have been from Captain Erskine's company; or they might equally have been from Captain Murray's mysterious two companies. In either case, it is one of the ironies of history that this brutal struggle, overlooked by historians for a century, was waged by the very men whom many at the time blamed for the disaster.

On the right, Durnford's black troopers had been left without their officers. Simeon Kambule, the Sergeant-Major of the Edendale Troop, took his men off to look for ammunition when they fell back from the donga. They could not find their own wagon, but came across one belonging to the 24th guarded by a drummer boy. Kambule tried to persuade the boy to issue him with cartridges, but he was adamant that he had been posted there to prevent anyone but his own Battalion from getting them. There were loose rounds lying in the grass, dropped in the hurry to distribute them, and the Edendale men gathered them up; Kambule tried to persuade the boy to come away with him, as the battle was clearly lost; but

he refused to leave, and the Edendale men rode on.

Perhaps when Davies saw Durnford he was trying to rejoin his men, but if so it was too late, and he made his way instead towards the group of Carbineers and other Volunteers who, joined by a few redcoats, where holding a position on the slope below the nek. Mehlokazulu kaSihayo of the iNgobamakhosi described their stand:

> The Carbineers were still fighting when the Edendale men got into the camp. When the Carbineers reached the camp they jumped off their horses, and never succeeded in getting on them again. When they got into the camp they dismounted, made a stand, and prevented our entering the camp, but things were then getting very mixed up and confused — what with the smoke, dust, and intermingling of mounted men, footmen, Zulus and natives it was difficult to tell who was mounted and who was not . . .
>
> It was a long time before they were overcome — before we finished them. When we did get to them, they died all in one place all together. They threw down their guns when their ammunition was done, and then commenced with their pistols, which they used as long as their ammunition lasted; and then they formed a line, shoulder to shoulder and back to back, and fought with their knives.

He heard someone shout the command "Fire!" repeatedly; he did not see Durnford's death, but after the fighting was over he saw "a dead officer with his arm in a sling and a big moustache", surrounded by the bodies of his men.

George Shepstone's grave on a rocky knoll at the south-western foot of Isandlwana. No details of his last moments are recorded; but judging by the number of bodies found in this vicinity he died at the centre of a determined last stand, probably by African auxiliaries, against the Zulu "right horn" which swung south down the west side of the mountain and cut off the route of retreat. (Author's photograph)

Captain George Shepstone, Durnford's Political Assistant. (Killie Campbell Africana Library)

Private John Power of the 1/24th served with the Mounted Infantry, and had distinguished himself in the earlier Griqualand West campaign. He survived Isandlwana; and was later awarded the DCM for gallantry at Hlobane in March 1879. (Royal Archives)

The Hon. Standish William Prendergast Vereker was a Lieutenant with Captain Barry's No.5 Company, 2/3rd NNC, and was killed at Isandlwana. A persistent story has him giving up his horse to an African trooper who claimed it. (Anne Ruffell/Vereker Family Collection)

Parties of the 24th, meanwhile, were still fighting desperately towards the nek:

One party of soldiers came out from among the tents and formed up a little above the ammunition-waggons. They held their ground there until their ammunition failed them when they were nearly all assegaid. Those that were not killed at this place formed up again in a solid square in the nek of Isandlwana. They were completely surrounded on all sides, and stood back to back, and surrounding some men who were in the centre. Their ammunition was now done, except that they had some revolvers which they fired at us at close quarters. We were unable to break their square until we had killed a good many of them, by throwing our assegais at short distances. We eventually overcame them all in this way.

Any surviving groups were pushed over the nek and into the dongas on the far side. Here one large group rallied, and "kept up such a fire that no Zulu dared show his head over the nek and the Zulus began to waver; but another *impi* (the horn) coming round the back of Isandlwana compelled the soldiers to retire across the road, and they had nearly reached the first spruit about half way between the road and where the spruit joins the [Manzimyama] stream where they were met by another *impi*, the Zulu left horn in overwhelming force, and pushed along the valley of the Manzimyama where they made their last stands and all perished but a few who had horses, and some of these were overtaken. This body of soldiers fought

well and whenever they faced about to retire fired over the shoulder at us."

Individual fragments, grim vignettes from this last brutal stage of the battle, survive to illustrate the slaughter. "Just as I reached the tents", recalled uMhoti of the uKhandempemvu, "a bald-headed man, unarmed, rushed me and tried to dodge round it but was assegaid. I then met a soldier whose bayonet pierced my shield and while he was trying to extract it I stabbed him in the shoulder. He dropped his rifle and seized me round the neck and threw me on the ground under him, my eyes felt as if they were bursting and I almost choked when I succeeded in grasping the spear which was still sticking in his shoulder and forced it into his vitals and he rolled over, lifeless."

Some of the Colonials in the camp, presumably civilians, called out to the warriors in Zulu, "Have mercy on us. Spare our lives. What wrong have we done to [Cetshwayo]?" The Zulus replied, "How can we give you mercy when you have come to us and want to take our country and eat us up? How can we give you mercy? *Usutu!*"

A warrior of the uMbonambi, uMbongoza, came across an unarmed man who grabbed him by the throat; the two were wrestling on the ground when an uKhandempemvu warrior came past and stuck his spear straight through him: "He groaned, loosened his grip on my throat and rolled off me, writhing with pain on the ground."

Kumpega Qwabe, a warrior of the uKhandempemvu, came across a man armed with a revolver — presumably an officer. "Dum! Dum! went his revolver as he was firing from right to left, and I came along beside him and stuck my assegai under his right arm, pushing it through his body until it came out between his ribs on the left side. As soon as he fell I pulled the assegai out and slit his stomach so that I knew he would not shoot any more of my people." Generally the Zulus were not impressed by revolvers: "For every man they killed," Vumandaba kaNtati told Bertram Mitford after the war, "they fired a great many shots without hitting anybody."

Muziwento had heard that some men covered their faces, "not wanting to see death come upon them", but most simply fought on in a desperate rage. Bertram Mitford was told that in the last moments, when their ammunition was gone, many defended themselves with pocket knives and even their fists. Mehlokazulu kaSihayo described some of the fighting on the nek, as the Zulus tried to break up the last formations:

Some Zulus threw assegais at them, others shot at them; but they did not get close — they avoided the bayonet; for any man who went up to stab a soldier was fixed through the throat or stomach, and at once fell. Occasionally when a solder was engaged with a Zulu in front another killed him from behind. There was a tall man who came out of a wagon and made a stout defence, holding out for some time, and when we thought all the white people had been driven out of camp. He fired in every direction, and so quickly as to drive the Zulus some in one way, some in another. At first some of the Zulus took no notice; but at last he commanded our attention by the brave way in which he fought, and because he had killed so many. He was at last shot. All those who tried to stab him were knocked over at once, or bayonetted; he kept his ground for a very long time.

Mehlokazulu thought this man was an officer because when he later examined the body, although the jacket had been taken, he had gaiters on. If so his identity remains a mystery, for the fate of very few individuals has survived. Lieutenant the Hon. Standish Vereker was apparently seen, handing over his horse to an African who claimed it; since Vereker had been without a horse earlier in the fight the man's claim may well have been genuine, and Vereker behaved like a gentleman to the last. His body was found later at the foot of the mountain, by the stands on the nek.

Smith-Dorrien was in the camp when the line collapsed, and he heard a civilian wagon-driver named Du Bois say, "The game is up. If I had a good horse I would ride straight for

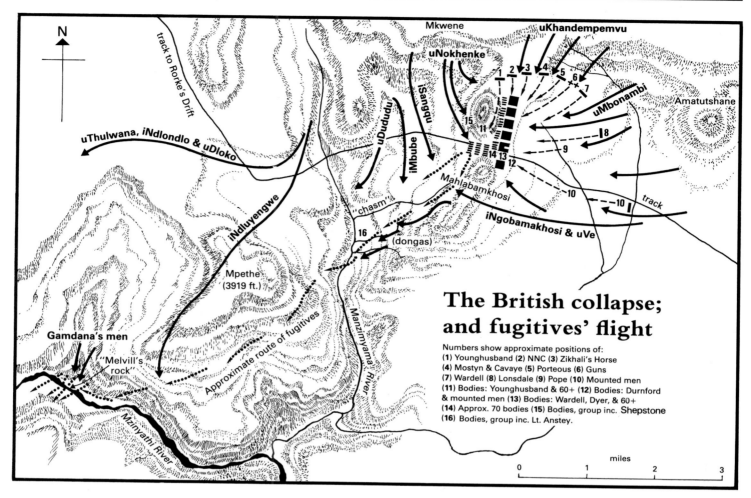

The British collapse; and fugitives' flight

Numbers show approximate positions of:
(1) Younghusband **(2)** NNC **(3)** Zikhali's Horse
(4) Mostyn & Cavaye **(5)** Porteous **(6)** Guns
(7) Wardell **(8)** Lonsdale **(9)** Pope **(10)** Mounted men
(11) Bodies: Younghusband & 60+ **(12)** Bodies: Durnford
& mounted men **(13)** Bodies: Wardell, Dyer, & 60+
(14) Approx. 70 bodies **(15)** Bodies, group inc. **Shepstone**
(16) Bodies, group inc. Lt. **Anstey**.

Maritzburg." Smith-Dorrien had a broken-kneed pony, but he took Du Bois' advice. The last thing he saw was Surgeon-Major Shepherd tending the wounded in a hollow. Shepherd was amongst those killed, though the exact circumstances of his death are not clear. Trooper Muirhead claimed to have seen him later:

> As we were riding for our lives, the Zulus pursuing us, my companion, a trooper named Kelly, staggered in the saddle, evidently hit with an assegai. I stopped my horse to see what was the matter, and tried to support him, but could not, and had to lift him off onto the ground. At that moment Dr.Shepherd came galloping past. I called out to him, and he dismounted to examine poor Kelly. After carefully examining him he said, "Ah, the poor fellow! Too late, too late!" I had just mounted my horse and Dr.Shepherd was in the act of putting his foot into the stirrup, when he was struck fatally with an assegai."

It may be that Shepherd had realised that there was no point in remaining in the camp; certainly the ambulance wagon tried to escape. Davies had seen it from the nek, trying to cross the rough ground to the left of the road before being overrun by the Zulus. Henry Harford, however, who had known Shepherd in the 99th, claimed to have found his body that evening amongst the wreckage in the camp. Clearly either he or Muirhead was mistaken, but the confusion is typical of that shrouding the last moments of many individuals at Isandlwana.

There are many stories about the deaths of the officers of the 24th, some of them obviously romanticised, others contradictory. A warrior named Maqeda kaNtshingwayo Mdlalose described how, during the rush through the tents, he

> saw before me a little tent standing apart from the rest, and I sprang in the door. There at the table was a man writing. As I appeared he looked up and put his hand down below the table. A little child of a gun [revolver] appeared in it and whispered death to me. But the bullet went into my mouth at one side and came out at the other side, and I sprang upon him and finished him with the assegai.

Years later, Maqeda still bore a puckered scar where the bullet had struck him. Because the tent, "apart from the rest", sounds like a Headquarters tent, his story has been taken to represent the end of Lieutenant-Colonel Pulleine. Yet Maqeda obviously did not know the identity of his victim; any number of men could have found a reason to write a note or an order in the last moments of the camp. There were several sightings of Pulleine; Captain Nourse thought he glimpsed him in the midst of a stand of the 24th some 800 yards down the Manzimyama valley. Both Colonel Glyn and Hamilton-Browne claimed to have found his body that night near the camp; it is likely that he was one of the men uGuku saw in the centre of the stand beneath the nek.

Of the other officers of the 24th, a Zulu *induna* who surrendered after Ulundi recalled that "on the neck of the plain" he had seen two officers with pieces of glass in their eyes. They both fired at him with their revolvers; one fell dead from a gunshot wound, the other kept firing, grazing the *induna* on the right side of his neck. The Zulu threw a spear which hit the officer in the chest; "by a supreme effort" he had almost succeeded in pulling it out ("here", continues the account, "the Zulu writhed his body in pantomime of the movements of the officer'), but the Zulu fell on him and finished him off with another spear. The officers of the 2/24th were later convinced that these two men were Lieutenants Pope and Godwin-Austen, both of whom wore eye-glasses. Lieutenant Daly was glimpsed at some point waving to the mounted men who rode past, then turning back to his men. The body of Paymaster White was found in the 2/24th camp.

The Zulus burst through the line at about 1.30 a.m. At about that time the moon passed in front of the sun, and the same eerie darkness which gave Trooper Symons at the Mangeni a premonition of disaster spread over the battlefield. The eclipse reached its height at 2.29 p.m. and, in the adrenalin rush of terror or bloodlust, the gloom added an apocalyptic touch to the confused nightmare around the foot of Isandlwana. "The tumult and the firing was wonderful", a warrior of the uKhandempemvu told Mitford, "every warrior shouted *Usutu!* as he killed anyone, and the sun got very dark, like night, with the smoke." A warrior of the uNokhenke noticed that it coincided with the last moments of the camp: "The sun turned black in the middle of the battle; we could still see it over us, or we should have thought we had been fighting till evening. Then we got into the camp, and there was a great deal of smoke and firing. Afterwards the sun came out bright again." In their frenzy some young warriors, who had been told to kill everyone in clothes and had never seen a white man before, stabbed and ripped at the sacks of mealies.

Durnford was probably dead by about 3 p.m. His brother and champion Edward Durnford observed that his watch had stopped at 3.20 p.m. and that it "*must* have stopped almost immediately after his death wound." It is difficult to see the logic of this statement, but in fact he cannot have survived much longer.

The company up on the shoulder of Isandlwana were among the last to succumb:

A lot of them got up on the steep slope under the cliff behind the camp, and the Zulus could not get at them at all; they were shot or bayonetted as fast as they came up. At last the soldiers gave a shout and charged down upon us. There was an induna in front of them with a long flashing sword, which he whirled round his head as he ran –it must have been made of fire. Weugh! (Here the speaker made an expressive gesture of shading his eyes). They killed themselves by running down, for our people got above them and quite surrounded them; these, and a group of white men on the "neck", were the last to fall.

In this last, desperate rush down the steep slope of the shoulder these men may well have been trying to link up with surviving groups on the nek and beyond. Some, at least, probably succeeded; the bodies of both Younghusband and his subaltern, Lieutenant George Hodson, were found in the group at the foot of the mountain. (This makes one survivor's story — that Younghusband had fought to the last, alone, by an empty wagon — seem unlikely.) At the very end, the killing had sunk to levels of primal savagery: "In the last struggle the butts of the rifles and stones were used, the soldiers having no cartridges."

The Zulus flushed out isolated individuals hiding in the camp and its confines throughout the afternoon. Thinking the fighting was over, uMhoti was eating sugar and watching Chelmsford's men returning in the distance when he was startled by a shot from the slopes of Mahlabamkhosi. "A soldier had been lying there and seeing a Zulu approach, fired at, and killed him, and then made a run for it; but was soon overtaken and speared."

High up on Isandlwana, another man was at last brought to bay. He was apparently a survivor from Younghusband's company who, rather than charge down onto the nek, had retreated up to the base of the cliff itself. Here he found a cave which he defended "until the shadows were long on the ground" — perhaps as late as 5 p.m. There are a number of shallow caves in the eastern face of Isandlwana, and one is sited directly above the shoulder. It is not deep, extending only two or three feet into the cliff face; but it is high enough to shelter a man standing, and the boulders projecting on either side and lying at its mouth would provide adequate cover. Long after every other white man in the camp was dead this anonymous soldier fought on, keeping the Zulus at bay with well-placed shots. There was no chance of escape, unless he hoped Chelmsford's force might return in time to save him; from his position he must have been able to see all too clearly the bloody ruin below. At last the Zulus grew tired of him, and brought up some men with rifles to fire into the cave and kill him. Perhaps it was a mercy.

"The Last of the 24th, Isandlwana", a painting by R.T.Moynan depicting the unknown soldier's defence of the cave at the foot of the eastern cliff. It combines a surprising degree of accuracy — both the 24th uniform and the Zulu costume are well represented — with classic Victorian iconography: the soldier's mystic expression and raised hand are suggestive of martyrdom, while the Zulus draw back before him in awe. The reality must have had a grimmer kind of poignancy. (Courtesy G.Corbett,Esq.)

Surgeon-Major Peter Shepherd, MB, the senior medical officer in the camp; he was apparently killed while tending the wounded, although accounts of the circumstances differ. (Royal Archives)

The cave where the incident is traditionally, and convincingly, said to have taken place. (Author's photograph)

CHAPTER EIGHT

The Hunting Trail

Those who survived had left the camp long before this. The first to go had probably been the men of Barry's NNC company, which broke shortly after the Zulus were discovered. At that stage the road to Rorke's Drift was open, though many of them must simply have scattered. Harry Davies of the Edendale Troop had seen the flood of fleeing NNC, "casuals" and civilian wagon-drivers go when the line collapsed. Unable to rejoin his men, he had asked Henderson, who was with him, what they should do; Henderson made no reply, but both of them then rode off across country. The interpreter Brickhill, too, had got out; like Smith-Dorrien he had met Du Bois, who asked him in Zulu how things looked; Brickhill replied, "Ugly". The two became separated in the confusion, and Brickhill rode off not knowing that Du Bois had also escaped from the camp.

The only body who seem to have made an organised retreat were the Edendale Troop. Brickhill had seen a group of "Basutos" keeping up a steady fire from under the rocks by the nek and, since the Edendale men were the only ones who had managed to secure a small supply of ammunition, it seems likely that these were they. They then joined the general movement across country. It was terrible country, as Brickhill described:

Our flight I shall never forget. No path, no track, boulders everywhere — on we went, borne now into some dry torrent bed, now weaving our way amongst trees of stunted growth, so that unless you made the best use of your eyes you were in constant danger of colliding against some tree or finding yourself unhorsed at the bottom of some ravine. Our way was already strewn with shields, assegais, blankets, hats, clothing of all descriptions, guns, ammunition belts, saddles (which horses had managed to kick off), revolver and belt and I don't know what not. Whilst our stampede was composed of mules with and without pack saddles, oxen, horses in all stages of equipment and flying men all strangely intermingled — man and beast apparently all infected with the danger which surrounded us.

Not all were simply fleeing: "Up to this time," claimed Trooper Barker of the Carbineers, "I had never thought of disaster, but only that we were retiring to a point to rally". Just beyond the road he met Trooper W. Tarboton; Tarboton's brother was also at Isandlwana, and he had lost sight of him in the confusion. He asked Barker to come back and help him search, and since Barker had been separated from his friend Hawkins he agreed. "As we got in sight of the camp," said Barker, "from a hill we both for the first time realised what had happened." Both Barker and Tarboton turned away, but many small groups of redcoats, even here and there an individual soldier, were making desperate stands on the slopes to the south-west of the nek. Some were pushed right down into the dongas by the banks of the Manzimyama; the body of Lieutenant Anstey of the 24th was found surrounded by a clump of redcoats amongst the dongas on the banks of the Manzimyama itself — nearly two miles from the camp.

While these knots of troops held together they probably had some idea of falling back on Rorke's Drift. The distinctive outline of Shiyane is clearly visible from the nek, and for most of the force it must have represented the only point where they knew they could cross the Mzinyathi safely, and where there was a garrison to support them. In the event, the route they actually took was dictated by Zulu pressure: cut off from the road by the right horn, the fugitives turned to the left in an attempt to go round the point. They had not gone far, however, when the left horn came over the ridge south of Mahlabamkhosi, and forced them sharply right again. The tips of the horns did not quite meet, and the fugitives made for the gap between them, which shifted as the warriors chased them on both sides. The fugitives were funnelled down the valley of the Manzimyama, still trying to head in the direction of Rorke's Drift, harried this way and that by their pursuers. Finally, they were spilled out onto the heights above the Mzinyathi where it enters the rough country about five miles south of Rorke's Drift.

When Lieutenant Davies was about 400 yards from the tents a Zulu stabbed his horse. Davies noted that the man wore a single red feather upright in his headdress; "in fact, all the natives had the red feather, no other ornaments." He thought it was a regimental distinction. A little further on, by a steep donga, Davies saw two soldiers stabbed, and he and a Carbineer who was riding by both fired, hitting one Zulu each. As the ground became progressively worse Davies had to dismount. He had caught up with Stafford by this time, and shortly afterwards two Zulus ran up, one of whom grabbed Davies' bridle. Davies had fixed the bayonet to his carbine on leaving the camp, and he lunged at the warrior, but the man simply grabbed his carbine and pulled it out of his hands "as if it were a toy". His horse shied, which carried him clear, though the other man threw a spear at him. Davies fired a shot with his revolver which, Stafford noticed, struck the Zulu in the head.

Stafford had already had adventures of his own; a little way down the hill he had come across a wounded man lying in a donga. Stafford stopped to help him — he said his name was Young, of Lonsdale's NNC — but it took several attempts before he could get his foot in the stirrup and climb up behind. The man had a bad stab wound under his arm, and was so weak from loss of blood that Stafford could hardly feel his grip. When Stafford drove his horse across a donga it faltered for a second climbing out the far side, and Young fell off. Stafford had no time to turn back for him.

(Stafford's account of Young's death has an interesting

The valley of the Manzimyama, looking roughly eastwards behind Isandlwana; Mahlabamkhosi is on the right, and the line of the deep donga or "chasm" can be made out running down towards the river, diagonally to bottom left. Most of the survivors fled around the top of the donga, right, only to be struck by the Zulu "left horn" coming over the Mahlabamkhosi ridge. Those who went too far down before crossing were trapped against the steep banks by the "right horn" advancing down the valley from the left of the picture. (Author's photograph)

Whitewashed cairns today mark where a concentration of bodies were buried on the Manzimyama side of Isandlwana; many of the last stands took place on the slopes down towards the stream (which is out of the picture, left). The angle of view is roughly north-east; on the skyline is the rocky southern shoulder of Isandlwana, with the nek to the right. (Author's photograph)

The bed of the Manzimyama, showing the broken ground on its banks which fatally slowed so many fugitives. The peak of Isandlwana is visible, left: note the distance — the last of the 24th were pushed over the nek and right down to the river before they were killed. Lieutenant Anstey's body was apparently found surrounded by a clump of dead redcoats in this area, some two miles from the camp. (Author's photograph)

sequel. Lieutenant L.D.Young of the 2/3rd NNC was indeed killed in the battle. His brother, Lieutenant H.C.Young, also claimed to have been in the camp. H.C.Young was posted missing for several days after the battle, and when he turned up at last in Durban he gave a detailed account of his brother's death and of his own escape. He claimed that L.D.Young had been shot through the head just as the line had collapsed, and that he had tenderly laid his body under a wagon wrapped in a blanket before riding off down the trail. When this story appeared in the press, however, Lieutenant Higginson wrote a letter saying that H.C.Young was never in the camp, being sick at Sandspruit on the day of the battle.)

Wally Erskine had left the camp without a horse. He had gone some way down the hill when, exhausted, he sat down to rest. He heard some Zulus killing soldiers nearby, and started up again. A little while later he overtook Stafford (Stafford says that this was after he met Davies) and, as Stafford had caught a spare horse, he gave it to Erskine. Erskine heard him say "Keep behind me", but when he looked round Stafford had disappeared. Erskine "watched where the contingent [men] were making for and followed them." He had gone about two miles when he saw a soldier, about ten yards away, run past a bush from which sprang a Zulu, who threw his stabbing spear into the man's back, knocking him forward onto his face. The Zulu ran up and, with a shout of *"Usuthu!"*, finished him off with the same spear. He had no sooner done this than he threw one at Erskine, hitting the calf of his leg. He shook it out, but another then hit his horse. Erskine pulled it out and threw it down when a bullet "whizzed about an inch from my nose." Miraculously, Erskine managed to struggle clear.

Six or seven hundred yards from the road a donga scars the western face of Mahlabamkhosi, flowing down towards the Manzimyama. About half way down the slope it opens into a narrow chasm, in some places 20 feet deep. Here many of the fugitives came to grief. Most of them went round the top of it, until the left horn, coming over the hill to their left, forced them down the length of it on the far side. The whitewashed cairns that mark their graves can still be seen today, spaced out at irregular intervals where some of them turned to fight or were simply caught and butchered. Shepstone's friend James Hamer struck this ravine too far down:

> I met it at the centre, we could not go above as the Zulus were too near, and we had to go to the end of it before we could cross. The Zulus saw this and large numbers tried to cut us off, I and four others were the last to get round, and we had to use our revolvers very freely, for the Zulus followed us up quickly, this ground being very bad for horses, and footmen had not the ghost of a chance.

Major Smith and Lieutenant Curling of the artillery had managed to get their guns through the camp, though Smith had been wounded in the arm and many of the gunners had been killed along the way. Curling saw Lieutenant Coghill nearby and asked him if "he could not rally some men and make a stand; he said he did not think it could be done." Seeing that the Zulus were already killing the men trying to flee along the road, the limbers turned off to the left, clattering across the stony country until they struck the donga. Here, according to Curling:

> When we had gone about 400 yards, we came to a deep cut in which the guns stuck. There was, as far as I could see, only one gunner with them at this time, but they were covered with men of different corps clinging to them. The Zulus were on them almost at once, and the drivers pulled off their horses. I then left the guns. Shortly after this I again saw Lieutenant Coghill, who told me Colonel Pulleine had been killed.

Curling's reference to Coghill is interesting, since it suggests that the latter had left the camp on his own. The heroic attempt by Coghill and the Adjutant, Melvill, to save the Queen's Colour of the 1st Battalion is, of course, one of the epic legends of Isandlwana. In the usual version of the story Melvill

William F.D.Cochrane photographed in the 1890s; attached to Durnford's staff, he escaped Isandlwana by "Damn all but my horse's ears", and was another of the only five Imperial officers to survive. (Natal Archives)

is depicted receiving the Colour from the hands of Colonel Pulleine, who charges him with its safety and the honour of the Battalion. Melvill and Coghill then cut their way through the Zulu hordes in a heroic death-ride.

In fact, there is no evidence one way or the other that Pulleine ordered Melvill to save the Colour. The story seems to have originated in a report which appeared in a Natal newspaper in January. Based on the account by "a gentleman whose testimony may be relied upon", it described how:

> When the loss of the camp seemed quite certain Colonel Pulleine called Lietenant Melville [sic] and said — "Lieutenant Melville, you, as senior Lieutenant, will take the colours, and make the best of your way." He shook hands with him and then turned round and said — "Men of the 1-24th, we are here, and here we stand and fight it out to the end."

It is difficult to know what to make of this account. It is significant that it is anonymous; the implication is that the writer was someone who knew the 24th well, and was with them when the camp collapsed. Several of the survivors might conceivably fit this description, but none of their accounts mention the incident although, if it were true, they could be expected to have made the most of it, since it showed both the 24th and the British Army in a very favourable light — which is, of course, precisely why it is probably just one of those heroic vignettes so beloved by the Victorians.

As Adjutant, the fate of the Colours did fall within Melvill's theoretical responsibility. (Each Imperial infantry battalion had two: the Regimental, which bore the regimental devices and battle-honours on a field of their facing colour; and the Queen's, which was basically the Union Flag. The Regimental Colour of the 1st Battalion was not in the camp; both of the 2/24th's Colours were, although it is not clear what part, if any, they played in the battle.) Pulleine may have ordered Melvill to save the Colour; Melvill may have taken it upon himself to do so; or he may have had some other purpose in mind, such as using them as a rallying point, which circumstances prevented him achieving. Whatever his intentions, they will never be known now. (The Colour, incidentally, was not flying; it was rolled on its staff inside a cylindrical black leather case with a brass top.)

Although Melvill left the camp at about the same time as Coghill they did not necessarily leave it together. Nothing is known of Coghill's movements in the battle; while he was probably acting as an ADC to Pulleine, his injury may have kept him out of the fight until it became serious. Near the end Private Williams, Colonel Glyn's groom, was ordered by Coghill to pack up the Colonel's tent; this was done, but in the event there was no opportunity to save his things. Williams later saw "Lieutenant Melvill leaving Camp with the Queen's Colours and Lieutenant Coghill close behind him; the latter told me to come on or I should get killed." Another survivor, Private Bickley, started off across country on foot, and after about a quarter of a mile caught a riderless horse. He had ridden on a little way when he came across Melvill with the Colour. "Mr. Coghill afterwards joined us and reported to the Adjutant that Colonel Pulleine had been shot." Curling made no mention of having seen Melvill when he met Coghill.

Undoubtedly, Melvill and Coghill caught each other up several times during their flight. Brickhill saw them together somewhere near the chasm:

A mounted infantryman, impatient of our indian file type of following one another put his horse at the gully. It was a noble looking grey but the horse fell far short and the rider lay crushed beneath his horse about 12 feet below. I have little doubt both horse and rider had found their grave. We found a crossing to the gully, but so steep that on coming out on this side I laced my arms round my horse's neck and threw my head as far forward as possible and even then it will remain a puzzle how our horses got out of this without falling over backwards. A little further I found Mr. Melvill carrying the Colours was just in front of me. We pursued our course for some distance when Melvill, in turning to me, said "Mr. Brickhill, have you seen anything of my horse back there?" After glancing back at our path for his satisfaction I explained that I had not . . . Going down to the Manzimyama Blackwater we had some very bad country, so bad that we all got off and led our horses. Here we were compelled to take one narrow pass. The flying party all converged there, there was a great crush. Seeing the danger of Melvill's position, for there was a steep precipice on his immediate left, I backed my horse and kept all the others back as well I could, as a collision there might have sent him and his horse rolling down for several yards. It was then that I became aware that Mr. Coghill was just behind, as he shouted "get on your horses there Mr. T — , this is no place to be leading a horse, get on your horses you fellows in front there." Someone near him said "you get off yours, this is no place to be riding one." I did not then know that he suffered from an injured knee and could not walk.

It is doubtful if any white men on foot survived the ordeal of the Manzimyama valley. A great many were killed amongst the dongas, where the chaotic terrain slowed them down and the Zulus caught them. A few, perhaps, crossed the stream, then foundered on the slopes on the far side. Even when spurred on by terror it was an exhausting journey for men on foot, many of whom had already been fighting throughout the morning. The fate of a few of them is known. Both Private Williams and Brickhill remembered seeing Band Sergeant Gamble "tottering and stumbling amongst the stones." Williams passed him, "but could give him no assistance." Gamble called out to Brickhill, "For God's sake give me a lift". Brickhill replied, "My dear fellow, it's a case of life and death with me", and, closing his eyes, put his spurs to his horse. It was a decision made on the instant, and it probably ensured that Brickhill, at least, survived, but years later he was still haunted by Gamble's pleas. Gamble was killed. A little later Brickhill came up to a soldier who simply sat down on a rock and said, "Well, I'm jumped, I'm done — the Zulus can just come and stab me if they like." Private Bickley saw Corporal Richardson, the 1/24th's Pioneer Corporal, ride up wounded,

James A. Brickhill, the interpreter for the Centre Column, photographed in later life. (Talana Museum, Dundee)

then fall off his horse and lie on the ground, unable to remount.

Crossing the Manzimyama, the fugitives came under a heavy fire as they climbed up the slopes of Mpethe hill beyond, but in fact the main Zulu pursuit seems to have spent itself in the valley. It took time to flush out the last survivors and to wipe out the stubborn knots of resistance, and this allowed the mounted men some respite. Their route took them over the top of Mpethe, striking the Mzinyathi, which lay like a brown ribbon winding through a steep gorge to their left. The summit of Mpethe gives rise to several springs; here and there the ground is marshy, and the fugitives scattered, "each seeking his own way out". Brickhill's horse bogged down for a second, and at the touch of the spurs he heaved and reared, and Brickhill's spectacles fell off. This was a serious loss, and Brickhill was peering down into the bright green grass trying to catch a glimpse of them when a bullet whistled past and reminded him that there were still Zulus nearby.

Smith-Dorrien saw Melvill near here, "in a red coat and with the cased Colour across the front of his saddle . . . I think the casing must have been half off, and hanging down." Coghill, he noted, was at least half a mile ahead. Lieutenant Higginson, who had met up with Durnford's transport officer Cochrane near the camp (when asked in later life how he escaped, Cochrane would simply say by "Damn all but the ears of my horse!"), came across Melvill and Coghill near the river; they had presumably just caught up with one another, and Higginson overheard them promise to stick together.

From the top of the hill Higginson saw that the river was alive with a struggling mass of men and animals. These must have been the NNC who fled early in the fight; there were Zulus already amongst them, and these seem to have been Gamdana's followers rather than men of the pursuing army — not all of that chief's adherents had approved of his decision to defect to the British, and many had remained in hiding in their

Private Samuel Wassall, 80th Regiment, served with the Mounted Infantry, and was the only Isandlwana survivor to be awarded the Victoria Cross — for turning back to rescue Private Westwood at Sothondose's Drift. (Royal Archives)

territory. Davies was told by his men who survived that "the Zulus left in the kraals as loyal men did more harm at the river than the men we were fighting with. It seems they let all the armed men pass and stabbed all the men without arms. I know some of the Zulus came out of some of the huts and chased us." There was no time to linger, however, for as they crested Mpethe the fugitives were struck by a fresh body of Zulus who came up from their right. These were almost certainly warriors of the iNdluyengwe *ibutho*. Along with the uDloko, the iNdlondlo and the uThulwana, the iNdluyengwe had been held back from the attack on the camp. They had swung round to the right of the Zulu advance, behind the right horn, moving across country west of the Manzimyama. The iNdluyengwe were despatched to mop up some of the survivors, and they struck into them just before they reached the river, literally forcing them down a steep precipice towards the water. Smith-Dorrien described the horror of that moment:

> We came to a kind of precipice down to the river Buffalo. I jumped off and led my horse down. There was a poor fellow of the mounted infantry (a private) struck through the arm who said as I passed that if I could bind up his arm and stop the bleeding he would be all right. I accordingly took out my handkerchief and tied up his arm. Just as I had done it, Major Smith of the Artillery came down by me wounded, saying "For God's sake get on, man; the Zulus are on the top of us." I had done all I could for the wounded man and so turned to jump on my horse. Just as I was doing so the horse went with a bound to the bottom of the precipice, being struck with an assegai. I gave up all hope, as the Zulus were all round me, finishing off the wounded, the man I had helped and Major Smith among the number."

This rocky precipice — the location of which is today lost under dense bush — cost the lives of many who had got thus far. Months later the bodies of horses and men were still lying amongst the boulders, and the marks made by horseshoes as the horses slid down the rocks could still be seen. At the bottom, the fugitives struck the river opposite a high cliff on the Natal bank. There was no hope of crossing there, but a narrow flat extended along the foot of the hill on the Zulu bank, and the fugitives fled through the long grass. Ahead of them, however, the Zulus were already extending in long lines to cut them off. There was no hope of getting further in that direction, and the only chance was to plunge into the river.

The spot where the survivors crossed was known as Sothondose's Drift, after a chief who lived on the Natal bank. (Since that day it has been known as Fugitives' Drift.) At low water the river flows over a rocky bottom and it is possible to pick one's way across. It was never, in the true sense, a drift, in that it was always a difficult crossing, as a large *isivivane* on the Natal bank — a pile of stones dropped by travellers to ensure good luck — bears witness. On 22nd January 1879 the river was in flood, and the water surged through the valley in a torrent 50 or 60 yards wide and six or seven feet deep. There was no obvious crossing point; the survivors crossed there because they had no choice.

Private Samuel Wassal, one of the Mounted Infantry, had just put his horse into the water

> and was urging him to the other side, when I heard a cry for help, and saw that a man of my own regiment, a private named Westwood, was being carried away. He was struggling desperately and was drowning. The Zulus were sweeping down to the river bank which I had just left, and there was a terrible temptation to just go ahead and save oneself. But I turned my horse round to the Zulu bank, got him there, dismounted, tied him to a tree — and I never tied him up more swiftly. Then I struggled out to Westwood, got hold of him, and struggled back to the horse with him. I scrambled up into the saddle, pulled Westwood after me, and plunged into the torrent again; and as I did so the Zulus rushed up to the bank, and let drive with their firearms and spears. But most mercifully I escaped them all and, with thankful heart, urged my gallant horse up the steep bank on the Natal side.

There were, indeed, some miraculous escapes. Trooper W. Dorehill of the Natal Mounted Police was approaching the drift when the Zulus ran to intercept him. Two were young men, the third older and wearing the headring. Dorehill was riding along the flat looking for a place to put in his horse when he heard the double report of a shotgun behind him. He felt no blow and assumed the shots had missed, but when he glanced round he saw the elder Zulu with a smoking gun in his hand, and the two young Zulus lying dead. The Zulu called out to him "Jump in the water!", which he did. He managed to get across to the far bank when he heard a voice crying for help. It was Trooper Hayes, his tentmate who had suffered premonitions of disaster the night before. Hayes had floundered into a patch of reeds and was stuck in the mud. Just then Sergeant Costello of the Artillery and a Mounted Infantryman named Gascoigne came past. Costello was on Major Smith's horse Black Eagle, though whether he had escaped from the camp on it, or whether he had just caught it after Smith's death, is unclear. The three men got Hayes out of the mud, but while they were doing so one of the NNC made off with his horse. Gascoigne went after him, knocked him off, and brought the horse back. While they were helping Hayes up about 20 or 30 Zulus loosed a volley at them from across the river, but the only casualty was Major Smith's cloak, rolled at the back of his saddle.

Smith-Dorrien admitted that he threw himself into the river on foot with "the strong hope that everybody clings to that some accident would turn up." He was being carried down the river at a tremendous pace when a riderless horse came past, and Smith-Dorrien caught its tail. It dragged him safely onto the other bank, but Smith-Dorrien was too exhausted to catch and mount it.

Lieutenant Vause of Zikhali's Horse had lost his mount, too, and on reaching the Natal bank he had sat down to rest when a young African boy — presumably a *voorlooper* — offered to let him ride behind him; Vause was convinced that this act saved his life. Davies found four Swinburne-Henry carbines discarded by the Zulu bank; he gave two to some wagon-drivers, and plunged into the water carrying a third. He lost it in the river, however, but on reaching the far bank noticed that some of his men were nearby, and joined them. The Edendale men, it seems, had managed to keep together along the trail, stopping periodically to fire a volley at the Zulus.

Wally Erskine had reached the river about the same time as Cochrane and Higginson. His horse was too tired to face the water, and he made way for Cochrane to pass. Erskine's horse then followed, but in midstream several men clung to its tail. Some Zulus were also in the water, however; they stabbed some of the fugitives, and the rest let go. As Erskine clambered onto the Natal bank he heard the Edendale men shout for him to lie flat on his horse's neck. He did so, thinking the Zulus were firing at him, but to his surprise the Edendale men loosed a volley which killed about a dozen Zulus across the river. "While watching this little skirmish", continued Erskine, "I saw one of our [men] brought to bay by a Zulu. After some preliminary guarding on the part of both, the Zulu stabbed the [NNC man] in the shoulder; thereupon our [man] jumped up into the air and stuck his assegai into the Zulu's heart. Both of them rolled into the river."

Brickhill had plunged his horse into the river — it was, he reflected, "no time for choosing the best crossing then" — and it began swimming well, but suddenly struck something beneath the water and stumbled. Brickhill hung on tight to its mane, all too aware that not ten yards downstream was "a waterfall and a seething pool in which three riderless horses were swishing round and round." Brickhill got safely out the other side, and caught a glimpse of Melvill in difficulties somewhere nearby. But Melvill's horse gave a plunge and Brickhill thought he was clear, "and I hastened on."

Higginson had put his horse in the water after Cochrane, but his mount too hit a stone in the water and

> he turned over and threw me off. I sank at once, as I had my rifle and ammunition with me, but on dropping them I managed better; the current carried me downstream a good distance, but I, fortunately, came on a large rock which I held on to: getting the water out of my eyes I looked round and saw [an African lad] mounting my horse on this side, I called out for someone to stop him, but no-one took any notice of me. I then saw Melville [sic] coming down stream towards me, he having also been thrown from his horse, he asked me to catch hold of the Colour. I did so and the force he was going pulled me off the rock into still water. Coghill, who had got out alright then rode his horse down to Melville to help him, but as he rode into the water, the Zulus who were on the bank we had just left, opened fire on us, and one of the first shots killed Coghill's horse; we were then all three in the water, and also I think the last white men to cross the river. We got out alright . . .

Those who managed to reach the far bank were utterly spent. Quartermaster Macphail of the Buffalo Border Guard was amongst them, and he found himself afflicted by the terrible thirst which strikes so many in the physical and emotional exertion of combat. He noticed a small stream flowing into the river just below the crossing on the Natal side, and "had a good drink. Somebody said, 'You're damned cool,' just those words. I said 'I am damned hot.'" Macphail noticed that Captain Essex had crossed the river nearby. Essex, Gardner and Cochrane had apparently met up on the Natal bank, and they conferred for a few moments. Essex was in favour of them making a stand on the Natal bank, but it was too late, the men were too exhausted. Macphail heard him say " 'We had better get into order to go to Helpmekaar', but there was no order at all. Nobody took any notice, but a lot did go to Helpmekaar." Essex gathered those about him who were willing, Stafford amongst them, and rode off in the direction of No.3 Column's old camp.

It seems clear that once on the Natal bank most of the

survivors thought they were safe from attack. The Zulus were still firing heavily from the other side but very few had managed to cross. Davies had seen two swim over, but they were stabbed by members of the NNC as they climbed out. Wassall had noticed that a few Zulus had braved the water, and that they "had a curious way of using their elbows which made them able to get across." Nevertheless, he thought that the current was running at the rate of six or seven miles an hour, and that "no ordinary man could swim it." Certainly it is doubtful if any of the fugitives had managed to get across without the help of a horse. The Zulus did not have a culture of swimming, and generally preferred to cross dangerous rivers in a mass, as Harford had observed when the NNC crossed at Rorke's Drift; but there is no evidence that they did so at Fugitives' Drift. Nor does it seem likely that those who did manage to swim across could have taken much in the way of weapons with them.

All of which makes the fate of Melvill and Coghill all the more intriguing. They had just crossed the river, Higginson said, when:

> Coghill called out "Here they come." I turned and saw only two men close to us, and turning to Melville said "For God's sake fire, you both have revolvers": they did so and I saw both Zulus drop; Melville then said "I am done up, I can go no further." Coghill said the same. I ran on, passed them, and got to the top of a hill, where a few Basutos on horseback had stopped, seeing me coming . . . I could see nothing of the two fellows behind me, so I guessed they had been overtaken.

Smith-Dorrien, emerging onto the Natal bank, had lain on his back and stuck his feet up into the air to let the water drain out

The fugitives plunge into the Mzinyathi River to escape the pursuing Zulus: an engraving based upon a sketch by Smith-Dorrien and Lieutenant W.W.Lloyd. Although the topography is not strictly accurate, this does give a convincing impression of the scene. (Author's collection)

Melvill's escape with the Colour, celebrated in spirited Victorian style by the illustrator Stanley Wood. This picture is more accurate than most, however, in that it at least shows the Colour cased. (Keith Reeves Collection)

Sothondose's Drift — now known as Fugitives' Drift — showing the large dark rock (centre) to which Melvill clung. On 22nd January 1879 the river was in flood, probably reaching to the line of bush at top right, and the top of the rock only just broke the surface. (Author's photograph)

of his boots. He struggled up and managed to catch a loose horse running by. He then noticed James Hamer lying exhausted on the ground, and offered the horse to him; Hamer hauled himself into the saddle, then rode off without waiting for his benefactor. (Hamer's own account omits this detail, perhaps out of embarrassment.) Smith-Dorrien then noticed that about 20 Zulus had managed to cross the river, presumably upstream, and were running round apparently to attack them. Were these the men who killed Melvill and Coghill? Possibly: there is, however, one other intriguing field for speculation.

There is a very strong local tradition amongst the farmers around Fugitives' Drift that Melvill and Coghill were killed by Africans living on the Natal bank. According to this story, some of Sothondose's people were watching the fight from the nearby heights when the Zulus called across to them to kill the white men; if not, the Zulus promised to cross the river upstream and come looking for Sothondose — a threat which must have seemed all too serious at the time. It is interesting to note that Higginson saw only two Zulus, and he does not suggest that they were particularly threatening; perhaps Melvill and Coghill provoked their own deaths by firing on men who were at that moment uncommitted to either side.

There are, of course, a number of drawbacks to this story. Sothondose had been called upon to provide a contingent for the border levy, and his followers could expect terrible reprisals should it ever be learned by the Colonial authorities that they had gone over to the Zulus at the crucial moment. Perhaps the Zulus harassing the fugitives on the Natal bank were Gamdana's followers, who had caused such havoc a few minutes earlier; some of them would presumably have known of safe places to cross the river, even in flood. When the Zulu reserve crossed the river upstream a little later, their warriors were seen hunting through the bush and firing into caves along the length of the river, searching out fugitives. Perhaps some had made the crossing in time to catch Melvill and Coghill. Sadly, there are no Zulu accounts of the incident apart from one collected in Qudeni as late as 1919. A warrior named

uMbulwane Mdine, who had fought at the battle, claimed that he had been wounded in the knee early in the fight by a Snider bullet accidentally fired "by one of my own side who did not know much about working his old [Snider] gun." Because of this uMbulwane did not see the end of the fight, but he was told some details by his friends who were

> *of the regiment that followed the fugitives to the Buffalo River. They told me they killed quite a number of soldiers along the path between Isandlwana and the Buffalo river. When my friends got to the Buffalo river they shouted to some Natal natives who were on the Natal side of the river and warned them not to allow the soldiers to get away — "if you don't kill them we'll kill you."*

(One last point before leaving Melvill and Coghill. According to the Regimental Records, Melvill's watch was later found to have stopped at 2.10 p.m., which the writer supposed was "probably the time he was washed off his horse." A stopped watch is no proof of anything — it might have run down days later, or even beforehand. Since the killing in the camp was at its height during the eclipse at 2.30 p.m., Melvill would have had to leave the camp very early to have reached the river by that time; given the number of men who saw him there, this seems unlikely).

Troopers Barker and Tarboton of the Carbineers had crossed the river safely and had climbed the hill on the Natal side, when they began to look around for any of their comrades. Barker saw a man behind him in the valley whom he thought was Hawkins, but when he went to fetch him he found it was Lieutenant Higginson. Barker allowed him to mount his own horse, which was too tired to take both of them; but once he was up Higginson rode off, leaving Barker to follow on foot. Barker had walked about three miles in a disgusted state of mind when Tarboton and some others rode back for him. They had met Higginson and recovered Barker's horse; Higginson had admitted frankly that he had been too exhausted to walk any further. Smith-Dorrien walked all the way, a distance he estimated at 20 miles, and got into Helpmekaar about sundown.

And so the remnants of No.3 Column straggled back to the very point they had started from just a fortnight before. Among them was not to be found a single one of the 1/24th officers who had laughingly drunk Degacher's and Porteous' toast, in their crate-and-tarpaulin mess, to "better luck this time". These remained with their friends and comrades, black and white — 1,357 of them — on the slopes of Isandlwana.

Lieutenant Nevill J.A.Coghill photographed just before the Anglo-Zulu War. His decision to return to Melvill's aid cost him his life, but subsequently won him one of the first posthumous awards of the VC. (Killie Campbell Africana Library)

Fugitives' Drift photographed from Mpethe hill on the Zulu bank; this is the view survivors would have seen as they reached the Mzinyathi River. They descended downstream and crossed the flats in the foreground, but were forced into the water by Zulus cutting them off from the right. Melvill and Coghill were killed, and subsequently buried, almost at the top of the heights on the Natal bank opposite — not down by the water, as so often imagined — and the very small white mark just visible at top left of this photograph is their grave. (Author's photograph)

Lieutenant and Adjutant Teignmouth Melvill, wearing the officer's forage cap and scarlet undress frock — this may even have been the jacket he was wearing when he was killed. (Royal Regiment of Wales Museum, Brecon)

CHAPTER NINE

The Butcher's Bill

By 3.30 p.m. on Wednesday, 22nd January 1879, the surviving troops of both the British No.3 Column and the main Zulu army were scattered over a wide area between the Mangeni gorge in the east, and Rorke's Drift in the west. There can have been no more than a handful of doomed white men left alive at Isandlwana, while the main Zulu attack had burnt itself out in the valley of the Manzimyama. It was at about this time that Lord Chelmsford learned from Hamilton-Browne that the camp was taken, and orders were given for his command to return to Isandlwana. At Rorke's Drift, the garrison left to guard the supply depot was still blissfully unaware of the storm about to break over them.

Although the sight of the survivors escaping across the Mzinyathi at Sothondose's Drift prompted a few Zulus to cross after them, the attack was largely spent by this time. Those who had fought in the battle had covered the five miles from the Ngwebeni valley to Isandlwana at a run, and then fought a battle which must have drained them both physically and emotionally. Those elements who had pursued the survivors had covered another six or seven miles of very rough country, fighting along the way.

If Natal lay exposed before them, they still had to cross the flooded Mzinyathi, and the king's prohibition on such attacks was general knowledge. There were some who advocated following up the attack; Prince Ndabuko kaMpane, King Cetshwayo's younger full brother, tried to urge the members of his own *ibutho*, the uMbonambi, to continue, but they refused, saying they had too many wounded to care for. Instead they marched slowly back to Isandlwana, singing a war-song which dated from King Dingane's time. Some of the iNgobamakhosi began to search for a way across, but the *induna* Vumandaba kaNtati called them back, reminding them of the king's orders. The *induna* Zibhebhu kaMapitha was amongst those who had joined in the chase, but he was apparently injured in the hand and he, too, decided not to continue. His response is probably indicative of a general feeling within the army that they had done enough for one day, and had nothing left to prove.

The same could not be said for the *amabutho* commanded by Prince Dabulamanzi kaMpande. The uThulwana, iNdluyengwe, uDloko and iNdlondlo regiments had been held back by the generals Ntshingwayo and Mavumengwana, and had then acted as their reserve. They had swung wide of the right horn, crossing the Rorke's Drift road west of the Manzimyama, where they seem to have divided. The iNdluyengwe were sent forward across Mpethe hill to cut off the fugitives, while the remainder of the force moved westwards across country, striking the Mzinyathi at the mouth of the Batshe valley. Only the iNdluyengwe, therefore, had seen any action in the battle, and their part in it had been limited to the slaughter of the survivors on the banks of the river. They were anxious to continue the fight; and moved upstream for a mile until they found a spot where they could cross en masse.

A contemporary eyewitness account suggests that they crossed "below the bend in the Buffalo", in an area where the valley is steep and narrow. At this point the Mzinyathi flows for perhaps a hundred yards through a fissure in the bedrock; when the water level is low it is perhaps ten feet below the top of the fissure, but in flood it fills it to overflowing. Although the water, compressed by the narrow gorge, flows through at a terrific rate, it would not be impossible for a large body of men to leap across at such a point; in any case, there are no other easy crossing places in the vicinity. Once across, the iNdluyengwe climbed the valley on the Natal bank and squatted down on a rise to rest and take snuff.

* * *

Back at Isandlwana, the victorious army had utterly ransacked the camp. "When it was over", recalled uNzuzi of the uVe regiment:

> we went into the tents and took what clothes and blankets we could find and also collected as many rifles as we could. The tents we cut into strips and left them lying there. We did not touch any of the food because we thought it might have been poisoned, so we cut open the bags and smashed the boxes, throwing the contents all over the veld. The oxen and mules that were left we took, but we killed all the horses because they were the feet of the white men and we had not been ordered to take those back to the king.

In the fury of the assault, hundreds of animals had been killed along with the combatants. Despite the value the Zulus placed on oxen, many were slaughtered in the frenzy of blood-letting which characterised the height of the battle; whole teams were later found dead in their traces. Apart from a few horses taken for sophisticated chiefs like Sihayo, who knew their worth, they were all killed, along with the camp dogs. (Many officers had taken their pets with them on campaign, and the 24th had collected dozens of strays on their march up from Durban. A number escaped, but where the Zulus caught them, they killed them).

All the rifles which could be found were taken, together with any cartridges found on the bodies. The Zulus prized open the reserve ammunition supplies; those who had acquired a Martini-Henry took away what ammunition they could carry, and those who possessed percussion or flintlock guns tore the bullets out with their teeth and kept the powder; in 1882 the traveller Mitford noted that the camp was littered with piles of empty cartridge cases which had not been fired. Useful strips of canvas from the tents were carried away, and the rest were burnt. A few wagons were dragged off that same day, though the rest, with the artillery battery's two guns, were left abandoned on the field. Tools — axes and shovels — were taken, together with money, watches, and any valuable looking trinkets. The rest, all the everyday impedimenta of camp life, was examined, discarded and scattered about: portmanteaux, boxes, boots, brushes, photographs and countless letters and papers.

After the terrible exertions of the fight many Zulus were desperately thirsty, and they searched the camp for drink. They were particularly keen to find "canteen", the name by which they called alchohol. "I found a bottle", remembered uMbongoza of the uMbonambi, "and I was so hungry for it that I did not wait to take out its stopper. I just broke the neck off and drank." Yet there were dangers in this, since most Zulus were unable to tell alcohol from the medicines stored in the hospital tent, or paraffin found in the camp. "We left the wagons but took all the canteen and paraffin we could get hold of", said Gumpega Qwabe of the uKhandempemvu. "Some of our men were so thirsty for the white man's drink that in their haste they started to drink the paraffin instead." Several were poisoned, and the shock caused by this unexpected injury was so great that the writer E.V.Morton found an echo of it lingering in the 1930s: he met a chief called *Nkantini* kaSitheku, whose father Sitheku fought at Isandlwana, and had named his son in memory of the terrible surprise sprung by the white man's "canteen".

The British dead were stripped of their jackets and shirts, and left where they fell. The Zulus believed that to cause a death in battle resulted in the release of evil forces, *umnyama*, which could only be countered by performing various cleansing rituals known as *zila*. According to Mpashana kaSodondo of the uVe, "Clothing was also looted. These were taken by the warriors who had killed. They zila'd with them. Every single corpse was stripped absolutely naked. I saw this."

Mehlokazulu, however, commented that "as a rule we took off the upper garments, but left the trousers, but if we saw blood upon the garments we did not bother." Certainly the bodies were found later in various states of undress, as each warrior who had killed had to remove some item of apparel from his victim; if he had killed more than one, he took something from each. He was required to wear it until the cleansing ceremonies were complete. The British found this shocking; but they were even more appalled by the Zulu habit of disembowelling the dead.

According to Mehlokazulu "all the dead bodies were cut open, because if that had not been done the Zulus would have become swollen like the dead bodies". It was necessary to dissipate the *umnyama* that lingered around the corpse by opening it from sternum to groin, an operation which, in the aftermath of a great battle like Isandlwana, was performed with varying degrees of precision and efficiency. Certainly most warriors were keen to disembowel their victims immediately — "after killing them we used to split them up the stomach so that their bodies would not swell" — to reduce the risk of any supernatural taint attaching to the slayer. Trooper Richard Stevens of the Natal Mounted Police had noticed that even at the height of the battle, as he was fleeing the camp, "They were not content with killing, but were ripping the men up afterwards." Each warrior was supposed to disembowel his own victim, but with some falling to shots fired a long way off, and in the utter confusion of the last mêlée, it was obviously impossible for many to claim their personal victims. Indeed, some corpses escaped mutilation altogether.

Prince Dabulamanzi kaMpande, leader in 1879 of the uNdi corps which crossed into Natal on the 22nd, photographed with the trader John Dunn (right) at Cetshwayo's "coronation" five years before. (Local History Museum, Durban)

Nevertheless, most of the dead presented a terrible sight. Most of those who had died by the spear had probably fallen to a flurry of blows; in the extreme excitement of the moment few warriors would have been content to make one clean stab, and it was natural to strike repeatedly to ensure that a man who went down, stayed down. Other Zulus coming past later also stabbed the bodies; this was a custom known as *hlomula*, observed when hunting powerful or dangerous animals, when some portion of the glory of stabbing the animal still attached itself to a man who stabbed such a fierce adversary even after it was dead. That the Zulus observed this custom at Isandlwana is a macabre testimony to the desperate resistance put up by the camp's defenders.

No medical reports were ever compiled on the dead of Isandlwana, but a description of the body of the Prince Imperial of France, killed in a skirmish some months later, suggests exactly the sort of injuries they must have sustained:

There was one longish wound on the right breast which was evidently mortal, for the assegai had passed through the body, and the point had penetrated the skin of the back. There were two hurts in the left side also which might well be mortal, and less serious wounds all over the upper part of the chest, and one in the right thigh. The eye was out, but whether by the thrust of an assegai or by the impact of a bullet of some kind it was impossible to say. If a bullet . . . it could not have been projected with any force. There was a large gash in the abdomen exposing the intestines, which were, as in the case of the trooper, uninjured . . . The gash . . . in the abdomen is not, I feel assured, inflicted with any idea of mutilating the corpse of a slain enemy, but simply because it is a belief among them that if this coup is not given, and the body swells, as it would by the generation of the gases of decomposition, the warrior who had neglected this precaution is destined to die himself by his body swelling . . . the gash was in every case inflicted after death, for no blood had flowed . . . Many of the wounds were so slight that I think they too must have been inflicted after death, all the members of the party probably "washing their spears", in pursuance of some ceremonious regulation on the subject of the enemy dead.

Later, the British were particularly concerned to find out if any parts of the bodies had been removed for use in later doctoring ceremonies. Human body parts from a defeated enemy could have an immense value as *intelezi* medecine in soliciting the help of the spirit world, as Mpashana observed:

The doctor then treats his own impi with these bits of human flesh . . . These bits are used by the doctor after the vomiting ceremony, eating of the meat strips, and washing at the drift, and just as the impi is about to move off, when the impi is brought into a circle formation and treated with the smoke of burnt medicines . . . It is not given out publicly that a doctor had succeeded in getting pieces of the enemy's flesh, but of course the information gets about and becomes generally known, but only by degrees.

Most warriors were reluctant to admit that this might have occurred at Isandlwana, although Mehlokazulu did admit the

"It's all bosh!": Brevet Major Matthew W.E.Gosset, 54th Regiment, one of Chelmsford's three ADCs in 1879. (Ministry of Defence)

possibility. "There was a man," he said, "whose head was cut off at the entrance to the camp, where the white people had held out, and formed back to back." (Curiously, one of the Carbineers later heard that one of his regiment who had died on that spot had been decapitated; it was Edward Tarboton, whose brother had returned with Trooper Barker in a vain attempt to find him.) Certainly the dark tales of mutilation which have survived would suggest that a limited number of body parts were removed. In the Zulu civil war of the 1880s Zibhebhu kaMapitha's war-doctors took from the corpse of an enemy "a piece from his forehead . . . His rectum, penis, bone of the right forearm (throwing arm), also the cartilege from the bottom of the breast-bone . . . the rectum is taken to cause fear by causing agitation in the stomach, and to bring on diarrhoea. This is the method of causing fear." It is instructive to compare this account with Archibald Forbes' observation that "some were scalped, and others subjected to yet ghastlier mutilations" (see Chapter Eleven).

It seems that facial hair from the European dead had a special significance as *intelezi* medicine; at the beginning of the 1906 Bambatha Rebellion, Bambatha's war-doctor Malaza had removed from the body of Sergeant Brown of the Natal Mounted Police, killed in the action at Mpanza, the left forearm, private parts, and upper lip bearing a moustache. At Isandlwana, the warrior uNzuzi recalled that "some of our bad men cut away the lower jaws of those white men who had beards and decorated their heads with them", although they were later reprimanded by án *induna* who told them contemptuously that "the mighty Zulus did not get their strength by cutting up dead bodies and carrying bits around with them." These grisly trophies were thrown away; and truly the area around Isandlwana must have resembled a slaughterhouse:

> The green grass was red with the running blood and the veld was slippery, for it was covered with the brains and entrails of the slain. The bodies of black and white were lying mixed up together with the carcasses of horses, oxen and mules.

For the Zulu dead and wounded there were no organised medical facilities or burial details. The wounded relied on friends or family to carry them away. Similarly, kinsmen were obliged to decently bury the bodies of the killed where they could find them, and many were tumbled into grain pits in the empty homesteads around the plain, or tipped into dongas. Many corpses were left in a donga along the line of retreat, at the foot of the spur; nearly a century later a heavy rain exposed some of their bones, and they were buried beneath the floor of a small chapel, "the tomb of the unknown warrior", at the nearby St. Vincent's mission. For those who had no friends or relatives to observe even these minimal last rights there was nothing to be done but to cover the bodies with a shield and leave them on the field.

How many Zulus died? It is impossible to arrive at a precise figure because the Zulus did not compile casualty lists, but assessed the cost of a battle by the number of important men killed; and although several chiefs of note fell at Isandlwana this does not give any reliable guide to the true losses. Wild British estimates placed the figure as high as 3,000, but this was optimistic; in fact the Zulus lost perhaps 1,000 men killed, though many more wounded. On reflection, after the war, many Zulus admitted that the victory had been Pyrrhic.

The pillaging of the camp took until late afternoon, by which time Lord Chelmsford's force could be seen advancing from the direction of the Mangeni; and the army began to drift away into the Nyoni heights, carrying its loot with it.

* * *

Out across the plain, Trooper Symons caught sight of the movement: "We perceived dark groups moving up onto the hills to the left of Isandhlwana which we concluded at first from the gleaming of the bayonets to be soldiers, but which proved to be Zulus driving cattle and wagons. Now the tents began to disappear one by one and the anxiety to know what had become of our friends became intense, and the suspense became maddening."

It will be remembered that Lord Chelmsford had ridden back towards Isandlwana, accompanied by the mounted men, to find out for himself what had happened — but with no great sense of urgency. Indeed, Harness and the two companies led by Captains Church and Tongue had been ordered to resume their march to the new camp site at the Mangeni. The Police and Volunteers started out ahead of the General, who was escorted by the Mounted Infantry; and were passed on the way by a rider, presumably one of Hamilton-Browne's messengers, looking for Chelmsford. He must have passed something on to the Volunteers, since Symons recalled that he had "intelligence of the destruction of the camp by the Zulus; or should I say capture, for the tents were still standing, as I could see." A little further on the troopers passed Harness' command, still marching in the opposite direction. "I can't describe my feelings at that time", wrote Symons:

> There was a mixture of anger and grief and foreboding. Anger in the delay in returning to camp, when the guns in the morning had warned us the camp was being attacked: foreboding as to the fate of the garrison for I knew the Zulus would not give quarter, that is not their way, and grief at the thought that we could do nothing to help.

Chelmsford and his escort came up and overtook them, but no fresh orders were given, and after another couple of miles they

Detail from group photograph of the band of the 1/24th at King William's Town, 1877/78; Bandmaster Burck (seated centre left) does not appear on the Isandlwana casualty roll, but most of the band died there, serving as stretcher bearers. Note the young band boys in the front row: were any of these the victims of the notorious atrocity? (Africana Museum, Johannesburg)

met Hamilton-Browne's NNC battalion. By now the camp's fate must have been common knowledge, and a little while later any doubts were dispelled when the party met Lonsdale. Despite everything, it was still difficult to believe that such a catastrophe had occurred: " 'Impossible!' said most, nevertheless a messenger was sent back to call up the guns, infantry and Police, and we went forward and halted about three miles from the camp to await those in the rear." Symons was tormented by that wait so close to the camp, seeing what was happening in the distance, and imagining that anyone left alive in the camp could see them:

> We stood for about three hours watching the sacking of the camp. My head, and my heart ached, too with the thought of how the survivors must be willing us to their help, for survivors there must have been when first we came to our present position, and how they must have cursed us for the delay. "When will the infantry come up?" was the universal groan. Noone stopped to think that it was not the infantry's fault, but the General's for leaving them behind and ignoring all reports about the enemy.

Back at the Mangeni, Chelmsford had ordered the "Assembly" sounded before his departure. The 2/3rd NNC were still engaged in flushing out the survivors from Matshana's party, and they broke off the fight and fell back on the flat above Mangeni gorge. Passing some homesteads where six elderly Zulus were taken prisoner — "we saw a few women and children also, but these were not interfered with" — Lieutenant Maxwell managed to catch a chicken. Most of the men had still not eaten since the day before, and when they were ordered to fall out Henry Harford was amused to see that "being hungry, they bounded off like a herd of scared deer in all directions in search of kraals and mealie fields, and were very soon out of sight." Maxwell had managed to pluck and clean his bird, and had just started to cook it over a fire when the assembly sounded:

> Needless to say how disappointed I was at being compelled to leave the bird behind. We fell in and I found myself with the rear guard on the road marching back to Isandhlwana. I imagined something was wrong — but was struck almost speechless when our Commandant having waited on the road for me, told me that the camp had been destroyed by the enemy during the morning and everybody slaughtered and that we were marching back to retake the camp or — He said no more, except requested me not to mention this to anyone.

Henry Hallam Parr was with the Regulars when the news broke:

> Some one said "Hallo! there's a man in a hurry. He ought to have a horse behind every hill at that rate." "Who's the man?" said another. "I can't see; have you your glasses?" said the first speaker. "By Jove! it's Gosset. I hope nothing has gone wrong." Interest in the rider being awakened, we watched him gallop up the hill toward us, his horse evidently blown and weary. "Well, Gosset, what is it? you seem in a great hurry." "The General's orders are that you are to saddle up and march towards Isandhlwana at once," said Gosset; "the Zulus have got into our camp." "The Zulus have! You're not joking?" "I wish I was. Lonsdale met the General about five miles from the camp, and had seen the enemy in amongst the tents. The General is waiting for you with the mounted men."

The road back to Isandlwana seemed to the weary men "a hundred times longer than when we had stepped it twelve hours before"; and it was dusk by the time the infantry caught up with the General's party, who were waiting on some low ground by a stream, where the men hastily refilled their water-bottles. Chelmsford addressed them:

> Whilst we were skirmishing in front . . . the Zulus have taken our camp. There are ten thousand Zulus in our rear, and twenty thousand in our front; we must win back our camp tonight, and cut our way back to Rorke's Drift tomorrow.

It was hardly reassuring news, but the men answered with a shout of "All right, sir; we'll do it." Trooper Symons noted that Chelmsford added, "No man must retire": "As there was no place to retire to, this last order was superfluous, but we cheered most heartily." Henry Fynn wasn't so sure; he thought the 2/24th refused to cheer.

Nathaniel Newnham-Davis of the Buffs, photographed as a Captain in 1884. He served with the Mounted Infantry in 1879; and aroused Henry Harford's wrath by refusing to share with his hungry comrades a tin of bully-beef he found on the battlefield. In later life he wrote books as a gourmet. (Buffs Museum, Canterbury)

The men were then formed up, Harness' guns in the centre on the road, with the 24th in fours on either side. To the right were the 2/3rd NNC in line of column, and on the extreme right were the Mounted Infantry and Police in troops. To the left of the 24th were the 1/3rd NNC, flanked by the Carbineers, Buffalo Border Guard and Newcastle Mounted Rifles. The 24th marched well, keeping up a steady pace, with the NNC silent on either side of them; "there was no gwia-ing or capering now, the only sound from them . . . was the rattling of their sticks or assegai handles, as they clicked against one another." After they had marched a little way a warrior with a shield suddenly stood up in the grass ahead of them, and "an active little Mounted Infantryman, scouting in front, no sooner saw him than he sprang from his horse and fired several shots, missing each time though, before he could be told to stop." It was just as well that this soldier was such a bad shot, for the warrior turned out to be a man from the NNC who had slipped away from the Mangeni earlier in the day and had lain hidden when he found his return to Isandlwana cut off. Several more appeared as the little column advanced. By this time it was getting quite dark,

> and we had to regulate our movements by the rumbling of the gun and cart wheels for that, and the clicking of sticks, and the swish, swish of the men's and horses' feet was all the sound we heard. Fires sprang up in the camp and hope began to revive in us that perhaps our men had held it after all or retaken it. Before darkness set in we had seen the Nqutu mountain so covered with Zulus that it looked like it would be in winter time when the grass had been burnt off freshly. I never saw such a crowd in my life.

On the outskirts of the battlefield the horses began to shie at the first Zulu dead, lying in the long grass with their shields over their backs. To Symons, it seemed as if they were marching into the jaws of death.

At about two thousand yards from the camp the line halted, and Harness unlimbered the guns. Against the fading glow of evening in the western sky the wagons could just be seen silhouetted on the nek, and there was a feeling that perhaps the Zulus had dragged them into a barricade. Harness' battery fired several shells into the camp to disperse them, and Symons thought the fires in the camp were extinguished by the first salvo. The burning fuses of the shells traced their trajectory through the gloom:

> It was a pretty sight to see the bright flash of the gun and the graceful curve of the shell as it passed like a meteor through the air, to fall and rebound over the nek. Sometimes the shell would strike Isandlwana and bring down the rocks with a crash. Some went into the valley beyond.

There was no response from the camp; so the 2/24th fixed bayonets, and the whole line advanced. By now it was quite dark, and since there was no moon the men were guided by nothing more than a faint starlight. Lieutenant Maxwell, out on the flank, followed his skirmishers into one of the deep dongas running across the front of the camp. Suddenly he found himself on his back with his reins in his hand and his horse nearby. Feeling rather shaken, he managed to remount and, calling out to his men, found they were nearby. Having got into the donga, however, they could not find a way out in the dark, and had to walk up it until they eventually struck a path.

On the other flank, Trooper Symons noticed his first man lying dead in a red coat, and the horses shied at more as they pressed on up the slope. Captain Shepstone's African servant was leading a packhorse, and stopped when the pack slipped. Thinking Symons was the last man in the troop, he begged him not to leave him alone; he was weeping with terror, but stuck to his charge. Symons and a few of his comrades stopped to help him rearrange the pack, when Shepstone rode back and urged them on, "so I presume he stayed to see the native off."

A little way out from the 1/24th camp they were halted again, and Major Wilsone Black was ordered to take the left half-battalion and to seize Mahlabamkhosi. At the head of his men he marched off into the night, and after a few anxious minutes the column heard them giving a loud cheer; they had occupied the hill without opposition. The remainder of Chelmsford's force then moved up, and prepared to bivouac just below the 1/24th camp. There were a few Zulus still lingering amid the wreckage; Maxwell's party found eight or ten of them lying drunk on a buck-wagon. He called over a party of the 24th, who "put the bayonet through them."

The accounts of that night spent on the battlefield have a surreal quality, a sense of unreality mixed with horror. The men were hungry and exhausted, and concern for the fate of their comrades mingled with a fear for their own predicament. Odd noises broke the still night; Trooper Cunningham of the Newcastle Mounted Rifles swore he heard jackals screaming for blood, while out in the darkness a wounded or drunken Zulu cried out at regular intervals. Symons thought that the crying of wounded mules sounded like children, and somewhere under the mountain a badly wounded man was groaning. The air reeked of death, "a cold unearthly smell which must have arisen from the numerous dead bodies". It was a smell which haunted Sam Jones of the NMR all of fifty years later:

> *And the stench! It was awful. I can still smell it at times. Some things remind me of it, as for instance a sweet potato that has been cooked when it is just beginning to go bad. And when I smell such things I become quite ill.*

Amongst the dead Jones noticed his horse, with its leg still wrapped with a red bandage. His keenness to go into the anticipated battle had saved him despite the efforts of his well-meaning brother.

The dead were, indeed, lying everywhere. Chelmsford's men were bivouacking on the site where some of the fiercest fighting had taken place, and Trooper Symons found himself lying near the corpses of three men he knew — Troopers Swift and Jackson of the Carbineers, and Trooper Guttrige of the Buffalo Border Guard. A Mounted Infantryman told Symons that he had nudged the man next to him and asked him for a drink; thinking him asleep, he reached out to take his water-bottle, "and his hand came in contact with the man's disembowelled body." In the morning Sam Jones noticed that several men's mackintoshes were caked with the bloody mud in which they had unknowingly lain down to sleep. Henry Fynn found himself close by the veterinary surgeon's wagons, which gave off a sickening smell from the bottles of chemicals which had been smashed there:

> *Many had drunk of these chemicals as war charms and eaten carbolic soap as biltong and died; one elderly Zulu on the ground, a Thulwana, becoming conscious thus explained to me the particulars, and died an hour or so later beside me.*

John Maxwell had a worse memory to live with. He had been awoken by a messenger telling him that Lord Chelmsford wanted to see him: the General wanted to inspect the NNC outposts, some of whom were reluctant to stay at their posts. Maxwell was not the officer on duty, but thought it easier to show him than to protest, and duly went the round accompanied by Chelmsford and Clery. Maxwell managed to find most of the picquets, but was compelled to explain his ignorance when he could not find the last one. Chelmsford apolo-

gised, and asked him to rouse out the real officer of the watch. Maxwell had gone a few paces when:

> *I tripped and fell down the mountain some 10 or 12 paces. Naturally I had my hands in front in the position I can remember of one about to take a dive, and a dive it was, for I found myself with my hands in the inside of what turned out to be the body of a 24th man, and my heels up hill. The Major [Clery] having heard the fall turned the lanthorn and discovered me in the above predicament. Luckily I was not hurt, but my hands and wrists were in a nice mess. I succeeded in somewhat cleaning them with the damp grass, and not until the morning on crossing the spruit did I succeed in thoroughly washing them.*

Many of the men were so exhausted that they fell asleep immediately, and even the issue of some beef and biscuits could not rouse them. Hallam-Parr was in charge of distributing the rations, and after the Regulars and Volunteers were given theirs they were issued to the officers and NCOs of the NNC:

> *One officer — I could not see his face and have no notion of who he was — asked leave to draw for six or seven of his comrades, and as he had forgotten to bring a haversack, and could not carry six or seven rations of loose biscuit and tinned rations in his hands, I told him he had better hold out his hat for the biscuit. "Sir," he said stiffly, "I must object to your suggestion. I should prefer to go without my rations than carry them in my hat." As it then seemed highly probable that before long there would not be many of us with either a head to put a hat on or a mouth to put a biscuit into, I sent this gentleman away in a hurry to fetch some one else to draw rations.*

Out on Mahlabamkhosi, Trooper Symons heard Major Black call out an intervals to steady his men: "Don't shoot, boys — cold steel is our motto." Symons was impressed, and contrasted Black's attitude with his own Captain Offy Shepstone, who began shaking hands with his friends and saying good-bye, " 'For we shall never see the sun rise again.' From that moment I lost confidence in the Capt. Major Black's the man for me, 'Cold steel is our motto', no going around saying goodbye about him." Trooper Cunningham was less impressed, however; he thought Black had gone mad.

Several times during the night there were false alarms. Hallam-Parr and the Regulars blamed the NNC, but neither Harford nor Hamilton-Browne mention a serious panic amongst their men, while Maxwell even commented archly that "there were two or three false alarms during the night, and they were not caused on this occasion by the Native Contingent."

Many men wanted to examine the camp in the hope of finding some friend or relative, but Chelmsford refused them permission; Seargeant-Major Dan Scott of the Carbineers set out to look for his brother, Lieutenant Durrant Scott, but was turned back. A few were allowed through to look for food or on other practical errands, however; and they returned with vivid tales of the horror beyond.

Harford, looking for his outposts, visited his tent, and came across the bodies of two dead drivers who appeared to have blacked their faces in a pathetic attempt to escape detection. Beneath a wrecked ambulance wagon stinking of chemicals he saw a body lying face down with a stab-wound in the neck; he thought it was Surgeon Shepherd.

The body of Signalman Aynsley of HMS *Active*, the naval ADC Milne's servant, was found by Lieutenant Newnham-Davis and some of his Mounted Infantry; his pockets had been rifled, and several photographs were strewn around him. Newnham-Davis gave the photos to Milne, but kept Aynsley's cutlass as a souvenir. Newnham-Davis also found an undamaged tin of bully-beef; and to Harford's disgust, "as we tramped in together to Rorke's Drift the following morning demolished the lot, never offering me or anyone else a mouthful. I don't think another officer, NCO or Private, in the whole column, would have been guilty of such selfish gluttony."

He was not the only one who took a souvenir. Rupert

Lonsdale kept a knobkerry to remind him of his narrow escape. The trumpeter of the Natal Mounted Police went to his tent and returned with his boots, and a story that he had seen "several wheels lying about, and most of them with the heads of our men pushed round them in a circle." Colonel Glyn and some of his officers searched about for the bodies of their comrades, and Glyn thought that he recognised Pulleine and Hodson. Hamilton-Browne also thought that he recognised Pulleine; if true, these reports tend to confirm that Pulleine had died with the men making their last stands on the nek.

During the night the occasional flare of burning farms or homesteads could be seen along the line of the Natal border. A faint glow burned behind Shiyane, and the distant crackle of musketry could be heard; for a while it was hoped that there might be some innocent explanation, but it soon became clear that the Zulus had crossed into Natal and the garrison at Rorke's Drift was under attack.

Chelmsford ordered the men to stand-to before dawn, and the column moved off before the men had a chance to witness the full horror of the camp. Nevertheless, as the sun came up they caught macabre glimpses. Civil Surgeon Thrupp, attached to the 24th, saw the body of an Engineer officer and, noticing his watch, took it from the body. Some time later, when he tried to trace the owner, it transpired that it had belonged to Durnford. In the camp Symons noticed a young black lad, apparently a *voorlooper*, "on his knees with his face buried in his hands on the ground, dead and stiff." Just beyond the nek one of the wagons was found half overturned in a donga by the right of the road. A team of oxen were lying dead in the traces, but one of them suddenly staggered to its feet

uninjured. The Carbineers cut it free, and it threw up its head, "cocked his tail in the air and ran off along the road to Rorke's Drift." Fynn believed it was later shot by the commissariat.

The atmosphere in the column was overwrought; the men were strained to breaking point by the horrors they had witnessed and the worse ones they imagined, and burning for revenge. The sense of shock pervades the accounts of those who experienced that terrible night. Sergeant W.E.Warren, one of Harness' detachment, wrote to his father:

> You could not move a foot either way without treading on dead bodies. Oh, father, such a sight I never witnessed in my life before. I could not help crying to see how the poor fellows were massacred.

A little further down the road the column passed a Zulu homestead. It had been deserted the day before, but now there were several men standing amongst the huts watching the column go by. Fynn claimed to have seen spears piled up outside, and a doctor burning medicine over a fire. Chelmsford gave strict orders that the men should not be molested, but the sight was apparently too much for the NNC, who fired into the homestead and killed one man. There may have been other killings; there is a suggestion that the mounted vedettes encountered a few Zulu stragglers in the Manzi-

A dramatic sketch by Trooper W.Nelson, Natal Mounted Police, of Chelmsford's departure from the scene of the massacre early on the morning of the 23rd. Presumably Nelson was working from memory, and the topography is exaggerated — particularly the hill behind Mahlabamkhosi, left background — but the condition of the corpses is all too accurate: stripped, disembowelled, and some skewered to the ground with spears. A sanitised version of this sketch, minus the nudity and mutilation, was published in The Graphic. *(Courtesy of the Director, National Army Museum, London)*

myama valley and showed them little mercy. Certainly the mood was grim; "we saw red", was how Trooper Jones remembered it.

On the march, stories of the sights witnessed in the camp began to circulate. One of the most widespread was that "Even the little boys that we had in the band, they were hung up on hooks, and opened like sheep. It was a pitiful sight." This horror has become part of the mythology of the battle, but it is difficult to know what to make of it. Certainly, there were few enough "little boys" in the camp. Most of the drummers of the 24th were mature men — the average age of those killed at Isandlwana was 24. There were only five who held the rank of Boy: Thomas Harrington and Robert Richards of the 1/24th, and Daniel Gordon, James Gurney and Joseph McEwan of the 2/24th. (A Private Denis Harrington was also killed in the battle, and may have been the former's father). Neither Harrington's nor Richard's age is recorded, but Gordon was otherwise the youngest, being 13 when he attested in 1877. Even if Harrington and Richards had joined the Battalion with the last draft sent to South Africa they would have been with it for 18 months before Isandlwana. Gurney and McEwan were 15 and 14 respectively when they attested in 1877. It is possible, of course, that the the dead boys were not drummers at all; it is quite feasible that some civilian contractor might have had his sons with him in the camp, and certainly not all of the black *voorloopers* were adults.

Trooper Sam Jones of the NMR was one who claimed to have seen the bodies: "One sight, a most gruesome one, I shall never forget. Two lads, presumably little drummer boys of the 24th Regiment, had been hung up by butcher's hooks, which had been jabbed under the chins, and then disembowelled; all the circumstances pointing to the fact that they had been subjected to that inhuman treatment while still alive." Visiting the battlefield some months later, Trooper Symons saw the bodies lying not far from the butcher's poles. Yet there is still something which does not ring quite true about this story.

That the Zulus would have killed and disembowelled boys as well as adults need not be doubted; but one wonders if they would have understood the significance of the butcher's hooks, especially in the heat of the moment; and on what evidence Jones supposed that the boys had been hung up living

one can hardly imagine. Although there were dark rumours of torture throughout the war, none of them proved well-founded. Captain Penn-Symons of the 24th, who was present with Chelmsford's force, stated quite categorically that "no single case of torture was proved against them. The wild stories current at the time, and repeated in the English papers, were untrue." There is a more telling reason, too, for being suspicious of this and other horror stories: as Maxwell pointed out, "on the way I heard some terrible stories about mutilated bodies. These were invented for the occasion, as it was impossible for those who told these yarns to have distinguished anything in the night, it being exceptionally dark."

That Jones and others glimpsed terrible sights in the dim starlight and the gloom before dawn was undoubtedly true; but what they saw, and what they thought they saw, cannot now be distinguished, and a significant question mark must hang over the true fate of the 24th's boy soldiers.

When the column reached the Manzimyama there was a chance for the men to fill their water-bottles. Maxwell took the opportunity to wipe the last of the gore from his hands, "and felt a good deal more comfortable." The men had marched only a little further, however, when another extra-ordinary sight met their eyes. The Carbineers were in the advanced guard, and Symons "perceived at short cannon range a large black mass of Zulus approaching directly to-wards us from our left front. They looked just like a ten-acre mealie field in blossom turned black." Fynn recognised some of the men as from the uThulwana regiment, and that they were coming from the direction of Rorke's Drift; they were clearly part of the attacking force in retreat. Harness ordered his guns to be unlimbered, "to reap a few" of the mealies, but Chelmsford forbade the men to open fire. Having left their reserve ammunition in camp the day before, many of the men were now running low, and they were hardly in an ideal condition to fight an *impi* in the open. The Zulus were no better off, as Maxwell, who was also with the vanguard, relates:

> Suddenly from the enemy on the ridge there sprang out a young warrior to the front, who by his actions and speech was endeavouring to urge the others to attack. Failing in which, he madly rushed down the hillside towards the centre of the column, and was shot dead at about 30 yards distance, not one having followed or even risen from their squatting position. In my opinion had we had sufficient ammunition we could have made great havoc amongst them in their then tired and disorganised state.

For the most part, however, the two forces were content to shout the occasional comment as they passed each other warily by.

> So we passed on observing the smoke rising from burning kraals on the Natal side of the river. What has become of mess-mates? each enquired of the other as we marched dolefully along . . . "All gone" we thought as we rode down the road we had traversed but three days before with fifteen days rations and enough ammunition to have brought half a dozen Cetywayo's and their armies to nought if properly applied. Vain boast! Where are they now?

A pall of smoke could be seen hanging over the buildings beneath the slopes of Shiyane. When the column reached the river they were surprised and delighted to find that the ponts had not apparently been molested. Chelmsford and his staff crossed by the ponts, while the mounted men crossed at the drift below them where they had entered Zululand just 12 days before. The Volunteers dismounted and lined the bank while the Mounted Infantry, with Russell and Walsh at the head, rode up the road to scout the mission station. From the drift, a mass of warriors could be seen in position on the slope of a hill to the south-west of Shiyane. Had the post fallen? As Russell's party drew near the Zulus on the hills drew off; and figures in red coats could be seen around the remains of the mission, one waving a flag.

Rorke's Drift had been held.

"Guilty or Not Guilty": an engraving in The Graphic *of two Zulus "suspected of torturing the poor little drummer boys of the 1st Battalion 24th Regiment" under guard at Helpmekaar. It is not clear on what pretext these two men were accused of that atrocity, if it occurred at all; however, feelings ran high among the survivors of the Centre Column, and the fate of these men, although unrecorded, was probably grim. (Author's collection)*

CHAPTER TEN

Rorke's Drift

When Lieutenant John Chard of the 5th Company, Royal Engineers visited the camp at Isandlwana on the morning of the 22nd, he had confirmed that his orders were to prepare an entrenchment on the Natal bank at Rorke's Drift to protect the crossing. Chard had left his Sappers with their wagon with Durnford's column, whom he passed on the way up; and on his way back he met them again, and ordered them to march the last stretch to Isandlwana while he returned to the drift with the wagon. He was back at Rorke's Drift by mid-morning, and rode up to the mission station to consult with Major Spalding, the Deputy Acting Adjutant and Quartermaster General, who had been left in command of the post.

A company of the 2/24th — B Company, under Lieutenant Gonville Bromhead — had been left to guard the mission station, and had pitched their camp behind the buildings, between them and the foot of Shiyane hill (called by the missionaries "Oscarsberg"). Although consisting mostly of young, short-service soldiers B Company and their officer had already seen active service in Africa, taking part in a number of sweeps through the bush country around the Xhosa strongholds. On one such occasion the company commander Captain A.G.Godwin-Austen (whose younger brother Fred was with Pope's G Company) was wounded when one of his men's rifles had discharged accidentally; he was invalided home, and command passed to the 33-year-old Lieutenant Gonville Bromhead. Bromhead (who also had an older brother, Captain C.J.Bromhead, serving with the Battalion), was the third son of a family from Newark in Nottinghamshire. He seems to have been a quiet and retiring character, which may have been due to the premature onset of deafnesss. In the absence of another subaltern he was effectively seconded by Colour-Sergeant Frank Bourne; only 5ft. 6ins. tall and not yet 25 years old, he had held his rank since the previous April, and was clearly an exceptional young soldier. Known among the men of his company as "the kid", Bourne had been nervous when first promoted, but after nine months felt that he was "getting along quite well".

A huge quantity of stores had been accumulated at the post in readiness to supply the column, and the wagons to fetch them were expected to arrive from Isandlwana later that day. The stores consisted of sacks of mealies weighing 200lbs. and big, heavy wooden boxes full of Army biscuits and tinned meat ration. They had been stacked into Jim Rorke's old storehouse, which the Reverend Witt had been using as a chapel, and were under the supervision of a handful of Commissariat officers led by Assistant Commissary Walter Dunne. Witt's house had been turned into a hospital, and housed about 30 men suffering from a variety of ailments ranging from wounds sustained in the action at Sihayo's stronghold to fever, diahorrea and blisters.

There was also a company of the 2/3rd NNC under Captain William Stevenson at the post. Some uncertainty hangs over this company, largely because none of the Regulars seem to have paid much attention to it until it was gone; its strength is variously given as 100, which should be about right, and 300. Nor is there any indication of where it was camped.

Chard's proposed entrenchment was intended for the use of Captain Rainforth's G Company, 1/24th, which had been ordered down from Helpmekaar to provide a guard over the ponts. When Chard arrived at the post, however, he found that Rainforth had not arrived, and that Spalding had directed six privates and an NCO from B Company, supported by 50 of Stevenson's NNC, to provide a temporary guard at the drift. Having heard the reports of Zulus in the vicinity of Isandlwana, and apparently having little faith in the NNC, Chard pointed out to Spalding that a guard of seven men would hardly prove sufficient in the event of an emergency; and Spalding decided to ride up to Helpmekaar to find out what had delayed Rainforth:

Major Spalding told me he was going over to Helpmekaar, and would see about getting it down at once. Just as I was about to ride away he said to me "Which of you is senior, you or Bromhead?" I said, "I don't know" – he went back into his tent, looked at an Army List, and coming back, said — "I see you are senior, so you will be in charge, although, of course, nothing will happen, and I shall be back again this evening early."

Chard went down to the drift, where his tents were pitched, and some time later Spalding departed. The camp went about its routine business. In the early afternoon the distant sound of gunfire could be heard, but did not cause any undue alarm. At the mission, Assistant Commissary Dunne and Lieutenant Bromhead had just settled down to lunch under an awning they had improvised from a tarpaulin and tent poles when "suddenly, we noticed at some distance across the river a large number of mounted natives approaching, preceded by a lot of women and children and oxen."

This is an intriguing remark. Since the post faces out towards the drift Dunne and Bromhead must have been looking in that direction, but it is doubtful if they could see much of the road to Isandlwana. The detail of the fleeing civilians seems convincing, but curiously Chard, who was down at the river, did not notice any black horsemen. It would be helpful to believe that these men were the survivors of Durnford's command who later appeared at the post; their movements between the Manzimyama and Rorke's Drift have always been uncertain, and if they crossed at Rorke's Drift itself they must have had an interesting ride across country.

Despite his earlier unease about the Zulus Chard does not seem to have spent an active day down at the drift. With no Sappers to supervise and no infantry, as yet, to entrench, he took a leisurely lunch and settled down to write some letters in his tent. By all accounts John Rouse Merriott Chard, a 31-year-old Devonian, was a very relaxed personality, given to peaceful pipe-smoking; indeed, his company commander, Captain Walter Parke Jones, later judged him "a most amiable fellow, and [an asset] to the mess, but as a company officer . . . hopelessly slow and slack." On this occasion his reveries were soon interrupted, however:

My attention was called to two horsemen galloping towards us from the direction of Isandhlwana. From their gesticulations, and their shouts, when they were near enough to be heard, we saw that something was the matter, and on taking them over the river, one of them, Lieutenant Adendorff of Lonsdale's Regiment, Natal Native Contingent, asking if I was an officer, jumped off his horse, took me on one side, and told me that the camp was in the hands of the Zulus and the army destroyed; that scarcely a man had got away to tell the tale, and that probably Lord Chelmsford and the rest of the column had shared the same fate. His companion, a Carbineer, confirmed his story — He was naturally very excited, and I am afraid I did not, at first, quite believe him, and intimated that he probably had not remained to see what did occur.

Brevet Major H.Spalding, 104th Regiment, the Centre Column's DAA & QMG, was in charge of the depot at Rorke's Drift. He rode off to Helpmekaar early on the afternoon of the 22nd with the immortal remark "Nothing will happen, and I shall be back again this evening early". (Courtesy of the Director, National Army Museum, London)

Adendorff, too, has attracted a certain amount of unnecessary mystery, and it has been suggested that he left Isandlwana early — before the right horn cut the road — and was later court-martialled for desertion. There is no evidence to support this, however; Adendorff was a Lieutenant in Captain Krohn's No.6 Company, 1/3rd NNC, and Higginson remembered seeing him during the battle. Years later, Stafford recalled that Adendorff had told him that he and his companion had avoided Sothondose's Drift because he could not swim, and had worked their way upstream to Rorke's Drift instead. Chard went out of his way to record that Adendorff was the only man amongst the fugitives who stayed to help in the defence; by rights, therefore, he deserves the distinction of being remembered as the only man to have fought at both Isandlwana and Rorke's Drift.

In the middle of this conversation, a messenger arrived from Bromhead. Dunne and he had been about to go down to the drift to investigate the mysterious horsemen when two Mounted Infantrymen, Privates Evans and Whelan, rode up with a pencil note from Captain Alan Gardner. It stated baldly that the camp had fallen, and that the Zulus were on their way to attack Rorke's Drift. When he heard the news Dunne had a curious sense of *deja vu*. No doubt it was simply shock; for a few minutes neither he nor Bromhead could quite take in the enormity of the disaster.

Acting Assistant Commissary James Dalton snapped them out of it, and suggested that they must make preparation for a defence. Dalton had formerly been a Sergeant in the 85th Regiment, and had earned a distinguished reputation on the Cape Frontier; this, coupled with a commanding personality, gave him a good deal of influence at this crucial moment. Bromhead gave orders for the sacks of mealies and biscuit boxes to be dragged out from the storehouse; B Company's tents were struck; and a water-cart was filled and dragged into the yard between the two buildings. Picquets were posted to give some warning of the Zulu approach, and Private Fred Hitch was sent up to the storehouse roof as a lookout.

By the time Chard arrived from the drift this work was well underway. He and Bromhead held a hurried consultation, but in fact the options facing them were limited. The exact strength of the Zulu force was unknown, but it was clearly larger than the garrison. There were two ox-wagons at the post which could be used to evacuate the hospital patients to Helpmekaar, but the Zulus were bound to overtake them on the road, and the chances of B Company making a successful stand in the open were slim. As one patient, Harry Lugg of the Natal Mounted Police, put it: "Nothing remains but to fight".

Chard went back to the drift to collect the guard at the ponts. Sergeant Millne of the Buffs, who had been one of a party supervising the crossing since the invasion, and a civilian pontman, Mr.Daniells, offered to man the ponts and moor them in midstream; but as their position would be completely exposed to Zulu rifle-fire, and since no men could be spared to guard the drift, Chard declined the offer. The ponts would have to take their chances; Chard ordered the guard to load his tents and equipment into the wagon, and together they went back to the mission.

If the mission buildings offered the only hope of a successful defence, however, nothing had previously been done to fortify them. Nobody hitherto had thought the Zulus any more capable of attacking them than Isandlwana. The mission station itself consisted of two large thatched buildings of brick and sandstone, built on a flat about 300 yards from the western foot of Shiyane. The storehouse, on the right, was the bigger of the two, some 80ft. by 20ft., and was set back so that its front was on a level with the rear of the hospital. The hospital — Witt's house — was about 60ft. by 18ft., with a neatly fenced verandah. The road from the drift ran past the front of the post, off towards the rear of Shiyane, but a track branched off to the front of the storehouse. Right across the front of the post the flat ground dropped in a shelf about four feet high. This ran close to the front of the hospital, falling away into a steep slope; but further along towards the storehouse, and on either side of the track, it formed an exposed rocky step about shoulder high. On the front right corner of the storehouse there was a well-built stone cattle-pen with walls four feet high, divided by an interior partition, and measuring about 50 feet square. Below the ledge to the right of it was another, larger cattle-pen, roughly built, with the stones piled up no higher than two or three feet. To the left of the track, stretching across the front of the hospital, was a clump of dense bush and grass, and in amongst it was a half-completed stone wall. Beyond the road was a neatly fenced orchard of fruit trees which covered several acres. Out the back of the post, only a few yards from the corner of the storehouse, there was a small cookhouse and two ovens.

It was relatively easy to secure the back of the post, facing the hill. The two ox-wagons were run into the gap between the front corner of the store and the back corner of the hospital and barricaded with biscuit boxes and mealie sacks. The front, however, was more open, and there was little choice but to build a barricade which ran the length of the ledge, from the corner of the cattle-pen to the far corner of the hospital. Along the middle reaches, between the buildings, this was actually quite secure, since a rampart three or four feet high on top of the natural barrier of the ledge provided an obstacle seven or even eight feet high — a formidable barrier to a man on foot. In front of the hospital, however, the slope of the ground made it difficult to build the barricade on a firm foundation. It was also the furthest point from the storehouse, and there is a suggestion that the defenders simply had not finished building it when the Zulus arrived; Dunne noted that "there was nothing but a plank to close the opening in one part."

When the first sounds of distant fighting had been heard, a party went up Shiyane to see if they could make out anything in the direction of Isandlwana. The Reverend Otto Witt, who had sent his family to a farmhouse a few miles away but stayed on himself, was among them, as were Surgeon James Reynolds, who was in charge of the hospital, and Chaplain George Smith, the Anglican vicar of Estcourt, who had volunteered to join No.3 Column as its Chaplain. The climb to the top of Shiyane is deceptive; a terrace of fractured strata runs round the base, pitted with shallow caves and strewn with huge slabs of rock, while above it the slope rises steeply. From this shoulder the summit rises gently towards the peak at the eastern edge of the hill. It is a stiff twenty-minute walk for a fit man, and on a day as hot as 22nd January it probably took this mixed party a good deal longer. From the summit, however, there is a magnificent view of the Mzinyathi below, stretching round from the Drift itself on the far left, past Ngedla mountain, and the line of cliffs marking Sihayo's stronghold. To the right Isandlwana stands out on the skyline above the slopes of the Manzimyama, while further to the right the Mzinyathi disappears into a narrow valley between the hills which block out the view of Sothondose's Drift. The party apparently had a telescope with them; and Witt claimed that he saw

> *the Zulus descend and draw themselves in long lines between the camp and river. From where I stood I could see the English forces advancing to the attack; but I could not see any hand-to-hand fighting. I observed that the Zulus were fighting heavily, and presently I saw that the English were surrounded in a kraal some distance from the camp.*

There is nothing inherently unlikely in this description. The haze and smoke must have obscured much, but from the summit of Shiyane it is possible to see something of the western slopes of Mkwene hill, the spur leading up to it, and the valley of the Manzimyama. Witt apparently witnessed the first phase of the battle, and the advance of the right horn.

Witt's party must have been up on the summit for some time. Later, they watched long lines of black troops moving down towards the Mzinyathi. These men were led by two

John Chard wearing his VC, photographed at the end of the war. He wears the RE officer's undress frock, which he was probably wearing on the day of the battle. ("SB" Bourquin)

commanders on horseback, and for a long time the observers thought that they were battalions of the NNC. Only when they got close enough to reveal that the officers, too, had black faces did they realise that these were Zulus. They scrambled back down to the post, and when asked by one of the garrison Witt confirmed that "The Zulus will be here in five minutes." Witt himself did not wait; he was concerned about the safety of his family, and rode off towards Helpmekaar to look for them. He took with him Lieutenant Purvis of the NNC, wounded in the action at Sihayo's stronghold, who, according to Chard, "was so sick that he could hardly mount a horse." The Reverend Smith stayed to help in the defence.

The exact number of men under Chard's command differs slightly in the various sources, but the most convincing estimate appears to be 152, excluding Stevenson's 2/3rd NNC company. The figure includes: Bromhead; Surgeon Reynolds; Dunne, Dalton, and Assistant Storekeeper Byrne of the Commissary Department; Adendorff; Chaplain Smith; 112 NCOs

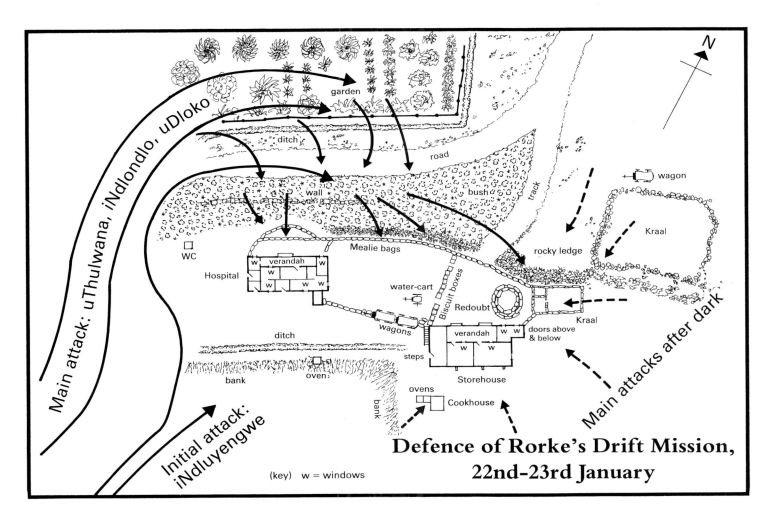

Defence of Rorke's Drift Mission, 22nd-23rd January

(key) w = windows

Lieutenant Gonville Bromhead, B Company's commander at
Rorke's Drift: a superb portrait taken late in 1879. (Royal Archives)

and ORs of the 2/24th, of whom 95 were from B Company; ten from the 1/24th, mostly hospital patients; three men of the Army Hospital Corps, and Reynolds' servant; four from the Royal Artillery and one from the Royal Engineers; three men of the Natal Mounted Police; one each from the Buffs, 90th Regiment, Army Service Corps, and staff (Sergeant Mabin, duties unknown); six individual NNC men, and the civilian Mr. Daniells.

The Zulus were, indeed, approaching the mission. The iNdluyengwe regiment, who had crossed at the fissure above Sothondose's Drift, began to move at a leisurely pace upstream, foraging about as they went, searching every potential hiding place for possible British survivors; they could be seen from the hill, firing into bush and caves. The other section, the senior men of the iNdlondlo, uThulwana and uDloko, crossed the river at a point near the junction of the Batshe. Here the river must have been wider, since it

flowed less fiercely and only came up to the warriors' waists. They formed long chains through the water, crossing in a leisurely manner, cooling off, and helping one another over. When they were all safely on the Natal bank they, too, paused to take snuff.

It seems quite clear that the Zulus were acting in accordance with no co-ordinated plan. Both their commander, Prince Dabulamanzi kaMpande, and the men themselves were well aware of the king's prohibition on crossing into Natal, but they felt justified in doing so because they had formed the reserve at Isandlwana and had missed the fighting. Dabulamanzi wanted to "wash the spears of his boys", and his men were determined not to return home without something to show for the day. There was certainly no plan to raid further into Natal — the men were too tired, and anyway could not have sustained a serious foray unsupported — nor was there any intention of cutting Chelmsford off from his bases. They simply expected to take advantage of the British defeat to raid the border region along the valley. Some sections had probably broken away already to do just this, since both black homesteads and a deserted white farmhouse downstream of Rorke's Drift were looted and put to the torch. Other parties pressed westwards as far as the foot of the Helpmekaar heights. The mission at Rorke's Drift was widely known as KwaJim ("Jim's place") from Rorke's trading days; the warriors probably hoped to catch the garrison off-guard and ransack the stores. It is difficult to say how many men actually went on to attack the post, but it was probably between 3,000 and 4,000.

The iNdluyengwe moved slowly towards Shiyane preceded by a screen of skirmishers. Further north, the men of the older contingent divided in two, one party moving up to follow the iNdluyengwe, the other sending out scouts upriver towards Rorke's Drift. Perhaps they thought to encircle the post and attack it from two sides; but in the event the topography of Shiyane made any approach from that angle difficult, and this party turned back to reunite with the other, led by two corpulent chiefs on horseback. One of these was probably Dabulamanzi himself who, taught by John Dunn, was both a skilful horseman and a marksman.

At least Chard had some warning of their approach. The defences around the mission were rapidly taking shape when a detachment of the Native Horse, perhaps as many as 100 strong, rode up with their white officer. Presumably this officer identified himself to Chard, but Chard did not record

The men who held Rorke's Drift: the survivors of B Company, 2/24th, photographed at the end of the war. The company is very understrength, and a number of the well-known defenders appear to be absent — some had been invalided home; but Colour-Sergeant Bourne sits on the extreme left, and Bromhead (looking to the left) is at the left of the front row. ("SB" Bourquin)

his name and it is difficult to be precise about his identity. However, since the men had escaped from Isandlwana the choice is limited, and it was almost certainly Lieutenant Henderson of the BaSotho Troop. According to Davies of the Edendale Troop, he and Henderson had parted company somewhere on the mad dash across country, and "Lieutenant Henderson I believe escaped by the road to Rorke's Drift; some of my men and his own accompanying him." The men were therefore presumably from the BaSotho unit — most of the Edendale men had stuck with Simeon Kambule and crossed at Sothondose's Drift — though a few of Zikhali's riders were no doubt with them. Quite how they reached Rorke's Drift is unlikely ever to be resolved. Chard asked them to "observe the movements, and check the advance, of the enemy as much as possible until forced to fall back."

They had not been gone long, however, when a spatter of shots behind the hill indicated that they were engaged. Henderson rode in with Bob Hall, a civilian meat contractor who had also escaped from the camp, and who shouted out "Here they come, black as hell and thick as grass!". Henderson reported that the Zulus were approaching, and that his men would not stay with him; indeed, Chard could see them in the distance, riding off towards Helpmekaar. Henderson and Hall fired a few shots in front of the advancing *impi*, then rode away after their men. Even Chard found it difficult to blame them; after their harrowing experiences of the morning they must

have been physically and emotionally drained, their ammunition was exhausted, and they can have had little faith in the garrison's chances. "I have seen several of these men behave so well since," commented Chard later, "that I have spoken with several of their conduct — and they all said, as their excuse, that Durnford was killed, and that it was no use."

Their retreat precipitated a more serious desertion, however. All of a sudden Stevenson's NNC company simply bolted. "I am sorry to say that their officer, who had been doing good service in getting his men to work, also deserted us." This sight was not greeted by the garrison quite so generously, and a few shots were fired after them. A white NCO, Corporal Anderson, fell dead on his face in the garden; he was the first man killed at Rorke's Drift. Whatever the fighting value of the NNC, it was a serious blow to lose them at this critical moment. The defensive perimeter was now too long to be properly held, and Chard ordered a new barricade to be built as a final bastion. A line of biscuit boxes was trailed from the corner of the storehouse to the front wall, bisecting the yard.

(opposite):
An aerial photograph, c.1940s, of the Rorke's Drift area, looking north-east across the Mzinyathi (centre) towards Zululand; Shiyane hill is on the right, with the mission complex at its base. The cliffs marking the western edge of Ngedla are visible at top centre. (Author's collection)

The mission at Rorke's Drift, c.1885: a Zulu rifleman's view, from the rocky terraces at the foot of Shiyane, looking south-west towards kwaSingqindi hill. All of the buildings here post-date the 1879 fighting; but the chapel (right) was built largely on the site of the storehouse, and Witt's new house (centre, in front of lone tree) was built over the hospital ruins. (Bryan Maggs Collection)

Acting Assistant Commissary James L. Dalton, a former infantry NCO, whom many believed played an important part in inspiring the defence.

Alfred Fairlie Henderson, a Lieutenant with the BaSotho Troop of the Natal Native Horse, survived Isandlwana, and was probably the officer whose men reported to Chard but fled at the start of the fight. (From Henderson Heritage*)*

Corporal William Allen (later promoted Sergeant) of B Company, 2/24th, photographed after the presentation of his VC. (Keith Reeves Collection)

Then the 24th's picquets came in, and Hitch gave a shout from the top of the store, and the Zulus were upon them. It was now about 4.30 p.m., some two and a half hours before nightfall.

* * *

The iNdluyengwe were in the van. They advanced at a flat run, screened by a line of skirmishers and fed constantly by the main body behind. As they moved round the slope of Shiyane they came straight at the back of the post, stooping very low and making the most of whatever cover was available. The defenders crouched behind the wagons or lining the back walls of the hospital and store opened fire at 450 yards. Trooper Harry Lugg "had the satisfaction of seeing the first man I fired at roll over at 350, and then my nerves were as steady as a rock. I made sure almost before I pulled the trigger. There was some of the best shooting at 450 yards that I have ever seen." Someone noticed that when they were hit the Zulus "would give a spring in the air, and fall flat down".

Private Henry Hook was one of the men detailed to guard the hospital, and he described this first attack:

The Zulus came on at a wild rush, and although many of them were shot down, they got to within about fifty yards of our south wall of mealie bags and biscuit boxes and wagons. They were caught between two fires, that from the hospital and that from the storehouse, and they were checked; but they gained the shelter of the storehouse and ovens, and gave us many heavy volleys. During the fight they took advantage of every bit of cover there was, anthills, a tract of bush that we had not time to clear away, a garden or sort of orchard which was near us, and a ledge of rock and some caves (on the Oscarberg) which were only about a hundred yards away.

Making no headway against the fire from the rear of the post, the rest of the iNdluyengwe veered to their left past the end of the hospital, and threw themselves into the protection offered by the garden and bush at the front. From here they opened a heavy fire on the defenders, and launched a rush against the barricade in front of the hospital. The bush extended to within as little as five yards of the hospital; with no ledge to slow them down, only a steep slope, and only an incomplete barricade across the front of the verandah, they ignored the fire poured into them at close range and closed in, hand-to-hand. The rush was met by Bromhead and his men at the point of the bayonet.

One warrior grabbed the rifle muzzle of a Private in the Army Hospital Corps, and was just about to stab him when James Dalton shot him dead. The fighting was so fierce that the defenders were forced back from the verandah to an improvised barricade on the corner of the hospital; but the Zulus could not sustain their position, and fell back into the cover of the bush.

Private Hitch, who had come down from the storehouse roof when the fighting began, was in the thick of that fight:

The Zulus pushing right up to the porch, it was not until the bayonet was

used that they flinched the least bit. Had the Zulus taken the bayonet as freely as they took the bullets, we could not have stood more than fifteen minutes. They pushed right up to us, and not only got up to the laager but got right in with us, but they seemed to have a great dread of the bayonet, which stood to us from beginning to end. During that struggle there was a fine big Zulu see me shoot his mate down — he sprang forward, dropping his rifle and assegais, seizing hold of the muzzle of my rifle with his left hand and the right hand hold of the bayonet. Thinking to disarm me he pulled and tried hard to get the rifle from me, but I had a firm hold of the small of the butt of the rifle with my left hand. My cartridges were on top of the mealie bags which enabled me to load my rifle and [I] shot the poor wretch whilst holding on to his grasp for some moments.

While this attack had been taking place, the rest of the Zulu force came up — the senior men of the uThulwana, uDloko and iNdlondlo regiments. Seeing that the fight was already begun, they avoided the back of the post, keeping to the left of the iNdluyengwe, and "occupied the garden, hollow road, and bush in great force. The bush grew close to our wall, and we had not time to cut it down — The enemy were therefore able to advance under cover close to our wall, and in this part soon held one side of the wall, while we held the other."

With the main body now up, the Zulus directed a series of attacks against the post's weak spot — the front of the hospital:

A series of desperate assaults was made, on the Hospital, and extending from the Hospital, as far as the bush reached; but each was most splendidly met and repulsed by our men with the bayonet. Each time as the attack was repulsed by us, the Zulus close to us seemed to vanish in the bush, those some little distance off keeping up a heavy fire all the time. Then, as if moved by a single impulse, they rose up in the bush as thick as possible, rushing madly up to the wall (some of them being already close to it), seizing, where they could, the muzzles of our men's rifles, or their bayonets, and attempting to use their stabbing assegais and to get over the wall. A rapid rattle of fire from our rifles, stabs with the bayonet, and in a few moments the Zulus were driven back, disappearing into the bush as before, and keeping up their fire. A brief interval, and the attack would be made again, and repulsed in the same manner. Over and over again this happened, our men behaving with the greatest coolness and gallantry.

Although it was not apparent to the defenders, the post was a very difficult place to storm. While the numerical odds were overwhelmingly in Prince Dabulamanzi's favour (at least thirty to one), the short front involved meant that he could not bring all his men to bear at once. Although the defenders were hampered by the extensive cover at the front, which the Zulus could use for concealment to within a few yards of the barricades, the warriors could nonetheless make little headway against barricades which gave the defenders such an advantage in height.

With the arrival of the older regiments, the Zulus took possession of the Shiyane terraces and began to put down a heavy volume of fire. Here they were able to settle behind boulders or in crevices, and fire straight down into the open courtyard between the two buildings. They could see little of the men sheltering behind the rear barricade except their helmets; but those at the front, who had their backs to them, were completely exposed. Chard could do nothing but encourage his men on the back wall, including several excellent marksmen, to try to suppress the Zulu fire.

In this they had a distinct advantage: at 300 to 400 yards the Martini-Henry was working at its most efficient range. Even if the Zulus were under cover the puffs of smoke from their old muzzle-loaders gave their positions away; and, with the onset of evening, the late sunshine would have shone onto the terraces like a floodlight. The Zulu snipers, for their part, were firing at ranges probably well beyond the accurate reach of most of their weapons, given the quality of their ammunition and the usual state of Zulu firearms. It is one of the myths of Rorke's Drift that the Zulus fired Martini-Henrys looted at Isandlwana; they did not, simply because none of the Zulus involved had either fought at the battle or taken part in the looting of the camp.

Several individuals had remarkable escapes at Rorke's Drift, and none more so than Chard's wagon-driver, a Cape Coloured man. He had fled from the post when he heard the first firing, and hidden in one of the caves on the terrace. After several Zulus had run by without spotting him some, to his horror, actually entered the cave and started firing at the post. None of these caves is more than a few feet deep, and it is extraordinary that he remained undetected. While he was cowering in the back of the cave several shots fired by the defenders actually struck the walls inside, and one of the Zulus was killed — which says something for the aim of B Company.

Even so, the sheer volume of fire poured down into a small and relatively crowded area was bound to take a toll, and several of the defenders were hit in the yard. Corporal John Lyons had leaned forward over the rear barricade to get a better shot when he was hit by a musket ball — which travelled down his spine and lodged in his back — and fell into a gap in the biscuit-box wall. He said to Corporal William Allen, close by, "Give it to them, Allen. I am done; I am

dying." Even as he spoke he saw a shot strike Allen, who walked away with blood streaming from his arm. Chard, who was also nearby, thought Lyons was dead; but Lyons called to him, "Oh, Sir! you are not going to leave me here like a dog?" He was pulled through behind the inner barricade, and Surgeon Reynolds attended to his wound.

Acting Assistant Commissary Dalton, the former Sergeant of Light Infantry, had been in the forefront of the defence, directing the fire and "dropping a man each time he fired his rifle". Spotting a man running up to the barricade he shouted "Pot that fellow", and aimed over the barricade at another, "when his rifle dropped, and he turned round, quite pale, and said that he had been shot." A bullet had passed clean through him above the shoulder-blade. He stood there quite coolly while Chard took the spare cartridges out of his pockets, and then allowed himself to be helped away.

Corporal Scammell of the NNC was shot through the back; he crawled a few yards to hand his cartridges to Chard, then asked for a drink of water. Assistant Storekeeper Louis Byrne bent down to give him one, and was promptly hit in the head and killed.

There were some lucky escapes, too: Surgeon Reynolds was taking ammunition across to the men in the hospital when a bullet struck his helmet. Chard was aiming at a Zulu marksman when Private Jenkins, yelling out " 'Look out, Sir!', gave my head a duck down just as a bullet whizzed over it. He had noticed a Zulu who was quite near in another direction taking a deliberate aim at me. For all the man could have known, the shot might have been directed at himself."

This heavy fire made the yard too dangerous to hold. Futhermore, the Zulus were beginning to extend their attacks further to their left: moving out from the bush, crossing the track, and attacking the barricade in front of the storehouse. Chard sent Bromhead with several men from the line over to meet the new rush. It was quite clear, however, that the defenders could not cover the entire perimeter; and at about 6 p.m. Chard ordered them to fall back to the line of biscuit boxes, the inner barricade in front of the storehouse. This effectively abandoned the hospital and its defenders to their own devices. The hospital, according to Private Hook,

was a queer little one-storeyed building, which it is almost impossible to describe; but we were pinned like rats in a hole; because all the doorways except one had been barricaded with mealie bags, and we had done the same with the windows. The interior was divided by means of partition walls into which were fitted some very slight doors. The patients' beds were simple, rough affairs of boards, raised only about half a foot above the floor. To talk of hospital beds gives the idea of a big building, but as a matter of fact this hospital was a mere little shed or bungalow, divided up into rooms so small you could hardly swing a bayonet in them. There were about nine men who could not move, but altogether there were about thirty. Most of these, however, could help to defend themselves.

Six men from B Company were told off to guard the hospital, along with those patients who were able to fight. Hook was with Private Thomas Cole, universally known as "Old King Cole." The only patient in their room was a soldier in the NNC, one of Mhungo's isiQoza, who had been wounded in the leg at Sihayo's homestead. Cole suffered from claustrophobia, however, and could not stand the cramped conditions in the room; he ran outside just as the first Zulu attack was developing, and was immediately shot through the head. (The bullet passed on and struck Private Bushe on the nose.)

Once the defenders had been driven back from the front of the verandah there was nothing to stop the Zulus storming the hospital building itself. Chard had "tried to impress upon the men in the Hospital the necessity for making a communication right through the building — unfortunately this was not done. Probably at the time the men could not see the necessity, and doubtless also there was no time to do it." The necessity soon became apparent when the Zulus burst through the doors and drove the defenders from room after room. In many cases the rooms had no interconnecting doors, and in some, no doubt, the defenders were slaughtered and no account has survived. If the experience of battle is disorienting at the best of times, it must have been bewildering in those cramped, stifling little rooms, lit by oil lamps if at all: the magnified roar of the rifles, the war-shouts of the Zulus, the cries of the sick and wounded; the "extraordinary rattle as the bullets struck the biscuit boxes, and queer thuds as they plumped into the bags of mealies . . . the whizz and rip of the assegais."

Once they had broken in, the Zulus set fire to the building in an attempt to force the defenders out, and the rooms began to fill with "fire and a thick dense smoke." The struggle began to take on that same nightmare quality which pervades accounts of the last moments at Isandlwana. Private Hook was forced back from his original room through an interior door:

> It was impossible to take the native patient with me, and I had to leave him to an awful fate. But his death was, at any rate, a merciful one. I heard the Zulus asking him questions, and he tried to take his bandages off and escape.
>   . . . In the room where I now was there were nine sick men, and I alone to look after them for some time, still firing away, with the hospital burning. Suddenly in the thick smoke I saw John Williams, and above the din of the battle and the cries of the wounded, I heard him shout "The Zulus are swarming all over the place. They've dragged Joseph Williams out and killed him." John Williams had held the other room with Private William Horrigan for more than an hour, until they had not a cartridge left. The Zulus then burst in and dragged out Joseph Williams and two of the patients and assegaid them. It was only because they were so busy with this slaughtering that John Williams and two of the patients were able to knock a hole in the partition and get into the room where I was posted. Horrigan was killed. What were we to do? We were pinned like rats in a hole. Already the Zulus were fiercely trying to burst in through the doorway. The only way of escape [was] the wall itself, by making a hole big enough for a man to crawl through into the adjoining room, and so on, until we got to our innermost entrenchment outside. Williams worked desperately at the wall with the navvy's pick, which I had been using to make some of the loop-holes with.

A revealing portrait of Private Fred Hitch, VC, suggesting the extent of his injuries sustained at Rorke's Drift. (Royal Archives)

Fortunately the interior walls were made of mud brick coated with plaster, and "these shoddy inside bricks proved our salvation." As Williams passed the patients through, Hook held the door, or the hole, through which they had just escaped. Once a spear struck him a glancing blow on the forehead, but was deflected by his helmet, "so that I escaped with a scalp wound which did not trouble me much then, although it has often caused my illness since." The Zulus could only come up to the door one at a time, and Hook shot or bayonetted each one in turn. One man grabbed hold of the muzzle of his rifle and tried to tear it from his grasp, but Hook had time in the struggle to slip a cartridge into the breech and shoot him at point blank range. In one room lay a patient named Conley, a big man with a broken leg. Conley was the last to be evacuated, and Hook held the door until the last possible moment, then dashed through dragging Conley after him: "His leg got broken again, but there was no help for it."

In the last room Hook and John Williams found that William Jones and Robert Jones — whose names reflect the high proportion of Welshmen in B Company rather than any blood relationship — had been defending seven patients. The room had a small, high window which looked out onto the yard; the two soldiers had, with difficulty, been passing their patients through this to the outside, where Corporal Allen and Private Hitch had been helping them across to the safety of the barricade in front of the storehouse. Hook and Williams in turn evacuated their patients the same way, though the Joneses' last man, Sergeant Robert Maxfield, who was delirious with fever, refused to move. "Robert Jones made a last rush to try and get him away like the rest, but when he got back into the room he saw that Maxfield was being stabbed by the Zulus as he lay on his bed."

Nor was the ordeal over once they reached the open air at last. As soon as the defenders abandoned the yard the Zulus had rushed up and taken possession of the outside of the barricades. The fire from the biscuit-box rampart made it difficult for the warriors to cross the yard, but every now and then one would risk a dash to try to get at the men leaving the hospital. They also kept up a heavy crossfire on the defenders from close range. According to Chard,

> Trooper Hunter, Natal Mounted Police, escaping from the hospital, stood still for a moment, hesitating which way to go, dazed by the glare of the burning hospital, and the firing that was going on all round. He was assegaid before our eyes, the Zulu who killed him immediately afterwards falling.

Under the circumstances it is remarkable that any of the patients survived at all. At least three men decided to take their chances in the night. Private John Waters was defending an isolated room with Private William Beckett. There was a large wardrobe in the room, and after shooting several approaching Zulus the two men crawled inside it. In the noise and confusion they were overlooked — although Waters was wounded in the shoulder and knee — and Beckett decided to make a break for it. As he rushed out, however, he was spotted, and a warrior stabbed him right through the stomach. He staggered out into the darkness and collapsed somewhere in the garden. Waters waited as long as he dared; then, wrapping himself in one of Witt's old black cloaks which was still hanging in the wardrobe, he too ran outside. It was quite dark by this time, and he was not seen. He crawled through the grass towards the cookhouse, presumably hoping to work his way back towards the barricades; but when he got there he found that there were Zulus inside, firing at the defenders. It was too late to go back; so Waters got close enough to grab a handful of soot which he smeared over his hands and face. He then lay down in the grass and waited until morning. "The Zulus must have thought I was one of their dead comrades", he marvelled, "as they were all round about me, and some trod on me."

Lady Butler's painting "The defence of Rorke's Drift, January 22nd, 1879"; men of the 24th returning from South Africa posed for the artist within months of the action, and her care over details is clear from her sketchbooks, though different incidents are concentrated into a single moment. The viewpoint is roughly west to east, and the foreground figures hold the barricade opposite the front of the hospital, with the storehouse in the background. Lieutenants

Bromhead and Chard confer in the centre. The heavily-bearded, dark-uniformed Corporal Schiess, NNC, turns to shout from the barricade, left; right of him the wounded Dalton lies against the mealie-bags. At right, Surgeon Reynolds kneels with a wounded Natal trooper; right foreground, the wounded Private Hitch carries ammunition. (Reproduced by gracious permission of Her Majesty the Queen)

Gunner Arthur Howard, Harness' batman, also had an extraordinary escape. He too ran out from the hospital, and hid in the garden at the front of the post. There were several dead horses nearby, killed by the Zulus at the beginning of the fight, and a number of dead Zulus, and Howard lay down amongst them. No doubt his dark blue RA uniform saved him, since he too escaped discovery.

The reduced position in front of the store was far more secure than the extended perimeter. The back of the storehouse effectively protected it from any fire that might still come from the Shiyane terraces, while the narrow front enabled Chard to deploy his men in greater concentration. Two large piles of mealie bags were still lying where they had been dragged out in front of the store, and Commissary Dunne set about converting them into a small redoubt to shelter a handful of riflemen. Dunne was a tall man, and he stood on top of the bags to do the work. Bullets and "clouds of assegais" whistled past him, but he was not touched; and the redoubt provided "a second line of fire all round."

Otto Witt's house at Rorke's Drift, photographed c.1883. This was built on the foundations of the destroyed hospital, and greatly resembled it, complete at this date with thatched roof. This is much how the hospital must have looked on the day of the battle; note the verandah, and the sloping ground in front of it. ("SB" Bourquin)

The one weakness in the position was that fire from the front of the barricade could not effectively reach under the rocky ledge, and now that the barricade along the front of the post had been abandoned the Zulus could creep along it unseen and attempt to enfilade the line of biscuit boxes from close range. In an attempt to counter this Bromhead and six men took up a position in the corner between the biscuit boxes and the front wall. Fred Hitch was one of them, and commented: "About this time all was pressed very much, Bromhead was using his revolver with deadly aim." One man got inside the barricade and was about to stab Bromhead; Hitch presented his rifle at him, knowing that it was not loaded, and the Zulu ducked back without delivering his blow. According to Hitch, four out of the seven men were killed and two wounded, and

A rare early portrait photograph of Private Alfred Henry Hook, VC, of B Company, one of the defenders of the hospital. (Keith Reeves Collection)

Bromhead was the only one who escaped unhurt:

It was in this struggle that I was shot. They pressed us very hard, several of them mounting the barricade. I knew this one had got his rifle presented at me, but at the same time I had got my hands full in front and I was at the present when he shot me through the right shoulder blade and passed through my shoulder which splintered the shoulder bone very much, as I have had in all 39 pieces of broken bone taken from my shoulder. I tried to keep my feet, but could not, he could have assegaid me had not Bromhead shot him with his revolver. Bromhead seemed sorry when he saw me down bleeding so freely, saying, "Mate, I am very sorry to see you down." I was not down more than a few minutes, stripping [to] my shirt sleeves with my waistbelt on and valise straps I put my wounded arm under my waist belt. I was able to make another stand, getting Bromhead's revolver, and with his assistance in loading it I managed very well with it.

Corporal Schiess, a Swiss NCO of the NNC who had been in hospital with severe blisters, and who had been hit in the instep by a bullet earlier in the fight, left the safety of the biscuit boxes to creep a few paces along the abandoned rampart to get at the snipers crouching below the ledge:

Slowly raising himself, to get a shot at some of the enemy who had been particularly annoying, his hat was blown off by a shot from a Zulu the other side of the wall. He immediately jumped up, bayonetted the Zulu and shot a second, and bayonetted a third who came to their assisstance, and then returned to his place.

At about dusk a rumour went round amongst the defenders that a column of troops was to be seen on the Helpmekaar road, and they responded with a cheer. Chard himself could see nothing, and no help arrived; but, curiously enough, two companies from Helpmekaar had been on the road at about that time.

With the onset of darkness, the Zulus completely surrounded the post; nevertheless, the limitations of this apparent advantage soon became clear. They could no longer use their firearms at anything other than close range, while the flames of the blazing hospital illuminated that side of the battlefield and made any rushes from that direction as conspicuous as they had been in daylight. Instead, the Zulus shifted the focus of their attack to the far end of the storehouse, where they could still muster for an attack amongst the shadows. A vicious fight erupted along the wall of the cattle-pen, and the defenders were gradually forced back, first to the interior partition, then to the wall in front of the storehouse. This victory was difficult for the Zulus to exploit, however, since the wall was high, and every time a man put his head over it he was shot by the defenders. At one point the desperate thirst of the defenders

drove Bromhead, Hook and a few others to make a sortie across the yard to drag the abandoned water-cart over to the biscuit boxes.

Chard's position throughout the night covered no more than a few square yards. Several times the Zulus tried to set fire to the storehouse, and had they succeeded it is difficult to see how the defenders could have survived; each time they tried, however, the warriors were dropped by Lieutenant Adendorff, Corporal Attwood of the Army Service Corps, and the handful of men at the loopholes inside the building. Many times the shouts of Zulu commanders and the cries of *"uSuthu!"* rose up out of the darkness; but the last charge took place at about 10 p.m., and by midnight the firing began to die away.

In fact, the Zulus probably began to retire as soon as the last attacks failed. They were completely exhausted, and the battle had been a terrible ordeal. They had covered about 15 miles of rugged country, mostly at a run, some of them engaged in a running fight. They had then fought for six hours hand-to-hand, in the teeth of a devastating fire; and, what was worse, they had nothing to show for it, since Chard's men seemed to be just as securely emplaced as before. Many, no doubt, simply began to drift from the field, but for the most part the retreat was orderly. The body of troops who passed Chelmsford at the Manzimyama drift were clearly spent, but not in disarray; they must have left Rorke's Drift at the latest two hours before dawn.

When the sun rose just after 5.20 a.m. the next morning the only Zulus in sight were the heaps of dead and dying piled in grotesque attitudes all around the barricade. A pall of dense smoke hung over the field from the burning hospital; and the yard was strewn with broken weapons, shields, helmets, paper cartridge packets, spent cartridges, and a yellow carpet of mealies spilt from the torn sacks. Chard immediately ordered out patrols to collect up the Zulu weapons, and to remove the thatch from the storehouse. To everyone's surprise, a Zulu suddenly stood up in the cattle-pen and fired a shot at close range — it missed — before running off towards the river: "although many shots were fired after him as he ran, I am glad to say the plucky fellow got off."

Gunner Howard and Private Waters stood up to be recognised — the soot-smeared Waters was almost mistaken for a Zulu and shot — and Beckett was brought in badly wounded. Private Hook was among those sent out to collect weapons. He wandered around the yard, marvelling at the terrible sights there. One soldier was still kneeling against the barricade, and Hook said "Hello, what are you still doing here?" He did not reply, and when Hook tilted back his helmet to look at his face he saw the blue mark where he had been shot through the head. Wandering down towards the river, Hook saw an apparently dead Zulu lying on the ground but bleeding freely from his leg. Hook had his rifle in his right hand and a bunch of spears over his left shoulder, and just as he passed the Zulu made a grab at the butt of his rifle. Hook dropped the spears, and managed to strike the Zulu in the chest with the butt — "the rest was quickly over."

A frightened African reported to the post, claiming to be one of the NNC from Isandlwana. Chard called on Mr. Daniells, who could speak Zulu, to interrogate him, and Daniells armed himself with Spalding's sword, "which he flourished in so wild and eccentric a manner that the poor wretch thought his last hour had come." At last, convinced by his story, Chard sent him off to Helpmekaar with a note asking for help.

The garrison was still in a dangerous predicament. The Zulu movements were not at all apparent; the fate of Lord Chelmsford was unknown; there was no sign of any relief column; and "although the men were in excellent spirits, and each man had a good supply of ammunition in his pouches, we had only about a box and a half besides." Then, at about 7 a.m., the

Zulus reappeared, and Chard called in his patrols.

A large body of warriors took up a position on the slopes of kwaSinqindi hill, out of range to the south-west, and the garrison waited anxiously for the attack. But none came; and, Chard later admitted, none had probably been planned. From their position the Zulus could see Lord Chelmsford's column approaching the drift. If their own retreat had been intended in that direction, they abandoned the idea; and after a while they rose up and retired away behind Shiyane.

From the top of the storehouse lookouts could now see the column at the drift. The long column of the 3rd NNC looked like Zulus, and for a while it was feared that this was the victorious Zulu army returning from Isandlwana, the helmets and red coats visible among them being loot from the dead. Then, a few minutes later, Russell and Walsh rode up at the head of the Mounted Infantry. The reunion was emotional: "We broke into roar after roar of cheering, waving red coats and white helmets, and we cheered again and again." Yet for Chelmsford's men the relief at finding the garrison alive was tempered by the terrible realisation that no part of the force from Isandlwana had reached it in safety:

> *Approaching cautiously at first, a mounted officer, when re-assured, galloped up and anxiously inquired if any of the men from the camp at Isandhlwana had escaped and joined us. Sadly we answered "No!" Overcome by emotion at the terrible certainty conveyed by that short word, he bent down to his horse's neck trying in vain to stifle the sobs which broke from his overcharged heart. No wonder his grief had mastered him, for he had passed during the night by that camp where hundreds of his brave comrades lay slaughtered, and the hope that some portion might have fought their way through was crushed forever.*

As Chelmsford's column came up the men fell out and walked about together, swapping stories of their experiences. Lieutenant Maxwell got talking to two men of the 24th who "bared their shoulders and I saw they were black and blue and swollen, caused by the recoil or kicking of their Martinis, proving to what extent they had been firing. In fact they told me that towards daylight they were unable to place the rifle to the shoulder, but held it out pointing to the front and firing. They had during the night to change shoulder constantly, which caused both being in this state."

Most of the defenders had minor injuries, cuts or scrapes, although their casualties were remarkably light. Maxwell had heard that a friend of his had been killed, and saw five bodies laid out in the cattle-pen, guarded by a sentry who kept him away. In fact, 15 of Chard's men had been killed outright, and two more mortally wounded; 16 others were wounded to various degrees of severity. Curiously, as Chard noted, very few of the injuries were caused by spear-wounds, reflecting the extent to which rifle-fire and the barricades had kept the Zulus at arm's length. Most of the wounds were from firearms, and many of them in the upper body, the most exposed part. Where the Zulus had killed men and been able to reach them, they had mutilated them in the usual fashion: Drummer Haydon's body in the hospital was found "stabbed in . . . sixteen places, and his belly cut open right up in two places, and part of his cheek was cut off."

The Zulu dead were a macabre spectacle; Chard noted that:

> *Some of the bullet wounds were very curious. One man's head was split open, exactly as if done with an axe. Another had been hit just between the eyes, the bullet carrying away the whole of the back of the head, leaving his face perfect, as though it were a mask, only disfigured by the small hole made by the bullet passing through.*

Hamilton-Browne, who had "been over a good many battle-fields," noted the extraordinary number of Zulus who "seemed to have dropped on their elbows and knees and remained like that with their knees drawn up to their chins. One huge fellow, who must have been, in life, quite 7 feet high lay on his back with his heels on the top of the parapet and his head nearly touching the ground, the rest of his body sup-

Private William Jones, VC, another of the hospital's defenders.
(Royal Archives)

ported by a heap of his dead comrades." Commissary Dunne noted that most of the dead Zulus wore the *isicoco* headring, suggesting the extent to which the senior age-group *amabutho* had suffered the brunt of the fighting. Fynn thought that they were mostly of the uThulwana regiment.

Although the Zulus had carried off as many of their wounded as possible, large numbers were found lying a little way off where they had crawled away or been abandoned by comrades who could carry them no further. Hamilton-Browne is explicit about their fate:

> *During the afternoon it was discovered that a large number of wounded and worn out Zulus had taken refuge or hidden in the mealie fields near the laager. My two companies of the Zulus [i.e. isiQoza in the NNC] with some of my non-coms and a few of the 24th quickly drew these fields and killed them with bayonet, butt and assegai. It was beastly but there was nothing else to do. War is war and savage war is the worst of the lot. Moreover our men were worked up to a pitch of fury by the sights they had seen in the morning and the mutilated bodies of our poor fellows lying in front of the hospital building.*

It seems that the Zulu losses were extraordinarily heavy. The bodies were dragged from around the ruins and buried at a number of spots a few hundred yards away, chiefly in two pits in front of the post. The NNC, with their dread of *umnyama*, would not touch the corpses, but dug the holes; white troops were compelled to collect the bodies. Over 300 corpses were disposed of in this way. Chard thought that this figure was an accurate reflection of their losses, but on mature consideration decided that they must have been higher. Bodies continued to turn up for weeks afterwards along the Shiyane terrace or down by the river, and a figure of 500 dead does not seem unlikely. No doubt the surviving wounded ran to scores, perhaps hundreds more. (The percentage of battle casualties suffered by any force before necessarily having a detrimental effect on its morale often strikes the casual civilian observer as surprisingly low — usually about ten per cent. The Zulu casualties at Rorke's Drift were between 12 and 15 per cent in total, but must have been much higher within particular groups committed to assaults on a narrow front. We should beware, however, of generalisations made across a cultural divide.)

Ironically, since Prince Dabulamanzi had led his men into Natal to save their reputation, the nation as a whole despised his performance. Mehlokazulu kaSihayo commented that "Dabulamanzi is not a good general; he is too hasty". Muziwento recalled how the story of the fight reached the country, and the general reaction to it:

> The Zulus arrived at Jim's house. They fought, they yelled, they shouted, "It dies at the entrance! It dies in the doorway! It dies in the entrance! It dies in the doorway!" They stabbed the sacks; they dug with their assegais. It was no longer fighting: they were exchanging salutations merely. (We were told this by Umunya who was present.) The Mbozankomo regiment [uThulwana] was finished up at Jim's, shocking cowards they were too. Our people laughed at them, some said, "You! You're no men! You're just

women, seeing that you ran away for no reason at all, like the wind!" Others jeered and said "You marched off. You went to dig little bits with your assegais out of the house of Jim, that had never done you any harm!"

It was a harsh judgement on men whom even their enemies came grudgingly to admire. In 1882, when the passions caused by the fighting had burnt out, the traveller Bertram Mitford met a warrior of the uNdi corps who had fought at Rorke's Drift. Asked why the Zulus had not triumphed there as they had at Isandlwana, the man smiled, and gave a perceptive reply: "The soldiers were behind a *schaans* [barricade] . . . and they were in a corner."

Sketch by Lieutenant H.G.Mainwaring, 2/24th, of Rorke's Drift the morning after the fight. The storehouse is on the left, with the redoubt of mealie-bags in front of it — note its height; the ruins of the hospital are on the right. (Killie Campbell Africana Library)

The storehouse photographed after the post had been abandoned; the thatch was stripped from the roof, and the loopholed stone wall added, immediately after the battle. (Keith Reeves Collection)

CHAPTER ELEVEN

Burying the Bones

On the morning of 22nd January, Major Harcourt Bengough's 2nd Battalion, 1st NNC marched up from Sandspruit to Msinga. Bengough's battalion had been part of Durnford's No.2 Column, and Bengough's orders were to cross the Mzinyathi at Eland's Kraal, downstream of Rorke's Drift opposite the Mangeni gorge. Bengough reported to William Beaumont, the Magistrate of Newcastle, who was temporarily in charge of the magistracy at Msinga during the absence of Henry Fynn, and asked him to guide his battalion across the drift. Beaumont ordered his border levies to guard the crossing on the Natal side, and led Bengough's men safely across.

His duty done, Beaumont ordered his levies to stand down and returned to Msinga. He had not been back long when he noticed Mrs.Fynn and her sister talking earnestly to a solitary rider, who turned out to be the interpreter James Brickhill. Living nearby, Brickhill had cut across country to the Gordon Memorial Mission to break the news to Mrs.Fynn, and assure her that her husband was safe, rather than accompanying the other refugees to Helpmekaar.

The implications of the disaster were not lost on Beaumont. Rorke's Drift was only 20 miles away, and so far as he knew there were only scattered pockets of troops between him and the border. If the victorious Zulus came raging into Natal Msinga lay directly in their path. At Fynn's insistence, however, the magistracy had been reinforced with loopholed steel shutters; and Beaumont decided to stick to his post. He sent messages out to recall the border levies (in vain), and set to work barricading the doors and windows. The only whites with him were Mrs.Fynn, who "very pluckily said she would throw in her lot with me", her children and sister, the gaoler Elkington and his family, "and two or three others who were strangers to me." By evening, however, as news of the disaster spread through the civilian population along the border, the first of a stream of refugees who had abandoned their missions and farms arrived seeking protection.

Colonel Bray of the 4th (King's Own Royal) Regiment was on his way up from Greytown to Helpmekaar, with just 22 men guarding 28 wagons, when a stream of refugees passed him on the road. The 4th, one of only two battalions sent out from Britain at Chelmsford's request, had arrived in Durban a week or so before, and the Battalion Headquarters had marched as far as Pietermaritzburg; the 4th's companies were slowly deploying along the line of communication, freeing the last of the 24th companies who had been left behind on garrison duties. Amongst Bray's wagons were no less than 15 full of ammunition. Feeling that his position was too exposed on the road, Bray halted when he reached Msinga, where the buildings at least offered something defensible. "I was greatly relieved at their arrival", admitted Beaumont. Bray's men formed the wagons into a laager around the courthouse, and set to work knocking connecting holes through the interior walls and making loopholes. They passed a tense night in expectation of attack, while a glow beyond the Biggarsberg and the distant crackle of gunfire confirmed that the Zulus had reached Rorke's Drift. There was still no sign of them as the dawn broke over Msinga, and Beaumont rode out with his binoculars; in the distance he could see "men, women, children and cattle streaming inland from the border."

If Bray's tiny garrison had felt isolated that night, the situation was even worse at Helpmekaar. Major Spalding must have left Rorke's Drift after lunch on the 22nd, for he had ridden up the escarpment beyond Vermaaks when he met D and G Companies, 1/24th under Brevet-Major Upcher and Captain Rainforth. Rainforth's company had been at Helpmekaar for several days, presumably delaying its ordered march to Rorke's Drift because bad weather had prevented Upcher arriving at Helpmekaar from Greytown until the 21st — Rainforth could not leave the depot unguarded. Now these officers broke the news to Spalding of the disaster at Isandlwana; fugitives cutting across country from Sothondose's Drift had reached Helpmekaar, and Upcher was marching down to find out the situation at Rorke's Drift. Spalding rode back with them as far as the foot of the escarpment, then pressed on with Dickson of the Buffalo Border Guard.

There were a lot of demoralised men streaming along the road; Spalding was pleased to note that they were "chiefly Basutos and people in civilian clothes, but there were one or two Mounted Infantry". He ordered them to accompany him, "but all except two slipped away when my back was turned." All whom he questioned assured him that Rorke's Drift had already fallen. "At about three miles from the same," Spalding reported, "I came across a body of Zulus extended across the road. They were fifty yards off. A deep donga . . . was behind them capable of concealing a large force. They threw out flankers as if to surround the party. Mr. Dickson agreed with me that they were Zulu, an appearance borne out by the 'horns' which they threw out. So we trotted back to the troops some two miles in the rear." From a rise on the escarpment the flames of the burning hospital could be seen at the foot of Shiyane; and the two companies turned back to Helpmekaar, convinced that Rorke's Drift was beyond help.

Most of the survivors had arrived at Helpmekaar between 5 p.m. and 6 p.m., while the infantry were absent, and found the supply depot completely unprotected. "I found I was the senior officer present," recalled Captain Essex,

so I took the command and caused some wagons to be drawn up at a short distance all round the storehouse, a zinc building, quite indefensible. I had sacks of oats placed under the wagons, and now had a barrier. We mustered, of those who had escaped, about 25 Europeans; the others, about 10 volunteers and camp followers, continuing their retreat. A few others, such as owners of wagons, two or three farmers with their wives and children, now arrived, and my little garrison numbered 48 men, of whom, however, only 28 had rifles. We expected the approach of the Zulus every moment, but we had plenty of ammunition, and I told every one to fire away as hard as he could in the event of attack, so as to deceive the enemy as to the number with whom he had to deal.

Essex's determination does him credit, especially after what he had seen that day; but few of the Volunteers had any fight left in them. In an apparent attempt to stop further desertions Essex ordered all the horses to be turned loose, and any that lingered near the camp to be shot. Quartermaster Macphail of the Buffalo Border Guard thought this a "foolish order" which merely lowered morale still further; many of the Volunteers had more faith in their horses than in Essex, and were anxious to secure the safety of their families in the border settlements and laagers. The order "cleared a lot of us out and left him to fight the Zulus by himself . . . You could hear a

A marvellously characteristic period photograph, c.1876, of Major Harcourt M.Bengough, 77th Regiment, who commanded the 2/1st NNC, which crossed into Zululand at Eland's Kraal on 22nd January. Fearing disloyalty after Isandlwana he disarmed his men, but Chelmsford countermanded his order to them to stand down. He led a reorganised NNC battalion on the border in the tense months which followed. (Ministry of Defence)

swear here and a swear there. Some muttered, 'If the horses go we go'. We could hear many breaking away so we came along." Macphail himself set off for Dundee. Lieutenant Higginson of the NNC had been surprised to discover Captain Stevenson and the wounded Lieutenant Purvis at Helpmekaar; Higginson decided that as he had no gun he was useless, and the three of them rode off towards Ladysmith. Stafford and Davies volunteered to carry the news to Pietermaritzburg.

Typically, the Regulars clung to their sense of duty to see them through. Captain Alan Gardner was concerned that the victorious Zulu army might strike north across country and catch Colonel Evelyn Wood's Left Flank Column unprepared. He tried to find someone to take a message to Wood; but no one would go, so he started out himself. Macphail passed him along the way: "He was off his head . . . Poor fellow, any sort of noise made him start suddenly." One wonders if many of the other survivors were any steadier. Macphail persuaded one Millward to take Gardner to Utrecht, from where he finally got his message through to Wood.

When Macphail reached Dundee he found the town deserted; the news had outpaced him, and most of the settlers had fled to the stone redoubt at Fort Pine. Indeed, the news spread rapidly along the exposed border; and many families who had waved their menfolk off to war enthusiastically enough were now left to fend for themselves with no idea of the fate of husbands, sons and brothers.

At Newcastle, a day or two before, Maud Bradstreet had helped her friend Mrs.Hitchcock deliver a baby girl, Georgina; now word came that both their husbands had been killed with Durnford. The two women set off for the safety of the Orange Free State, accompanied only by a young black servant. (It was a week before they found a safe refuge; the baby survived on a diet of water strained through mealie meal.) Back down the road, behind the Biggarsberg, 16-year-old Ruben Jones was leading a wagon and span when he met Jim Rorke's widow coming in the opposite direction; she had abandoned her farm at Knostrope, and now broke the news of Isandlwana to Ruben, leaving him to wonder about the fate of his two brothers with the Newcastle Mounted Rifles.

Those who stayed at Helpmekaar passed a terrible night. It was pitch black, and all along the border the glow of spreading fires marked the progress of the Zulus among Natal African homesteads. The distant thud of gunfire (when Harness

shelled the deserted camp at Isandlwana) suggested further heavy fighting. In the early part of the night the men manned the rampart of mealie-bags, straining to catch any sound of movement on the road from Rorke's Drift. At about 10.30 p.m. they were astonished to hear wagon-wheels; it turned out to be Spalding with the two companies of the 1/24th. "I had had a long enough day," wrote Smith-Dorrien, who was among the little garrison, "having been on the move, including a stretch of twenty miles on foot, much of it at a run, for forty-two hours, and directly Lieutenant Clements . . . told me he had relieved me, I lay down then and there on two sacks of grain, and was fast asleep in a second."

No attack occurred that night, and the dawn of the 23rd saw the heights wreathed in mist. Groups of warriors suddenly loomed up along the road out of the gloom, and the garrison hurredly stood-to and fired several shots before they were recognised as men of the 3rd NNC. At about 9 a.m. Chard's messenger arrived with his note begging for assistance; and Spalding rode down to investigate with a small group of mounted men, including Smith-Dorrien. On the road they met Major Russell and Henry Fynn riding back up, and learned from them that Rorke's Drift had held. When he arrived at the post which he had left only 24 hours earlier Smith-Dorrien was shocked at the scene: "All round lay dead Zulus, between three and four hundred, and there was my wagon, some 200 yards away, riddled and looted . . . Dead animals and cattle everywhere — such a scene of devastation! To my young mind it appeared impossible that order could ever be restored . . ."

Chelmsford had not stayed long at Rorke's Drift. As soon as he had learned the details of the fight, and satisfied himself that none of the Isandlwana garrison had been able to escape, he rode off via Helpmekaar to Pietermaritzburg. He left the mounted men and Harness' artillery at Helpmekaar. Although the sight of exhausted warriors in retreat from Rorke's Drift suggested that there was no immediate peril of a raid into Natal, the Colony remained largely defenceless, and the civil administration would have to be reassured by prompt action. Not only did Chelmsford need to co-ordinate a proper defensive strategy; he also had to break the news to the Home Government, which had only recently learned that it was at war at all. Colonel Glyn was left in charge at Rorke's Drift with what remained of No.3 Column.

The first night after the battle there was not a pleasant one. The fear of a renewed Zulu attack was very real, and the men had spent the day dragging away the enemy dead and repairing the barricades. The entire column slept in the immediate confines of the mission station. With the destruction of the camp they had lost their tents, greatcoats and blankets — everything, in fact, except what they stood up in. The sentries were reduced to improvising greatcoats from empty mealie sacks, cutting holes for their heads and arms. The Natal Carbineers found themselves posted in the cattle-pen for the night, and were disgusted to discover in the morning that the straw they had been sleeping on concealed the swollen bodies of several dead Zulus.

The men of the 3rd NNC were posted behind the mission, on the slopes of Shiyane, to give some warning of a Zulu approach; their officers and NCOs, however, joined the other whites behind the barricades. At one point there was an alarm when an NNC picquet fired at an imaginary enemy, and the whites manned their posts. The NNC not unnaturally felt that they were being abandoned to their fate outside the laager, and by morning large numbers were openly deserting. Chelmsford consulted with their officers, whose general opinion of their men was that "the majority were worse than useless." Lonsdale addressed them and asked how many of them were prepared to return to Zululand with their officers; to his disappointment only a handful said they would. Chelmsford thereupon gave the order for them to be disbanded.

Their officers and NCOs collected their rifles, ammunition belts and red headcloths — most were allowed to keep their blankets — and the 3rd NNC officially ceased to exist. Its end seems entirely in keeping with its short, unhappy history; the men were as keen to leave their officers as the latter were to see them go. The men were told to keep together until they reached Msinga, after which they could disperse to their homes.

Feelings within the exhausted and overwrought garrison were still running high, and the widely-circulated stories of disembowelled drummer boys made the area around the post unsafe for anyone with an unfamiliar black face. Within a couple of days of the fight Smith-Dorrien was shocked to see an ageing Zulu hanging from the poles he had erected to stretch reims:

> It was found that it was a case of lynch law performed by incensed men, who were bitter at the loss of their comrades. Other incidents of the same sort occurred in the next few days before law and order were re-established.

In his memoires Hamilton-Browne characteristically excused his own orders to hang a "spy" on the grounds that he was in a bad temper at the time, having just barked his shin; and there are dark hints that a number of Zulus were killed more or less arbitrarily. At Helpmekaar Curling wrote in a letter home that "all spies are shot; we have disposed of three or four already". It is, of course, quite possible that individual Zulus had crossed the river to scout around the British garrisons, but the likelihood must be that these men were perfectly innocent subjects of the Lieutenant-Governor of Natal.

When Chelmsford passed through Helpmekaar he gave orders for a fort to be built around the storehouses. On 29th January the 5th Company, Royal Engineers arrived there, under the command of Captain Walter Parke Jones and accompanied by Colonel F.C.Hassard, RE; with the Sappers were four companies of the 2nd Battalion, 4th Regiment who marched up from Greytown. Half of Jones' company went on to Rorke's Drift, while the remainder set about building an earthwork to protect the sheds. It was not ideally sited — being overlooked by hills on two sides — but when a deep trench had been dug all round, and the earth piled up inside into a formidable parapet with bastions at the corners, it was largely impregnable to Zulu attack. Clery, in his usual acerbic style, commented that Hassard had "shut himself up in it and strongly recommended everybody else to do the same". In fact Hassard did not feel himself up to the task of command, and soon handed over to Colonel Bray of the 4th Regiment. Despite its strength, life at Helpmekaar was far from pleasant, as Curling described:

> Those who have escaped have not a rag left, as they came away in their shirtsleeves. We always sleep at night in fort or laager, and in the open air. It is very unpleasant as it rains every night, and is very cold. We none of us have more than one blanket each, as you can see we are having a rough time. The first few days I was utterly done up, but have pulled up alright now. We have made a strong entrenchment, and are pretty safe even should we be attacked. The only thing we are afraid of is sickness. There are fifty sick and wounded already, who are all jammed up at night in the fort. The smell is terrible, 800 men cooped up in so small a place. Food, fortunately, is plentiful, and we have at least three months' supply.

Amongst the sick were the wounded from Rorke's Drift, who were sent up to Helpmekaar on the 26th in the expectation that the facilities there would be better. In fact there was nowhere to put them but in beds made from mealie-sacks inside the zinc storage sheds, which stank of rotten grain. Surgeon D.Blair Brown, a thorough and conscientious medical officer, took a detailed interest in his patients. Corporal Lyons, for example, was in a bad way when Brown examined him; he was in great pain, and one side of his body was paralysed. The Zulu bullet had not been located; Brown administered chloroform and "made a prolonged attempt" to find it. The ball had passed

down the spinal column, smashing two vertebrae, and Brown had to give up his attempt to recover it when Lyons' vital signs faltered. Lyons was later sent down to the base hospital at Ladysmith where, a month later, Brown examined him again. By this time the Corporal was in such pain in his arms that he was begging to have them amputated. Brown searched for the ball once more, and found it lodged close to the spinal cord; he extracted it, and Lyons made a remarkable recovery.

Blair Brown was less able to treat the shattered nerves of those whose visions of Isandlwana returned by night. Several times the garrison was disturbed by someone screaming out, over and over again, "Are they coming yet?" Curiously, the tormented Trooper Hayes of the Mounted Police had used those words the night before Isandlwana; Hayes was in the camp at Helpmekaar, where he died of fever a few weeks later.

Conditions were no better at Rorke's Drift. When Jones' Engineers arrived they began building high loopholed walls around the old storehouse; the post was named Fort Bromhead. Stone was taken from all along the Shiyane terraces, and the bodies of many dead Zulus were found in the process, as late as two months after the battle. Henry Harford described life at the post:

> To make matters worse, we had a lot of rain, and the interior of the Fort became a simple quagmire from the tramping of so many feet. Fatigue parties were employed for the best part of the day in carrying liquid mud away and emptying the slush outside. In this state of filth we lived and ate and slept for more than two months, no-one being in the possession of anything more than a blanket or the clothes he stood up in. An exception was made, however, with B Company, 2nd Battalion, 24th Regiment, who had made such a gallant defence, and they were housed in the attic of Rorke's house with a tarpaulin thrown over the rafters (from which the thatch had been removed) to shelter them from the wet, a well-deserved honour.

In such appalling conditions it is scarcely surprising that the health of the garrison deteriorated. John Chard himself was among those who fell sick, and was sent back to Ladysmith to recuperate.

* * *

While the infantry manned the Imperial outposts on the borders, panic swept through the civilian population of Natal, both black and white. The magistrate Beaumont had noticed it first, on the morning of the 23rd, and it spread through the Colony at the speed of a galloping horse. Stafford and Davies rode into Pietermaritzburg that night, but somehow a rumour had already circulated among the town's black population, and many citizens of Pietermaritzburg woke up on the morning of the 24th to find themselves without domestic staff. When the first news of the losses was posted the Colonial capital was stunned; the Natal Carbineers had recruited heavily amongst the sons of the metropolitan gentry, and many well-known Colonial families were bereaved. People began flocking in from the countryside; and Lieutenant-Colonel Mitchell, the town commandant, hastily organised a town laager, ordering prominent buildings to be loopholed, and linking together blocks of houses and shops with barricades. The panic extended to Durban itself, where volunteers were posted on the outskirts of the city, and a barricade was built across the Point, a tongue of land enclosing the harbour, to shelter non-combatants.

* * *

The expected Zulu invasion failed to materialise. King Cetshwayo was as committed to his defensive policy in victory as he had been at the beginning of the war, and in any case his army was preoccupied. Isandlwana had been won at such a cost that the regiments needed weeks to recuperate, and there were important post-combat cleansing rituals to perform. Immediately after the battle at Isandlwana the army spent the night bivouacked in the same valley of the Ngwebeni where they had slept before the battle. Many of the wounded were too badly injured to move, and the army drifted away over a period of days. It was customary for a victorious army to report to the king, but so traumatic had this victory proved that many warriors, particularly those caring for wounded relatives or friends, simply went home.

Those who did return to the king were not allowed into his presence for several days, until they had been freed from the lingering and malignant influence of the dead. Those who had killed in the battle, or stabbed the dead bodies (known as *izinxwelera*), were sent to their respective *amakhanda*, still wearing items of their victims' clothing, or to special homesteads appointed by the king. Here they were fed on cattle captured during the battle. Every morning they were required to report to a nearby stretch of river, carrying their spears point-upwards and singing their war-chants. They washed thoroughly, and on returning to the homestead were told to stick their spears in the ground and dip their fingers in a specially prepared medicine, the ingredients of which included some from the amulets worn by warriors into battle. They then had to suck the medicine off their fingertips *(ncinda)*, and squirt it in the direction of the enemy, casting out the evil influences with it.

After several days of this the army was summoned to Kwa Gqikazi on the Mahlabatini plain, near the king's favourite homestead of Ulundi; the *izinxwelera* took with them stripped willow sticks. It was then that the boasts and challenges issued before the war were recalled, the deeds of brave warriors recounted, and cowards publicly identified and mocked. There had been much argument between the regiments as to who had been first to "stab" the enemy — who had been the first to get amongst them. After carefully weighing the evidence the king took a length of willow and, drawing it back like a throwing-spear, hurled it in the direction of the uMbonambi and their *induna*, Ntuzwa kaNhlaka. "The king's doing so is a public acknowledgement of the king accepting such men, headed by their *induna*, as having really been the first to come up to the enemy and begin stabbing." The men so recognised were entitled to use their willow sticks to make necklaces of small, interlocking wooden blocks. These necklaces *(iziqu)* were worn as a distinction of service in a particular campaign. "If one cuts fresh ones, one asks, 'Have you gone once more and killed others in a fresh battle?' Hence one always keeps the old *iziqu*."

Despite these ceremonies, the king was disappointed in his army's showing. The return had been half-hearted, more suggestive of a defeat than a victory, and once the full implications of the casualties sank in the nation was stunned. "The dead are not to be counted there are so many," said a Zulu named uCajana kaMatundeka, "the whole Zulu nation is weeping and mourning." In the days after the battle the wounded made their way home to their families, and to the care of the *izinyanga*, the Zulu medical doctors. These had a wide array of herbal treatments and poultices for the sorts of injuries that were sustained in everyday life, but there was little they could do to treat some of the appalling wounds inflicted by Martini-Henry bullets. Shortly after the war Captain William Molyneux noted the grim evidence of the damage inflicted by British firepower — and also the lack of rancour apparently displayed towards their conquerors by the defeated warriors:

> One large kraal I visited . . . was full of wounded men, who were as friendly as possible . . . as merry as could be. One had lost two brothers at Isandlwana, and had been wounded at Ulundi himself; his regiment was the Nkobamakosi . . . commanded by Usicwelecwele. How he had got home in a fortnight he scarcely knew; it was very hard work, for he had been wounded in the thigh, but the other boys had helped him . . . An old man, who had lost half his right arm . . . had fought . . . at Inyezane and Ginghilovo, and at the latter place the bone of his arm had been smashed by

The expedition to recover wagons from Isandlwana, 21st May 1879, after sketches by Melton Prior. Although the mountain has been shown too small the sketch otherwise accurately reflects the search through the desolate camp. (Author's collection)

> a bullet below the elbow; but he had cut the loose part off, and the wound had healed now. The many little mounds outside, covered with stones, told how many of the poor fellows had crawled home simply to die.

Henry Harford met a man who had fought at Isandlwana, and suffered an extraordinary number of wounds:

> One bullet had gone through his hand, three had gone through his shoulder and smashed his shoulder blade, two had cut the skin and slightly into the flesh right down the chest and stomach, and one had gone clean through the fleshy part of the thigh. The others were mere scratches in comparison with these, but there he was, after about eight months, as well as ever and ready for another set-to.

These descriptions reflect an observation made by British medical officers: that due to the comparatively high velocity the Martini-Henry bullet made clean flesh wounds which healed easily; but when the bullet struck bone the injuries caused were massive. Blair Brown wrote: "When the shaft of a long bone is struck by a round bullet, long fissures and splitting up into fragments do not occur in the way they do when a conoidal one [i.e. such as the Martini-Henry's] hit a like bone." The Martini-Henry projectile splintered major bones into fragments, and death from shock often followed. Such injuries tested the skill of British surgeons to the full, and were beyond the abilities of the *izinyanga*.

Nevertheless, John Gill, a medical officer serving with Wood's Column, primly noted that Zulus wounded in the battle of Khambula preferred their own treatment to that offered by British doctors:

> The few wounded Zulus under our care absolutely refuse any operation or treatment; they even take off splints as soon as they are applied. But in spite of their stupidity, they do very well, and one has an opportunity of observing the natural history of gunshot wounds and fractures. They somehow crawl out of doors every day and nurse their fractured limbs with both hands, squeezing the wounds a good deal, and constantly washing them with a small stream of water, which they very cleverly manage to eject from their own mouths on to the wounds, though held at a distance of two feet or more. One man, shot through the head of the tibia — a fearful smash, knee-joint opened in all directions — has got quite fat under the above treatment and ordinary soldier's rations; the joint is of course in a very bad position, but I suppose he will eventually recover.

Surgeon Blair Browne was also surprised at the extent to which individual Zulus had survived serious wounds with a minimum of treatment:

> For two months I was detained in Zululand after the war, and saw many of our former enemies come in to camp to get the written passes to enable them to return to their homes. Not a few of them were wounded. The number of

simple penetrations of muscles was remarkable. I found one with the most distinct marks of a gunshot wound of the knee, which anyone would have said, from the line of flight the bullet must have taken and from the situation of wounds of entrance and exit, must have penetrated the joint. The bullet had hit the inner border of the patella grooving it distinctly, and made its exit posterially half an inch internally to the tendons forming the outer upper margin of the popliteal space. A month after the injury it was completely healed, the joint being perfectly mobile, without aid of surgery. Through an interpreter he told me all about the progress of healing and the means adopted to get it well. There is a small flat-leaved orchid which grows plentifully on the Veldt. A leaf of this was secured on both wounds and changed occasionally; this was all that was done. A piece of oil-silk would have answered the same purpose and been followed by the same result.

Yet these optimistic anecdotes are essentially misleading. The wounded who made such remarkable recoveries and were still alive to intrigue British witnesses were almost certainly a small minority. In 1882 the traveller Bertram Mitford interviewed many Zulu survivors of the war, and his conclusions regarding the wounded summed up the grim lottery which faced them:

While on the subject, I was surprised at the fewness of the wounded men I fell in with during my progress through the country. Whether, owing to rude surgery, numbers died whom the most ordinary skill could easily have saved, I cannot say, but considering that every man with whom I conversed had taken part in one or more of the battles, the fewness of those who had wounds to show was rather remarkable.

* * *

With the bulk of the nation's manpower recovering from the shock of battle, the Zulus lacked the capacity for a major incursion along the border. Small parties — mainly, it seems, Gamdana's followers — slipped across the Mzinyathi to loot the almost deserted Natal bank, and occasionally there were skirmishes with the black Border Police or Guards.

Although fear of a Zulu attack remained very real for at least two months, the garrison at Rorke's Drift made its first tentative forays from Fort Bromhead within a fortnight of the disaster. Colonel Glyn, who was clearly deeply shocked by the fate of his Battalion, had become more withdrawn than ever, and it fell to the resourceful Wilsone Black to organise patrols along the border. Since there were no mounted men left at the post Black called on the services of those officers and NCOs of the 3rd NNC who had horses. For the most part these patrols were merely intended to give advance warning of any Zulu movements towards the Mzinyathi, but "Maori" Hamilton-Browne secured permission to make a few offensive strikes across the river. These chiefly consisted of attacks on Zulu homesteads and the theft of Zulu cattle. They became so irritating to the local civilian population that two *izangoma* were brought in to discourage them by occult means. The pair burned medicinal charms on a fire on the Zulu bank on days when the wind carried the smoke towards the garrison. Unfortunately they had the opposite effect to that intended, since Hamilton-Browne and his colleagues crept up on them one day and shot them both dead; Hamilton-Browne noted with satisfaction, on examining the bodies, that his victim was

a woman. (There is something almost reassuring about the absolute consistency of this officer's repulsive character.)

One of the earliest of these patrols made a significant find which greatly lifted the morale of the garrison. Rumours of the fate of Melvill and Coghill had circulated amongst the troops shortly after Isandlwana, and Glyn was under pressure from his officers to search for their bodies and for the Queen's Colour. For some reason he was reluctant, but he gave Major Black permission to mount a patrol to Sothondose's Drift on 4th February. The afternoon before Black rode out with Harford to scout the vicinity. The party paused on the heights on the Natal side, deciding where to place covering parties the following day; then, as it was still mid-afternoon, they decided to go down a little way towards the river. Harford recalled that they were

following as well as we could over the stony and precipitous ground, the . . . path by which, it was said, the fugitives had made their way. Suddenly, just off to the right of us, we saw two bodies, and on going to have a look at them, found that they were those of Lieutenants Melvill and Coghill! Both were clearly recognisable. Melvill in red, and Coghill in blue, uniform. Both were lying on their backs about a yard from each other, Melvill at right-angles to the path and Coghill parallel to it, a little above Melvill with his head uphill. Both had been assegaied, but otherwise their bodies had been left untouched.

Major Black at once said, "Now we shall see whether they have the Colours on them," and proceeded to unbutton Melvill's serge, while I opened Coghill's patrol jacket, but there were no Colours. Presently Major Black said, "I wonder if Melvill's watch is on him! He always carried it in the small waist-pocket of his breeches!", and, on looking, there was his gold watch, which was subsequently sent to his widow. Nothing was found on Coghill, but his bad knee was still bandaged up. Undoubtedly, Melvill must have stuck to him and helped him along, otherwise he never could have got so far over such terrible ground.

Black and Harford covered over the bodies with stones until a proper burial could be arranged, and returned to Rorke's Drift. The news caused a good deal of excitement and there was no shortage of volunteers for the next day's expedition; in the event the patrol was commanded by Black and Commandant Cooper, and accompanied by Harford and several subalterns of the NNC.

Watched by picquets posted on the top of Shiyane, the party rode down river towards the drift, and Black posted his covering party on the heights. Chaplain Smith read the burial service over the grave of Melvill and Coghill; then Harford, together with Captain Harber and Lieutenant Wainwright, was ordered to go down to the river and search the banks and shallows. After a stiff scramble down through undergrowth and boulders, the three men posted themselves at intervals and began to walk downstream. The river level had dropped considerably since the 22nd, and all manner of military debris, along with the usual driftwood and other flotsam, was trapped amongst the boulders.

The party had begun searching quite some distance below the large coffin-shaped rock to which Melvill and Higginson had clung, almost as far as the bluff of the gorge on the Natal bank, when Harford

Consistently misidentified as a sentry of the 2/24th at Isandlwana on 21st May 1879, this photograph in fact shows a Dragoon, which dates it to the burial expeditions of late June. He holds a spade, and the ground at his feet is disturbed. (Author's collection)

stumbled on the Colour case mixed up with a heap of other things, and picking it up I said to Harber, who was closest to me, "Look here, here's the case! The Colours can't be far off!" We all three then had a look at it, put it on a conspicuous boulder, and went on. Then, as Harber was returning to his position, I noticed a straight piece of stick projecting out of the water in the middle of the river, almost in line with us, and said to him, "Do you see that straight bit of stick sticking up in the water opposite to you? It looks to me uncommonly like a Colour pole." He waded straight in, up to his middle, and got hold of it. On lifting it out he brought up the Colour still adhering to it, and on getting out of the water handed the standard to me, and as he did so the gold-embroidered centre scroll dropped out, the silk having more-or-less rotted from the long immersion in the water.

And thus, in a fitting end to a story ripe with portents and symbolism, the Queen's Colour of the 1/24th, the epitome of the Regiment's honour and its commitment to the Empire and Crown, was found in the waters of the Mzinyathi River — upside down. The finders let out a cheer which brought Major Black scrambling down the steep hillside. "I handed him the Colour amidst ringing cheers in which he joined", and Black led them back up the slope, "he carrying the Colour".

The party rode back to Rorke's Drift with the Colour carried erect, so that the picquets on Shiyane could make no mistake. To Harford's surprise they found a guard of honour waiting for them, "and the whole garrison turned out to give us an ovation." Black presented the Colours to Colonel Glyn, for whom it was clearly an emotional moment: he had received the same Colours when they were first presented to the Battalion at the Curragh in June 1866. Glyn thanked the party "with tears in his eyes." At Glyn's insistence the party escorted the Colours up to Helpmekaar the next day, where they were formally handed back to the surviving companies of the 1/24th. Glyn himself rode up to receive them. Arthur Harness witnessed the ceremony: "Poor Glyn, in speaking to the two companies under Major Upcher, fairly broke down. He said that fourteen years before, he and Upcher were the

officers to receive that colour, and they were again receiving it being almost the only officers left with the regiment." At Black's suggestion Harford, who had first spotted them in the river, carried them for the last part of the journey:

It was the proudest moment of my life, and I shall ever consider it so. I very much doubt whether such another case has ever occurred that an officer on duty and belonging to another Regiment has been given the honour of carrying its Queen's Colour.

* * *

At Helpmekaar, the inquest into the disaster had already begun. At Chelmsford's request a Court of Inquiry was convened on 27th January under the presidency of Colonel F.C.Hassard, RE; its members were Lieutenant-Colonel Law, RA, and Arthur Harness. Their brief was "to inquire into the loss of the camp", and the evidence of Clery, Crealock, Essex, Gardner, Cochrane, Curling, Smith-Dorrien and Nourse was recorded. The choice of Harness, who was clearly an important figure in the story, was subsequently criticised in the press, but Harness was not the sort of man to allow his personal involvement to influence his duty. Nevertheless, he interpreted the Court's role in a very literal sense, insisting that it was not there to pronounce a judgement, nor to analyse the circumstances surrounding the battle, but merely to list what he considered reliable evidence concerning the loss of the camp itself:

I am sorry to find that it is thought more evidence should have been taken. Of course, I know Lord Chelmsford thought so, for he sent an order that it should be done: but he does not know, nor does the general public know, that a great deal more evidence was heard, but was either corroboratory of evidence already recorded or so unreliable that it was worthless. I wrote it

A famous image of the nek at Isandlwana, taken in late June 1879; the bones of dead oxen lie in the centre, and in the centre foreground is a human skeleton. (Author's collection)

Isandlwana photographed from Mahlabamkhosi, late June 1879. Some of the wagons are still on the site. (Royal Regiment of Wales Museum, Brecon) all myself, and indeed I think I managed the thing entirely and might have recorded or rejected nearly what I liked; it seemed to me useless to record statements hardly bearing on the loss of the camp but giving doubtful particulars of small incidents more or less ghastly in their nature. We were assembled to inquire into the loss of the camp and I still think that the evidence we took was the very best living evidence, and that nothing more was necessary. I am sure that no more light will be thrown on the matter. I am glad to think that I stuck out most determinedly against giving an opinion, for you will hardly believe that Hassard and Law really thought it should be given. I said, "You may give an opinion but I decline to do so, and I will not sign the proceedings unless it is recorded that I have not given an opinion." However, it ended by no opinion being given, as you know. The duty of the court was to sift the evidence and record what was of value: if it was simply to take down a mass of statements the court might as well have been composed of three subalterns or three clerks.

Of course, the modern historian is left to ponder by what criteria Harness decided which statements were unreliable and worthless. Harness, at least, clearly felt that any criticism of the General or his staff was outside the court's remit; nor was any evidence taken from anyone but officers. Certainly, in the aftermath of the disaster, the old antagonism between the Imperial troops and the Volunteers flamed up again. Curling wrote a private letter to his family, which they subsequently passed on to the London *Standard*, in which he commented that "most of those who escaped were volunteers and Native Contingent officers, who tell any number of lies." The publication of this letter caused an outcry in Natal, and Harness was forced to advise Curling to apologise.

Indeed, although Harness clearly believed that the main function of the court had been to obtain information for Chelmsford, it is difficult to see now what useful purpose it did serve. It presented no very coherent picture of the camp's last hour, and, since no conclusion was drawn, the inferences remain obscure. It did, however, enable blame for the disaster to be placed squarely at the feet of the two convenient scapegoats: the NNC, and Anthony Durnford. The evidence formed the basis of a confidential report compiled in March 1879 by Lieutenant W. James, RE, which in turn influenced the official history of the war. Yet neither of these reports tallies with the broader range of evidence — that not selected for inclusion by the Court of Inquiry — and, indeed, they seem to have misinterpreted some of the recorded evidence.

In both accounts the NNC are placed on an angle separating the two wings of the 24th, and it is their rout which enables the Zulus to burst through the line and overrun the infantry. This conclusion was apparently drawn from Essex's testimony, yet Essex himself freely admitted that he was not at all sure where the NNC were posted. Having black skins, the Native Contingent were, of course, ideal scapegoats. Another was Anthony Durnford: because he was the senior officer present, because he was not an infantryman, and because he was dead. As early as 3rd February a cable from Frere to the Home Government included a reference to "poor Durnford's misfortune." Chelmsford and his staff were keen to obscure the deficiencies in their own planning by highlighting Durnford's shortcomings. The statements of the Court of Inquiry did not contradict this position; indeed, the Deputy Adjutant General, Colonel William Bellairs, passed on the court's findings to Lord Chelmsford in just those terms:

From the statements made before the court . . . it may clearly be gathered that the cause of the reverse suffered at Isandhlwana was that Lt.Col. Durnford, as senior officer, overruled the orders which Lt.Col.Pulleine had received to defend the camp, and directed that the troops should be moved into the open, in support of a portion of the Native Contingent which he had brought up and which was engaging the enemy.

There may, certainly, be some truth in this accusation; but whatever errors Durnford had made, they were committed within the framework of ambiguity created by Chelmsford and his shoddy staff work. It was not Chelmsford who ordered Pulleine to "defend the camp" – the order had come

from Clery, and the General was later greatly relieved to hear that it had been given. Crealock's carelessness was also a factor: his written order to Durnford to move up to Isandlwana was lost on the field and, speaking from memory, Crealock insisted that it had included the phrase "take command of the camp". When the order later turned up on the battlefield this phrase was missing; nor was there any indication of what Durnford was to do on his arrival.

The Natal press, whose attitude to Durnford had changed radically since the days of Bushman's Pass, sensed a conspiracy. On 29th May the *Natal Witness* reported that it was common knowledge that "certain members of Lord Chelmsford's staff . . . came down to' Maritzburg after the disaster, prepared to make Colonel Durnford bear the whole responsibility, and it was upon their representations that the High Commissioner's telegram about 'poor Durnford's misfortune' was sent."

Clery, for one, believed that the detested Crealock was the villain of the piece, and, indeed, claimed to detect his hand behind an apparent move to shift part of the blame to Colonel Glyn. Some weeks after the battle Glyn apparently received an anonymous memorandum from Headquarters which innocently asked him to clarify how he had followed the regulations with regard to the establishment of the camp. Glyn merely passed the note to Clery with no more comment than, "Odd the general asking me to tell him what he knows more about than I do." Clery, however, saw the trap: if Glyn replied, he was tacitly accepting responsibility for the defence of the camp. Under Clery's guidance, Glyn's reply suggested that such a request should be addressed to the General. A flurry of correspondence ensued, in which Glyn "accepted all responsibility for details, but declined to admit any responsibility for the movement of any portion of troops in or out of camp." Chelmsford rather unfairly suggested that it was Glyn's duty to protest at any decisions with which he did not agree; Glyn replied that it was his duty to follow his commanding officer's instructions. And there that particular fox went to earth.

Durnford's supporters continued to defend his reputation for years afterwards. His brother Edward, supported by Anthony's friend Frances Colenso, challenged Lord Chelmsford's public statements on the battle. The ommissions and errors in Chelmsford's case became all too apparent, but the military establishment rallied behind him, and he enjoyed the Queen's support. He weathered the storm, and Frances Colenso's increasingly impassioned accusations steadily eroded her own credibility.

* * *

While the apportioning of blame preoccupied the living, the dead still lay out on the field of Isandlwana. In the weeks after the battle Zulu civilians began to return to homesteads around the site, and looters continued to visit the battlefield to pick over the debris. The king was angry that the artillery pieces had been left on the field, and sent men down to fetch them; they were dragged away by hand, and the broken limbers left where they lay. Generally, however, the presence of so many unburied dead discouraged casual visits. For Muziwento, the Zulu boy whose father had fought at the battle, the site had a macabre fascination, and despite the obvious disapproval of his family he went to explore it with his playmates. It proved, however, an unnerving experience:

We went to see the dead people at Isandhlwana. We saw a single warrior dead, staring in our direction, with his war-shield in his hand. We ran away. We came back again. We saw countless things dead. Dead was the horse, dead too the mule, dead was the dog, dead was the monkey, dead were the wagons, dead were the tents, dead were the boxes, dead was everything, even to the very metals. We took some thread for sewing and a black pocket-book; we played with the boxes; we took the tent ropes and played with them. We thought to return home. As for Umdeni he took

Battlefield relics from Isandlwana: a 24th Regiment helmet plate, and a handful of coins apparently fused together by the flames of the burning tents. (Local History Museum, Durban)

some biscuit, but I and my brother declined. We said, "We don't like them." We went off, they carrying them. We moved out of sight of the place where they [the dead] were. We asked for some. Said Umdeni, "O! we don't choose, for you said you didn't like them." We retorted, "O! sit there, if you please, with your little bits of bread smelling of people's blood!" This we said, being with envy. We then returned home.

At daylight we came back again. We saw some boys who had died in a tree, [lying] underneath it. They were dressed in black clothes. We saw white men dead (they had taken their boots off, all of them), and the people also who had served them, and fought with them, and some Zulus, but not many . . .

In the end Muziwento successfully looted a new pair of brown trousers. Nevertheless, the apocalyptic vision of the camp clearly stayed with him for years afterwards.

It seems likely that most of the dead left on the field were British. Many of the Zulu dead and wounded were removed while the army was still in the vicinity, the bodies carried away by friends and relatives; those that remained were either men with no kinsmen present, or others who were simply missed in the confusion. It was not always necessary to include the corpse in Zulu mourning rituals; what mattered was the spirit of the departed. The sprigs of certain trees and shrubs were believed to have the power to catch the spirit of the dead so that it could be carried back to his homestead. Although many of the mourning rituals were not observed in the case of warriors killed in battle, it seems likely that a trickle of people from across the country made their way to the battlefield to fetch the spirits of their dead kinsmen and bring them home.

Many of the most exposed bodies naturally suffered the attentions of scavengers. Cape vultures were still found in the region in the 1870s, and, despite the systematic destruction of wild game that came with European farming methods and a high population density, there may still have been jackals, and even hyenas, in the more inaccessible parts of the Mzinyathi valley. Kites, crows and rodents doubtless did their part; most of the damage to the bodies was probably caused, however, by domestic dogs, both those from nearby Zulu homesteads and also, perhaps, surviving pets of the massacred column. Several accounts speak of these dogs roaming the outskirts of Rorke's Drift and even Helpmekaar; a few, including some bearing spear-wounds, returned to domesticity and were nursed back to health, but most of them simply ran wild in packs. Maxwell was attacked on patrol one day by "a pack of dogs about 20, consisting of various breeds, Newfoundlands, Pointers, Setters, terriers etc, a few with collars." These became such a nuisance that they had to be shot. There were, however, far too many corpses to be disposed of by the small number of scavengers, and most of the bodies remained intact despite exposure to contant downpours and baking sunshine. It seems that the Zulu habit of disembowelling corpses may have served as a primitive encouragement to a degree of mummification.

* * *

For the first month after the battle it was quite impossible

for Chelmsford to consider organising an expedition to bury the dead: his priorities lay elsewhere. Once it became clear, however, that no large-scale Zulu incursion into Natal was likely, and once the hastily improvised Colonial defence measures had been implemented, both the press and elements within the Army began to agitate for the dead of Isandlwana to be decently buried. By the beginning of March it was possible to take a more positive initiative, and on the 14th Major Black made his boldest foray to date. Accompanied by three officers and a Sergeant of the 24th, Commandant Cooper and 12 officers of the NNC, and ten Natal Mounted Police under Major Dartnell, Black was ferried across at Rorke's Drift. Two companies of Bengough's NNC were moved down from a new fort at Msinga to the Natal bank in support. (By now Rorke's Drift had lost two of its most prominent personalities: Rupert Lonsdale had been sent down to the Cape to raise a fresh troop of irregulars; and "Maori" Hamilton-Browne, the terror of the 1/3rd NNC, had gone to join him. Rorke's Drift had seen the last of him, for which many on both sides of the river were no doubt grateful.)

The patrol followed the road through the Batshe valley, and when it drew near Isandlwana a handful of Zulu scouts were seen. They fired a few shots and ran off, lighting two signal fires which brought a body of warriors running to cut the patrol off. Black's party stayed just long enough to experience the terrible smell rising from the battlefield, and to see that many of the bodies were only partially decomposed, before they rode back to Rorke's Drift, galloping part of the way to avoid the Zulu musket-balls fired after them. Black reported that it was advisable to delay sending out burial parties for at least another month.

This suited Chelmsford's plans. By the middle of March the strategic situation was daily changing in his favour. When Chelmsford notified the Home Government of the disaster he had tentatively asked for reinforcements to make good his losses. Whilst the Government was shocked to find that Frere had precipitated a war without securing prior consent, it was clearly impossible to review British policy until the reverse at Isandlwana had been avenged. A steady stream of reinforcements began to pour into Durban, and by the end of March Chelmsford was able to contemplate a limited offensive. Of his original three invading columns only one, Colonel Wood's No.4, was still operating in the field. The other, Pearson's No.1 Column, had advanced to the abandoned mission station at Eshowe, nearly 40 miles from the Thukela, brushing aside Zulu opposition at the Nyezane River on the same day as Isandlwana. The destruction of the Centre Column left Pearson unsupported, however, and he had remained cooped up at Eshowe under increasing Zulu pressure. At the end of March Chelmsford prepared to march to his relief, and ordered the garrisons along the border to make diversionary attacks.

On 28th March, therefore, Wilsone Black made another move in the direction of Isandlwana. With 35 men from the NMP and ten officers of the old 3rd NNC he advanced through the Batshe valley. Bengough's battalion was moved down to a crossing downstream of Roke's Drift, where it was joined by the local Border Guard. The Mzinyathi was too high for the black infantry to cross, however, so the raid had to be cut short. Another foray was planned for early April; but in the meantime significant events took place elsewhere in the country.

On 29th March the main Zulu army attacked Wood's base at Khambula hill. It was clear to Cetshwayo that the British were recovering from their reverse. He had made a number of diplomatic overtures, but these had been rebuffed; neither Chelmsford nor Frere could afford to forgo revenge for Isandlwana. The king had little choice but to call up his army once more. Wood's Column was selected as the target since it was the strongest and most active. The Zulus went into battle full of confidence, shouting "We are the boys from Isandlwana!"; but after four hours of heavy fighting they were driven off with massive casualties. Curiously, some of their old adversaries were fighting against them again: the Edendale Horse, with William Cochrane in command, had been attached to Wood's Column; and Alan Gardner was now on Wood's staff — he was wounded in the fighting.

Before Cetshwayo had time to digest the implications of this disaster, Chelmsford defeated the Zulus investing Eshowe at Gingindlovu on 2nd April. Within a few days the Zulu armies had been badly defeated at opposite ends of the country; and at Khambula alone their losses may have been higher than at Isandlwana.

As the British garrisons began to operate along the border with more confidence, a wood-cutting party made an intriguing find. In the garden of a deserted farmhouse some four miles downstream from Rorke's Drift they came across the crown finial from one of the 2/24th's Colour poles which had been lost at Isandlwana. How it came to be dropped there remained a mystery, but it seemed to have been unscrewed by someone familiar with such things.

With the change in British fortunes the patrolling from Rorke's Drift became bolder. On 9th April Major Dartnell commanded the largest force assembled there since Chelmsford had crossed on 11th January: the Mounted Police, Carbineers, about 200 of Teteleku's Mounted Natives, and 1,000 of Bengough's NNC, supported by a further 1,000 men from two border levies. The party crossed at the drift early in the morning, and systematically swept up through the Batshe valley destroying all the deserted homesteads they came across. Their advance was not opposed — they saw only a few scouts in the distance — but a rumour that a large force was gathering at Isandlwana prompted them to return via Sothondose's Drift early in the afternoon.

Although this string of successful forays helped to improve British confidence along the Mzinyathi border, it was still another six weeks before any attempt was made to bury the dead. By that time Lord Chelmsford's army had been reinforced to such an extent that he was able to plan a second invasion. Rather than advance by the melancholy field of Isandlwana, he decided to make his new thrust from a point further north, to advance in tandem with Wood's Column. Designated the 2nd Division, the new column was to cross the Ncome 20 miles north of Rorke's Drift, skirt Isandlwana, then

cut down to join the route to Ulundi originally planned for the Centre Column. At Dundee the 1st Battalion, 24th Regiment was reconstituted from Upcher's and Rainforth's companies (B Company, under Captain Harrison, remained in southern Natal) and from drafts sent out from Britain. Another column of fresh troops, the 1st Division, was assembled on the Lower Thukela.

Throughout early May patrols swept the country north of Rorke's Drift, clearing the Zulus away from the border and scouting a route. At Rorke's Drift itself the garrison was at last reduced and moved away from the old mission confines. A new fort had been started in March down by the river, on the rise overlooking the ponts; an oblong structure with loopholed stone walls, this Fort Melvill was guarded by four companies of the 2/24th under Wilsone Black, recently promoted Lieutenant-Colonel.

Before dawn on 15th May Black led another party out from Fort Melvill. They reached Isandlwana just after sunrise, and, after posting vedettes, "Colonel Black gave us twenty minutes to roam about; long enough as there was nothing of value to be found, and the grass, which in places had grown to a great height, hid the remains of the brave fellows till we almost trod on them. We counted over 100 wagons and vehicles of all sorts still there, and most of them sound." The party then moved off down the fugitives' trail, marked "here and there by a bit of paper, a shield, a pack saddle, etc", until they came to the steep descent down the face of Mpethe towards the river. Passing on, they descended the hill by an easier route, and then divided; one group crossed the drift, and the other went down the flat on the Zulu bank for half a mile. Here they left their horses and scrambled up to the foot of the bank where the fugitives were said to have come down:

> Lieutenant Mainwaring soon found the body of Major Smith almost concealed in the rank grass. It was clearly identified by the uniform, and had not been touched since the gallant officer was slain. Captain Symons [of the 24th] proceeded alone to the top of the cliff, it was very steep climbing, and he came every few yards on skeletons of men and horses, and at one point where there was a sheer drop of fifteen feet, two men and three horses were lying in the bottom, and the marks on the face of the rock showed where they had crashed down headlong.

The party was just covering Smith's body with stones when some 30 Zulus opened fire on them from the top of the ridge

A historic photograph of the two 7-pdr. RML guns lost at Isandlwana, taken at Wolseley's camp at Ulundi in September 1879. (John Young Collection)

The 1/24th Colour Party under Lieutenant-Colonel Tongue (far left), Lieutenants Weallens (left) and Phipps (right) which presented the recovered Queen's Colour (centre left) to Queen Victoria at Osborne House on 28th July 1880. Colour-Sergeant Wilson (behind the Regimental Colour, right) and Private Roy, DCM (far right), were both at Rorke's Drift. (Royal Regiment of Wales Museum, Brecon)

two hundred yards away; lookouts posted on Shiyane later said that the Zulus had shadowed Black's men all the way from Isandlwana. Fortunately, Bengough's battalion had been ordered up to the heights on the Natal bank overlooking the drift to cover such an eventuality, and they opened a heavy fire which suppressed the Zulu snipers until Black's men had retreated safely across the river.

This latest patrol was a prelude to a major expedition to the site. Two days later it was announced that Chelmsford had authorised the newly formed Cavalry Brigade under General Frederick Marshall, which consisted of the 1st (King's) Dragoon Guards and the 17th Lancers — both new arrivals from England — to visit Isandlwana to bury the dead and, more pragmatically, to bring away any of the wagons or other equipment which was serviceable. With a new campaign in the offing Chelmsford's need for transport equipment was urgent. By 20th May the necessary troops had gathered at Fort Melvill: the Lancers and Dragoons were to form the backbone of the force, supported by the mounted units which had fought in the battle — the Natal Carbineers, Buffalo Border Guard, Natal Mounted Police and Newcastle Mounted Rifles. Arthur Harness was also present, with two 7-pdr. guns from N/5 Battery; as was a recently raised irregular unit called Carbutt's Rangers.

The column set off in two divisions early on the morning of the 21st. Each unit had been spilt in half, and the first division crossed the Mzinyathi at about 4 a.m. It headed up the Batshe valley, circling round Ngedla mountain, and came at Isandlwana from the north. The second division, led by Marshall himself, left at about 5.30 a.m. and followed the old road across the Manzimyama and up to the nek. Bengough's NNC battalion was moved up to cross the drift in their wake, and advanced in a leisurely fashion up the Batshe, destroying any homesteads that had escaped the previous sweeps; while Lieutenant-Colonel Black led two companies of the 2/24th to the southern end of the Batshe valley. It was a very cautious movement, a far cry from the carefree days of January; a Zulu force was rumoured to be gathering at the Mangeni valley, and the British were in no mood to take chances. As it was, the

sight of the battlefield had a deeply unsettling effect, and "it was with the greatest difficulty the mounted natives were induced to skirmish properly for being in such a funk they huddled up as close as possible, until they began to think there were no Zulus near." No doubt they were not the only ones.

The force was also accompanied by two of the great British war-correspondents of the day, Archibald Forbes and Melton Prior. The Zulu War had created little interest in the press at home until the news of Isandlwana and Rorke's Drift broke. Norris-Newman, the only reporter on the spot, had scooped his better-known rivals, but editors had then lost no time hurrying their best men to the front. Melton Prior was a "special artist", the equivalent of today's war-photographer, who specialised in drawing from life sketches which were then shipped home and worked up for publication by a team of engravers. Forbes was a true journalist, whose strong, dramatic style and appetite for adventure made him one of the most highly regarded reporters of the age. Certainly his account of the approach to Isandlwana must rank as one of the most striking pieces of writing produced by the whole extraordinary saga, and is worth quoting at length. Forbes described how the column made its way across the Manzimyama, and up towards the nek:

Already tokens of the combat and bootless flight were apparent. The line of retreat towards Fugitives' Drift, along which, through a chink in the Zulu environment, our unfortunates who thus far survived tried to escape, lay athwart a rocky slope on our right front, with a precipitous ravine at its base. In this ravine dead men lay thick, mere bones, with toughened, discoloured skin like leather covering them, and clinging tight to them, the flesh all wasted away. Some were almost wholly dismembered, heaps of yellow, clammy bones. I forbear to describe the faces, with their blackened features and beards bleached by rain and sun. Every man had been disembowelled. Some were scalped, and others subject to yet ghastlier mutilations. The clothes had lasted better than the poor bodies they covered, and helped to keep the skeletons together. All the way up the slope I traced by the ghastly token of dead men, the fitful line of flight. Most of the men hereabouts were infantry of the 24th. It was like a long string with knots in it, the string formed of single corpses, the knots clusters of dead, where (as it seemed) little groups might have gathered to make a hopeless, gallant stand and die. I came on a gully with a gun limber jammed on its edge, and the horses, their hides scored with assegai stabs, hanging in their harness down the steep face of the ravine. A little further on was the broken and battered ambulance wagon, and around lay the corpses of the soldiers, poor helpless wretches, dragged out of an intercepted vehicle, and done to death without a chance for life.

Still following the trail of bodies through long rank grass and amongst stones, I approached the crest. Here the slaughtered ones lay very thick, so that the string became a broad belt. Many hereabouts wore the uniform of the Natal Police. On the bare ground, on the crest itself, among the wagons, the dead were less thick; but on the slope beyond, on which from the crest we looked down, the scene was the saddest, and more full of weird desolation than any I had yet gazed upon. There was none of the stark, blood-curdling horror of a recent battlefield. A strange calm reigned in this solitude of nature. Grain had grown luxuriantly round the waggons, sprouting from the seed that dropped from the loads, falling in soil fertilised by the life-blood of gallant men. So long in most places had grown the grass, that it mercifully shrouded the dead, whom four long months tomorrow we have left unburied.

As one strayed aimlessly about, one stumbled in the grass over skeletons that rattled to the touch. Here lay a corpse with the bayonet jammed into the mouth up to the socket, transfixing the head and mouth a foot into the ground. There lay a form that seemed cosily curled up in calm sleep, turned almost on its face, but seven assegai stabs have pierced the back. Most, however, lay flat on the back, with the arms stretched widely out, and the hands clenched. I noticed one dead man under a waggon, with his head on a saddle for a pillow, and a tarpaulin as if he had gone to sleep, and died so.

Among the party were both Trooper Fred Symons and Norris-Newman. "I cannot describe my feelings," wrote Symons, "upon entering the field and seeing the remains of men, cattle and wagons lying in strange confusion." Norris-Newman

had the melancholy satisfaction of discovering my own tent, or rather the disjecta membra of what had once been mine; and immediately behind it were the skeletons of my horses, with the bodies of my servants, just as I had left them picketted on the 22nd January, when I accompanied the reconnoitering force with Lord Chelmsford. But I could find nothing of value remaining; my papers, letters and books were lying about, torn up. I found, and brought away with me as mementoes, some of my wife's letters, a book and some of my ms. stories, and a photograph that had reached me just two days before the massacre.

Forbes, wandering about the campsite sickened by the "sour odour of stale death",

chanced on many sad relics — letters from home, photographs, journals, blood-stained books, packs of cards. Lord Chelmsford's copying book, containing an impression of his correspondence with the Horse Guards, was found in one of his portmanteaus, and identified in a kraal two miles off. Colonel Harness was busily engaged in collecting his own belongings. Colonel Glyn found a letter from himself to Lieutenant Melvill, dated the day before the fight. The ground was strewn with brushes, toilet bags, pickle bottles, and unbroken tins of preserved meats and milk. Forges and bellows remained standing ready for the recommencement of work.

At a homestead two miles from the camp Lieutenant Sadlier's Dragoon vedettes found one of the 2/24th Colour poles, apparently the one from which the recovered finial had been removed; he returned it to the Regiment, but to their disappointment the homestead was burned before any further search could be made.

Naturally, the searchers were anxious to identify the bodies of men from their units. Durnford's body was found lying in the long grass just below the 1/24th camp, "the long moustache still clinging to the withered skin of the face." Offy

Shepstone recognised him, and searched for relics to send to his family; he found a penknife in his pocket, and gently took two rings off the withered fingers. (Veterinary Surgeon Longhurst of the King's Dragoon Guards saw him, and later mentioned to Edward Durnford that he thought Shepstone had removed papers from the body. Edward, seizing on the hope that these might have been orders from Chelmsford which justified his brother's actions, wrote to Shepstone demanding to see them. Shepstone denied having removed any papers, and Durnford backed down; Frances Colenso pursued Shepstone for months, however, until he demanded an inquiry which cleared his name.)

Round Durnford lay a cluster of Volunteers, Mounted Police, and a few men of the 24th. The Carbineers were particularly anxious to identify their own, since stories about their dead had been circulating since the disaster. Trooper Swift, it was said, "had died hard; they killed him with knobkerries. Mackleroy was shot through the side whilst fighting with the others . . . After he was wounded he managed to get on his horse and ride about half a mile when he fell, and nothing more was seen of him." Lieutenant Scott was found near Durnford, "hidden partially under a broken piece of waggon, evidently unmutilated and untouched. He had his patrol jacket buttoned across, and while the body was almost only a skeleton, the face was still preserved and life-like, all the hair remaining, and the skin strangely parched and dried up, though still perfect." Nineteen-year-old James Adrian Blaikie was recognised by the size of his particularly large head, and his brother-in-law gently placed a hat over the skull. In the same clump of dead were Troopers Borrain, Dickinson, Moodie, Tarboton, Lumley, Davis, and R.Jackson; Swift, Moodie and F.Jackson were lying further towards the nek. Earlier reports had suggested that Tarboton had been decapitated, but if he was the burial party did not mention it; perhaps it was hard to tell. Captain Bradstreet lay nearby. All were "struck with the noble way in which they stuck to their officers." The irony that it was the Carbineers, of all people, who had rallied to Durnford at the end was not lost on their comrades. The condition of the bodies varied; some remained quite recognisable, while those most exposed to the elements and scavengers were badly damaged. Trying to identify the latter was a gruesome business, as Melton Prior found:

The individuals could only be recognised by such things as a patched boot, a ring on the finger-bone, a particular button, or coloured shirt, or pair of socks in a few known instances. And this could only be done with much difficulty, for either the hands of the enemy, or the beaks and claws of vultures tearing up the corpses, had in numberless cases so mixed up the bones of the dead that the skull of one man, or bones of a leg or arm, now lay with parts of the skeleton of another. The Lancers went about all over the field, often here and there quietly lifting the clothes off the skeletons, or

The Queen's Colour of the 1/24th, laid up today in Brecon Cathedral; it has been heavily restored, and the battle honours post-date the Anglo-Zulu War. (Author's photograph)

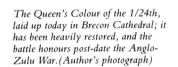

The original wreath of immortelles placed on the Colour by Queen Victoria. (Author's photograph)

Brevet Major C.J.Bromhead, 2/24th — Gonville's brother — who commanded the burial detail in September 1879. (Royal Archives)

One of three cairns erected on the battlefield in September 1879 by Bromhead's party. This one stands on the nek; another was in the area of the 1/24th camp; and the third still stands on the shoulder where Younghusband's company rallied. (Natal Museum)

gently pushing them on one side with their lances, to see what regiment they belonged to. I almost regretted to see this done, for it seemed like sacrilege. But this is a time of war.

Colonel Glyn had asked that the 24th be allowed to bury their own dead, and with some misgivings General Marshall had agreed. Archibald Forbes did not approve:

One has some sympathy with the claim of the regiment to bury its own dead; but why postpone the interment till only a few bones can be gathered? As the matter stands, the Zulus, who have carefully buried their own dead, who do not appear to have been very numerous, will come back tomorrow and find that we visited the place, not to bury our dead, but to remove a batch of waggons.

He had a point. The Volunteers and Artillery roughly covered over their own dead, but all those in red coats were left where they fell. Durnford's body was wrapped in a tarpaulin, and buried under the side of a donga.

By about noon, the expedition had selected some 40 wagons which were worth salvaging, and Harness had recovered the limber stuck in the donga (the other one could not be found). There were still rumours that Zulus were lurking in the vicinity, and Marshall had no wish to stay any longer than necessary. By early afternoon the entire force was on the march back to Rorke's Drift, and the battlefield was abandoned to the dead once more.

The next morning Harness set out with a squadron of the Lancers and went down to Sothondose's Drift. The cavalry were left to guard the crossing while Harness took a party down to find the body of his friend Stuart Smith, which Mainwaring had identified on the 17th.

Some two hundred yards up we found poor Stuart Smith's remains and we dug a grave. One of us read the service and marked the place with stones and a wooden cross. Melton Prior was with us and he took four sketches so you will see them in the Illustrated London News. *We also buried another artillery man we found.*

Sadly, Prior's sketches did not appear, and the site of Smith's grave is now lost amidst the dense bush which covers the final reaches of the fugitives' trail.

* * *

Over the next few days the troops who had made the expedition were moved back to their original stations; and the tide of war moved away from Isandlwana and Rorke's Drift. Chelmsford's 2nd Division built its new border depot at Landman's Drift on the Ncome, and it was from here that the second invasion began a fortnight later. The British Army had learned its lesson expensively, but well; this new advance was slow and painstaking, with each halt along the way protected by a stone or earthwork entrenchment. Nevertheless, such was the reputation the Zulu army had by then achieved that false alarms were common, especially at night. King Cetshwayo, convinced by the terrible losses at Khambula and Gingindlovu that defeat was inevitable, tried with increasing desperation to "ward off the falling tree" by diplomatic means. But neither Chelmsford nor Frere was interested in a settlement before a last conspicuous victory to wipe out the stain of Isandlwana. The final advance towards Ulundi was particularly destructive, as Chelmsford was prepared to take the war to civilian homesteads and food supplies in an attempt to starve the Zulus into submission. British patrols took satisfaction in recovering relics of Isandlwana from civilian homesteads, and this eased any consciences which may have been troubled by the wholesale destruction meted out. Two artillery wagons turned up at one homestead, and Lieutenant-Colonel Harness had the last laugh on those who had teased him when he had meticulously painted the battery number on all its property; they still bore the unarguable designation N/5.

By the beginning of July the combined 2nd Division and Wood's Flying Column had reached the south bank of the White Mfolozi River. Beyond it lay the Mahlabatini plain, the great heartland of the Zulu nation, encircled by *amakhanda* including Ulundi itself. There was a final flurry of diplomatic activity, but when Cetshwayo attempted to send a herd of the royal white cattle to the British camp as a peace offering it was intercepted and sent back by his own uKhandempemvu regiment: the victors of Isandlwana were not prepared to see the nation humiliated without one last fight. On 4th July all talking ceased, and Chelmsford marched his troops in a huge hollow square out onto the plain. For perhaps three-quarters of an hour the Zulu army launched a spirited assault, only to be driven back by a hail of rifle and cannon fire. When their rushes at last faltered Chelmsford unleashed the 17th Lancers, who harried them from the field. By nightfall Chelmsford had retired back across the White Mfolozi leaving Ulundi in flames.

The 1/24th were cheated of their revenge, being left behind to guard the forts on the lines of communication; nevertheless, a few of those who had been through the flames at Isandlwana were in at the kill. The Natal Native Horse were there, with Cochrane in command. Both Essex and Gardner were present within the square, as was Chard, who had recovered from his bout of sickness. Private Wassall was present in the ranks of the Mounted Infantry with, perhaps, one or two other survivors. Harness had the satisfaction of commanding N/5 during the battle and, while noting with disappointment that the enemy did not come within 400 yards of his position, nevertheless congratulated himself that "my two seven-pounders made excellent shooting." Smith-Dorrien missed the battle, but must have heard the boom of the guns from the British fort on the banks of the White Mfolozi. Neither the Carbineers, Police, Buffalo Border Guard or Newcastle Mounted Rifles were allowed to accompany the final advance; to their disgust they too remained on guard along the supply lines.

Chelmsford resigned his command immediately after the victory. He had, in fact, already been superceded; the Home Government had been prepared to allow him the chance to vindicate himself, but his relationship with the civil administration in Natal had deteriorated. He was finally removed from his command not by any action of the Zulus, but by the misgivings of the Exchequer over the ever-escalating transport costs. His replacement was General Sir Garnet Wolseley, the Army's arch-reformer. Wolseley had arrived in South Africa a week or two before Ulundi, and had tried to halt Chelmsford's advance; to his bitter disappointment Chelmsford politely ignored him, and he could not reach the front in time to claim Chelmsford's victory. He was left with little more than the mopping-up operations. King Cetshwayo had fled, and patrols were organised to capture him; royalist chiefs in the more remote parts of the country also had to be intimidated into submission.

In the middle of August, as Wolseley's patrols scoured the countryside looking for the king, they came across the two 7-pdr. RML guns which N/5 had lost at Isandlwana, abandoned on the veld; they were undamaged, though the Zulus had tried to make them serviceable by screwing rifle percussion caps into the vents. They were taken back to Ulundi, and stood menacingly by the Headquarters tent as Wolseley received the submission of the *izikhulu*. Harness was somewhat embarrassed by them: "I hope Sir Garnet will not think of saying a few words, etc., in returning the guns, for then I should have to reply and I really do not know what to say except to express a hope that we shall take better care of them." Eventually it was decided to ship them back to England, "although I have really not much feeling in the matter."

* * *

As the war passed into its last and successful phase, the British gave out their laurels for the events of 22nd January. No less than eleven of the defenders of Rorke's Drift received the Victoria Cross; it is hard today not to feel that so high a number reflected not only the bravery of individuals but also the perceived propaganda value of the victory. By elevating Rorke's Drift to the level of a major strategic victory the more damaging significance of Isandlwana was obscured. Most of the awards were announced in May 1879, before the start of the second invasion, and provided a welcome fillip to morale.

The Army had at that time no means of recognising gallantry apart from the VC and the Distinguished Conduct Medal; and, as Smith-Dorrien later pointedly hinted, incidents recognised then by the award of a VC might, in the light of standards accepted in the Great War, have been more appropriately marked by a Military Cross in more recent times. The

awards to the Rorke's Drift defenders also reflect a desire to recognise each branch of the services represented there. Chard received the VC, as did Surgeon Reynolds, Commissary Dalton, and Corporal Schiess of the NNC. In B Company they went to Bromhead, Corporal Allen, and Privates Hitch, Hook, William Jones and Robert Jones, and John Williams. Hook alone had the distinction of being presented with the award by Sir Garnet Wolseley at the mission station itself on 3rd August. Colour-Sergeant Bourne of B Company, Private William Roy of the 1/24th (a patient in the hospital), Gunner John Cantwell, and Corporal Francis Attwood of the Army Service Corps were all awarded the DCM.

The presentation of awards to survivors of Isandlwana was more problematic. Clearly the subject was an embarrassing one, and in any case there was at that time no provision for the presentation of posthumous awards; so the Army had a rather limited choice of potential recipients. Alan Gardner was considered a possible candidate, because after his escape he had ridden on to warn Wood of the disaster. Chelmsford, however, felt that while his services "deserved recognition", the ride itself "was not one of danger but of fatigue, and consequently could not be construed as a gallant act deserving the VC." Smith-Dorrien was apparently recommended for one, for stopping to help the wounded Mounted Infantryman on the Fugitives' Trail; he did not recieve it, however, because the "proper channels for correspondence had not been observed." Since the recommendation for the award had to be approved by a candidate's commanding officer, it may well be that he paid the price for securing a place in the war despite his Colonel's disapproval. In the end the only Isandlwana survivor to receive the supreme award was Private Samuel Wassall of the 80th Regiment, attached to the Mounted Infantry, in recognition of his gallantry in returning to save the drowning Westwood at Sothondose's Drift. He was presented with the award by Wolseley at Utrecht on 11th September 1879.

There was considerable pressure for some sort of award to Melvill and Coghill, whose experiences in the flight, dubbed "the dash with the Colours", had caught the public imagination. On 2nd May 1879 the *London Gazette* published an official notice that both Melvill and Coghill "would have been recommended to Her Majesty for the Victoria Cross had [they] survived." Mevill was recommended for attempting to save the Colours, and Coghill for returning to his aid at Fugitives' Drift. There was, however, clearly some embarrassment about awarding the supreme honour to men who had, after all, been fleeing from the camp. Chelmsford summed up the dilemma in a letter to General Sir Alfred Horsford at the War Office, dated 14th May:

As regards poor Melvill and Coghill the case is even more difficult. The latter was a Staff Officer attached to Col.Glyn, and had every right to leave the camp when he realised the fact that nothing could be done to save it. It is, however, most probable that Melvill lost his life in endeavouring to save Coghill rather than vice versa.

Coghill had strained his knee and remained in camp on the 22nd as a consequence. He could hardly walk, and any exertion such as walking or riding would have been likely to render him helpless. He could not have assisted, therefore, in saving the colours of the 1/24th, and as I have already said I fear he was a drag to poor Melvill.

As regards the latter, I am again puzzled how to reply to your question. I feel sure that Melvill left camp with the colours under orders received. He was too good a soldier to have left without. In being ordered to leave, however, he no doubt was given the best chance of saving his life which must have been lost had he remained in camp. His ride was not more daring than that of those who escaped. The question, therefore, remains had he succeeded in saving the colours and his own life, would he have been considered to have deserved the Victoria Cross?

Sir Garnet Wolseley, whose comments were coloured by an apparent dislike of the 24th and by a resentment towards Chelmsford and his staff, at least expressed his views with commendable logic and clarity:

I am sorry that both of these officers were not killed with their men at Isandlwana instead of where they were: I don't like the idea of officers escaping on horseback when their men on foot are killed . . . .Heroes have been made of men like Melvill and Coghill, who, taking advantage of their having horses, bolted from the scene of the action to save their lives . . . it is monstrous making heroes of those who saved or attempted to save their lives by bolting or of those who, shut up in buildings at Rorke's Drift, could not bolt, and fought like rats for their lives which they could not otherwise save.

It was a point of view not calculated to gain much support amongst an Army and public accustomed to thinking of such incidents in terms of unqualified glory. Coghill's father continued to campaign for recognition of his son's supposed heroism for years afterwards. In 1906 Melvill's widow Sara was one of several who petitioned King Edward VII to recognise the principal of posthumuous awards; and on 15th January 1907 the *London Gazette* published the names of those whose families were to be sent the award — amongst them were Melvill and Coghill. (It came too late for Sir Jocelyn Coghill, who had died the year before.)

The 1st Battalion brought home the tattered Queen's Colour in October 1879. Queen Victoria expressed a wish to see it; and on 28th July 1880 Lieutenant-Colonel J.M.G.Tongue, Lieutenants Weallens and Phipps and four Colour-Sergeants from the Battalion carried the Colours to Osborne House on the Isle of Wight. Colour-Sergeant Edward Wilson, and Private Roy, DCM, who was also present, had been among the defenders of Rorke's Drift. The Queen placed a wreath of immortelles to the Colour in memory of the gallantry of Melvill and Coghill. The Colours were carried on parade by the Battalion until 1933, when they were laid up in Brecon Cathedral. The original wreath of immortelles was kept in a silver-mounted box in the Officers' Mess, and later in the Cathedral. (It was stolen in 1980, apparently for the silver, although both wreath and box were recovered; the wreath, however, had been thrown into a ditch, and the original flowers were ruined — those currently on display in the Cathedral are replacements.) Subsequent Colours of the Battalion have been decorated with a silver wreath in commemmoration of this honour.

* * *

At the end of June 1879 the bodies of the 24th were finally buried. On the 20th Lieutenant-Colonel Black took a party of 30 mounted and 50 dismounted Dragoons, 140 men of the 2/24th, 360 Border Guards and 50 of Teteleku's Horse to Isandlwana. They were accompanied by Major Dartnell and representatives of the Mounted Police and Volunteer units, including the Carbineers. Black's description of where the bodies were found is revealing:

As I reported in March last, the bodies of the slain lay thickest on the 1-24th camp; a determined stand had evidently been made behind the officers' tents . . . seventy dead lay here. Lower down the hill in the same camp another clump of about sixty lay together, among them Captain Wardell, Lieutenant Dyer, and a captain and subaltern of the 24th unrecognisable. Near at hand were found the bodies of Colonel Durnford, Lieutenant Scott, and other Carbineers, and men of the Natal Mounted Police, showing that here also our men had gathered and fought as a recognised body. This was evidently a centre of resistance, as the bodies of men of all arms were found converging as it were to the spot, but stricken down ere they could join the ranks of their comrades. About sixty bodies lay on the rugged slope, under the southern precipice of Isandlwana, among them those of Captain Younghusband, and two other officers, unrecognisable; it looked as if these had held the crags, and fought together as long as ammunition lasted.

"Many of the dead", commented Black, "lay on the Buffalo side of the nek", and the grim remains still bore testimony to the desperate nature of the fighting. Three men of the 24th lay by three dead Zulus, "confronting each other, as living they had stood." The body of a Mounted Policeman was still entwined with the body of a Zulu. One man was found

beneath the cliff face with his skull smashed; he had probably died under a blow from a knobkerry, but Black thought "that he had fallen or been hurled from the top." Lieutenant Maxwell recognised the bodies of Lieutenants Gibson and Vereker of the NNC; he removed them to the foot of the mountain, facing the sun, and covered them over.

It was generally impossible, however, to recognise most of the dead, and the troops simply scooped out shallow graves in the hard, rocky ground and covered the remains with stones. They returned again on the 23rd and 26th to finish the job. The Carbineers at last found the rest of their dead; Willie London was lying near the 1/24th camp and Quartermaster Bullock in the 2/24th; one wonders if they had been helping to distribute ammunition. One of the artillerymen who had escaped took a party down the trail, and they at last found the body of Trooper George Macleroy; today his is the only grave on the trail which is individually marked. On 26th June Black was able to report "I have just completed burying the dead after four days' work. Some of the out-lying dead may remain, but those on the field of battle are now interred." However, one observer commented that "most of the white men's bodies in camp are buried now, but in a most superficial way, and the first heavy rain will expose them again."

The last sentence was prophetic, since the dead of Isandlwana have refused to stay buried for more than a century. As early as September 1879 Brevet Major C.J.Bromhead — Gonville's elder brother — was ordered by General Sir George Colley, then Chief of Staff in South Africa, to visit the site and "carefully clean up the field, collecting and burning and burying all debris still remaining, and you will bury all remains still lying unburied and bury afresh those bodies which were hastily and imperfectly buried on previous visits. You will endeavour, as far as possible, to identify the graves and erect cairns over the graves of our officers and soldiers." Bromhead accordingly camped at Isandlwana on the night of 19th September with F and H Companies, 2/24th; and the next day his men swept across the battlefield, collecting all the debris that still remained. Some bodies had been missed by Black's party, and these were decently interred, together with those which had been exposed by the weather. It was, by now, quite impossible to identify any individual graves, so Bromhead ordered stones to be piled up in three large cairns where the largest stands had been. One of these was placed in the centre of the 1/24th camp, not far from where the bodies of Durnford and the Volunteers had been found, and another above it on the nek. The third was placed on the shoulder beneath the south-west edge of Isandlwana itself, where Younghusband's company had been brought to bay. Two poignant relics came to light while Bromhead's men were in the vicinity; part of a broken Colour pole from one of the 2/24th Colours was found on the battlefield, and one of the Colour cases was found in the bed of the Manzimyama.

Despite Bromhead's endeavours, Wolseley complained in early 1880 that the summer rains had again washed open many of the graves. Lieutenant M.O'Connell of the 60th Rifles was sent out from Pietermaritzburg with the Chaplain of the Forces, G.M.S.M.Ritchie, and a Sergeant and ten men of his Battalion. Guided to the site by Sub-Inspector Phillips and seven troopers of the Natal Mounted Police, they arrived on the evening of 14th March. Over the next five days they, too, tried to cover over the exposed remains. O'Connell's methods were nothing if not practical:

Each man was provided with a sack to carry any bones he might find, and every third or fourth man had a spade or pick to dig up bones in those places where they had not been properly buried, and where the ground did not seem to be such as to make the re-covering of old graves desirable. I extended my men in a line across the place where Lord Chelmsford's camp had been, and moved them slowly backwards and forwards. They put all the uncovered bones they could find into the sacks, and renewed the stones

Redcoats at Isandlwana: the Mounted Infantry Company of the 1st Welsh Regiment (ex-41st) visit the battlefield in 1884. The men are standing on the site of Durnford's last stand, already marked by memorials to the Colonial dead. The height of the grass suggests that the photograph was taken at about the same time of year as the battle. (Bryan Maggs Collection)

1927: Dugald Macphail of the Buffalo Border Guard poses on the battlefield with two reputed Zulu veterans of Is ndlwana. The cairn on the shoulder of the mountain is just visible, top right. (Talana Museum, Dundee)

and earth over the graves that required it. As soon as three or four sacks of bones had been collected in this way, I caused them to be carried to [a specified spot] and there buried them in two large deep graves . . .

O'Connell's parties roamed the field as far as the Ngonyane, and down the fugitives' trail. There were a lot of exposed remains around the dongas above the Manzimyama, but most of those buried at the Mzinyathi end were still covered over. O'Connell was thorough in his work, but he admitted that "a few stray bones will be found at Isandlwana for many years to come."

* * *

The Anglo-Zulu War had ended long before. On 28th August 1879 a British patrol had captured King Cetshwayo in the Ngome forest, and he was taken to the coast and thence by sea to Cape Town. With his capture even the most ardently royalist chiefs began to submit. Most of the Volunteers, who had been mobilised for a period of six months, had already returned to their civilian lives. Wally Erskine had visited Fred Symons when his time was up, and took home with him a haversack of souvenirs picked up at Isandlwana; to Symons' disappointment the haversack proved to have a hole in it, and the relics were scattered unnoticed along the way. The Natal Carbineers had returned to Pietermaritzburg at the end of July to be mustered out, and on 8th August the Newcastle Mounted Rifles returned to Newcastle; William Beaumont was back at his courthouse, and he and the townsfolk gave them a warm welcome. Both they and the Buffalo Border Guard had seen enough of the soldier's life, and they disbanded for good. None of the Volunteers had received the farms in Zululand Lord Chelmsford had promised them when the war began, and only the civilian contractors had grown rich on the profits of looted Zulu cattle.

By October the last of the British troops had left Zululand, either to sail away to new trouble-spots around the Empire, or to take up the mundane duties of peacetime garrisons. The people of the Mzinyathi border were left to pick up the pieces of their lives.

Ironically, Isandlwana had proved a spear-thrust in the belly for both the Zulu kingdom, and the Confederation scheme. It drew political attention within Britain to the South African question; and when the Disraeli government fell in 1880, given a sharp push by Gladstone's spirited attack on Frere's policies, its Liberal successor refused to countenance further intervention in Zulu affairs. Having deposed the king, destroyed the political and economic structures which held the country together, razed the great centres of royal authority, killed thousands of warriors and maimed countless others, burned and looted the homes of many non-combatants, Britain turned her back on the consequences. In a deliberate attempt to break down the support of the regional *izikhulu* for the king Wolseley imposed a peace settlement which divided the country into 13 self-governing chiefdoms under British appointees. The nation soon split between pro- and anti-royalist factions, and within a few years a brutal and deeply destructive civil war consumed the lives of many of those who had distinguished themselves in 1879. Zibhebhu kaMapitha, who had led the uDloko regiment at Isandlwana, became bitterly opposed to the royal house, and when King Cetshwayo was finally restored to a portion of his old country in an

131

attempt to restore order it was Zibhebhu who defeated him and drove him out. Cetshwayo died, a broken man, in 1884. Prince Dabulamanzi continued to support his brother's cause, and for his pains was murdered by the Boers in September 1886. The strip of country opposite Rorke's Drift was given to Hlubi and his Sotho in recognition for their services at Isandlwana and elsewhere, and Sihayo and his son Mehlokazulu were driven out of the Batshe valley. Mehlokazulu continued his vigorous support of the royalist cause; he was involved in several incidents during the civil wars of the 1880s, and was killed fighting with the rebel leader Bambatha at the battle of Mome Gorge in 1906, when a number of Natal and Zulu groups launched a forlorn rising against the Colonial regime.

Neither Frere nor Chelmsford came well out of the war. Frere did not long survive the collapse of his policies; he died in 1884, his hitherto glittering career brought low, like so many, at Isandlwana. Lord Chelmsford returned to England and a hero's welcome, the success of Ulundi having almost wiped out the stain of Isandlwana. Almost, but not quite: although he continued to enjoy the support of the Queen and the military establishment, he never commanded an army in the field again. The controversy over his conduct of the campaign continued to dog him, on and off; when Archibald Forbes attacked him in a piece in *Nineteenth Century Magazine* in February 1880 Harness sprang to his defence in *Fraser's Magazine*. Chelmsford died in the middle of a billiards match in the United Services Club in 1905, at the age of 81.

For most of the British professionals the end of the war meant a move to pastures new. Edward Essex served as a staff officer throughout the 1881 Transvaal War, and narrowly escaped death in two more disastrous battles, Laing's Nek and Ingogo; his capacity for hairsbreadth survival earned him the nickname "Lucky Essex". He went on to become an instructor at the Royal Military Academy at Sandhurst, and commanded the Gordon Highlanders. William Cochrane went on to a distinguished career in the Anglo-Egyptian Army. Horace Smith-Dorrien's subsequent service spanned almost every theatre in which the late Victorian army campaigned. He fought on the North-West Frontier, in Egypt and the Sudan, and returned to South Africa for the Anglo-Boer War. As a General during the early months of the First World War he commanded II Corps during the retreat from Mons; and although successful, his defence of Le Cateau against the orders of his superior Sir John French (who had resented him for years) led to his losing his field command in May 1915.

Illness cost him the command in German East Africa. He was killed in a car crash outside Bath in 1930.

Crealock's career was successful but undistinguished; he commanded his regiment, the 95th, in Gibraltar and India before accepting a series of home appointments. Clery, for all his theoretical knowledge, proved no better at South African warfare than Chelmsford; he served as Sir Redvers Buller's second-in-command during the disastrous campaign to relieve Ladysmith in the Anglo-Boer War, and retired from his command in 1900. "Maori" Hamilton-Browne continued to roam southern Africa in search of adventure, and cropped up at the diamond fields and in Bechuanaland before joining Cecil Rhodes' private enterprise empire north of the Limpopo.

Henry Fynn stuck to his post at Msinga throughout the rest of the war, although his experiences that night on the field of the dead had brought him to the verge of a breakdown, and after the war he remained in the Natal civil service. For men like Trooper Fred Symons, the Jones brothers and Dugald Macphail, peace meant a return to the everyday hardships of settler life.

* * *

The first tourists began to visit the Anglo-Zulu battlefields almost before the echo of the last shots had died away. The Empress Eugenie of France, whose son Louis Napoleon had been killed on patrol while accompanying the second invasion as an observer, made a pilgrimage on the first anniversary of his death to the spot where he was killed. She was followed over the next few years by a steady trickle of travellers. As early as the end of 1880 R.W.Leyland, a Fellow of the Royal Geographical Society, visited Zululand prompted by nothing more than an interest to see the country which had so recently been in the news. His visit to the battlefields was a cursory one, but he noted that Fort Melvill was now occupied by a civilian trader; and that the Reverend Witt had reclaimed the remains of his home at Rorke's Drift, where he was building a new house on the site of the hospital, and demolishing Fort Bromhead to provide the stone for a new chapel built almost over the foundations of the storehouse. At Isandlwana Leyland saw "the most unpleasant sight . . . many unbleached human bones. They had been washed by heavy rains out of the shallow graves in which they had been interred . . . We noticed some bodies partially exposed, portions of skeletons

A poignant group: Zulus who fought in the battle gather with their families at Isandlwana for the 50th anniversary commemoration in 1929. (Killie Campbell Africana Library)

visible. In one instance the leg bones, encased in leather gaiters, protruded at the bottom of a grave, and close by were the soldier's boots, containing what remained of his feet.''

A year later Bertram Mitford made a more comprehensive expedition to the battlefields, and his subsequent book — *Through The Zulu Country, Its Battlefields and Its People* — is one of the most delightful reads in all the comprehensive literature of the Anglo-Zulu War. Mitford found the campsite still strewn with cartridge cases, rotting boots, old brushes, smashed boxes and debris of all kinds, suggesting just how much had been missed by Bromhead's cleaning party. The bones of dead oxen and mules still lay scattered about, and four dead horses lay lightly covered over in the ravine where the gun-limber had come to grief.

It was partly as a result of reports such as these that Alfred Boast was asked by the Lieutenant-Governor of Natal to bury the dead once and for all. Boast's party stayed on the site from 12th February to 9th March 1883, and exhumed all except a few individually identified graves. The remains were reburied in graves 3ft. deep and 18ins. wide, each marked by a cairn of stones. Boast's meticulous report lists a total of 298 graves each containing between two and four bodies; his cairns, now whitewashed, remain a feature of the site today.

Not all those who were killed in the battle were buried on the site. Edgar Anstey's brother Captain T.H. Anstey, who served with the Royal Engineers in Zululand and was commissioned to produce a survey of the battlefield, took his remains home for interment in the family plot at Woking, Surrey. Louis Phillipe Dubois, who had been shot on the Natal bank at Sothondose's Drift within reach of safety, was buried on his family's farm "Giba" at Helpmekaar.

In October 1879 Bishop Colenso had the remains of his friend Anthony Durnford exhumed, and on the 12th they were buried with full military honours in the garrison cemetery at Fort Napier in Pietermaritzburg. It was an appropriate final scene in a career bedevilled by ironies; there were over 2,000 soldiers in attendance, representing practically every Volunteer and Imperial unit in Natal, and the guard of honour was provided by 300 men of the 24th. Whatever Durnford's faults as a commander, his hero's death had overshadowed them.

In November 1879 a party led by Canon Johnson and accompanied by Archdeacon Usherwood, Chaplain George Smith and Henry Fynn visited Isandlwana with a view to establishing a mission church near the sight in honour of the fallen. They held a service on the site of the 1/24th's camp, and erected an iron cross to mark the spot. Canon Johnson then selected a spot beneath the spur, at the foot of Mkwene hill, for the site of the church. There was a spring rising out of the hillside nearby, and Cannon Johnson used the iron ferrules from the tent poles, which were scattered all around the camp area, to make pipes to divert the water. The church subsequently built on the site, St. Vincent's, is still a functioning mission; part of the complex, the fine old Colonial-style building of the one-time Bishop Mackenzie College, has recently been opened as a small museum and on-site visitors' interpretation centre.

Memorials to the Colonial dead began to appear on the site not long after the war, erected by grieving relatives. A white-washed stone cross, almost overgrown with sisal and aloes, marks the place on the rocky shoulder at the foot of the mountain where George Shepstone died; and there are individual monuments to many of the Volunteers (including James Blaikie) who fell with Durnford. It was not until March 1914 that a memorial to the 24th was unveiled by General Sir Reginald Hart, VC, KCB, KCVO.

In 1929, the fiftieth anniversary of the war, hundreds made a pilgrimage to the battlefield. General Sir Duncan MacKenzie, who in 1906 had put down the last hopeless Zulu uprising, laid a wreath at the monument to the Natal Carbineers. Most of the dozens of veterans of the battle who attended were Zulus; but Dugald Macphail was there, still going strong. Their conversations must have been worth overhearing.

Isandlwana today is still a mournful place, with a deeply moving atmosphere for those sensitive to it. A steady trickle of tourists are prepared to go out of their way to visit the site; and in the late 1980s the battlefield suffered a spate of vandalism apparently at the hands of unscrupulous relic-hunters. Both the South African and the local Zulu authorities have taken steps to protect the site for future generations. Rorke's Drift, across the river, is still a working mission; and it was only in January 1992 that the first museum was opened there, in the building which Witt raised over the foundations of the old hospital.

* * *

And what of Henry Harford, with whom we began this extraordinary tale? He returned to the 99th Regiment in July or August 1879 and resumed the Adjutancy, his friend Davison having died of disease during the siege of Eshowe. Harford had a successful career with the 99th, rising to the rank of Colonel and commanding the lst Battalion from 1899 to 1902. He retired to the village of Crawley Down in Sussex, and died in March 1937. He never lost his interest in natural history, nor forgot his experiences in Zululand.

When Harford left the NNC to return to his Regiment he spent a few days at Pietermaritzburg. He was told that an African had been looking for him for some time, and when at last they met he found that the man had served with the 3rd NNC. After its disbandment this man had joined another levy battalion, and had fought at Ulundi. When the battle was over and the NNC were scouring the field to finish off the wounded, he had come across a British boot lying amongst the Zulu dead, and had immediately recognised it as belonging to Harford. It was one of the pair of field boots made by Dean's in the Strand for the anonymous gentleman traveller which Harford had commandeered at the start of his adventures, and which had been lost with all the rest of his kit at Isandlwana. It had found its way back to Ulundi with the victorious Zulu army and, separated from its companion, had somehow ended up on the final battlefield. Harford was delighted:

> *Ulundi is about eighty miles as the crow flies from Isdandlwana and about two hundred via the Coast road to Maritzburg, so the Zulu army had the honour of carrying my boot (or boots) for over 150 miles, and this good chap had tramped with it another 200 miles on an off-chance. To him, of course, it was of no value whatever, but to me that boot is greatly treasured, both for the remarkable circumstances under which I got it back and as a reminiscence of my days in the 3rd NNC.*

It was not the least extraordinary of the stories which have gathered around the events of 22nd January 1879 below the remote African rock called Isandlwana.

Lost and found: Henry Harford's boot. (Local History Museum, Durban)

ACKNOWLEDGEMENTS AND SOURCES

This book is the result of a fascination with the battle of Isandlwana which dates back more than fifteen years, long before I hoped I might one day be able to write about it. In that time many people have shared with me their knowledge and enthusiasm, and it is no exaggeration to say that I could not have written this book without them.

My oldest debt is to that great Natal expert on Zulu history and culture, "SB" Bourquin, who first took me camping on the battlefields, and brought the past of old Zululand alive for me. Since then SB has allowed me free access to his remarkable library and collection of historic photographs with unfailing generosity; he has acted as my host and guide on many occasions, and I cannot thank him enough. On my travels to South Africa, Graham Dominy, the Historian with the Natal Museum in Pietermaritzburg, has greatly smoothed my path in my dealings with both the Museum and the Natal Archives, and, with his wife Anne and son James, proved the most entertaining of hosts, as did Professor John Laband and his family. Dr John Vincent of the Natal Museums Service, together with his colleagues Gilbert Torlage and Mark Coghlan, allowed me the fullest access to their work at Rorke's Drift, as did Graham Smythe, the curator of the museum there. Dr. Barry Marshall of the KwaZulu Monuments Council was most helpful during my visits to Ulundi and Isandlwana. Gillian Berning and her colleagues at the Local History Museum in Durban; Jenni Duggan and her staff at the Killie Campbell Africana Library; Pam MacFadden at the Talana Museum, Dundee; and Mrs. Nagelgast at the Africana Museum in Johannesberg, were all most generous with their time and assistance. My great friends David and Nicky Rattray provided me with accommodation at Fugitives' Drift Lodge, many stimulating evenings' conversation, and one or two adventures on the battlefields themselves. David and Wendy Rosenhahn revealed much of Zulu culture to me through Thomas Fakude and his family at kwaBekithunga. Stephen Coan searched the archives of the *Natal Witness* on my behalf.

In Britain, F.W. David Jackson shared with me his perceptive thoughts about the battle, even though he was about to go to press with his own book on the subject: rare generosity. Sonia Clarke, editor of the Harness and Alison papers, also discussed the battle with me. Col. Ian Bennett of the Royal Corps of Transport gave me many crucial insights into Chelmsford's transport problems. Ian Castle, a regular travelling companion in Zululand, allowed me access to his researches on the Natal Volunteer units in the Anglo-Zulu War. Keith Reeves and Rai England, both serious students of the war, shared with me not only their thoughts, but their collections of rare publications. I am also indebted to Tim Day and Ian Woodason for their advice and support; and I have benefited greatly over the years through correspondence with the members of the Zulu War Study Group of the Victorian Military Society. Major Bob Smith and his Archivist, Diana Roberts, allowed me the fullest access to material at the Royal Regiment of Wales Museum, Brecon; and the staff of the National Army Museum, London, and the regimental museums of the Buffs, Sherwood Foresters and 9/12th Lancers were more than helpful. It goes without saying, however, that any errors of fact or interpretation are entirely mine.

On a more personal level, my fiancée Carolyn helped me through the difficult times when the midnight oil burned low to no avail; and my parents have been consistently encouraging and supportive.

SOURCES

Unfortunately it has not been possible to include comprehensive footnotes due to the confines of space. However, sources consulted are listed below for each Chapter; titles have been given in full the first time they are mentioned, thereafter in abbreviated form.

Chapter One: Africans and Colonials
Harford's account can be found in *The Zulu War Journal of Colonel Henry Harford, CB*, ed. Daphne Child, Pietermaritzburg, 1978. For life in the 3rd NNC, see also Charles L. Norris-Newman, *In Zululand with the British Throughout the War of 1879*, London, 1880; and George Hamilton-Browne's *A Lost Legionary in South Africa*, London, c.1913. A general history of Natal can be found in Edgar Brookes and Colin Webb's *A History of Natal*, Pietermaritzburg, 1965. On the Cape Frontier see Noel Mostert's *Frontiers*, London, 1992. H.L. Smith-Dorrien's autobiography is *Memories of 48 Years' Service*, London, 1925. On Natal's relationship with the Imperial power, see *Kingdom and Colony at War*, by John Laband and Paul Thompson, Pietermaritzburg, 1990. For the economic impetus behind the Anglo-Zulu War, see Jeff Guy, *The Destruction of the Zulu Kingdom*, London, 1979, and C.W. DeKeiwit's *The Imperial Factor in South Africa*, Cambridge, 1937. Graham Dominy's paper *Awarding a 'Retrospective White Hat'? A Reconsideration of the Geopolitics of 'Frere's War' of 1879*, 1984, is a perceptive assessment of Frere's culpability. More thoughts on the origins of the war can be found in A.H. Dumminy and C.C. Ballard's *The Anglo-Zulu War; New Perspectives*, Pietermaritzburg, 1981. For Chelmsford's experience on the Cape Frontier see *The Frontier Journal of Major John Crealock*, ed. Chris Hummel, Cape Town, 1988. Baden-Powell's comments on Hamilton-Browne are in *The Matabele Campaign 1896*, London, 1897. For a general history of the Anglo-Zulu War see Ian Knight's *Brave Men's Blood*, London, 1990. A copy of Trooper Symons' diary and letters are in the Talana Museum, Dundee, Natal. The dispute between Russell and the Volunteers is described by the *Natal Mercury's* Biggarsberg Correspondent, 6th January 1879. For the Mounted Police see H.P. Holt, *The Mounted Police of Natal*, London, 1913, and W.J. Clarke, *My Career in South Africa*, ms. in Killie Campbell Collection. John Maxwell's account is in *Reminiscences of the Zulu War*, ed. L.T. Jones, Cape Town, 1979.

Chapter Two: The Second Baron
For Chelmsford, see Chelmsford Papers, National Army Museum, London; also Hon. Gerald French, *Lord Chelmsford and the Zulu War*, London, 1939. Also Crealock's *Frontier War Journal*; and *Guilty As Charged? Lord Chelmsford and the Isandlwana Debacle*, Jeff Matthews' 1984 University of Natal Workshop paper. For the Ninth Cape Frontier War, see J. Milton, *Edges of War*, Cape Town, 1983; and Cunynghame's *My Command in South Africa*, London, 1979. For Crealock and Clery see the Alison letters in Sonia Clarke's *Zululand At War*, Johannesburg, 1984; also *The Road to Ulundi; The Water-Colour Drawings of John North Crealock*, ed. R.A. Brown, Pietermaritzburg, 1969. Wolseley's views can be found in Adrian Preston (ed.) *The South African Journal of Sir Garnet Wolseley, 1879-81*, Cape Town, 1973. For transport problems see Ian Bennett's *Eyewitness in Zululand*, London, 1989; Jeff Matthews' *Lord Chelmsford and the Problems of Transport and Supply during the Anglo-Zulu War of 1879*, unpublished MA thesis, University of Natal, 1879; and Smith-Dorrien's *Memories*. For the Mzinyathi border see *The Buffalo Border 1879* by J.P.C. Laband and P.S. Thompson, with Sheila Henderson, Pietermaritzburg, 1983; and Henderson's "The Turbulent Frontier" in *The Zulu War and the Colony of Natal*, Mandini, 1979. For Natal Police see Holt's *Mounted Police*. Fynn's *My Recollections of a Famous Campaign* appeared in the *Natal Witness*, 22nd January 1913 (Killie Campbell Library). Samuel Jones' account appeared in the *Natal Mercury*, 22nd January 1939. On the crossing, see Harford, Norris-Newman, Hamilton-Browne; also reports dated 11th January 1879 from "Biggarsberg Correspondent" and "Witness" in the *Natal Mercury*.

Chapter Three: The Red Soldier
For a masterly analysis of the 1/24th in South Africa see "The First Battalion, Twenty-Fourth Regiment Marches to Isandlwana" by F.W.D. Jackson, in Ian Knight (ed.) *There Will Be An Awful Row At Home About This*, Shoreham-by-Sea, 1987. Standard sources on the 24th during this period are Paton, Glennie and Penn Symons, *Records of the 24th Regiment*, 1892; and the *Historical Records of the 2nd Battalion 24th Regiment for the Campaign in South Africa 1877-8-9*, published privately by the Regiment in Secunderbad, January 1882. Biographical details of the officers killed can be found in *The South Africa Campaign 1879* by J.P. MacKinnon and S.H. Shadbolt, London, 1882.

Norman Holme's *The Silver Wreath*, London 1979, contains invaluable details on officers and rank and file taken from rolls, pay lists etc. For a popular history of the 1st Battalion in SA see *The Road To Isandlwana*, by Philip Gon, Johannesburg, 1979. Cunynghame's comments are in *My Command in South Africa*, London, 1880. See also Crealock's *Frontier War Journal*. The Coghill Papers are in the National Army Museum; the best of them are published in *Whom the Gods Love*, by Patrick Coghill. Owen Ellis' letter is one of several of interest in Frank Emery's *The Red Soldier*, London, 1978. For the Mounted Infantry, see Newnham-Davis' *The Transvaal Under the Queen*, London, 1900, and Julian Whybra's roll in *Soldiers of the Queen*, Issue 58/59, January 1990. Harness' letters are published in Sonia Clarke's *Invasion of Zululand 1879*, Johannesburg, 1979. For N/5, see "N Battery 5th Brigade At Isandhlwana" by P.E.Abbott in the *Journal of the Society for Army Historical Research*, Vol. LVI. A letter by Lt.Col.E.Wray, published in *The Times* of 14th February 1879, assessed the value of the 7-pdr. gun. For Clery and Crealock's comments see the Alison letters in Clarke, *Zululand At War*. Hallam-Parr's account is *A Sketch of the Kaffir And Zulu Wars*, London, 1880; selections appeared in *Major-General Sir Henry Hallam-Parr, A Recollection*, London, 1917. An ms. account of the 24th's role written by W.Penn Symons is at Brecon; it contains a few insights not found elsewhere. For the Volunteers at Sihayo's Kraal see Trooper Symons and Holt. Hamilton-Browne and Harford discuss the NNC's role. For Chelmsford's views see French, *Lord Chelmsford and the Zulu War*. For Dixon see *The Zulu War and the Colony of Natal*; Field Force Regulations were published in Pietermaritzburg in November 1878 and February 1879. I am indebted to that great Zulu linguist SB Bourquin for a detailed explanation of the meaning of Isandlwana; Fynn and Brickhill concur. For Matshana see *History of the Zulu War and its Origin*, F.E.Colenso, London 1880. Also E.Unterhalter in *Anglo-Zulu War; New Perspectives*, and John Laband's *Kingdom in Crisis*, Manchester, 1992. For Fynn, see Fynn's *My Recollections*, and Laband and Thompson's *Buffalo Border*. For movements of Chelmsford and staff see Fynn and Milne's *Report on the Proceedings of 21st, 22nd, 23rd January, 1879* (copy in Killie Campbell Library). Also Crealock's report, published in *The Times*, 17th March 1879. Trooper Dorehill's story was recalled by Col.Lewis in a radio broadcast in 1939 (transcript in Killie Campbell Library).

Chapter Four: A Day in the Hills
For the events at the Mangeni, see Hamilton-Browne, Harford and Maxwell. On Chelmsford, see Milne's report, Crealock's, Clery's letters to Alison, and report in WO 33/34. Symons' account is the clearest on the Volunteer movements; for Russell's movements see his report of 1st April 1879 in WO/7731. Stafford, writing in 1929 and 1939, remembered the heat. For Hamilton-Browne's movements, see also his report of 2nd Feb. in WO/7726. Church's account is in E.Durnford's *A Soldier's Life And Work in South Africa*, London, 1882. For the 24th see *Historical Records of the 2/24th* and *Records of the 24th*. Lonsdale was quoted by several — including Norris-Newman, Hamilton-Browne and Harford — but seems to have left no account himself.

Chapter Five: Pulleine and Durnford
I have followed F.W.D.Jackson's masterly analysis of Pulleine and the 1/24th in "The First Battalion . . .". For Chelmsford's orders to his Column Commanders, and analysis, see *Isandlwana and the Durnford Papers* by F.W.D.Jackson and Julian Whybra in *Soldiers of the Queen* Issue 60. For the movements of the NNC see Higginson's report of 18th February in WO 32/7726. Barker's account is included in *The Natal Carbineers, 1855-1911* by Rev.John Stalker, Pietermaritzburg and Durham, 1912. For the movements of the 24th see the accounts of Private J.Bickley, John Williams and E.Wilson, all survivors, quoted in Holme's *The Silver Wreath*. A copy of Brickhill's account was published in the *Natal Magazine*, September 1879. For a thorough analysis of Durnford, see R.W.F.Drooglever, *A Figure of Controversy: Colonel Anthony Durnford in Natal and Zululand, 1873-79*, D.Litt. thesis, University of South Africa, 1982; much of this has been reworked in *The Road to Isandlwana* by Robin Drooglever, London, 1992. Some of Durnford's letters are included in his brother's eulogy, *A Soldier's Life and Work in South Africa*. For Smith-Dorrien see his *Memories*. On Durnford's Column, see Davies' report in WO 32/7726; Cochrane, quoted in Durnford's *A Soldier's Life*; Cochrane's report at the Court of Inquiry, published in *The Times* of 17th March 1879 and Blue Book C2260, and his supplementary report in WO 33/

34. Also Raw's report, WO 32/7713, Nyanda's report, WO 32/7713, and Vause's diary (Killie Campbell Africana Library). Davies left several accounts: his official report, WO 32/7726, a letter in the *Natal Mercury*, 31st January 1879 (reprinted in the *Illustrated London News* 29.3.79), and a later account in the *Natal Mercury*, 22nd January 1929. Chard's movements are mentioned in Durnford's *Soldier's Life* and his own letter written at Queen Victoria's request in February 1880, published in Holme's *The Silver Wreath*. The messages from the picquets and conversations between Durnford and Pulleine are quoted by Cochrane. For the movements of the Ngwane foot, see Stafford's and Nourse's reports to the Court of Inquiry. Stafford left a number of longer but rather muddled accounts in later life — see *Natal Mercury*, 22nd January 1929. Another account by Nourse appeared in the *Natal Witness*, 19th January 1929. A letter by Wally Erskine was published in *Times of Natal*, 26th February 1879.

Chapter Six: Cetshwayo's Kingdom
The starting point for any analysis of the Zulu state and army in 1879 must be John Laband's *Kingdom in Crisis*, Manchester, 1992. See the same author's contributions to *Kingdom and Colony at War*, with Paul Thompson. For a perceptive analysis of the economic base of political power within the kingdom see Jeff Guy's *Destruction of the Zulu Kingdom*. For an insider's view see H.Filter and S.Bourquin (compiler and translator) *Paulina Dlamini: Servant of Two Kings*, Pietermaritzburg, 1986. Mpashana kaSodondo's account is in C.deB.Webb and J.B.Wright (eds.) *James Stuart Archive*, Volume 3, 1983. For firearms, see "A Note of Firearms With Special Reference to the Anglo-Zulu War 1879" in the *Journal of African History*, xii, 4, 1971. Also the *Natal Mercury*, 12th February 1879. For the king's strategy see *A Zulu King Speaks*. Wood's comments are in his autobiography *From Midshipman to Field Marshall*, London, 1906. For Zulu costume see Samuelson's *Long, Long Ago*, Durban, 1929; I.Knight's *The Zulus*, London, 1989, and I.Knight (ed.) *There Will Be An Awful Row*. The deserter from the Nokhenke's account is in WO 33/34. For Muziwento, see C.deB.Webb (ed.), "A Zulu Boy's Recollections of the Zulu War" in *Natalia*, December, 1978. J.Y.Gibson's *The Story of the Zulus*, London, 1911, includes references to Zibhebhu and Ndabuko; uGuku's account is in F.E.Colenso's *History*. I am indebted to David Rattray for information concerning place names and their relevance.

Chapter Seven: Isandlwana
For the initial stages of the battle, see Raw and Nyanda's reports, Hamer's account (Chelmsford papers), Brickhill. Both Curling's and Gardner's account were recorded by the Court of Inquiry. For Bickley and Wilson see Holme, *The Silver Wreath*. Essex gave a report to the Court of Inquiry; see also his letter in *The Times*, 2nd April 1879. For Vause see his diary, and his (anonymous) letter in the *Natal Mercury*, 1st February 1879. On the war-cries of the uKhandempemvu, see Samuelson's *Long, Long Ago*. For the movements of the 1st NNC, see Erskine's letter and Stafford. For the Rocket Battery, see Nourse's COI report and 1929 account, and the evidence of Privates Grant, Trainer and Johnson quoted in Holme, *The Silver Wreath*. Barker's account is in Stalker, *Natal Carbineers*. Mehlokazulu's account is given in full in the *Natal Mercury*, 27th September 1879, and slightly edited in Norris-Newman. For uGuku see Colenso's *History*; for uMhoti see the Trooper Symons papers. Several Zulu accounts are included in Bertram Mitford's *Through The Zulu Country; Its Battlefields and Its People*, London, 1883. Jabez Molife's account is reproduced in full in Jackson and Drooglever's *Isandlwana and the Durnford Papers* in SOTQ. The anonymous survivor's letter was published in *The Times* for 10th April 1879. Shepherd's pamphlet was published by the St. John's Ambulance Brigade c.1880. For troop deployments, see the *Field Exercises Manual*, 1877. For the 24th see the *Historical Record of the 2nd Battalion*, the *Records of the 24th Regiment*, and Penn Symons unpublished ms. An invaluable analysis is F.W.D.Jackson's "Isandlwana: The Sources Re-examined" in the *JSAHR*, March, September and December 1965. Chief Zimema's account appeared in the *Natal Mercury* of 22nd January 1929, together with Kumbeka Gwabe's, uMbongoza's and uNzuzi's. Smith-Dorrien's letter to his father was published in the *Illustrated London News* for 29th March 1879; see also his *Memories*. Driver Elias Tucker's letter was published in Frank Emery's "Isandlwana; a Survivor's letter" in *Soldiers of the Queen*, Issue 18, September 1979. Wood's comments on ammunition expenditure are in *From Midshipman to Field Marshall*. For ammunition boxes see the List of Changes, and J.A.Verbeek and V.Bresler in the *Journal of the Historical Firearms*

Society of South Africa, December 1877. I am grateful to Lt.Col.Ian Bennett for some professional thoughts on the question of ammunition supply. For the stand in the donga see Jabez Molife, Davies, Gardner. For the *izinduna* encouraging their men, see H.C.Lugg's *Historic Natal and Zululand*, Pietermaritzburg, 1949; and Mpashana's and Muziwento's accounts. For the rout of the NNC see Malindi and Higginson; for the British collapse see Barker, Davies, Brickhill, Wally Erskine, Essex and Gardner. Trooper Sparkes' account is published in W.H.Clements, *The Glamour and Tragedy of the Zulu War*, London, 1936; a brief account also appeared in the *Natal Mercury* of 22nd January 1879. The positions of the dead are to be found in Black's reports on the burial expeditions of 20th, 23rd and 26th June, quoted in Norris-Newman. For Simeon Kambule's part in the battle, see *They Fought For The Great White Queen* by the Rev. Owen Watkins, published in the *Methodist Recorder*, reprinted in *The Zulu War and the Colony of Natal*. Mackinnon and Shadbolt's *The South Africa Campaign 1879* includes some information on the last moments of some of the officers, usually couched in suitably heroic terms. Maqeda's account is quoted in *The Story of the Blood Drenched Field of Isandlwana*, a "form of service" published on the 60th anniversary of the battle (1939); it includes references to accounts gathered by "The Bishop of Zululand". The song sung by the iNgobamakhosi is also quoted both here and in 1929 accounts; that a song was sung during the attack is remembered in local tradition (information: Dr Barry Marshall). For the "Zulu *induna*" questioned at Ulundi, see Norris-Newman. The story of the last survivor is told by a warrior of the uVe in the 2nd edition of Colenso and Durnford's *The Zulu War and its Origins*.

Chapter Eight: The Hunting Trail
For the fugitives' flight see Brickhill, Smith-Dorrien (letter and memoires), Stafford, Hamer, Curling, Davies, Henderson, Cochrane, Williams, Bickley, Vause, Erskine. Martin Foley, a wagon-driver, also left an account, published in the *Times of Natal*, 3rd February 1879. John Maxwell's *Reminiscences* suggest Brickhill was troubled by Gamble's death. The anonymous account of Pulleine giving the Colours to Melvill is quoted in D.C.F.Moodie's *History of the Battles and Adventures of the British, the Boers and the Zulus*, Adelaide, 1879. L.D.Young's account was published in *The Echo* of 24th February 1879; Higginson refuted it in the *Natal Mercury* of 16th May 1879. The anecdote about Cochrane is quoted in *Hathorn Family History* by Amy Helen Young, Pietermaritzburg, c.1970. Dorehill's story is included in Col.Lewis' radio talk; many incidental details are confirmed by other sources. The position of Anstey's body is from a family source mentioned by F.W.D.Jackson in *Isandlwana: The Sources Re-Examined*. For Wassall's account see Walter Wood, "The Last Stand of the 24th at Isandula; The Story of Samuel Wassall" in the *London Magazine*, No. 38-Vol.XXXI. Dugald Macphail's account was published in the *Natal Mercury* of 22nd January 1929. The account by Mdine is in the Talana Museum.

Chapter Nine: The Butcher's Bill
For Ndabuko's and Zibhebhu's movements see Gibson, *Story of the Zulus*, for the latter also Lugg's *Historic Zululand*; for uNzuzi, Kumbeka Gwabe and uMbongoza, *Natal Mercury*, 22nd January 1929; for disembowelment and *hlomula*, see Trumpeter Stevens, quoted in Emery; also Mpashana and Mehlokazulu. For Zulu military customs, see also Mstasphi kaNoradu in Webb & Wright, *James Stuart Archive*, Volume Four. The medical examination of the Prince Imperial was published in the *Times of Natal*, and is included in Moodie. For Bambatha see C.T.Binns, *Dinuzulu*, 1968. Forbes' account was published in the *Illustrated London News*, 12th July 1879. For the return to Isandlwana, see the Symons papers, Hamilton-Browne, Maxwell, Hallam-Parr, Fynn, Sam Jones, Milne's report, Harford. Trooper Cunningham's account was published in *The Natal Witness*, 19th January 1929. Some brief anecdotes by Newnham-Davis appeared in *Chums* in 1900. For Thrupp see Durnford's *A Soldier's Life and Work*, and Drooglever *The Road to Isandhlwana*. Sgt.Warren's letter appears in Emery's *The Red Soldier*. For "band boys" see Emery, Jones and Symons. For the return to Rorke's Drift, see Symons, Maxwell and Fynn.

Chapter Ten: Rorke's Drift
Chard left two accounts of Rorke's Drift: his official report, quoted in *Records of the 24th Regiment*, and a letter written in February 1880 at Queen Victoria's request. This is published in Holme's *The Silver Wreath*, with Hook's 1905 account from the *Royal Magazine*, and accounts by Hitch, C/Sgt. Bourne, Lyons, Sgt. Smith, Pte. Jobbins and Waters. A slightly different account by Hook, and brief accounts by William and Robert Jones, appeared in *The Strand Magazine* January-June 1891. Reynolds' account appeared as an appendix to the 1878 Report of the Army Medical Department. The Rev.Smith's account is published in *Padre George Smith of Rorke's Drift* by Canon W. Lummis, Norwich, 1978. Smith was also apparently the author of "The Defence of Rorke's Drift by an Eyewitness" in the *Natal Mercury*, 7th April 1879. Witt's account appeared in the *Illustrated London News*, 8th March 1879. For Henderson and Wall see Paul Thompson, "The NNC at Rorke's Drift", in Laband and Thompson, *Kingdom and Colony At War*; and also *Henderson Heritage*, published privately, Pietermaritzburg, 1972. For Howard, Parke Jones and a different account by Hitch see Emery, *The Red Soldier*. For Lugg see Emery, and also H.C.Lugg's *A Natal Family Looks Back*, 1970. For an analysis of the Zulus during the battle, see Laband's *Kingdom in Crisis*. For Adendorff see Chard's letter and Higginson. For the aftermath, see Hamilton-Browne and Harford. Zulu reactions can be found in Webb's *Zulu Boy's Recollections* and in Mehlokazulu. Also see Mitford.

Chapter Eleven: Burying the Bones
For Bengough's movements see his *Memories of a Soldiers' Life*, London, 1913. Beaumont's account appeared in the *Natal Mercury*, 22nd January 1929. For Helpmekaar, see Essex, Smith-Dorrien, Macphail, Higginson, Stafford, Davies. For civilian reactions see *The Zulu War and the Colony of Natal* and *The Buffalo Border*. For Rorke's Drift immediately after the battle see Hamilton-Browne, Harford, Symons. Curling's letter is quoted in Emery, *The Red Soldier*. Clery's comments are in Clarke, *Zululand At War*. For Blair Brown's reports, see "Surgical Notes on the Zulu War" in *The Lancet*, 25th July 1879, and *Surgical Experiences in the Zulu and Transvaal Wars*, London, 1883. For the reaction of the civil administration, see Paul Thompson's articles on the defence of Pietermaritzburg and Durban in *Kingdom and Colony At War*. For Zulu purification rituals, see Mpashana. The comments by uCajana on Zulu casualties are in Blue Book C2269. W.F.Molyneux's memoires are *Campaigning in South Africa and Egypt*, London, 1896. John Gill's observations were published in *The Lancet* for 15th August 1879. For movements along the Mzinyathi border, see Laband and Thompson, *The Buffalo Border*. For the recovery of the Colours see Harford. For Harness see Clarke, *The War in Zululand*. For Muziwento, see Webb, *Zulu Boy's Recollections*. I am indebted to Dr.Ian Player for information concerning Zulu spiritual beliefs and mourning, and David Rattray and Dr.Barry Marshall for information regarding wildlife. For the dogs see Maxwell. On the mummifying effects of disembowelling, see A.N. Montgomery, "Isandlwana: A Visit Six Months After The Battle" in *Leisure Hour*, 1882. For the recovery of the 2/24th Colours, see C.J.Bromhead's report of 19th April 1881, quoted in the Glennie/ Paton/Penn Symons Records of the 24th. Norris-Newman includes various accounts of the May visits; both Forbes and Melton Prior described the field in the *Illustrated London News*, 12th July 1879. See also Symons papers. Drooglever's *Road to Isandhlwana* considers Sheptone and Durnford's papers. For details about Blaikie, see *Hathorn Family History*. For Harness and the COI, see Sonia Clarke, *Invasion of Zululand*. For Chelmsford on the VCs, see French. Wolseley's comments can be found in A.Preston (ed.), *The South African Journal of Sir Garnet Wolseley*, Cape Town, 1973. Black's reports are quoted in Norris-Newman. See also Maxwell's *Reminiscences* and, for the Carbineers, the Symons papers. For C.J.Bromhead and O'Connell see C.2676. For a description of the battlefield at the end of the war, see W.E.Montague, *Campaigning in South Africa*, London, 1880. For the Zulu Civil War see Jeff Guy, *Destruction of the Zulu Kingdom*. For post-war descriptions, see R.W.Leyland's *A Holiday in South Africa*, London, 1882, and Mitford's *Through The Zulu Country*. Boast's report, with an interesting but curiously drawn map, is in the Natal Archives Depot. For the removal of Dubois' body, see *The Zulu War and the Colony of Natal*. Canon Johnson's report is quoted in Lummis, *Padre George Smith*. Finally, the story of Harford's boot is in Daphne Child (ed)., *The Zulu War Journal of Col. Henry Harford*.